The
Wrestling Archive Project

Classic 20th Century Mat Memories

Volume 3

Other publications from Crowbar Press

Inside Out
by Ole Anderson, with Scott Teal

Wrestlers Are Like Seagulls
by James J. Dillon, with Scott Teal & Philip Varriale

Assassin: The Man Behind the Mask
by Joe Hamilton, with Scott Teal

"Is That Wrestling Fake?"
by Ivan Koloff, with Scott Teal

Bruiser Brody
by Emerson Murray, edited by Scott Teal

Wrestling with the Truth
by Bruno Lauer, edited by Scott Teal

The Solie Chronicles
by Bob Allyn, with Pamela S Allyn & Scott Teal

Wrestling in the Canadian West
by Vance Nevada

Long Days and Short Pays
by Hal West, edited by Scott Teal

Drawing Heat
by Jim Freedman

ATLAS: Too Much, Too Soon
by Tony Atlas, with Scott Teal

The Last Laugh
by Bill De Mott, with Scott Teal

HOOKER
by Lou Thesz, with Kit Bauman

The Last Outlaw
by Stan Hansen, with Scott Teal

NIKITA
by Nikita Koloff, as told to Bill Murdock

The Strap
by Roger Deem

BRISCO
by Jack Brisco, as told to Bill Murdock

The Mighty Milo
by Phillips Rogers

"I Ain't No Pig Farmer!"
by Dean Silverstone, with Scott Teal

The Hard Way
by Don Fargo, with Scott Teal

Whatever Happened to Gorgeous George?
by Joe Jares

"It's Wrestling, Not Rasslin'!"
by Mark Fleming, edited by Scott Teal

BRUISER
The World's Most Dangerous Wrestler
by Richard Vicek, edited by Scott Teal

The Mat, the Mob & Music
by Tom Hankins, edited by Scott Teal

BREAKING KAYFABE
THEY CALL ME BOOKER
by Jeff Bowdren, edited by Scott Teal

BATTLEGROUND VALHALA
by Michael Majalahti, edited by Scott Teal

Florida Mat Wars: 1977
by Robert D. VanKavelaar, with Scott Teal

When It Was Real
by Nikita Breznikov, with Scott Teal

The Annotated Fall Guys
by Marcus Griffin,
annotated by Steve Yohe & Scott Teal

Pain Torture Agony
by Ron Hutchison, with Scott Teal

Raising Cain: From Jimmy Ault to Kid McCoy
by Frankie Cain & Scott Teal

Master of the Ring
by Tim Hornbaker

Tonight! Tonight! Tonight!
by Bert Prentice & Scott Teal

— Wrestling Archive Project —
by Scott Teal
Volume #1 • Volume #2

– Through the Lens ... Through the Ropes –
Compiled by Scott Teal
— Volume #1 —
Southeastern Championship Wrestling
— Volume #2 —
Championship Wrestling from Florida
— Volume #3 —
All South Wrestling Alliance

— The Great Pro Wrestlng Venues —

Volume #1 — Madison Square Garden
by Scott Teal & J Michael Kenyon

Volume #2 — Nashville, volume 1
by Scott Teal & Don Luce

Volume #3 — Alabama: 1931-1935
by Jason Presley

Volume #4 — Japan
by Haruo Yamaguchi,
with Koji Miyamoto & Scott Teal

Volume #5 — Knoxville: 1905-1960
Volume #6 — Amarillo: 1961-1991
by Tim Dills & Scott Teal

— Classic Arena Programs —

Volumes #1-2 — SLAM-O-GRAM
Volumes #3-4 — Florida
Volume #5 — Knoxville, Tennessee
Volumes #6-9 — St. Louis, Missouri
Volumes #22-24 — Jacksonville, Florida

— Wrestling Archive Project —
by Scott Teal

The Wrestling Archive Project

Classic 20th Century Mat Memories

Volume 3

by Scott Teal

CROWBAR PRESS

Gallatin, Tennessee

The Wrestling Archive Project

Classic 20th Century Mat Memories

Volume 3

Published by Crowbar Press
106 Tattnal Court
Gallatin, Tennessee 37066.

http://www.crowbarpress.com

Book layout and cover design by Scott Teal
Cover photo by Scott Teal

Library of Congress Cataloging-in-Publication Data

Teal, Scott

The Wrestling Archive Project, volume 3 / by Scott Teal

1. Teal, Scott. 2. Sports—United States—Biography. 3. Wrestling—United States—Biography. I. Title.

Printed in the United States of America
ISBN 978-1-940391-45-8

First Edition / August 2022

Table of Contents

Acknowledgements

To everyone featured in this volume, I extend a hearty *thank you* for taking the time to talk with me and allowing me to ask questions both professional and personal. It's an honor for me to have the privilege of preserving your stories and history for fans who remember "the good old days."

To Jim Ruehrwein, who spends hours researching wrestling results to create ring records that often function as an outline for me to follow when I do the interviews.

To J Michael Kenyon, my mentor and the man who probably was the greatest champion of my work. The world is a lonelier place with his passing. J Michael is the person I consider to be the greatest of all wrestling historians, and I can only hope to come close to filling *one* of his shoes.

Finally, to my wife, who, even though she never watched wrestling and knew absolutely nothing about it, puts up with my obsession of recording the history of the greatest sport in the world. At the same time, she has given so much to the wrestlers through her work at our Tennessee Wrestling Legends Reunion. They have come to love her, as do I.

To all the guys we know as "carpenters" or "jobbers." It was you who made "superstars" out of the main-eventers and made professional wrestling exciting for those of us with our butts in the seats.

Foreword
by Scott Teal

It's hard to believe that more than three years have passed by since volume 2 of *Wrestling Archive Project* was published. The older I get, the faster time passes. In fact, 54 years have sped by since I saw my first pro wrestling program on television, and it was more than 27 years ago that I started doing interviews for my *Whatever Happened to ...?* magazine.

As I worked through this volume, I was excited about updating the status of those I interviewed, but as I got further into the narrative, I came to the realization that every one of them are now gone. Several of the guys — Al Costello, Buddy Wayne, Al Costello, Ox Baker, Pat Barrett, and Rip Tyler — were very close friends. As I researched and checked some of the things they told me, I couldn't help but wish I could pick up the phone and ask them about things I failed to ask when we did the interviews. In fact, I've love to talk to them just one more time about anything! It's a reminder that we need to tell those we love how much they mean to us ... before they're gone and the opportunity passes. These interviews, however, give me a little satisfaction in knowing their legacy will live on.

In this third volume of *Wrestling Archive Project* — the 60th book published with my Crowbar Press imprint — I'm excited to be presenting a short bio on the man — The Great Malenko — whose actions on the *Championship Wrestling from Florida* TV show one Sunday afternoon was the catalyst for my interest in pro wrestling. I'll tell you more about that in the pages ahead.

My plans are to publish at least one more volume before the end of 2022. Future volumes will be a mix of new, never-before-published interviews and those that appeared years ago in my now-out-of-print *Whatever Happened to ...?* magazine. For many, the interviews are the sum-total of their life stories, so it's important that we talk to them and get their stories in print before it's too late. As J Michael always told me, *"Talk to old people."* In saying that, he meant we should mine their brains for information, because they are the curators of history, and they can teach us life lessons through their personal experiences.

Scott Teal

THE GREAT MALENKO

by Scott Teal

Lawrence "Larry" J. Simon
June 28, 1933 – Sept. 1, 1994

One of the problems historians and researchers face when preparing a story on one of the Golden Age pro wrestlers is determining who was who when two — or more — wrestlers used the same name. That's the case with Larry Simon, who worked for the biggest part of his career in Florida as "The Great Malenko."

The "original" Great Malenko was a man named Frank Fozo. At various times, he wrestled as either Frank Fozo, Fozo Malenko, The Great Malenko, or Fozo (The Great) Malenko. His career seems to have begun in 1955 and he main-evented regularly from that year through 1958 in Tennessee, Alabama, Louisiana, and Mississippi. In early 1958, he split his time between wrestling in Detroit, New York, Ohio, and Ontario, Canada, as plain "Frank Fozo" and the Southern circuit as "Fozo Malenko." From Feb. 1959, he spent the remainder of his career, which ended in Feb. 1963, in the Northern states.

One year before that, on Feb. 3, 1962, a "Great Malenko" made his debut in Cincinnati and Dayton, Ohio. It's unclear as to whether or not it was Fozo, but several facts lead me to believe that this was the first appearance of Larry Simon as "The Great Malenko." Two other newcomers — Don Curtis and Karl Gotch — appeared on the cards in Dayton with Malenko during that month. Less than two months later, all three men appeared on the April 2 card in Orlando and made regular appearances throughout the state after that. The "Great Malenko" in Orlando definitely was Larry Simon. In his match with Joe Scarpa, Malenko was disqualified for refusing to stop choking his opponent on the ropes.

That was the beginning of a 13-year run for Malenko, who was billed as having been "barred from action in his own country due to his savage style."

My introduction to professional wrestling came about when I was just a junior high school student. While visiting with a girlfriend one Sunday afternoon, I was invited by her family to stay and watch professional wrestling (or *pro rasslin'* as they called it). At the time, I had never watched the sport, but I was instantly captivated by what took place during the next hour. My most distinct recollection of that show was of one man ... a tough individual who spoke slowly and confidently, yet with an air of menace. He talked with one eye closed, spoke with a foreign accent, and referred to the television announcer (who I would later learn was Gordon Solie) as "Mr. TV Announcer Man."

Tampa TV • Malenko tells Gordon Solie what he has planned for his opponent.

My first impression was, "*What a strange character!*", but from his expression and the tone of his voice, I immediately summed him up as someone I wouldn't want to cross. He reminded me of the principal during my days at Southeast High School – a stocky man who was built like a bull ... a man rumored to have an "electric paddle" in his closet that he used on unruly students ... a man who students passed by on the opposite side of the hallway.

The entire wrestling show revolved around that personality. His presence alone seemed to infuriate the television audience, who vented their outrage against him with boos and hisses.

"Mr. TV Announcer Man" referred to him as The Great Malenko – or Professor Boris Maximilianovitch Malenko. I was so fascinated by the antics of this so-called Russian that I not only started to watch the show every Saturday evening, but I refused to miss the Sunday afternoon repeat.

It was many years later before I would discover that Malenko grew up as Larry Simon in Irvington, New Jersey. He played a little football and threw the shot put at South Side High School [renamed Malcolm X Shabazz High School in 1972]. In 1954, Larry was approached by a pro wrestler who convinced him to take up amateur wrestling at the YMCA. Later, he was lucky enough to train with Henry Wittenberg, a gold medalist in the 1948 Olympics.

Driving a truck in the daytime and wrestling in clubs at night, Larry's wrestling skills increased steadily. Finally, as a nervous 17-year-old, he made his professional debut on Dec. 30, 1955, against Steve Gob. Only one other match can be found in the first two months of 1956 — a Feb. 29 match in Patchogue, New York, against Kenny Ackles — but by March, Larry seems to have hit his stride as he was appearing regularly in Newark, Yonkers, Baltimore, Philadelphia, and Camden. On March 23, 1956, in Newark, New Jersey, for promoter Vince McMahon Sr., Larry teamed up with Soldier Barry — who later changed his name to Ed Sharpe — against Tony Martinelli and

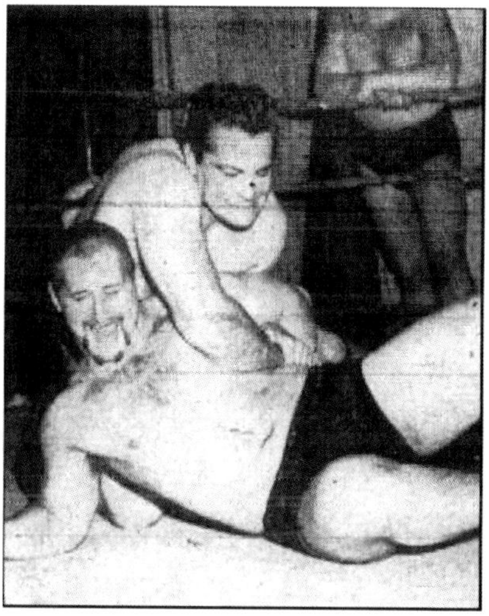

(l.) Wilmington, Delaware: April 29, 1957
(r) Yonkers, New York: March 27, 1957 • Larry Simon vs Gene Dubuque

Lou Scarpa. No results were published in the newspaper, but a repeat of that match took place in Yonkers, New York, on April 5, with Simon and Barry winning a decision.

For the next eighteen months, Larry learned his trade by wrestling in preliminaries held in both small and large arenas throughout New Jersey, usually losing to the more-established wrestlers. He appeared in his first main event on April 29, 1957, losing to undefeated Ricki Starr in Wilmington, Delaware. Shortly after that, he scored his first singles victories when he defeated Tony Martinelli in 18 minutes, 24 seconds in New Brunswick, New Jersey, on May 20, and on July 3 in Baltimore, he defeated Harry Lewis in the Coliseum.

From 1957 to 1960, while he was in the Northeast, newspapers referred to Larry as "Larruping Larry Simon." Larruping means "to beat, flog soundly, or thrash." Newspapers also called him the "disliked Irvington grappler" and/or "one of wrestling's bad boys."

In late 1957, Larry left the Northeast to work as Crusher Dugan for wrestling promoter Morris Sigel in Houston, Texas. His first outing was in Galveston on Oct. 31, at which time a *Galveston Daily News* reporter wrote:

> "Newcomer Larry (Crusher) Dugan conquered Marco Polo in two minutes with a neck-breaker and press. Dugan showed a wild and rough style of action that reminded the fans of the famed Bull Curry. Dugan claims that he is a rougher grappler than Curry."

Bull Curry was a legend in that part of the country, so that was high praise, indeed.

The following week in Galveston, the newspaper ad promoted the semi-final match between Larry (Crusher) Dugan and Texas junior heavyweight champion Billy King as "This Bout May Steal the Show." That was high praise again since the main event featured a return match between Pepper Gomez and Duke Keomuka, which was one of the hottest feuds ever to take place in the state.

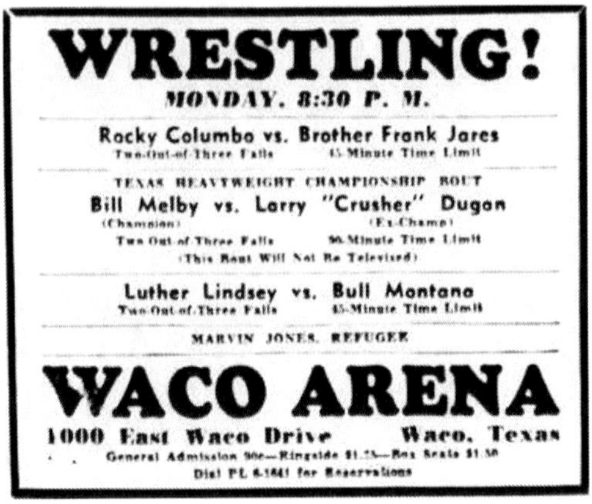

Waco, Texas: Dec. 16, 1957

While there, Larry won his first regional championship — the Texas heavyweight title — from Pepper Gomez on Nov. 8th in Houston, but dropped it to Bill Melby one week later.

In 1958, he set up shop in the Central States area, wrestling as German villain Otto von Krupp for promoters George Simpson in Kansas City and Gust Karras in St. Joseph. In his first outing, Jan. 3 at Memorial Hall, he defeated Bobby Bruns with a body-smother. It was during this time that he really learned his trade and trained with Joe Dusek, the promoter in Nebraska, who would prove to be the biggest influence on Larry's future in the business. He also made his first appearance in St. Louis during this time, teaming with Mighty Atlas [Morris Shapiro] in a losing effort against Ronnie Etchison and Larry Hamilton [later the Missouri Mauler]. While there, he wrestled Don Curtis several times, a man with whom he would feud years later in Florida.

From the June 1, 1958, *Sedalia Democrat*:

> Otto Von Krupp, whose "goose-step" has angered a few of the fans, has promised promoter Gust Karras that he will refrain from this when he wins, although it is his sign of victory. Von Krupp really raises the body temperature and tempers of a few who don't like it and hence, Karras, wanting no trouble, has asked him not to do it again.

Larry's highest-profile match to date had to have been his Oct. 9 match against former world heavyweight champion Lou Thesz in Kansas City. The *Kansas City Times* reported:

> Thesz won the first fall in 17:04 with a flying scissor and body-smother, Von Krupp won the second fall after 8 minutes with a knee-lift and smother. The final fall went to Thesz in 5:15 with a flying drop kick and body-smother.

Larry's next stop was West Texas. When he arrived in Oct. 1958, newspapers didn't seem to know what to call him. In Odessa, it was either "Otto Von Krupp" or "Kurt Von Krupp." He was introduced to San Angelo wrestling fans as "Bruiser Dugan." By the second week, everyone seemed to settle on simply "The Bruiser," although reports in the *Abilene Reporter-News* mistakenly said he was Dick Afflis, aka Dick the Bruiser.

On Dec. 1 in San Angelo, Larry had his first encounter with a wrestling bear. The *San Angelo Standard-Times* reported:

> Brownie beat The Bruiser, a heavyweight who refuses to tell his Christian name and where he's from. The Bruiser was the aggressor — and as a result got slapped around a lot and pinned by a lot of bear. The time was 4:45.

Larry left West Texas and made a stop in St. Joseph to put over Mighty Atlas on Dec. 19, and then returned to the Northeast. Once again, he was plain, old "Larry Simon," and once again he languished in the openers, but on Tuesday night, Jan. 6, 1959, in New York's Sunnyside Garden, Larry teamed with Al Smith to wrestle Miguel Perez and Pedro Escobar in what appears to be his first high-profile main-event match in the Northeast.

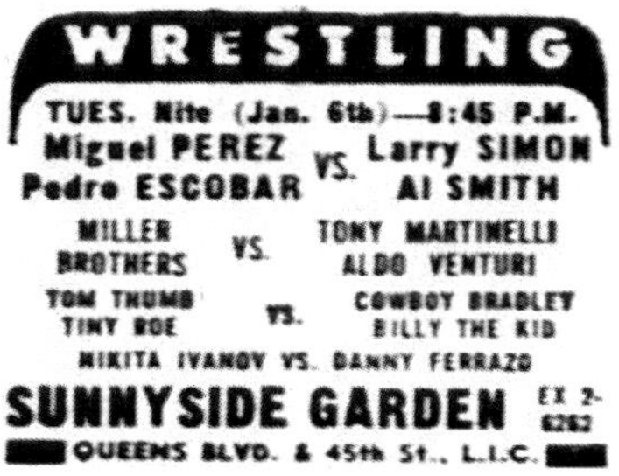

The Feb. 14 card at the Paterson [NJ] Armory brought Simon face to face with ... Sandor Fozo, aka Frank (The Great Malenko) Fozo. I wish I could have been a fly on the wall to hear what they talked about. It's very possible that Fozo gave Larry the idea for the "Great Malenko" moniker on that night, but that's just guesswork.

An interesting mention of Larry appeared in the March 18 edition of the Yonkers *Herald Statesman* as he was listed as Larry "Spaceman" Simon. The nickname had no reference to anything, other than the fact that the author of the article gave nicknames to several of the wrestlers, including "Dastardly" Dan Miller, Arnie "The Quarry Heights Crusher" Skaaland, and Lou "The Prince of Pepperoni" Albano.

In April 1959, Larry returned to the Central States where the title of "Baron" was bestowed on him, and he spent a considerable amount of time wrestling in Omaha and Lincoln, Nebraska ... both towns promoted by his mentor, Joe Dusek. Newspapers latched onto a new nickname for the Baron ... The Horrible Hun. For the next two and a half years, Larry divided his time between the Central States and the Northeast, but he was never given any kind of a push in the New York/New Jersey territory.

While in the Northeast, Larry wrestled in Bridgeport, Connecticut on May 20. Two nights later, he was in Charlotte, North Carolina, to put Sweet Daddy Siki over, and then wrestled in the Baltimore Coliseum the following night.

October 1961 found Larry working in the Midwest as Otto Von Krupp. On Nov. 23, he and Bob Geigel beat Dale Lewis and Pat Kennedy to win the AWA world tag team title. But before the New Year began, Larry unexpectedly packed up and left without giving any notice. The promotion fabricated the storyline that Von Krupp had been injured and ordered a tournament to determine new champions.

Once again, back in the Northeast, Larry was relegated to doing jobs [losing matches] on curtain-raisers. In fact, on March 21 in Bridgeport, a town in

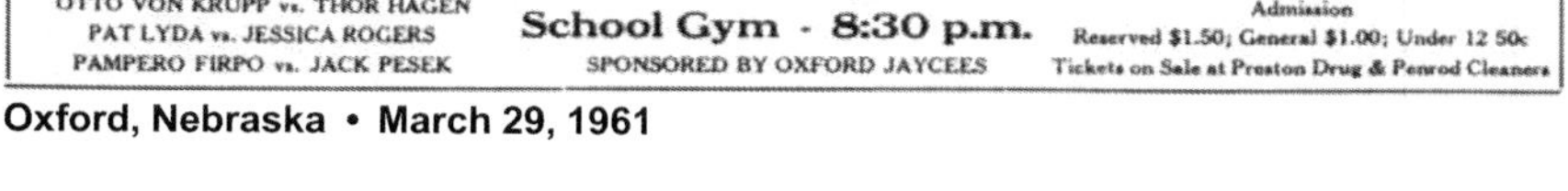

Oxford, Nebraska • March 29, 1961

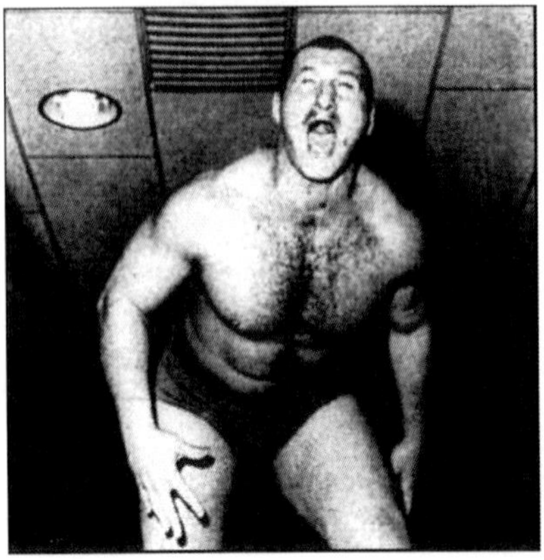

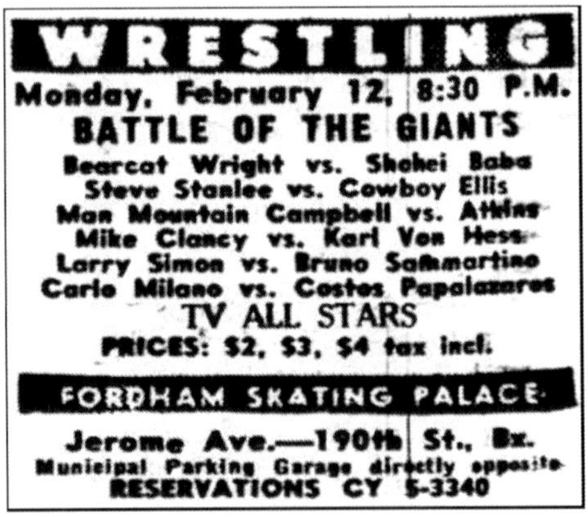

(left) Larry looks upset after his match with Gregory Jarque at the Roll-a-rama Arena in Brookly, even though he won in 21 minutes, 23 seconds.

(right) New York, NY • Feb. 12, 1962

which Larry appeared regularly, the newspaper noted that Pete Sanchez scored a rare victory, beating Larry Simon in straight falls.

One of the up-and-comers Larry put over in Brooklyn, New York City, and Washington D.C. was a young Bruno Sammartino. Another interesting fact was that promoters couldn't decide exactly where he was from. At various times, he was billed as being either from New York, New Jersey, or Israel.

Nobody paid more dues that Larry Simon. Interestingly enough, even when he was given a huge push — in Texas, Nebraska, Minnesota, etc. — he seldom had his hand raised. And yet, even after a big loss, he drew exceptionally well in the weeks that followed.

As noted earlier, in Feb. 1962, Larry appeared in Ohio as "The Great Malenko." In April of that year, Larry decided that a change of scenery might allow him to make a fresh start in the business. While on vacation in Clearwater Beach, Florida, he wrestled for promoter C.P. (Cowboy) Luttrall, and found that the fans accepted him from the start. More accurately, they hated him and his heel persona. That proved to be the turning point of his career. Larry decided to make his home in Florida, and in the process, "Larry Simon" disappeared. Taking his place was —

— The Great Malenko from Moscow, Russia —

On July 25, 1962, shortly after settling down in the Sunshine State, Malenko won the Southern heavyweight title. Less than two months later, Malenko and the Crusher [Tony Angelo] won the world tag team title. On Oct. 13, Tony Baillargeon and Maurice LaPointe took the belts from Malenko and Crusher at the Tampa Sportatorium in what is believed to be the first title change to ever take place in a television studio.

Another interesting detail about Malenko's career took place during the week of Jan. 10, 1963. He left Florida for a month and made appearances in Washington D.C. and three towns in Connecticut — New Haven, Bridgeport, and New Britain. He won his first three matches, defeating Pete Sanchez (finally!), Miguel Torres and Eugenio Marin. He wrestled Karl Von Hess in New Britain, but no results were reported. In all appearances, he was billed as "Boris Malenko, the Mad Russian."

The Great Malenko, 1964

It was a name that would soon make him famous, and respected, worldwide. Not so much in Northeast, though. Larry played the part of the Mad Russian to the hilt, but the fans just wouldn't buy it. Larry Simon was too well known in the Northeastern market as a local jobber, generating chants of "*Simon is a bum*" whenever he made an appearance as "The Great Malenko."

He didn't fare as well during a return to the Northeast in March through May 1963. He lost almost every match in which he appeared, with a short-list of his opponents being Tim Woods, Argentina Apollo, Great Scott, Arnold Skaaland, Dory Dixon, Johnny Barend, and Pat Barrett. Subsequent returns that year and in 1964 proved to be just as unfruitful.

The stories of Malenko's career in Florida, though, are legendary. The one that stands out above all others happened during his 1966 feud with Eddie Graham, who later took over the territory when Cowboy Luttrall retired in the early '70s. At the TV taping on Saturday, April 15, 1967, Malenko was dishing out punishment in the ring to a helpless and bloody Sam Steamboat. Eddie hit the ring and caught Malenko with an uppercut to the jaw. Malenko's false teeth popped out of his mouth, flew through the air, and landed on the mat. The packed studio of frenzied wrestling fans screamed with delight as Graham proceeded to stomp them to tiny bits in the center of the ring.

In addition to his continuing and profitable feud with Graham, Malenko engaged in bloody campaigns against Joe Scarpa, Sam Steamboat, Danny Miller, Jose Lothario, and Jack Brisco. At various times, fellow mat villains Bob Orton, Johnny Valentine, Tarzan Tyler, Hans Mortier, and the Missouri Mauler worked alongside him as his tag team partners and they packed out arenas throughout the state. Acknowledged by his peers as the wrestler who built Florida into the top territory in the nation, Malenko was the first heel in Florida whose appearance on a show practically guaranteed a sellout house. This was true wherever he appeared, and no matter who he worked against, from the early 1960s to the mid-'70s.

Malenko's first match in Florida
Orlando, Florida • April 2, 1962

"I first met Malenko when he was wrestling as Otto Von Krupp," said Bob Orton, who became a close friend of Malenko in the '60s. *"He really seemed to like me. It was probably because he heard I was a right-winger. When I went*

to New York, he was in the preliminaries and they wouldn't do anything with him. McMahon sure missed the boat. Malenko had talent just waiting to be tapped, and he took it down to Florida and made the territory. Malenko and I kept in touch right up to the end."

The following is an excerpt from an interview I conducted with Bob in Oct. 1994.

The riot that most people remember is the one with The Great Malenko.

What a night. That was in Richmond. Again, it was a case of not enough cops. That was when Eddie [Graham] was trying to push the Southern heavyweight title into other NWA territories ... Georgia, Charlotte. The people hated the fact that I was teamed up with a Russian.

The houses were way down at the time, maybe 25 percent full (pause) ... or 75 percent empty, however you want to look at it. On TV before the card in Richmond, Malenko slammed a chain over a chair back. That was all it took. The house took a big jump and almost sold out. We pushed it too far, though, because we had too much heat. The place was going bananas. When we realized things were going to get out of hand, we backed off and tried to let things settle down, but no matter what we did, things just got hotter. Malenko and I were leaving the ring and got separated. I got hit and was down and out for the count on the arena floor. There are several conflicting stories about this, and I can't be sure which is correct because I was unconscious.

The story I've heard most often is that Malenko saw you go down and fought his way over to you through the crowd. He grabbed you by the foot and began dragging you towards the dressing room, all the while punching people with his other hand. While he was in the middle of the crowd, somebody stabbed him in the stomach. He was so beat up and in shock that he didn't realize what had happened to him. The dressing room wasn't too far, so he ran back for help.

That's pretty much the way it went. Homer O'Dell took over at that point. He pulled out a .44 Magnum that wasn't even loaded, stood over me, and that's what kept the people back. Two or three guys then pulled me out, but it was Homer standing his ground that kept the crowd away. Malenko was leaking like a sieve and took 33 stitches in his abdomen.

Friends tell me that when Malenko got back to the dressing room to get help, everybody just stood there with their fingers inserted, so he turned around and walked back into the crowd. This time, when the fans saw him coming, with that blood pouring down, they couldn't get away fast enough. By that time, O'Dell and the others had gotten you back into the dressing room.

That's the way Malenko was ... absolutely fearless. If it weren't for Malenko and O'Dell, I'd probably be a dead man that day. I heard that O'Dell was driving a cab in Nashville. I always wanted to do something nice for him to thank him, but never had the opportunity.

Malenko also had successful runs for Jim Crockett Sr. in the Carolinas and Paul Boesch in Houston, where he set an attendance record for a match against Wahoo McDaniel. The stipulation for the match was a Russian chain match, a match in which two men were coupled together with a six-foot length of steel chain strapped by leather to their wrists. There were no falls, no disqualifications, and no time limit. The match continued until one man

Houston, Texas

dragged his opponent around the ring, touching all four corner posts, two times in a row.

The first Russian chain match took place in Jacksonville, Florida, on June 10, 1965, when Malenko faced arch-rival Eddie Graham. Billed as the inventor and master of the chain match — a stipulation that guaranteed a violent and bloody showdown — Malenko claimed that he had never lost that type of match. Promoters in other territories would bring him in to work a series of matches with their local hero (or themselves), culminating with a chain match to end or wind up the program. The Russian chain match caught the attention of promoters everywhere, and within a short period of time, wrestling promoters in other territories were featuring the Russian chain match — but without Malenko's — or even Russian — involvement.

On a personal note, my all-time favorite angle involving Malenko took place in May and June 1970. After returning from a successful nine-month run in Texas, Malenko wrestled and defeated Louie Tillet in Tampa on June 2, but he used a "foreign object" to accomplish the deed. As a result, Malenko was handed a "30-day suspension and a $1,000 fine by the National Wrestling Alliance." The following week, a masked wrestler known only as "The Masked Muscovite" was booked in the main event against newly-turned babyface Hiro Matsuda … in a "Russian chain match!" Thunderbolt Patterson, who was teaming with Malenko at the time, claimed that the Muscovite was the man who originally taught the chain match technique to Malenko. "Muscovite," by the way, is a person from Moscow.

There was no pretense made to fool fans into thinking it was anyone other than Malenko. In fact, the picture of the Muscovite in the arena program was the same picture of Malenko that had been used in publicity hundreds of times, but this time, a mask was drawn over his face in black ink. Malenko appeared to have won the match with Matsuda, but due to interference by Dale Lewis, the decision was reversed by special NWA referee Dick Kroll. Matsuda unmasked the Muscovite and revealed him to be Malenko, resulting in Malenko receiving an additional $1,000 fine for violating his suspension.

A huge turning-point in Malenko's career began in Feb. 1971 when he and Rene Goulet were put together as a tag team. They made a formidable team, but by May, cracks began to appear in their alliance. The problems began when the two were scheduled to compete on a May 27 six-man tag team match on television with Original Grappler as the third man. For whatever reason, Malenko failed to show, so a substitute partner was added to the team.

That next Tuesday night, a column by Rene Goulet, titled "Where were you, Boris?", appeared in the *Championship Wrestling ACTION* arena program. A portion of what he said was:

> "Now, I ask you, Boris. How can we be effective as a team when one of us does not show up for an important match? I had to get a substitute partner at the last minute."

Before publication, program editor Jerry Prater "contacted" Malenko for his response to Goulet's remarks and included it after Goulet's statement.

> "Tell me, Rene, can it be possible that you were not able to function as captain of our team in my absence? Did you really have that much trouble with Bob Roop and the Fuller brothers, three schoolboys? I would remind you that Ronny Garvin, the young man who took my place, has been wrestling professionally longer than any one of your three opponents.
>
> "I am sorry if I let you down, Rene. I hadn't realized that you depended upon me that completely. Hereafter, I shall endeavor to make even greater efforts in order to assure our success as a team. It appears that the responsibility for leadership rests more heavily upon my shoulders than I had thought. But never fear, Rene. The Great Malenko is equal to the task."

Wrestling fans who had been around, if even for a short time, knew what this was all leading up to ... a split between the two men with one of them turning babyface. Obviously, it wasn't going to be Malenko. Wrestling fans *hated* Malenko more than any other villain that had ever wrestled in Florida. Goulet, on the other hand, had an air about him that was somewhat likeable, despite his heel persona.

What actually happened, though, illustrates the genius in the events that followed. Whether Eddie Graham was the author of the storyline, or if Malenko himself came up with the idea, it was a brilliant series of moves.

The following Tuesday night in Tampa — June 1 — after being defeated by Louie Tillet and Bob Roop, Malenko and Goulet argued in the ring ... each blaming the other for the loss. Later that same night, Dick Murdoch was battling Jack Brisco in a Texas death match in the main event. When Murdoch found himself in trouble, Malenko got involved. Malenko climbed to the top turnbuckle and jumped off, intending to come down with a knee across Brisco's back. Brisco moved at the last second and Malenko landed on Murdoch, making him an easy victim for Brisco. Another argument followed, with both Murdoch and Goulet chastising Malenko.

Two days later, during a six-man tag team match at the Tampa Sportatorium TV tapings, Goulet and Murdoch left the ring, leaving Malenko to take a beating from their opponents. A few minutes later, they returned to the ring and themselves attacked Malenko.

The execution to this point was flawless. However, the program took a strange course. Instead of bringing Malenko and Goulet and/or Murdoch back in a grudge match the following week, Malenko was paired with fellow heels Dale Lewis and the Original Grappler against The Grappler, Hiro Matsuda and Buddy Fuller in a six-man elimination tag team match that meant next to nothing.

The following week, Malenko was booked against Goulet in what should have been a match hyped to the moon. Instead, it was billed third from the top, even taking second seat to Dick Murdoch vs. Klondike Bill, another match that meant nothing since Bill wasn't even a regular in the territory.

Two weeks into the program, nobody had turned. All participants continued to work as heels. This, in and of itself, was fine. Rather than going down the

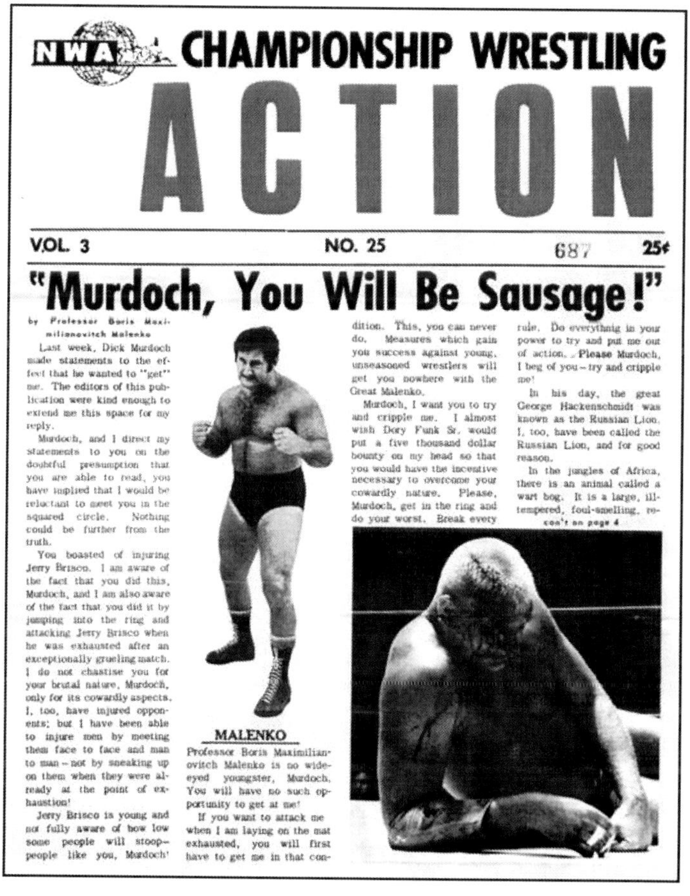
NWA CHAMPIONSHIP WRESTLING

ACTION

VOL. 3 NO. 25 687 25¢

"Murdoch, You Will Be Sausage!"

by Professor Boris Maximilianovitch Malenko

Last week, Dick Murdoch made statements to the effect that he wanted to "get" me. The editors of this publication were kind enough to extend me this space for my reply.

Murdoch, and I direct my statements to you on the doubtful presumption that you are able to read, you have implied that I would be reluctant to meet you in the squared circle. Nothing could be further from the truth.

You boasted of injuring Jerry Brisco. I am aware of the fact that you did this, Murdoch, and I am also aware of the fact that you did it by jumping into the ring and attacking Jerry Brisco when he was exhausted after an exceptionally grueling match. I do not chastise you for your brutal nature, Murdoch, only for its cowardly aspects. I, too, have injured opponents; but I have been able to injure men by meeting them face to face and man to man – not by sneaking up on them when they were already at the point of exhaustion!

Jerry Brisco is young and not fully aware of how low some people will stoop – people like you, Murdoch!

MALENKO

Professor Boris Maximilianovitch Malenko is no wide-eyed youngster, Murdoch. You will have no such opportunity to get at me!

If you want to attack me when I am laying on the mat exhausted, you will first have to get me in that condition. This, you can never do. Measures which gain you success against young, unseasoned wrestlers will get you nowhere with the Great Malenko.

Murdoch, I want you to try and cripple me. I almost wish Dory Funk Sr. would put a five thousand dollar bounty on my head so that you would have the incentive necessary to overcome your cowardly nature. Please, Murdoch, get in the ring and do your worst. Break every rule. Do everything in your power to try and put me out of action. Please Murdoch, I beg of you – try and cripple me!

In his day, the great George Hackenschmidt was known as the Russian Lion. I, too, have been called the Russian Lion, and for good reason.

In the jungles of Africa, there is an animal called a wart hog. It is a large, ill-tempered, foul-smelling, re-

con't on page 4

Tampa program
June 22, 1971

road that had been traveled many times in the past — that of immediately turning someone babyface, which was something the fans would expect — the feud was relegated to Murdoch and Goulet against Malenko and whatever heel partners he could find, which included Dory Funk Sr. or the Missouri Mauler. Even Jack Brisco — in an effort to keep the fans in the dark regarding the ultimate goal — chimed in with an article in the arena program titled "You Can't Trust Malenko."

From the time the program began, a full five weeks had passed before the promotion began to lift the veil that hid their plans. Fans in Miami Beach were probably the first to realize something special was happening. On July 7, the main event there was a Tornado team match with Murdoch and Goulet against Malenko and ... Louie Tillet, *a babyface*! By the end of the night, fans were cheering Malenko with as much gusto as they had booed him during his most despicable moments.

Six nights later in Tampa, wrestling fans came to the same realization when one of the most beloved wrestlers in the territory — Jack Brisco — sided with Malenko in that night's main event. And on July 21 in Miami Beach, Malenko joined forces with none other than ... Eddie Graham! That match alone set the stage for Malenko's turn to a full-fledged babyface. There was no doubt left in anyone's mind, and from that point forward, the fans loved Malenko as much as they had hated him in the past. Granted, he didn't change his style of wrestling too much, but his style never was that of what most people think of as the typical heel-wrestler style. Malenko was a highly skilled wrestler, so even when he worked as a monster heel, he relied on more than just punching and kicking, as most heels were inclined to do.

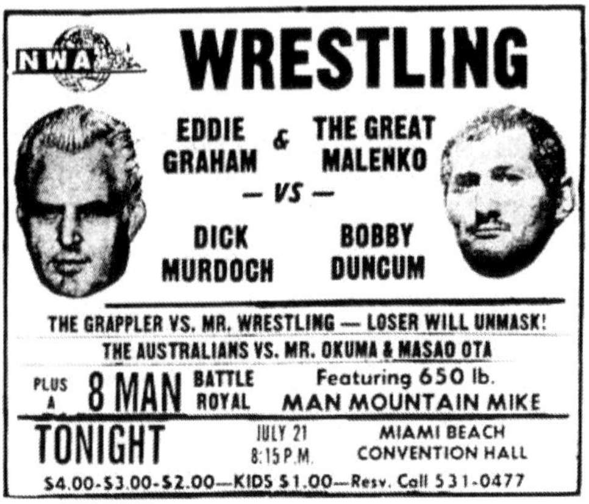

Malenko was a fixture in Florida rings for the next four years, although he made short tours for promoters in other territories:

Oklahoma, Sept.-Oct. 1971
Dallas and Houston, July-Aug. 1972
Japan, May-June 1973 and Oct.-Dec. 1974
West Texas, July-Aug. 1973
Georgia, May-June 1974

Other than that, he was booked as a top babyface in the Florida territory and was figured into many angles and programs.

In June 1975, Malenko went to work for the Charlotte office and stayed there for six months. On Dec. 16, he was booked to wrestle in Tampa's Fort Homer Hesterly Armory. His appearance that night sparked life back into the promotion and the Armory sold out – just like old times, despite the fact that Malenko wrestled and lost to Bob Orton, Jr. At the end of the evening, Graham handed Malenko a check for 100 dollars. The payoff was a slap in the face to Malenko and marked the beginning of the end to a business relationship between Graham and Malenko that had lasted more than a decade – an affiliation that had netted Graham millions of dollars.

The following night, Malenko was booked in Miami Beach to wrestle The Destroyer for the Southern heavyweight title. Always one to fulfill his commitments, regardless of the circumstances, Malenko appeared as scheduled, but wrestled Billy Robinson. That was Malenko's final match for the Championship Wrestling from Florida promotion.

Graham repaid Malenko's loyalty by telling everyone that he fired Malenko that night, claiming an impropriety on Malenko's part involving an airplane ticket. The boys working in the territory disclosed a different scenario ... that Graham was resentful of Malenko's popularity with the fans, while Graham's own star was just as quickly fading. Graham, a powerful player with the National Wrestling Alliance, had Malenko blacklisted.

Graham's influence, however, wasn't as great as he thought. One week later, Malenko was once again wrestling in the Charlotte territory for promoter Jim Crockett, Jr., the elder Crockett having passed away two years earlier. Malenko had an amazing two-year run there, both as an in-ring talent and as a manager for the Masked Superstar [Bill Eadie] and Kim Duk.

In April 1978, Malenko wrestled for Southeastern Championship Wrestling, the Knoxville-based promotion owned by Ron Fuller. While there, he met and helped train Buddy Landel, who was just a teenager at the time. Landel later went down to Jacksonville to wrestle as Buddy Roop for Sunbelt Wrestling, the promotion run by Don Curtis and Louie Tillet.

At the end of the decade, Malenko made the decision to retire from active competition and opened The Malenko School of Wrestling. The original school was held in a karate school and they just put down mats for the students to work out on. He later moved the school to North Tampa. At one point, he operated two gyms ... one in Tampa and the other at Highways 60 and 39 in Plant City.

This was when Malenko saw his opportunity to hit Graham where it hurt the most — in his pocketbook. He started his own promotion and ran opposition. He filmed his television at Channel 3 in Tampa, the PBS affiliate, and aired the show on Channel 28, an independent station that is now an NBC affiliate. It wasn't long before Graham was calling Malenko, trying to smooth things over, and wanting to know what it would take to get him off the air ... but Malenko wasn't about to back down.

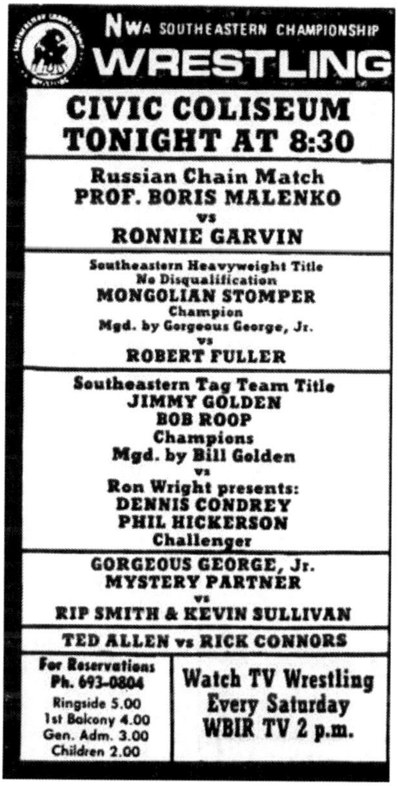

Knoxville, Tennessee • Aug. 11, 1978

Announcers on Graham's *Championship Wrestling from Florida* program began making on-the-air remarks, criticizing Malenko and his promotion. Dusty Rhodes, who was Graham's top draw during that time, got cute during one of his interviews and began to ridicule the boys that Malenko had working for him. Malenko responded on-the-air by challenging Rhodes to a match with all proceeds going to charity. In addition, Malenko's sons, Joe and Dean, were just starting their pro careers. Having learned the art of shooting and hooking from Karl Gotch, they issued challenges of their own to Eddie and Mike Graham. For some reason, "Graham and Co." suddenly refused to comment on the subject.

Malenko was considered to be a great teacher and, with the help of Karl Gotch, passed along the art of shooting and hooking to many students, including his sons, Joe and Dean. Most of the talent that came out of Florida during the '80s was trained by Malenko and his sons, including Johnny B. Badd [Mark Mero], Barry Horowitz, Al and Lou Perez, 1-2-3 Kid [Sean Waltman], Jumbo Baretta, Chris Champion, Ricky Santana, Gangrel, Norman Smiley, Alex G, and many others. Malenko launched several wrestling promotions, including Global Wrestling ['88] and Championship Wrestling Federation ['91], which gave his students the opportunity to practice their skills before paying audiences. He also helped place talent with promotions in Japan.

Malenko promoted a card on Oct. 14, 1981, in a tent at Gulf View Square Mall in Port Richey. The more than 700 wrestling fans who lined up to buy tickets were rewarded with a Russian death match won by Malenko over Tom Laxton. The card also included a young Dean (wrestling as Dino) Malenko and Luis Astea, and the legendary Karl Von Stroheim was in attendance.

The last reference to Boris Malenko wrestling was a Russian chain match against Rusty Brooks in Hollywood, Florida, on July 30, 1988. The match,

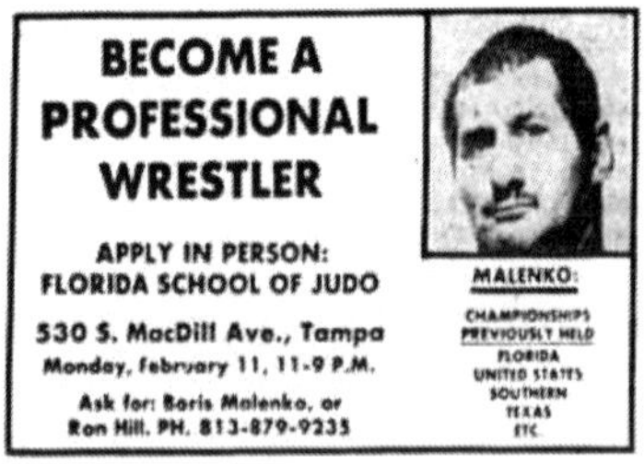

BECOME A professional wrestler, Apply in person, Thursday, January 17th, 9-5PM, Tampa Bay Amateur Boxing Gym, 1915 E. Broadway (7th Ave.) Ybor City. Interviews only. Ask for Professor Malenko.

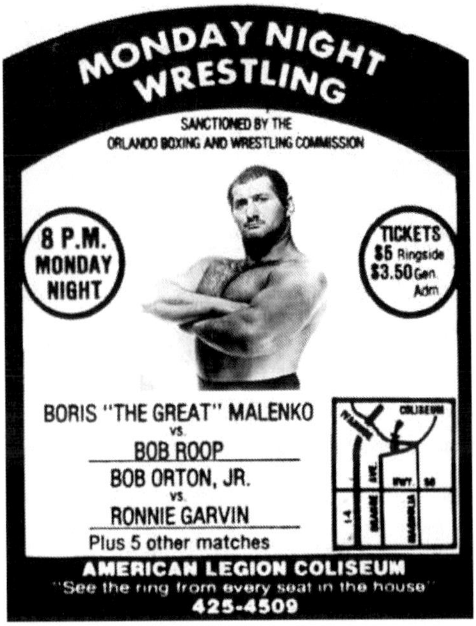

(top) *Tampa Tribune*
Feb. 10, 1980

(bottom) *Tampa Tribune*
Jan. 15, 1980

(right) *Orlando Sentinel*
Feb. 25, 1980

under the auspices of the Global Wrestling Alliance, was promoted in the *Miami Herald*. No report on the show has been found, though, so it's unknown as to whether or not the match actually took place.

Perhaps the best testimonial of Malenko's success as a heel comes from a quote from one of Malenko's son, Jody, in a 2020 *Tampa Bay Times* feature article.

> "People would come up to my dad and say 'It's fake.' Rather than argue, he'd say, 'Yeah,' because he knew what would happen next. The same fan would argue with him that it *wasn't* fake.
>
> "Once, an old woman approached him as he strolled Miami Beach. She said, 'I know your name is Larry Simon and you are Jewish and born in New Jersey. You're not Russian.' And then later she's in the audience screaming, 'Kill that Russian! Kill him!'"

Newspaper columnists often referred to "The Great Malenko" in their writing. Bill Sheldon, writer for the *Miami Herald*, quoted the athletic director at Sunland Training Center as saying, "The kids here see a lot of pro wrestling on television, and they ask, 'Is the Great Malenko coming today?' They love it."

In his May 25, 1971, column in the *Fort Lauderdale News*, Sports Editor Bill Bondurant wrote about an altercation that took place between Cleveland Indians pitcher Sam McDowell and New York Yankee shortstop Gene Michael.

> "McDowell, who is 6-foot-6 and weighs 245 pounds, lifted the 165-pound Michael shoulder-high and threw him to the ground, following with a full body press that would have made even the Great Malenko proud."

Another story related in the *Tampa Bay Times* looked back to a time when former Tampa Mayor Dick Greco wanted a personal trainer.

> "He went to The Great Malenko. Between sets of calisthenics, Malenko had Greco run up and down the stairs of his house. Later, Greco said the knee-bends and all that running left the muscles in his legs as solid as a piece of wood."

Even football players mentioned the Great Malenko. Charlie (Horse) Williams, one of the hardest hitting linebackers in University of Florida Gators football history, was influenced by Malenko. In Tom McEwen's *The Morning After* column, Williams said:

> "In our back yard, we'd play like we were wrestlers like Eddie Graham and The Great Malenko. We'd chain ourselves together for a death match, until mama came out and made us quit."

In the April 25, 1977, edition of the *Miami News*, sports editor John Crittenden featured a pop quiz on football. Question number three was:

> 3 — The Dolphin player who ran the team's first kickoff back for a touchdown was (a) Joe Auer (b) Wahoo McDaniel (c) The Great Malenko (d) Red Grange.

To this day, the three names frequently mentioned in newspaper articles written about the heyday of professional wrestling in Tampa are Jack Brisco, Dusty Rhodes, and Eddie Graham. But the name that is almost *always* mentioned is … you guessed it. The Great Malenko! And old-time wrestling fans still imitate his mannerisms. If you ask them about Malenko, they'll inevitably bring up the Russian chain matches, his two-fingered eye-poke, and the interviews he did with one eye closed.

Malenko's two sons, Joe and Dean, were his pride. Joe got into the wrestling business around 1974, but chose to focus on Japan for most of his career. He has been a pharmacist in cancer care for more than 25 years. Dean became one of the best in-ring technicians of his day, working for every major promotion before going behind the scenes for WWE, and now AEW. The Malenko family collectively trained some of the top talent of the day.

There are so many great moments in Malenko's career that I personally remember, but none as well as a humorous incident that took place in the early '70s. One afternoon, as the *Championship Wrestling from Florida* program faded to a commercial break, the picture changed to Malenko in the ring. He charged across the ring to meet his opponent ... a queen-size mattress. In an attempt to defeat his stuffed opponent, he bodyslammed it. He stomped on it and punched it. But it was all to no avail. The mattress was too comfortable. Malenko fell over backwards and fell asleep on the mattress. One-two-three and it was over. It was a classic moment that showed me a lighter side of Malenko that I never knew existed.

Boris Maximilianovitch Malenko was one of those rare individuals who was both a great worker *and* shooter, and when it came to ring psychology and interviews, there was none better. He convinced the fans beyond any shadow of a doubt that he was an unstoppable, killer heel. And, unlike the so-called prima donna "superstars" of the modern era, he wouldn't hesitate to put a guy over "one-two-three" in the middle of the ring and come back the next week with more heat on him than the week before.

On the other hand, he was a much different person outside the ring. As *Tampa Bay Times* staff writer Richard Danielson put it:

> *"The Great Malenko, a pro wrestling villain who was cold and hated inside the ring, was warm and caring outside it."*

The Great Malenko died on Sept. 1, 1994, at the University of South Florida's H. Lee Moffitt Cancer Center, after a long battle with leukemia. He turned 61 years old just five weeks before his death. Larry had undergone experimental chemotherapy, a process which made him very sick and destroyed his immune system. He fought bravely and made it through the ordeal, built his system back up, and went home to regain his lost weight. The doctors convinced him to undergo another series of treatments, a strategy which went tragically wrong, as he succumbed to a viral infection.

David Whitley, a staff writer for the *Tampa Tribune*, wrote a series of articles about Malenko's fight against leukemia.

> The great villain sits in a blue gown in the corner of a darkened hospital room, awash in his memories and suffering. Thirty years as a professional in pain barely prepares a man for this. "Nothing is like it," he said. "Nothing can compare. Chemotherapy is like a crap shoot. If it takes … if it's able to destroy the cancer cells. If, if, if …"
>
> You don't beat leukemia. You try to fight it to a draw as long as possible. That's a different equation for Malenko, who spent his life winning or losing five nights a week.

More than 200 people attended his memorial service on Sunday, Sept. 4. in Tampa, including close friend Karl Gotch, Don Curtis, Gordon Solie, Hiro Matsuda, George Scott, Danny Miller, Cyclone Negro, Stu Schwartz, Bonnie

Watson, Angelo and Lanny Poffo, 1-2-3 Kid, Tony Marino, Masao Hattori, and Steve Keirn. Hans Mortier, a long-time friend who lives in Holland, flew in a few weeks before Malenko's death to spend time with him during his first round of chemotherapy.

As someone who spent many years watching *Championship Wrestling from Florida*, I have a great deal of respect for the genius and talent of The Great Malenko ... so much so that I had a hard time referring to him in this article as "Larry," or "Larry Simon." It's feels like sacrilege to call him by that name. To me, and to the thousands of fans who were entertained by his antics for decades, he will always be "The Great Malenko."

I saw him wrestle many times at house shows in Florida, but one of my big regrets in life is that I never had the opportunity to actually meet Boris Maximilianovitch Malenko and tell him just how much of an influence he had been in the life of a young, high-school student. If I hadn't seen that dastardly Russian on television when I was introduced to professional wrestling on that Sunday afternoon, it's very likely that I never would have developed an interest in the sport. At least, not to the extent that I have.

This account is just a small tribute to a great man who left an indelible mark in the wrestling business. The Great Malenko will be missed, but the memories he left behind will always be an important part of wrestling history.

TITLES

Texas ['57 as Crusher Duggan]
AWA world tag
['61 as Otto von Krupp w/Bob Geigel]
World tag [FL '62 w/Russian Crusher]
Southern [FL '62]
Florida ['67]
Brass knucks [FL '68-72, 9x]
Southern tag
[FL '68 w/Johnny Valentine]
American tag [Texas '69
w/Lord Charles Montague]
Texas tag ['70 w/Killer Karl Kox]
American [Texas '70]
Florida tag ['72 w/Bob Roop;
'72 w/Johnny Walker]
Southeastern [Knoxville '78]
Southeastern TV [Knoxville '78]
Southeastern tag
[Knoxville '79 w/Assassin]

ALIAS

Larry Simon
Crusher Duggan [TX '57]
Otto von Krupp [MN '61]
Professor Boris
Maximilianovitch Malenko
Masked Muscovite [FL '71]

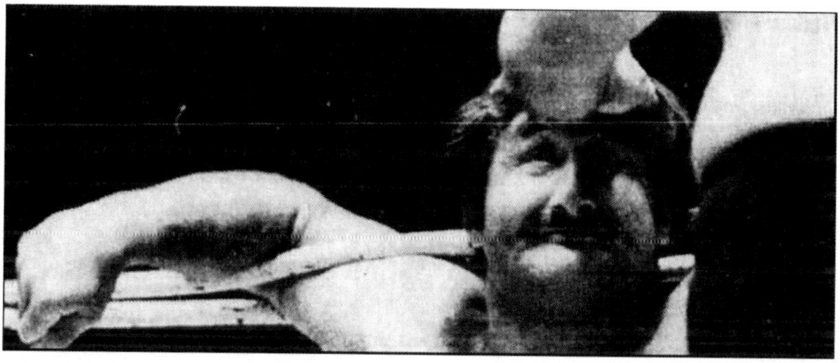

***Palm Beach Post* staff photographer Emil Fray entered the photographic series in the 21st Annual Southern Short Course at Columbia, S.C. and won first place in the sports picture story category with the above photo of the Great Malenko.**

THE GREAT MALENKO PHOTO ALBUM

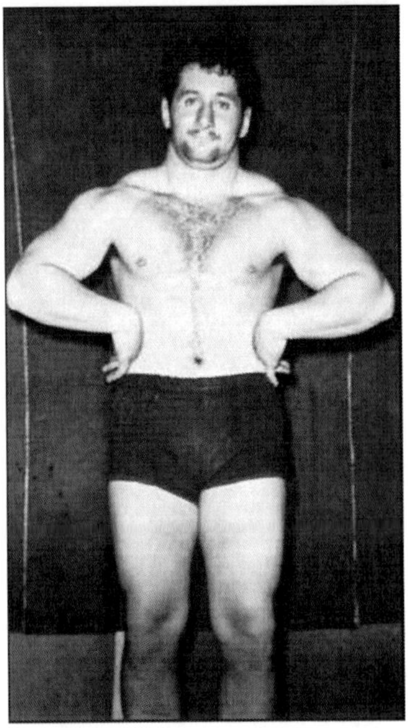

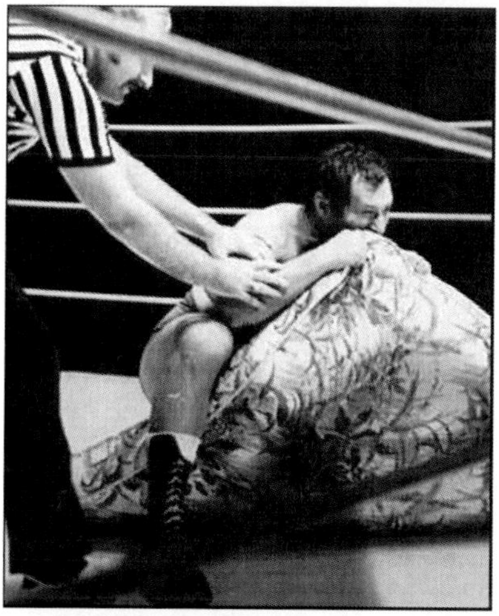

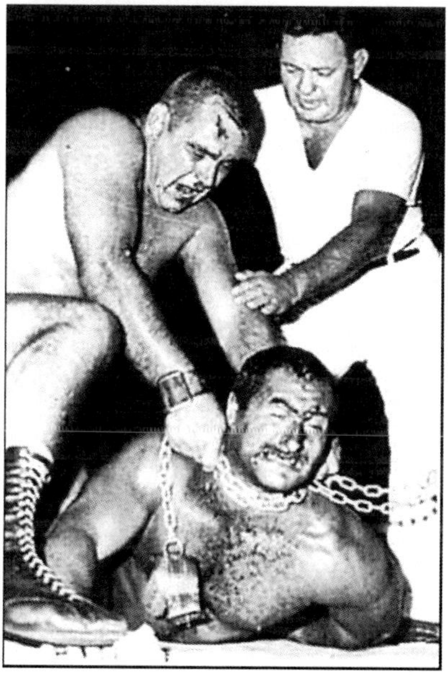

(page 26, top l. clockwise)
Malenko vs The Gladiator (Orlando, 1968)
Malenko vs Bruiser Ben (Tampa, Jan. 7, 1969)
Early photo of Larry Simon
Malenko with his team of The Mongols

(above, top l. clockwise)
Malenko after losing a hair match
Otto Von Krupp
Bob Orton, Malenko & Hans Mortier
Danny Miller vs. Malenko
Russian chain match (Tampa, Aug. 24, 1965)
Malenko vs. The Mattress

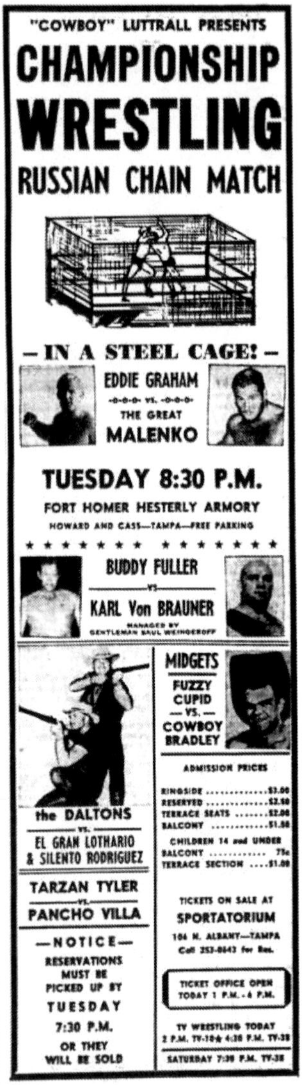

(top l. clockwise)
Malenko publicity photo
Tampa, Aug. 8, 1967
New York NY, March 7, 1959
Kansas City, Aug. 6, 1958
Kansas City, May 22, 1958

This is a side of The Great Malenko that most people have never seen!

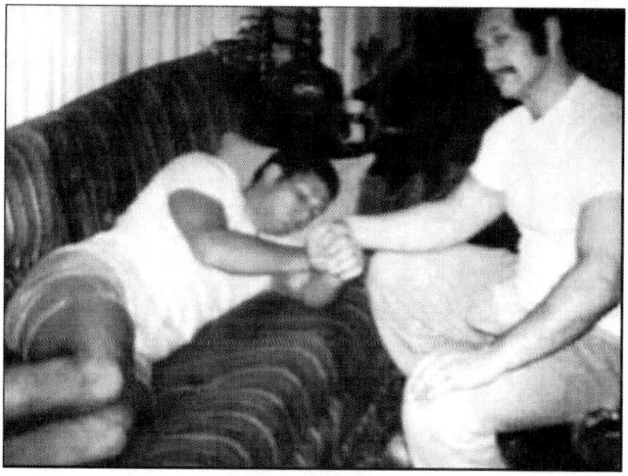

(top l. clockwise)
Malenko, Dean, Joe, Sandy
Dean, Malenko & Joe in front of Malenko's school
Joe's favorite picture -- Joe was sick, so Malenko holds his hand and comforts him
Malenko in a Russian chain match with Wahoo McDaniel in Houston.
Dean, Malenko & Joe

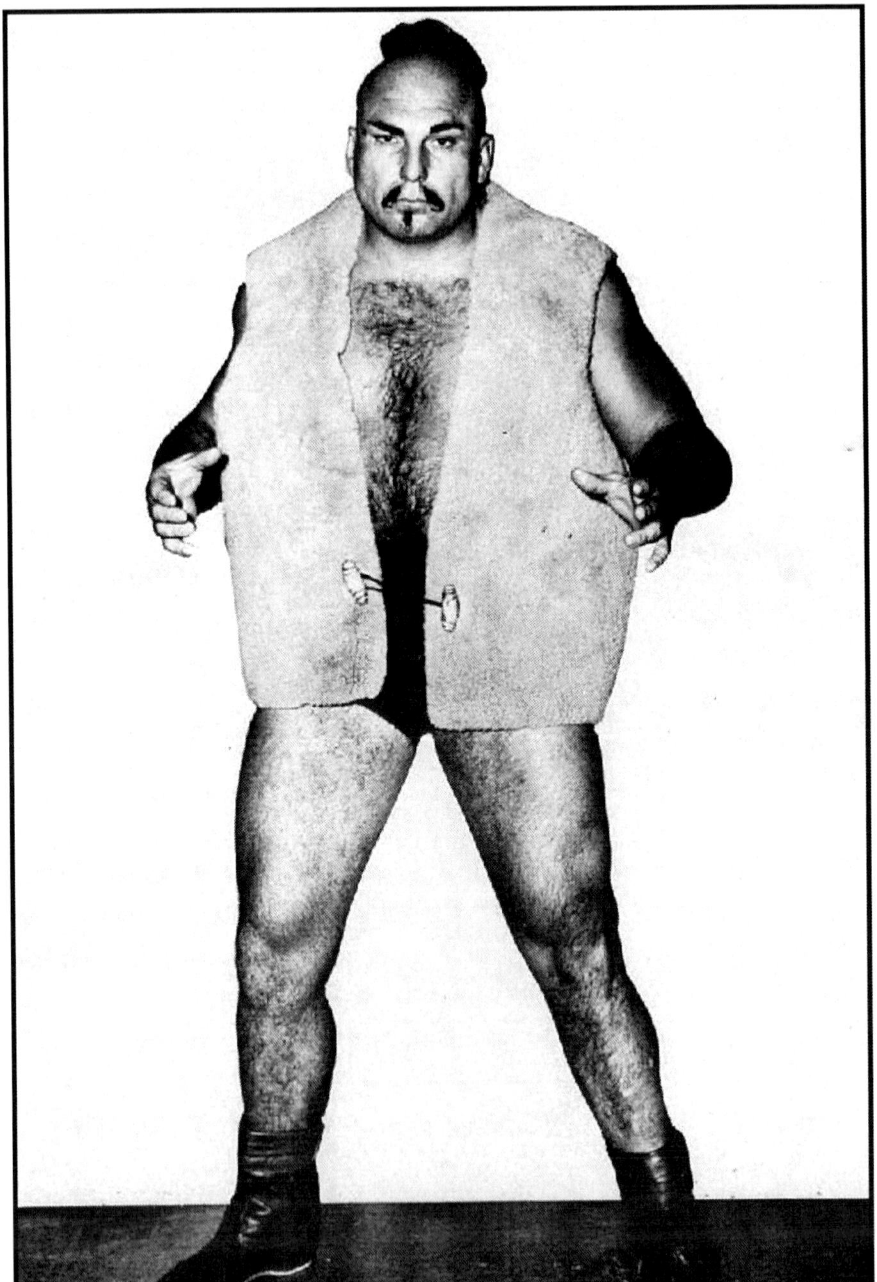

ARCHIE GOULDIE
The Mongolian Stomper

Archie Gouldie

This interview, conducted in Knoxville by Scott Teal in Dec. 1993, can also be found on video as part of Scott's *Shooting with the Legends* video series.

Why don't you start out by telling us about your childhood ... where you were born, where you grew up, and a little about your parents.

I was born in Carbon, Alberta, Canada. [Nov. 22, 1936] I was raised on a farm. I was the youngest of eight children. My daddy passed away when I was three years old. We lived two miles out of town. When I got in my teens, I had two brothers that really loved wrestling. Calgary, Alberta, which is 60 miles from Carbon ... it's a big city, which is where Stu Hart lived. My brothers used to take me to the wrestling matches, Friday night in Calgary. The first few times I went, we just bought tickets and sat. My brothers knew that I wanted to get into wrestling. They kept pushing me. *"Go up and talk to Stu ... talk to Stu."*

So, one week, I just went up and talked to Stu. I said, *"Mr. Hart. I'd like to be a professional wrestler. How do I get into it? Do I jump in the ring tonight and challenge somebody?"*

He said, *"No, don't do that. I'll let you know. I'll get you started."*

So, two or three more weeks went by. Finally, he came up to me one night and said, *"Come on up to my house. Do you know where I live?"*

I said, *"Yes."* The next day, I went up to his house.

Were you a pretty big guy at the time?

Yeah. I was about 220 when I was 19.

Were you pretty muscular?

Yeah. I worked out a lot.

Did you play any sports in high school?

Well, we played ice hockey ... a lot. We had an outdoor place there, you know, where we used to play hockey. Other little towns would come in and we'd go to their towns. That was the main thing in Canada. Anyway, I went out to Stu's. He lived in a big old house up on the hill. It was about four miles from my mother's house. She had moved to the city of Calgary and I was living there with her. I didn't have a car or anything, so I used to walk out to Stu's. Stu had a workout room in his basement. He had a wrestling mat ... just a mat, but it was wall to wall. He would get me on that mat. (laughs) He was sadistic. He'd get a hold on you. You would scream and beg, trying to get out of it. I spent three years in that ... I called it The Dungeon.

Tell me about the very first time you were down there.

(laughs) I didn't know what he was going to do, you know. All he did was just roll me around, take me down, tie me up, you know? I said, *"Stu I never see any of this on Friday nights."*

"Oh, we don't do that yet. You have to start at the beginning and learn all this first."

"Yes, sir." (laughs) I just went along with it. I tell you, he had a hold on me. He had me sitting down, and he had his arm wrapped around my neck. I couldn't move. Stu was funny when he had a hold on you. His tongue would hang out of his mouth and he would bite on it. (makes grunting noises) So he had this hold on me and was doing that with his tongue. . I had one arm that was movable ... my right arm. I saw that tongue, so I brought my elbow up under his chin, and that old tongue started to bleed. Blood was flowing all over the place. That's what saved me. His wife [Helen] come downstairs. She hollered through the door, *"Stu, you have a long-distance call!"*

She didn't know anything about the tongue yet. He still hung on. She went back upstairs. He never moved. Gruntin' and blood flying. She come back down stairs. *"Stu! Long-distance call."*

So he let go of me. I took off out of there and I run to my mama's place. It was winter. There was about a foot of snow. (laughs) I walked in the house. Of course, the blood from his tongue was all over me. Mama said, *"What are you doing?"* (laughs)

How long before you went back?

Two weeks. (laughs) In fact, he called me. He called my mom.

So he saw something in you?

Oh, yeah. You see, another thing used to happen there. At the end of football season up there — the Canadian Football League — those big lineman like to stay up there in Calgary until the spring season began. A lot of them were from the States and other places. So, a couple of them went to Stu and tried to get in like I did. He took them big lineman after a season of football. They used to squeal. You could hear them for half a mile. He was putting those sadistic moves and holds on them. Everything to him had to be a shoot. Like I told you, the night that I worked with him, and I had that sore knee ...

Tell that story again.

He was out there interviewing one night. We had this worked out. I was gonna sneak around to the other side of the ring and — they used to interview right on the floor standing up in front of the ring — so I went around the ring and I nailed him from behind. I didn't know whether he'd go down or not, but he did. I put the boots to them and I left. I knew he'd put the stranglehold on me if I hung around. Well, the next week, we had the match. It was sold out. We turned about 500 people away. We get up in there and, like I said, I had this knee I twisted. I jumped out of the ring, landed on it, and twisted it again. So I got back in the ring and I told him, *"Get a hold, Stu."*

My leg was really bothering me. So he got ahold of the leg and he's whispering to me, *"I'll put it back in place for you."*

I said, *"Leave the damn thing alone!"* If he had put it in place, he would've tore it right off.

So what did you do when you went back to the dungeon the second time? Did he stretch you again?

No, actually, he surprised me. He was okay. He started showing me some working moves. Of course, later on, when Bret started, I used to work out a lot down there in the basement. I was doing high spots and stuff. I was showing Bret and Stu was showing both of us. Stu was kind of refereeing for us. It worked out good.

How long did it take before he actually smartened you up?

Stu?

Yes.

Oh, I would say six months.

So, up until that time, you were pretty much just learning wrestling and the moves.

Yeah, yeah.

What did he say when he first started to clue you in?

Well, remember when I said, *"They don't do this on Friday nights, Stu."* Then he said, *"I'm gonna show you some stuff that we do in the ring."* That's the way I started. It was okay.

There was a legend that you jumped in the ring against Al and Tiny Mills years before you were smartened up.

Yeah, that happened. I forgot to tell you that. My brothers kept egging me on. One night, I did it. It just so happened that Stu was out there watching the matches. Just as I went to go under the bottom rope, he pulled me back. (laughs) He pulled me back.

So there was something to the story. You just didn't actually get into the ring.

Yeah.

How old were you when you first worked out with Stu?

I was twenty.

What were you doing during that time? Did you work a regular job?

I worked for the power company. They handled both power and natural gas. I worked for them and I would wrestle when I first started wrestling. For Stu, I wrestled part-time.

When you were training, did any other wrestlers help train you?

Yeah. There was one guy who really stands out ... Riot Call Jim Wright. Have you heard of him?

Oh, yeah.

He was a real nice guy. He would come out to Stu's and work with me ... Bret and me. He would show us different things.

So he was somewhat of a mentor to you?

Yeah. In fact, he was the one who got me booked in the United States — in North Carolina — when I first went there. He called Jim Crockett.

From the time you started training, how long was it before you had your first match?

Up there in Canada?

Yes.

Let's see … about eight months.

Did you have your first match in Calgary?

Yes.

Archie made his wrestling debut on Friday, Nov. 2, 1962. He wrestled and defeated John Dane at the Victoria Pavilion.

Do you have any memories of that first match? Were you nervous?

Yes. I was a little nervous.

Do you have any memories of that match that stand out?

My opponent got me out on the floor and threw me into the ring post. When my head hit that ring post, it shook the whole ring. I thought, *"Well, you've gotta make this look good."*

Was that the first time you were allowed in the dressing room?

No. No, I had been in there before and talked to the guys. All the guys were good to me.

Did you find it exciting to be in there?

Yep. The only other place I had ever seen them was in the ring.

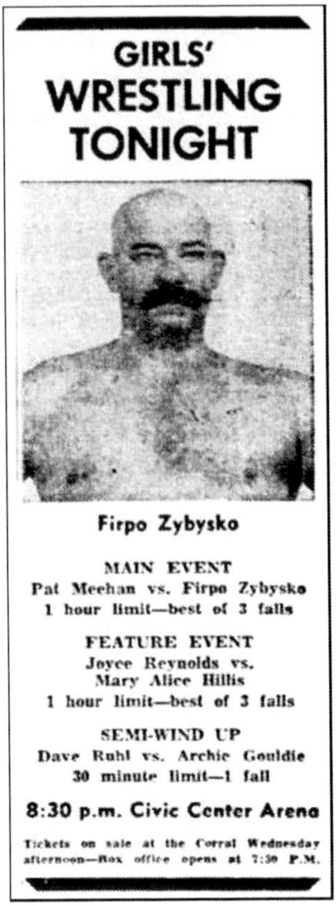

Great Falls, MT • Nov. 7, 1956

Did anybody try to discourage you?

No, they sure didn't. I didn't have any problems. You know, when you're starting like that, if you mess up a high spot or something, you feel kind of stupid. Of course, you go back to the dressing room and apologize to your opponent. Most of them were all right. We all had to start somewhere.

Did anybody give you any indication that you might be a main eventer?

Yeah. Jim Wright was a real pusher. He used to sit me down. I used to go to his apartment. He would tell me to come over. He told me, *"Keep fit and listen to everybody. It won't do you any good listening to some people, but listen to them anyway."* That's what I did.

What did you do to keep in shape?

I worked into heavy weights, but I never was a real heavy weight person. I worked out a lot with dumbbells and did a lot of dumbbell presses. I did a lot of stretching.

What did your mother think about you being a wrestler?

I have to tell you a story about my mom. I got going pretty steady there. It was when I came back in for Stu. I went in and out a few times. I went to other territories, but I would come back to see my family. I talked to one of my sisters. She said, *"You should see mom on Saturday morning. She always watches you on TV."* She said, *"But whenever anybody asks her if she watches you on TV, she says,* 'No, no, no! I can't stand it!'*"*

One Saturday morning, I snuck in. I walked around the corner and she was in the chair watching wrestling on TV. She was hollering at the TV. I said, *"Mom, I didn't think you watched this stuff."*

"I don't, but it was on." (laughs)

Nobody ever admits it.

No, no. It was on.

Did she ever express any worry that you might get hurt?

Oh, yeah … all the time.

Did you ever notice the guys talking carny and wonder what they were saying?

Yes. When I first went into the dressing room there in Calgary, somebody came in … a photographer or newspaper guy. *Kayfabe!* I looked around. I couldn't understand. I guess that word isn't even used today.

(laughs) No. There is no kayfabe.

You know, back then, it was pretty strict. I mean, especially starting like I was. You went down the line, or else, and I respected that, and they respected me for it.

Did anybody sit you down and give you a little talk about protecting the business?

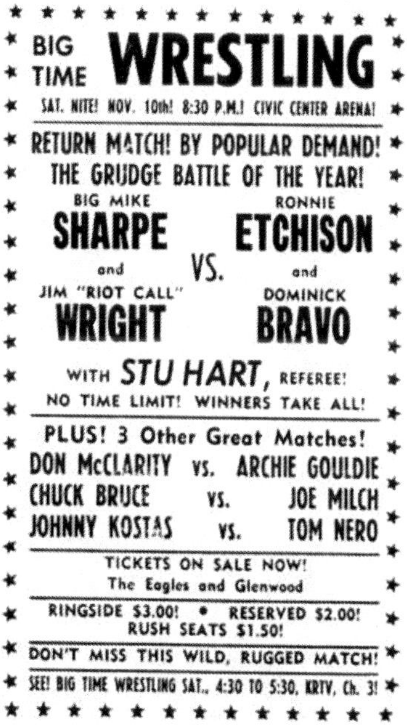

Great Falls, MT • Nov. 7, 1956

Oh, yeah. Several of 'em. Stu was one. Jim Wright was one. Jim had been in the business for 20 years by that time. That kind of information helped you. It gets you going the right way.

What was the toughest thing you had to learn?

Timing in the ring. Highspots, where you … maybe you were working on highspot where a guy gets you in a headlock and throws you off. You drop down and get up, he hip-tosses you. You can't remember it all. Of course, when you're first starting, a lot of guys don't do real long highspots. But timing is one of the hardest things … and knowing when to do something. If you have a good guy leading you, you're okay, but if you have to lead yourself, it's kind of tough sometimes.

Now, you started out as a baby face, right?

Yeah. Of course, you go over a lot of it in the dressing room. Not when to use 'em, but what to use, so when the time comes up, it's comeback time or selling time, or whatever, you have an idea of what to do when.

Did you have a hard time in places like Florida, where Eddie Graham had long, complicated finishes?

Jim Crockett! [Charlotte territory] He'd sit out there in a chair, not far from the ring. Anybody messed up, he'd go back to the dressing room and start hollering.

I never heard that before. You're talking about Jim Crockett Sr.

Yep.

What was the easiest thing for you to learn?

Bodyslams, slamming guys, hitting them with tackles, taking bumps. I was a good bump taker from a tackle. I could hit the turnbuckles. That's why I've got ten pinched nerves in the small of my back right now.

Did you have trouble learning how to go into the turnbuckle when someone whipped you into one?

Yeah. The thing of it is, some promoters who put the ring up, instead of leaving the three turnbuckles all even — I don't know why it was always the middle one — was left out a little bit. Like I said, when you take a turnbuckle — and I used to take them hard, shake the ring — a lot of times, that center turnbuckle would catch you right in the small of the back.

Did it have something to do with the way the hook was made?

I don't know … it was just the way it was put up, you know? Now, Stu was good because … you know, you tell a promoter sometimes. You say, *"Hey, them turnbuckles are sticking out. They're gonna break someone's back."*

How long did it take before you didn't feel scared to death when he went to the ring?

It wasn't too long. It really depended on who I was going in with. I used to watch the guys, so I knew the things they would do. When you're getting started in wrestling, once you work with a guy a few times, the match improves. Every time you go in with him, it gets better, because you know how he does it, what he does, and how his timing is.

Did your mother ever come to the matches live?

My brothers tried to get her to. One night, Stu promoted matches in my hometown of Carbon. It was just a little town, you know … 600 people. The people came out from all around, the farmers. It was a good crowd.

Kansas City KS • Oct. 3, 1963

As a rule, promoters didn't give a wrestler a push in their home territory because the people knew the person, and weren't likely to believe he was a tough guy. Your situation was different because you grew up in the area, but you still got a huge push.

Well, the thing of it is — I may be bragging when I say this — but I actually knew what Stu wanted. That was always the way. Just like when I got my big break in Kansas City. I knew what Bob Geigel and Pat O'Connor wanted. They wanted good, solid, believable stuff. Stu was the same way. Stu liked all that grabbing and pulling and tugging. But he also wanted the heel to do good, solid moves. If someone threw punches, he wanted to hear them pop. If you throw a guy in for a boot, or a kick to the stomach, you want to make sure it lands. The guy comes off the rope and tightens up his stomach … they better tighten it up when they worked with me.

(laughs)

You know, because I laid them in! That's how I got over … everywhere I ever worked. I made everything look believable.

Did any of the veterans ever tell you to loosen up?

Yeah, they would once in a while. I tell 'em in the dressing room, *"I'm not trying to hurt you, but I lay my punches in. I lay my kicks in."* I said, *"My finish is a stomp to the head. I won't kick you in the face. It'll be on the forehead. It'll go up high and I'll come right down on the forehead. When you get up after I get the three-count on you, sell that head. Hold on to it."* That's the way I worked. Just like when I went to Kansas City. They carried the first five guys I wrestled out on stretchers. Hauled 'em right out. I'd do the head stomp and they'd get the medical guys to put 'em on and haul 'em out.

How and where did you come up with the idea for the head stomp?

Actually, it was Jim Wright again. I keep mentioning Jim Wright. Jim told me he thought it was a good finish for me. Jim seen that I could go up high and come down with my boot. He was the one who mentioned it. I wore size 16, Triple E boots.

You were a babyface at the time. That just doesn't seem like a babyface move.

No, but at the time, I was turning [heel].

Okay. Did you turn before you left for Charlotte, or later on?

Before. I don't know if I told you before about my first break. I left Charlotte and went to Alabama.

Tell me about Charlotte first. Jim Wright got you in there?

Yeah. I stayed there about three months. I was in quite a few tag matches. It didn't suit me there. I don't like tag matches. I worked them, but I didn't like them.

Who did you work for in Alabama?

Lee Fields. Mobile was a pretty good territory, but it wasn't doing good. It was way, way down. I was talking to somebody in the dressing room one night. He said he was going to Texas and wanted to know if I wanted to go. He said he was pretty good friends with Dory Funk Jr. Of course, Dory Funk Sr. was the promoter in [West] Texas. He called Junior up and he said, *"Yeah, bring him in."*

So I went in there. Of course, Dory Senior knew Bob Geigel really well, and Geigel would go into

Kansas City KS • Jun 2, 1965

Amarillo to work. Geigel and Pat O'Connor were there one night when I was working. They came over to me and said, *"We just bought into Kansas City. We needed a top heel. We figure you can do it. We've watched you in several matches."*

On April 13, 1963, a wrestler named Billy Romanoff wrestled in Amarillo. The identity of Romanoff was unknown until, one day, I received a photo of Archie with the name "Billy Romanoff" written on the back. A search through my Amarillo wrestling programs led to an article about "Billy Romanoff" that included a picture of Archie. Archie's last match in Amarillo was Aug. 15. Seven days later, he was in Kansas City, where he was renamed "The Mongolian Stomper".

You were heeling there in Amarillo?

Yeah. So I went to Kansas City. Like I said before, they stretchered them out for me. I was a heel for a long time and then turned babyface.

Was Gust Karras still running the territory at that time?

No, he brought Geigel and O'Connor in as partners. He let them do all the finishes and stuff at the towns.

Did you have much interaction with Gust?

Yes. Gust was a good fellow. He was a funny, old man. We were sitting in Sedalia, Missouri, one night … a little town. I think the only reason Gust used to book the town was, his buddies were Masons or something, and they sponsored it in some way. Anyway, he booked Sedalia. He never drew nothin'. You could have cut a foot off and it would draw.

(laughs)

So, this one night we were in the dressing room. One guy said, *"Ain't nobody out there again tonight. No pay again."*

Gus was sitting there with his pipe, puffing, puffing. He was hearing this. *"Well, Sedalia at least pays the rent."*

I walked up about that time. *"You think we live in a damn tent, Gust?"*

So he got phased out when Geigel and O'Connor came in?

Not really. He still (pause) … St. Joseph, that was his town. He booked it.

He booked Omaha, too, didn't he?

He booked people in Omaha. Like me, I went up to Omaha. Oh, who was the promoter …

Dusek. Joe Dusek.

Joe Dusek. Good guy, too. Super guy. Now there was a town that done good. I made some money in Omaha, just by going in and out. Another thing Gust would do. He'd take my TV tapes and send them to Dusek. Dusek would play them and we'd work the same angles we did in Kansas City. Joe would bring the same guys up.

How did you get the name Mongolian Stomper?

Pat O'Connor. He came in the dressing room and said, *"We need to talk. I have a name for you. It's a gimmick. The Mongolian Stomper. We want you to shave your head, leaving a knot on the top back, and grow a Fu Manchu mustache."*

You didn't keep the top-knot for long, did you?

No. The boys used to get ahold of it. That little bit of hair hurts more than if they got ahold of (pause) ...

A great big handful.

Yeah, right.

Who were some of the guys you remember working with during that time?

Cowboy Bob Ellis. He was a good one. Shoot man, when he was a baby ... he would come in there as a babyface. He'd walk out of the dressing room and that house would come down. He was my favorite... Of all the babyfaces I ever worked against, he was my favorite.

You went to Australia at one point during your Kansas City run. How did that come about?

Pat O'Connor booked me out. I enjoyed Australia. Long trips, but we flew most of the time. I worked a lot over there with Tex McKenzie. He was a big card babyface over there. Jim Barnett was the promoter. I was there for about five months.

Saskatoon, Saskatchewan
May 15, 1968

Early in your career, was there anybody in particular that you watched for ideas or psychology, or someone who was a big influence on you?

For babyface, it would be Bob Ellis. Heel, there was a few of them. I liked Bob Geigel's way of wrestling. When I went to Kansas City, he put me over, and I used to watch a lot of things Bob did. He used to talk to me a lot in the dressing room. He was a big help. I really liked him. I enjoyed working with him. Probably better than anybody I ever worked with. I just felt comfortable. Guys like Geigel and O'Connor were just like the boys. They didn't act like promoters. That makes it a lot better.

When I switched babyface in Kansas City, this GM dealership called the wrestling office one day. They asked if they could talk to me. Bob called me and gave me their number. I talked to them and they asked me if I would be interested in doing a commercial. I said, *"Sure."*

I went out there and the owner of the company said, *"You got any ideas for this commercial?"*

I said, *"Yeah, I got a good one. You and I will be standing here in front of the camera. We'll start talking about prices of cars and I'll say,* 'You better give me the price that I want or I'll do this.'*"* And I said, *"I'm gonna scoop you up for a bodyslam and I'll hold you right up here. I'll say,* 'Now, are you going to give me the price I want for that car?'*"*

"Yes, yes, yes! Let me down! Let me down!"

I let him down. Anyway, they gave me a new Pontiac convertible. They played that commercial for a little more than two years in Kansas City.

In the early days as the heel Stomper, did you act like you couldn't speak English?

In some places I did, but I didn't do that too long. It was kind of rough living like that.

Sure. People would see and hear you talking in the outside world. That kind of kills the gimmick.

True.

Do you remember going to Hawaii?

Yeah. I'll tell you a strange thing about Hawaii. We used to go to Japan, and back in them early days, the plane would always stop in Honolulu to gas up. They had to gas up going to Japan and coming back. Coming back from Japan, all the boys would get off in Honolulu and stay there for a week or so because Japan was hard work. So (pause) … I forget who it was, but we got off the plane, checked into the motel, and all them guys went to the beach. There was four of 'em. I said, *"I'll be out in a little bit. I'm going to make a couple calls home."*

I made my calls and I'm going out to the beach. One of 'em said, *"See that blanket over there? The one with the cooler? There's a nice cold beer in that cooler. There's something to eat. Just sit there and relax. Have a sandwich."*

They were all out on the water, right? I sit down by the cooler, got a beer, a sandwich … or whatever was in there. Here comes this couple out of the water. This guy says, *"What the hell are you doing here … in our cooler, eating our food?"* I look out to the water and the guys were all laughing. (laughs)

A couple of the guys there at the time was Johnny Barend and Ripper Collins.

Collins was the guy.

Yes, he was a real ribber. Was the United States title in Gust Karras' territory your first title?

Yes. St. Joseph would be the first one. That's the first break I got … the first place someone really put me over. I've had a few since then.

Stomper won the title from Enrique Torres in St. Joseph, Missouri, on Friday, Dec. 20, 1963.

That's the understatement of the year. (laughs) When you were in Calgary, did Stu Hart like wrestling heels, or the kind of heels who punched and kicked?

He liked both, I guess … as long as it drew money, he really didn't care. (laughs) I never did see a real wrestling heel, somebody who made a lot of wrestling moves, draw a lot of money. It's great to use them in-between, but two guys going in there and just wrestling …

Did you ever work under a mask?

Yes, I did … one time. I forget where it was, but I was barred from the building. Did I ever tell you about guns being pulled on me in Kansas City?

No.

When I was in Kansas City, I took my two kids with me to the matches one night. I never did that. It was very rare. But this night, I took them. In Kansas City, Kansas, the wrestlers park in the basement of the auditorium. A lot of the cars outside were getting the tires cut and windows broken. I was on last that night. I showered and got dressed, got my kids, I'm in the car, and the overhead door was open. I was driving towards the door and here come these two guys with guns. They stand right in the doorway. Well, that basement was all concrete. I had a .38 in the glove box. I reached over, got it, and started shooting at the walls. Bullets were zinging off that concrete. You talk about two guys taking off. They were gone! (laughs)**You had serious heat when people did things like that.**

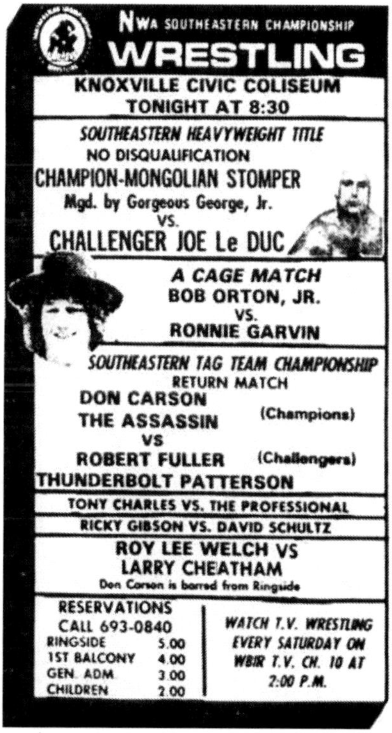

Knoxville TN • Dec. 9, 1977

Oh, yes. Harlan, Kentucky, was the worst. I was shot at, knifed at. Of course, Gorgeous George [Jr.] was my manager then. The first time ... Harlan was the roughest town anywhere I ever worked for its size. When we started running Harlan, we used the city police. We had to use the county police, too. This night, we were going back to the ring after the match. George was behind me and cops were all around us. You know how we walked down the aisle past the ringside seats. I told the sergeant, *"Sergeant, that guy's got something in his hand."*

He was walking out to the aisle. The sergeant took off and met the guy just as he got to the end of the seats. The guy had an army .45. The guy lifted it up to shoot me and the sergeant went [knocks his hand down]. He shot into the floor.

Another time, George and I were coming back from the same situation. This girl — I never even seen her because she come up the side — she had a knife with an eight-inch blade and she was gonna to stick it in my neck. George seen it, whacked her arm, and the knife flew. The police didn't see the knife. They grabbed George and put the handcuffs on him for hitting that girl. They took him back to the dressing room. George said, *"What are you guys doing? That girl had a knife to stick in his neck."*

"We didn't see no knife."

So, they went out to look ... like the knives just gonna be laying around. *"There's no knife out there."* So they took George to jail. You should see the jail in Harlan. I asked the jailer, *"Have you got a bond on George?"*

"No bond." The jailer said, *"... but if I was you, I'd get him out of here before morning, or you may not get him out of here alive."*

So I went out and I got on the phone. I called Ron Fuller. You know, he was the promoter here. I told him the situation. Ron, at that time, was going with the daughter of the mayor of Knoxville. I can't remember his name. Ron called the mayor and the mayor called the governor of Kentucky. They got a bond on George. It was one o'clock in the morning before I got to the jailhouse and bonded Georgia out. Every time we went to Harlan after that, George would start eating Rolaids about 20 miles out. (laughs) And I don't blame him. After a while, the deputies and the city would pat everybody down when they came in.

Were you ever cut anywhere else?

My back. In fact, it was in Oakland, California, when I was out there. The same deal, coming back from the ring. That was always the most dangerous spot. As long as you're in the ring, you're all right, but that walk back. I was doing the same thing that night in Oakland. Cops was all around me, here comes this little … of course, I didn't see him. He was behind me. He was a little, short Mexican. He run under the arms of the police and stuck that knife in my back. The police knocked his hand off. It went in for about an inch, and then it came out, but the scar was pretty long. It was very close to cutting my spinal cord.

How long did it take you to recover?

Not too long, but like I said, the one spot was deep, but the rest was skin deep. That one deep spot, though, was less than an inch from my spinal cord. I've had some close calls.

Tell me about leaving the ring with Dick Slater in Puerto Rico.

(pause) Oh, oh, oh. Okay. Yeah, that was out at the ballpark. They had the ring in the middle of the field. The ringside chairs were on the field around the ring. Slater and I were in there and we did some TV interviews, so we had some pretty good heat on us. Those fans over there were crazy, too. We was working against these two Puerto Ricans. It was getting hot. I could tell by looking around ringside … people were getting up. I said, *"Dick, come on, let's go."*

"We can't go. We gotta do the finish."

I said, *"Dick, do what I tell ya."*

We took off. We had about a 40-yard walk to the dressing room. About halfway there, I seen this Puerto Rican run inside and slam that door shut. I said, *"Dick, I'm gonna hit that door right now."*

We hit that damn door and it flew open. There he was. We were nice to him. We asked him if he wanted something to eat. Anyway, we were in the dressing room and here comes Carlos Colón, the promoter. *"Oh, boys. I never seen that much heat here ever. EVER! When are you two coming back?"*

I said, *"Never! That rhymes with ever!"*

"What you mean?"

I said, *"Give us our pay."* He paid us.

Was he upset about you not finishing the match?

No. He knew they were coming. The whole ringside was on their feet and half of them was holding chairs. Oh, and I forgot to tell you this. As we were going back to the dressing room, one of them caught Dick on his temple.

With a fist?

No, a chair. A steel folding chair. I got a couple on the back. I just told Colón, *"When you see us walk out the door, that's it."*

Is that the only time you went to Puerto Rico?

Yes. It's not worth it. I mean, they don't have the security to start with, that they need. I think there was four police that night and they were standing around like fans. Did I ever tell you about the time I went to Japan with Andre?

No.

I made five trips to Japan.

In late 1966, early 1967, you were in Northern California for about seven months.

They tagged me up with Ciclon Negro. I just couldn't get along with the promoter (pause) …

Roy Shires?

Yes. He would holler and scream. The first time he did that to me, I just walked out of the dressing room. It was nothing major. It didn't have to be with him. Any little thing would set him off … anything that wasn't just perfect.

Where did you first meet Andre the Giant?

I met him in Canada. Andre and I would be working some town. We'd go afterwards and get a cold beer in a bar. Here come the drunks. Andre was a nice guy. Andre would never get mad at you, but he would get drunk and say, *"There's two of us here! We can handle you!"*

I'd say to the drunks, *"Do you want him to eat you for breakfast?"*

They'd turn around and go right back where they came from. (laughs)

Where did you first work with him?

Canada, I think. He was a good guy to work with. You know, he could move for his size. He had that … what's it called? That giant disease?

Acromegalia.

He didn't tell a lot of people this, but he told me. Him and I were close. He told me that when he was 14, the doctors told him that he would never make it through his twenties. But he did, and you'd never know he had it. I don't think I seen him get mad but maybe once, and I was around him a lot. He was always in a good mood. Most people with a disease like that would have been depressed. I heard he went home to bury his dad in France and

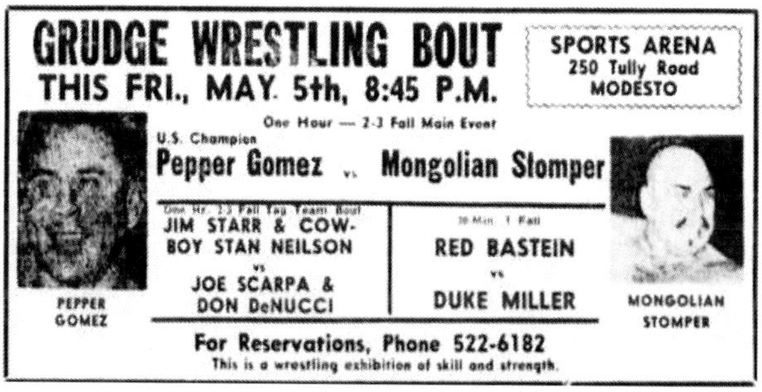

Modesto CA • May 5, 1967

he died about two weeks later. I was in North Carolina when the plane came in with his casket.

You made a good opponent for him because you were pretty tall. How tall were you?

Six-two. He was over in Japan. Oh, man! The crowds were always good in Japan, but when he came, they were super good. He was unreal.

You worked for Inoki in Japan, didn't you?

Yes. I worked for Baba, too. They were both good guys. The first time I went over, the U.S. promoter had sent tapes. The Japanese were in awe of us. When we landed in Tokyo, there was probably 150 media people there. It took us three hours to get out of the airport.

Archie first appeared in Japan on Jan. 4, 1971, in Tokyo, with Ricky Hunter as his tag team partner against Antonio Inoki and Great Kojika. They finished up on Feb. 6.

When we walked down the streets of Tokyo, there would be traffic jams. People would actually stop their cars and look. Japanese weren't used to seeing anybody as big as we were. I used to get a kick out of that.

In real life, in what ways are you like your wrestling character, the Mongolian Stomper?

Quite a bit like me. You know, when you're wrestling steady, you kind of get into that mode.

Who did you travel with most of the time?

I traveled a lot by myself. Sometimes I'd take somebody with me, but most of the time, by myself. I traveled a lot of miles. I used to keep a logbook because the IRS would allow so much a mile. I wore out 18 new cars. I mean, wore 'em out!

What were some of the injuries you received during your career?

Pinched nerves, I guess. I worked with Bret Hart one time. It was hot. It was in late summer and the air conditioner in the arena wasn't working, and Bret and I were sweatin'. We was out on the floor. He picked me up for a piledriver. Just as he got me off the ground, I slipped through his arms and my head hit the floor.

The worst injury I ever had happened when I was working in Japan. One of the Japanese wrestlers threw me out on the floor. He came out after me and we started fighting. Finally, he cut me off and picked me up for a slam. He slammed me down, which was alright, but there was a water bucket on the floor. The small of my back landed on that water bucket. I couldn't move either leg. They took me to the ER in Tokyo. Thank God, in Japan, they have chiropractors on duty at the ERs. He worked on me for about twenty minutes. I walked out of there. This leg here was numb for ten years.

One day, I was working out and I looked in the mirror at the leg. I thought, *"That leg is smaller than the other."* I got a tape measure and measured it. It was an inch and a half smaller. I went to several doctors after that. There was no feeling whatsoever. You could stick a pin or a nail in it and I wouldn't feel anything. I finally run across this doctor. He says, *"I'm gonna tell you how to fix that."* He says, "You need to do one-legged squats ... all on this leg, your whole body weight." He said, *"You don't go past 90 degrees with your leg."* I did that, and in four to five months, I measured them and they were back. I still do 'em.

I remember you doing squats all the time in the dressing room.

I got that from Japan. Everybody told me on my first trip to Japan, *"You'd better be fit ... because they like to show up people."* I thought I was pretty fit until I got over there. Anyways, about the third time I went over there, I went to the training facility. The head guy was there and I said, *"Show me what you do for fitness. I've never seen anybody as fit as you guys are."*

He said, *"There'll be two guys out here in about five minutes. I'll show you."*

Those two guys stood about 20 feet apart, facing each other, and they started doing free squats. They'd do about 90 degrees on both legs. 2,000 ... nonstop ... an hour and 15 minutes. I started doin' 'em. I still do. I don't do that many, but I got up to 900 one time. Nonstop, and I thought that was pretty good.

And they did 2000.

Yeah, unbelievable. But you know what they used to say? Japanese doctors used to say this in the dressing room. Those free squats is the best exercise in the world. It don't just keep your joints in good shape, because you're just using your body weight, it works your heart. After about 100 or so squats, your breathing (pause) ... let me tell you, you're breathing hard. That was the deal.

Nashville TN • 1976
Photo by Scott Teal

Did you ever blow-up during a match?

Oh, yeah. That happened several times.

At what point in your career were you in the best cardio shape?

Probably when I was going to Japan.

Out of self defense. (laughs)

(laughs) Yeah.

Tell me about going into Halifax and how that came about.

Those Kay boys — the ones you were talking about yesterday — used to come into Calgary to work for Stu. They talked me into it and got a bunch of our tapes from Calgary and played them down there on the East Coast. I had a good run there. It was a good little territory. I went there two or three summers. That's the only time they ran there, from spring until fall.

I show you making just one shot into Tulsa. Did you wrestle for Bill Watts?

(laughs) You would have to mention Bill Watts, didn't you? He was just (pause) ... he was just hard to get along with, especially when he started promoting. He thought he was the king of the hill. I just went in there one time. I think I wrestled in three different towns.

I went in for Vince ... the original Vince. Vince McMahon, Sr. He said he wanted me for six TVs. He was gonna put me in the main event at Madison Square Garden against Bruno Sammartino. So I went in for five weeks and made the tapes. I got a call from a doctor up in Canada about my 12-year-old daughter there. The doctor said, *"You better come home. I have to remove your daughter's spleen."* He says, *"I'm being truthful with you, I don't know if she'll make it or not. She's laying there crying and hollering for you."* So I go in to Vince's office. You can imagine how he took that. *"Vince, it's my daughter! She's hollerin' for me."*

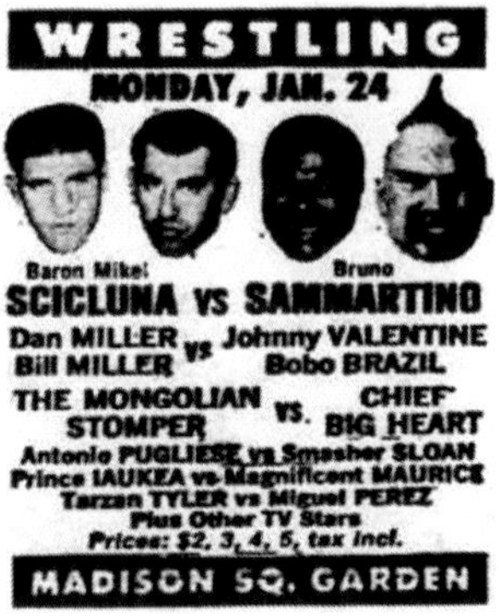

New York NY • Jan. 24, 1966

"You can't go. You can't go. I built it up. You're gonna kill Madison Square Garden."

Yes. I have clippings in which you were already advertised.

Yes. I talked to him and he wouldn't accept it. I finally just said, *"Vince, I'm going."* I went there and she made it, but barely. I stayed there for a while. I knew there was no more calling Vince.

Did you try to call him?

Yeah, but he wouldn't take the call. When I got hooked up with Bearcat Wright, as my manager, we had four sellouts in a row in Memphis, Tennessee ... which, at that time, was a record. Four weeks in a row. Bearcat and I were driving home one day and he said, *"Why don't I call Vince McMahon and see if I can get us into New York?"*

Bearcat Wright was one of the biggest babyfaces New York ever had. I said, *"Go ahead, Bearcat."*

I had already told him the story. *"Well, let me talk to him."*

He talked to Vince and Vince told him what I did. Bearcat said, *"I know it, but it was his daughter, man. You'd do the same."*

Vince said, *"Well, I'm not saying yes right now. Call me back."*

It never happened.

Stomper & Bearcat Wright

How did Bearcat come to be your manager?

I knew Bearcat quite a while. I had met him in different territories when he was a babyface. I went up to work for the Sheik one time in Detroit ... and Bearcat was up there.

He was still wrestling at the time?

Yeah. He was just about ready to quit. I didn't have a manager at the time. Bearcat said, *"Why don't you let me manage you?"* In fact, we went to Detroit that night and he managed me. The people didn't know what to think. He came out there managing a heel. And being a heel, they had never seen him like that. We went on from there. He was great.

What was the first territory you went in together?

Memphis. Bearcat called Jerry Jarrett. Bearcat did all the calling. He fixed everything up.

The two of you came in and worked for Nick Gulas in Chattanooga. You stayed, but Bearcat disappeared after a very short time.

Bearcat's health was bad. He was a good manager, though.

How did you get hooked up with Don Carson as your manager?

He was in the territory.

What led to you making Knoxville your home?

I was doing good and I liked it here ... short trips.

You never had a desire to go back to Canada?

To live, you mean?

Yes.

No, not really. I like to go back and visit, you know. It's too cold. (laughs)

Did you like working in Florida for Eddie Graham?

So-so. Eddie Graham was a little bit like Bill Watts. *"I'm the boss here."*

Who was the booker when you were there?

The guy who was the shooter. (pause) Bob Roop.

Who are some of the people you can say you were really good friends with?

[Gorgeous] George [Junior], Bearcat, Bob Geigel. There were a lot of guys I liked.

What led to you calling JJ Dillon to be your manager in Dallas?

Somebody told me about him. I can't remember who it was, but it was a friend of JJ. In fact, he called him and put him on the phone with me. JJ was a good guy.

What happened there? He said he went to your house one day and everything was gone.

Stomper & Gorgeous George Jr.
Knoxville TV • 1977

That's when I came back from Australia. My wife had moved everything out. The house was empty. I went to the neighbor's and they said she just backed a moving truck up to the house.

The wrestling business was hard on families.

Very hard. I'll tell you what's really hard is relationships with your children. I was traveling up and down the highway most of the time, and I missed a lot with my kids.

When was the first time you use the blade?

Calgary, I guess. Jim Wright showed me. He had the thing where he was gonna (pause) ... now, a lot of people carried it taped to their finger. I always had the referee carry mine.

The first time you used one, did you do it yourself or let somebody else do it?

No, I wouldn't let nobody do it. I did it myself. It was a [ring] post deal.

Were you apprehensive about doing it?

Yeah, a little bit. I was scared of cutting into the veins, which I did twice. I had to go to the hospital and they had to tie them off.

Do people ever ask you about the scars on your forehead?

Yeah.

What do you say?

I fell down in the gravel. (laughs)

Did you ever accidentally drop a blade in the ring?

No, but I had the referee drop 'em ... or they couldn't get it out of their pocket.

Do you think a booker can do a good job of booking while pushing himself as a wrestler, too?

I think that's hard to do. Instead of thinking about what's going on here, he's thinking about himself. He don't just have his own match. He has the other matches to take care of.

What do you remember about the trips in the Calgary territory?

Calgary to Regina ... 500 miles one way. I used to stay over. Have you heard of Bob Leonard?

Yes, I know Bob.

He's a good friend of mine. I used to stay at his house a lot and go back the next morning.

As a main eventer, did you ever get tired of staying until the last minute and getting home so late?

Yeah. The good part about that was, all the people were gone. I had a lot of tires slashed, windshields broke, and convertible tops cut off. One night, I came out and there was no canvas at all. All that was left was a frame.

Were you ever financially well-off, or did you work paycheck to paycheck for most of your career?

Well, I made pretty good money, but the thing of it is, you have a home at home and a home on the road. You have to buy gas, tires, food, hotel. At home, you have expenses there.

Did Stu pay well?

Yes, but I always made sure I got a guarantee from Stu. He'd try to nickel and dime you to death, but he always paid me.

What was your average weight during your career?

260.

Did anything ever happen during one of your matches that caused you to lose it, as in breaking out in laughter over something that happened?

Tex McKenzie. He was making a comeback on me. He had a thing where, when he made a comeback, he would run around the inside of the ring ... two or three times. The second time around, he crossed his legs, tripped over his feet, and fell down. Have you ever seen the size of Tex's feet? (laughs) But he was over! Let me tell you. The people loved him.

What point in your career would you say was the most memorable?

There would be two of 'em … Kansas City and Japan. They were two nice, happy places I worked.

Did it ever get to a point where wrestling became a job to you?

It never did … if the business was good. When it would fall off, it wasn't as fun.

You once told me a story about a plane where the landing gear didn't come down.

Coming back from Japan. I used to fly back to Canada. My family was there. We were coming in on Vancouver, coming into the airport, coming down low to the land. All of a sudden, the pilot guns the engines. We go back up and he comes on the speaker and says, *"The automatic landing is busted. It won't put the wheels down. We have to crank 'em manually."* They flew around the little more. He said, *"The manual won't take the wheels down, either. We have to do a belly-landing. I'm gonna to fly around up here until the gas is about all gone. They're gonna foam the runway."*

I was in the bar then. So was everybody else. (laughs) People were crying. Kids were crying. Oh, it was awful. We come in and, I'll tell you what. That guy did one heck of a landing. He come down. That foams about that thick when they put it on and it acts as a cushion. We just slid along. The only thing that was a little scary was, we started to spin around because there's nothing to hold the plane straight. It didn't hurt nothin'. We finally stopped. I hated flying, anyway.

Every time we went to Japan, we'd go through about two to three hours of turbulence, the same spot all time. I mean, you'd have to keep that belt done up tight. Man, that thing would just drop, like this. Awful, awful.

Tell me the story about Stu and the trailer.

Stu, in all his weekly towns, he had rings there. He just left them there. Spot shows, he had this old limousine, and this limousine had four doors on each side. It was an old one. And he had a trailer. To spot shows, he'd take the ring. He'd pull it with the limousine. He had a limousine to haul all his kids because he had 12 kids. (laughs) I don't know why he'd take it to … I guess he thought he needed it to pull that trailed.

Anyway, he was going to this spot show one night. He had this guy — and I can't think of his name — but he was a Polish wrestler who could hardly speak English. He had been over too long. I'd never heard of him or seen him. Anyway, Stu would pick somebody to go with him to the spot shows. So, we had the show that night, and we were coming back. Stu had the same thing he'd do. He'd get a few miles out, maybe halfway home, and he'd get sleepy. He'd holler at the Polish guy. He'd say, *"Can you drive? I'm tired. I'm sleepy."*

"Yeah, me drive."

The Polish guy got behind the wheel of that car — and you can imagine how far back that trailer and ring parts were. Well, they had a small town to go through. This guy was coming up to a red light … all of a sudden the light turned green. He hit that pedal and that gas. He jerked that trailer hitch right off. But he kept going. He didn't know. It was so far back there. So we get to the next town and he stops for a hamburger or something. Stu looked back and said, *"Echhh, where's the ring and trailer?"*

The Polish guy said, *"It's not there?"*

(laughs) They had to turn around and go back.

When did you first realize wrestling was being exposed to the general public?

Well, when I was wrestling, even at the height of my career, the word kayfabe was used a lot. You didn't let anything out. That's why we all drew money. Now, what I see on TV is skipping around like they're in a ballet dance or something. All it is is high spots and tumbling. What does that tell ya? It's like somebody said the other day, *"Oh, they drew $21,000 here."*

Sure, if you go into a town every three or four years. If you don't draw that, you're in bad shape. Try to fill it every week.

Like you guys used to.

Yeah!

How many people did Chilhowee Park hold?

Let's see, we used to get right under 4,000. We filled that up week after week after week.

At what point in your career did the bumps begin to bother you?

I guess when I started working part-time. I had a lot of tests and the doctors told me I had eighteen pinched nerves in my body. They said, *"Well, we can do exploratory surgery on your back."*

I said, *"No, I don't think so."*

They wanna cut a hole in your back. *"Oh, it's not there. Let's cut over on this side."*

I just live with it. I stretch a lot and work out a lot. That helps. Like I said, I still do the one-legged squats.

Was there a definitive time when you realized your career was winding down?

Yeah, when I got on with the Sheriff's Department.

Tell me how that came about.

That guy you were talking about the other day, Chris Powers. He still works there. He told me to come on and got me an application. I started out with medical transportation. I took inmates to the doctor, the hospital, or wherever they had to go. I took one guy out of his cell one day. The lieutenant told me, *"This guy has a bad ankle. You have to take to Baptist."* I took him and he was limping. We went inside, the doctor worked on him, and coming back, outside coming out of Baptist, there's a double door. He was ahead of me. The guy took off across Alcoa Highway. He could run like there was nothing wrong with his leg. He ran through a red light. I had to run it, too, or he would've been gone. Over there, there's a field of about 20 or 30 acres … grass about knee-high. I hollered, *"You sucker! I'll chase you to Maryville if I have to!"* He got about halfway across that field and he fell right down. He had long hair, all the way down his back. I went over there, grabbed that long hair, wrapped it around my fist, and put it over my shoulder. (laughs) His feet hit the ground about every 50 feet. *"My hair! My hair!"*

"That's right, you sucker! You may be bald by the time I get you back to the cruiser. You won't be running anymore, will ya?"

I took him up in the elevator, and when the door opened, I threw him out across that floor ... and he skidded. The guys there couldn't believe it. *"Archie, what's goin' on?"*

I said, *"That sucker run on me."*

Stomper served as a deputy sheriff in Knox County, Tennessee, for several years. When his health began to fail, he worked as a guard at a prison. Archie told Greg Oliver, author of many books on pro wrestling, "There's more fans in prison than there are on the street."

The *Calgary Herald* featured Archie in the Dec. 3, 2004, issue of the newspaper and said, "He still cycles up to 80 km a day, pulled his grandkids behind him in a trolley, and wrestled to raise money for kids."

Tell me a little about your cancer and what you've been through.

Five operations. They think they got it all now, so ... I just keep going in and getting checked. It started with the chemo because I had throat cancer.

What do you do now?

I work out, stretch a lot.

Looking back at your career, do you have any regrets?

Just the time I missed with my kids.

Thanks for taking the time to do this, Archie.

No problem. I've had a good time reminiscing.

Archie battled Alzheimer's for several years before he died. On Jan. 9, 2016, he fell and broke his hip. Two weeks later, he went into the hospital for surgery, but didn't recover and died in his sleep on Jan. 23. He was 79 years old.

TITLES

National [Atlanta '80]
Southern [FL '74]
Brass knucks [AL]
Southern [TN '75]
CWA International [TN '85]
Southeastern [Knoxville '76]
Southern States [Kingsport TN '94]
U.S. [IA/MO '65]
Central States [KS/MO '65]
Central States tag
[KS/MO '66 w/Bob Ellis]
North American
[Calgary '67,'68,'69,'73,'74,'77, '83]
North American [New Brunswick '84]
North American [Nova Scotia '84]

ALIAS

The Mongolian Stomper
Midnight Stallion [AL '83]

BILL MCDANIEL

Bill McDaniel

This interview, conducted by Scott Teal in June 1995, was originally published in issue #13 of *Whatever Happened to ...?*

Tell me a little about your childhood.

I was born on Oct. 7, 1924, and grew up in St. Louis, a place where a host of wrestlers got their start. My father was a salesman, while my mother was a housewife. I went to Roosevelt High School, where I played a little football, but I was a little too light to do much of anything. I was just a small, skinny kid. On the swim team, I did the breast stroke, relay, and 50-yard dash.

I remember my dad took me to Kiel Auditorium when Bill Longson won the championship from Sandor Szabo in '42 [Feb. 19]. Later, I started amateur wrestling in '46 at the Boys Club of St. Louis. Since we didn't have wrestling in high school, I hadn't done any wrestling before that. One day, when I was up at the Southside YMCA, I met Warren Bockwinkel, who was working out with another amateur wrestler. He was getting ready for a match with Bill Longson. Bockwinkel was a great friend, and really was the one who got me interested in wrestling. He helped me a great deal throughout my whole life. I didn't wrestle amateur very long, because I had a job at Union Electric and it was shift work.

If I wrestled at any of the meets, I had to take off work, and I didn't want to lose the money. I wasn't making any money wrestling amateur, so I kind of got with Bockwinkel and worked out, learned some moves. Plus, there was always local guys in St. Louis looking for someone who wanted to work out. Then, at that time, a lot of guys learned in the carnivals. You took on all comers. We'd either go wrestle fellows from the audience, or we'd use plants out in the crowd. It was good money on the side.

When I finished with that, I went over to St. Paul Social Center in East St. Louis, Illinois. That's where almost all the St. Louis boys had their first match. There was a Reverend there who promoted the shows at St. Paul's. I think his name was Gunn. If I'm not mistaken, that's where Lou Thesz had his first match, but don't quote me on that.

According to Lou, Gunn was a Baptist minister who ran regular shows in the church using junior heavyweights. Joe Sanderson, an old-time wrestler and right-hand man to promoter Tom Packs, helped book Lou in that church for his first match.

Well, I had my first match with George O'Brien there. [Nov. 27, 1947] George was just a local guy, a nice guy who wrestled on the side. He had a job at a printing company. While I was there, I met Leo "The Lion" Newman. He was the booker for Al Ritchie down in Florida and he said, "Sometime when you get vacation, come down for two weeks and we'll book you." So, I did that and got a taste of it. Leo and I became very good friends. In fact, he died about a year ago. He wanted me to go down the Mississippi with him. I said, no, I didn't want any part of it. Leo was a real character and a fine, fine guy.

I came back and quit my job at Union Electric, which was taking a big chance, because in those days, I was making good money with them. But, I loved wrestling and started on the road. I came back to St. Louis, which most of us did whenever we could. Local guys could get booked, but none of us really got a good break in here. We had to get out of here to really make any money. Lou [Thesz] had it all sewed up, and he wasn't about to let anybody else get too popular.

I came back to St. Louis, then went into Tennessee for Nick Gulas and Roy Welch. I didn't stay there long. There wasn't much there. I wrestled Herb Welch, Tex Riley, Babe Rodriguez. From there, I went to North Carolina for Jim Crockett Sr. for six to eight months. That was a long time for me, because I was single, and I'd go back home to wrestle.

My good break came when I went to Toledo for Jack Pfefer. Up until that time, I used my real name, Bill McDaniel. He changed my name to Tom Marshall. Pfefer changed everybody's name, except Billy Darnell. I think Billy was the only guy who didn't have his name changed by Pfefer. Jack was a great promoter and manipulator. He would buy ads in the paper and get publicity. This was before television. He didn't want you to capitalize on the publicity he spent for you. Pfefer had his own [world] champion, too. I won it from Dave Levin, then dropped it to The Demon, who was Jack O'Brien. O'Brien was a bald-headed guy with mutton chops [sideburns]. I stayed with Pfefer for about a year and a half.

I was fortunate enough to get to L.A. By the way, I enjoyed the articles on Lord Blears in your magazine. I really hadn't thought of him in years. But, anyway, I went there and was going to stay six weeks and go back home and go to San Francisco. I must have stayed there two years. While I was there, Gino and Leo Garibaldi, and George and Bobby Becker, were prominent tag team partners. Jules Strongbow and Johnny Doyle said, *"Freddie Blassie wants to come out and spend a few months. Why don't you and him team up as partners?"*

I said, *"Fine."*

So that's how we started out as the McDaniel Brothers. We look on each other as brothers and we still stay in contact. In fact, I got a letter from Fred today. He's doing better [since his heart attack] and he's back to work at Titan. Doyle and Strongbow were high-class guys. They made you money … like Jack Pfefer. A lot of people didn't like Jack, but he

Akron OH • Dec. 17, 1949

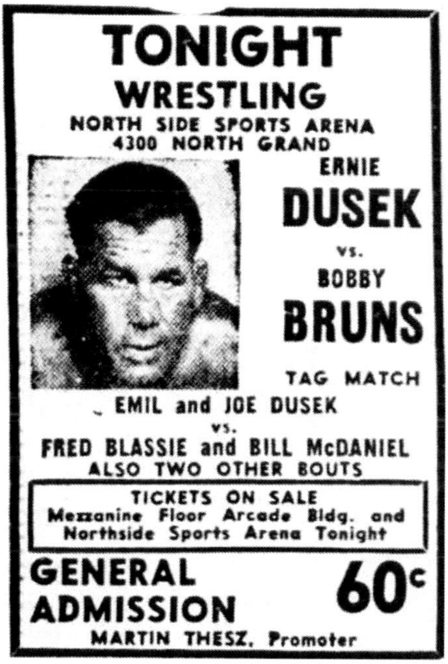

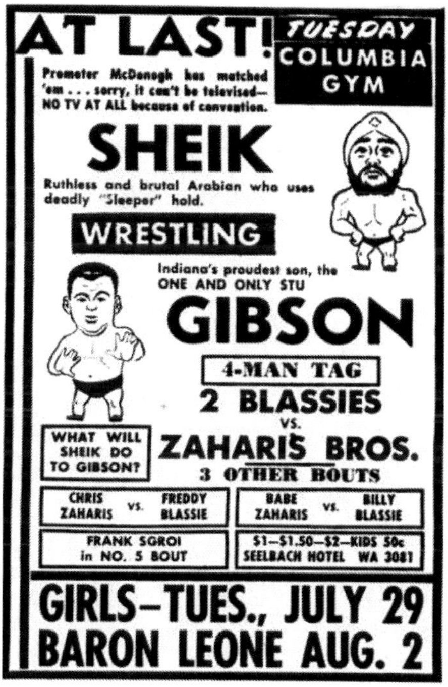

(above) St Louis MO • June 2, 1950
(right) Louisville KY • July 22, 1952

treated me great. He saw that you got every penny that you agreed upon.

What was the criteria for deciding whether you used the "McDaniel" name or the "Blassie" name?

Whenever we'd go to territories where he was established, we'd use his name. We were in L.A. for about six months, so we used McDaniel there. From there, Fred and I went to Houston, still as the McDaniel Brothers. We didn't stay but a week or so because we didn't like the way they were handling us. We went up to Buffalo, but left when the territory began to nose-dive. Fred and I were a big card in Louisville [KY]. We were the Blassie Brothers there, because Fred had been there before. We did very well. That's was when Frances McDonough promoted it. Fred and I split up then and I came back to St. Louis. I was in and out [of St. Louis] all the time. I'd pick the phone up, call Sam Muchnick, and ask for work.

Did you use the McDaniel name when you weren't with Fred?

Right. The only time I used the Blassie name was when we worked as a tag team. I used to go up to Chicago to work for Jim Barnett. I was up there one time and Jerry Meeker saw me. He was the booker in Des Moines and said they'd try me out. I told him I'd try it for six weeks, and wound up staying about a year and a half. I'd also work for Wally Karbo up in Minneapolis, Frank Tunney in Toronto, and Eddie Quinn in Montreal. I went into Columbus, Ohio. Al Haft wasn't booking much then. It was Buddy Rogers and Frankie Talaber. I was pleased with how they handled me there. In my opinion, Buddy Rogers was the greatest of all the boys in my day.

While I was in Columbus, Fred called me. It was getting winter time. Fred asked, *"Why don't you come down to Atlanta? We'll go as the Blassie*

Dec. 1949
Tom Marshall being presented with the "world" title belt.

Brothers." I went down there and ... oh, I must have stayed there a couple of years. When Fred left, I went over and promoted Augusta, Georgia. I found that I could make more money wrestling than I could with that, because there was no money in Augusta at that particular time. Somebody else had control of the town and the only industry there was textiles and lumber. Those were all depressed wages, so I decided not to fool with it too long. I went back to St. Louis and quit. I was tired of the travel and wanted to get some kind of profession. Wrestling was in a decline at the time and things didn't look like they'd pick up.

I was wrestling one time at the Chase and I asked Joe Garagiola if he could get me on at Anheuser-Busch. Busch sponsored "Wrestling at the Chase" and he was working for them. In fact, I was interviewed for the job that he got. Dave Martin was there and got me on with Consolidated Forwarding. I stayed in the trucking business for 30 years, then retired. I worked for four different truck lines, working my way up to vice-president with one of them, and never missed a day's work. They all went bankrupt later. Good job, good people. Good retirement? No. It's a good thing that I saved my money. In management, you know, you can't belong to the Teamsters, so I'm living on my investments.

Tell me a little about your personal life and what you do with your time.

I got married 41 years ago. Don't ask me the date. Pat O'Connor introduced me to my wife, Ann, in Minneapolis. She came to the matches with a lady news reporter that covered the matches. Ann and I each owned a Tennessee walking horse on a ten-acre farm where we kept them. We rode them all over Southern Missouri and Illinois. I was on the board of directors at the Missouri-Tennessee Walking Club for about twenty years, until it got to where there was hardly no place to trail ride anymore. They don't want you in the national parks. So, we sold the horses, joined the country club, and took up golf. I don't play worth a damn, but I get out there two or three times a week.

The *St. Louis Globe* wrote a real nice article on my career recently. A guy named Jack Rice called me and wanted to know if he could talk with me. I thought it was gonna be a little spread. Hell, they sent photographers down, took pictures, and did a three-quarter page spread.

Do you remember who you wrestled in your final match?

Bill Longson … who was like a father to me. We were very, very close. On the way to Evansville [IN], I didn't know who I was going to wrestle. I picked him up, and on the way down there, I said, *"Who am I wrestling?"*

He said, *"Oh, you're wrestling some new guy that's just breaking into the business."*

I said, *"That's good. I'll polish him off and we'll get the hell out of there."* Then I said, *"Who have you got?"*

Longson said, *"Oh, I've got some old guy."*

I said, *"Well that's good. That won't take long."*

Well, later on, I found out that we were wrestling each other. (laughs) It was a very emotional thing and we went like hell. In fact, they wanted to rebook it. I said, *"No, I'm going to quit."*

It was an honor to be a pallbearer at Bill's funeral because … I don't know what you know about the Mormon religion. They only have the immediate family, so when they asked me to be a pallbearer, when we were coming back, his nephew said, *"You realize they consider you part of the family."*

Any final words?

Just say hello to everyone and tell them that I'm retired and loving it!

TITLES

Southern Tag Team (GA as Bill Blassie w/Fred Blassie)
Ohio world

ALIAS

Tom Marshall (OH)
Billy Blassie

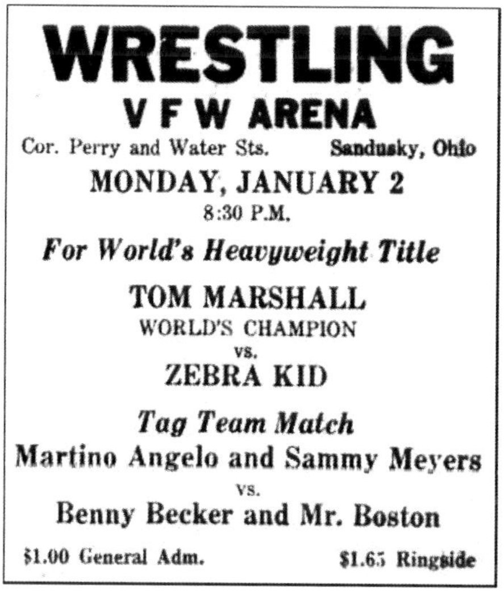

Sandusky OH • Jan. 2, 1950

St. Louis MO TV • Oct. 30, 1954

BUDDY WAYNE

Dwayne Peal

This interview, conducted by Scott Teal in Dec. 2001, was originally published in issue #47 of *Whatever Happened to ...?*

When and where were you born, Buddy?

I was born on Aug. 9, 1934, in Memphis, Tennessee. I was born at home on Pearce Street.

By a midwife?

No, it was a doctor. I was born right after the Depression. You couldn't have but three kids at the city hospital, which was also called the charity hospital. I was the fourth one, so I had to be born at home.

What were your parents' names?

Daddy's name was John Aubrey. Mother's was Euline.

Was the last name Peal?

Oh, yeah. My dad worked for the sheriff's department for about 26 years. He worked mostly in the courts.

Did you grow up in Memphis?

Yeah. I went to Bartlett High School, but I grew up in Frayser. Bartlett and Millington was the high schools you went to when you lived in Frayser. At that time, Frayser didn't have a high school. They only had elementary through the eighth grade.

In a 1950 essay contest on Christmas seals and tuberculosis, Dwayne, a high school junior, won honorable mention for his essay.

***Commercial Appeal*, Memphis TN Dec. 18, 1950**

Bartlett is really growing now.

Oh, it was the country then. It doesn't look anything like it did. We used to go to the creek and swim, ride horses, steal watermelons, and all that. Now it's all shopping centers and office buildings.

Did you play any sports?

No. Believe it or not, I was real little in high school. I only weighed a hundred pounds when I started the ninth grade and I was about five-foot. Wrestling just started on TV in Memphis about '48 or '49. I'd watch it comin' live from Ellis Auditorium every Monday night. That was when TVs first came out and most people didn't have one. Back then, there wouldn't hardly be one neighbor in twenty that had a TV, so we'd all go to Howard Van Eaton's house. He lived across the street and was the only kid in the neighborhood that had a TV. He had a pretty big house. They used his living room as a place for their church to meet on Sunday morning. We'd set chairs up, just like it was a movie or something, and we'd all sit and watch wrestling. There would be fifteen, sometimes 20 or 30 people, kids and grown-ups, sittin' around eatin' popcorn and watching wrestling.

Then Daddy started going down to the wrestling matches. Some of the guys that worked for the sheriff's office worked there, so they invited him to come down. We started going every Monday night. We'd get in free because Daddy worked for the sheriff's office.

That was when wrestling was still held at the old Ellis Auditorium. Do you remember who was on the card that first night?

I can give you a pretty good idea. Joe Wolfe, Jimmy Lott, Wild Bill Longson, Billy Rayburn, Lou Thesz, LeRoy McGuirk.

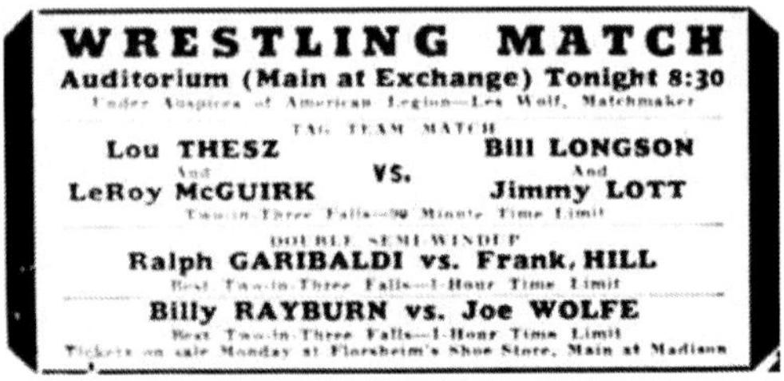
WRESTLING MATCH
Auditorium (Main at Exchange) Tonight 8:30
Under Auspices of American Legion—Les Wolf, Matchmaker
TAG TEAM MATCH
Lou THESZ And LeRoy McGUIRK vs. Bill LONGSON And Jimmy LOTT
Two-in-Three Falls—90 Minute Time Limit
DOUBLE SEMI-WINDUP
Ralph GARIBALDI vs. Frank, HILL
Best Two-in-Three Falls—1-Hour Time Limit
Billy RAYBURN vs. Joe WOLFE
Best Two-in-Three Falls—1-Hour Time Limit
Tickets on sale Monday at Florsheim's Shoe Store, Main at Madison

Memphis TN • June 20, 1949

You have a good memory. Did you do any amateur wrestling at all?

No. I went to a county school, so we didn't have wrestling. There was a boy named Jim Jamison who won the lightweight title in the city schools. I tried to get in the city school tournament, but I had to get all the coaches to give me permission since I lived outside the city limits. I couldn't get ahold of them all in time, so I didn't get to wrestle. I knew Jim. We used to work out a lot, and I could beat him, so if I had been in the tournament, I guess I'd have been the lightweight champion. Of course, I didn't do it, so I can't say for sure that I would have, but we worked out a lot.

Everybody laughed, Scott, when I said I was gonna be a wrestler. I was a hundred pounds! In the tenth grade, I sent a quarter in the mail to George F. Jowett for a little book. In fact, I still have it. It shows a few exercises. If you want the whole course, you have to pay $24.95. I never did get the whole course, but the sample only cost a quarter and had a whole bunch of exercises. In fact, one of the books had pictures of the old-time weightlifters — Louis Cyr, Milo Steinborn. Milo looked a whole lot like [his son] Dickie.

I had a little piece of iron. It was like a small piece of railroad iron. I'd curl that thing. I'd pull it over, press it. I had a cousin that got killed in Italy during World War II. He had some barbells, so I called my uncle and asked if I could borrow them. He let me have 'em. Back then, you could buy 425 pounds of weights from Ben Weider for $48.95. That included the course and everything. I had a little old shed I'd work out in. There wasn't any gyms in Memphis at that time. In fact, everybody laughed at me in school because

I was workin' out. Everyone thought it was a big joke. "*You shouldn't lift weights. It'll make you musclebound.*" I got disgusted because everybody was laughin' at me and makin' fun.

There was a boy named Buddy Craig who was a year or two older than me who was good friends of mine. He was a big star in football, baseball, basketball. He was just an all-around athlete. Everybody would rib me about workin' out. One day, he said, "*Hey, man! You still got your weights?*"

I said, "*Yeah.*"

He said, "*Can I come over and start workin' out?*"

I said, "*Yeah, Buddy, if you want to.*"

After that, nobody kidded me. I reminded him of that at a reunion. He said, "*I was real serious. I was gonna do it.*"

I said, "*Well, I appreciate you doing that. At the time, I didn't realize what you were doing.*"

Where did you get the money to buy the weights?

I worked! I worked for a veterinarian. I made fifteen dollars a week. I worked after school, five days a week, all day Saturday, and two hours on Sunday. In fact, I worked with him so long that a lot of people thought I was a veterinarian. They'd call and say, "*Is Dr. Coscia in?*"

I'd say, "*No, he's not.*"

They'd say, "*Who is this?*"

I'd say, "*Dwayne.*"

They'd say, "*Oh. Well, Dr. Wayne ...*" (laughs)

We did a lot of large animal work ... horse, cows, sheep. He would go out and take care of that, so I'd do most of the small animal stuff. I ran the clinic by myself for three months. At the time, we were the only veterinarian in the whole north end of Shelby County. There was a naval station out in Millington, so we got all that business. A lieutenant came in one time and said, "*Hey, boy. You're getting quite a reputation at the base.*"

I said, "*What do you mean?*"

He said, "*Well, a guy came in and said,* 'That friend of yours down in Frayser is really a good doctor. He knows what he's doing.'"

I told him, "*Yeah, Dr. Coscia is good.*"

He said, "*No, not him ... the young guy.*"

Did you ever consider going into that line of work?

Yeah, but I was interested in wrestling. You know how that goes. Not only that, but when I got out of school, everybody was getting drafted to go to Korea. It was 1952 when I graduated. I weighed 185 when I got out.

Buddy entered the South Memphis Golden Gloves elimination tournament on Jan. 7, 1951. He fought in the Novice Lightweight division, but lost via technical knockout to Guy Davidson in 1:45 of the second round.

Did you attend the wrestling matches at Ellis Auditorium on a regular basis?

Oh, every Monday night! Oh, yeah!

Who was the first wrestler you talked to?

That would be Karol Krauser. I just walked up and started talking to him. Then I met Sonny Myers and Mario Galento. In fact, Mario is really the one that got me into the business. He'd call me up. *"Hey, kid! What are you doin' tonight?"*

"Nothin'."

"Do you wanna go to Jonesboro?"

"Yeah!"

"You got a car, haven't ya?" (laughs)

The first time I went, Scott, I got me a map and studied it for about an hour. I got my oil changed and had the car greased. (laughs) Jonesboro wasn't but 80 miles away. (laughs) Mario would say, *"Bring your stuff. Somebody may not show up."* Sure enough, quite often, the guy wouldn't be there.

Which Karol Krauser did you meet? Karl Gotch or Karol Kalmikoff?

Kalmikoff. They used to advertise him as the model for the Superman comic strip.

Where did you first meet Mario?

We just got to talkin' at Ellis Auditorium. He saw that I was interested in wrestling. He hadn't been wrestling too long at the time. He'd call me and wanted to know if I wanted to go someplace with him.

How did your training come about?

There was another guy named Henry Allen. Henry had wrestled years before and he wasn't doin' much at the time. He got me and about half a dozen other guys. We'd work out in his back yard every night for hours. We didn't use a ring. It was just two-by-sixes driven into the ground, made into a twelve-foot square, with ropes pulled around the posts. The mat was just a canvas stretched out and nailed down over sawdust. We didn't hit ropes or anything like that. We just learned how to wrestle. We did the basics for a year before we ever had a match.

Did Mario or Henry try to discourage you from getting into the business?

No, not at all, but they were tough with me. Back then, when you went in that ring, you'd better know a little bit. If you didn't, you got taken down pretty good. Fortunately, I was smart enough to be respectful of the guys. I didn't act like a know-it-all and run my mouth. I'd listen. I wouldn't talk. Most of them liked me, so I never really had that problem. I've seen them take guys down and rub their nose into the mat until their nose would bleed. It would rub the skin right off. Now, Mario showed me a lot of stuff to do like that, but he didn't try to hurt me.

There's a funny story about that. Donnie Fargo said he went to Al Haft in Columbus and said he wanted to wrestle. When they asked him if he could wrestle, he said, *"Yeah!"* Then they asked him if he was smart.

He said, *"Well, I finished high school."*

He said everybody really laughed. He couldn't figure out why they were laughing. He really hadn't finished high school and thought somehow they knew it, but he couldn't figure out how *they* knew it. (laughs) He said they got him in there with Frankie Talaber. Frankie made him hurt in so many ways. He said he went back home and lifted weights a little more. He went back and they put him in with someone else. That guy hurt him. Finally, Larry Chene said, "*Hey, kid. If you want to get in the business, I'll help you.*" So, Larry Chene helped him get in.

Where did you have your first match?

Once a month, at Kennedy Veterans Hospital, which was out on Getwell and Park at the time, they would have benefit matches. If Mario or someone was in town, they'd feature him. Of course, we didn't get paid, but I'd have paid *them* to let me wrestle. I'd go out there once a month just to get a little experience. There was usually two or 300 patients in there, along with their families.

Independent wrestlers from the Memphis area appeared on shows at the hospital from 1948 until 1951. No one of note, other than Mario Galento, wrestling at the time at Butch Boyette, appeared on those shows. Some of the names in the area at the time, though, include Robie Hodges, Wild Bill Watts, Speed Miller, Henry Allen, and Shorty Lewis.

Those were your first matches?

Yeah. That was the first place. The first place I wrestled and got paid was in Jonesboro, Arkansas. I don't know the date, but I know it was on a Tuesday night. I still have the ad, but I don't have the year. It was held in the Earl Bell Community Center, the same building they were wrestling in when Randy [Hales] quit.

You wrestled a guy named Ronnie Allen in that first match. Who was that?

He was going to college at Arkansas State. Virgil [Hatfield] called and wanted to know if I wanted to be on the card. He booked Ronnie in the hopes that it would bring some of the college people in. Yes, that was the first match that I actually got paid for.

At that time, we didn't use but four men on the card. That night, though, there was six. He added me and Ronnie. Normally, when there was only four guys, there was three matches. For example, when we only had four guys on the card, Ronnie would go out and wrestle Lee Fields, then I'd wrestle Don Fields, and we'd all come back in a two-out-of-three-fall tag match.

Who were some of the guys you worked with on the hospital benefit shows?

Henry Allen, J.T. Rogers. I wrestled a guy named Robie Hodges. He wasn't wrestling full-time. He was a barber and cut hair for a living. He'd leave once in a while and go someplace like Kansas, then come back.

Did any of the other guys from that training class turn pro?

No, they never did. Well, they may have had a few matches, but I'm talking about making a living out of it.

In the early months of your training, was Mario open with you about the business?

No! I wrestled several months and I still wasn't sure what was goin' on. Mario was in a working mode his entire life, up until the day he died. Mario had been in Pensacola to wrestle Lee Fields. We was goin' to Jonesboro and his wife, Marie, was with us. She said, "*Bonnie* [Mario], *you know you're wrestling Lee Fields tonight.*"

"*Yeah, that son-of-a-bitch tried to break my arm in Pensacola the other night! That no-good so-and-so!.*" Mario looked at me and said, "*You know he's a shooter!*" I didn't know what a shooter was.

You didn't?

No, but I didn't ask him. I just said, "*Oh, really?*"

He says, "*Yeah, he's a pistol man.*"

I still had no idea what he was talkin' about, and I had been in the business several months by then. A few years ago at the reunion, I told Lee, "*Lee, when I first met you, I didn't like you. All the way over to Jonesboro that night, Mario kept talkin' about what a low-down skunk you were and how you tried to break his arm.*" (laughs)

When you did the VA benefit shows, were you working or wrestling?

A little bit of both. We used a lot of wrestling moves, but we were performing. I was refereeing in Blytheville [AR] one night. Back then, you didn't just jump in the ring and start wrestling. You started out as a referee and learned a lot from watching the guys. (laughs) Today, you wouldn't learn nothin'. (laughs)

We were in Blytheville and Karl Kowalski was wrestling as a tag team with someone. He'd come in the ring and I'd put him out. "*Why are you puttin' me out of this ring?*" Blah-blah-blah. A few minutes later, here he comes again ... and I'd put him out. By the time I put him out four times, he yelled, "*If you put me out one more time, I'm gonna hit you right in the nose.*" A few minutes later, he came in again. Shit! I got busy on the other side of the ring doin' somethin'. (laughs) I wasn't gonna put him out and get punched in the nose. Back then, they didn't sit you down and smarten you up. They just didn't. I had an idea of what was goin' on, but I wasn't sure.

Seminole OK • Nov. 12, 1954

And back then, you were afraid to ask.

Exactly! If you asked a guy, "*How are you gonna beat me,*" if it was somebody like Herb Welch, they'd say, "*You'll know.*" That's all they'd say! They wouldn't have a conversation with you. If a punk ever came in runnin' his mouth ... whooo! He was in trouble.

I remember one night when Red Roberts and someone were wrestling Don Wayne [Fields] and Albert Lee [Fields] for the Jonesboro tag team title. That night, they exposed the fact that Don and Lee were brothers. They went two falls, it got down to the finish, and everything went perfect. I counted Don out, or Lee, whoever. He jumps up, grabs me, and starts screaming at me. "*You blankety-blank, blank-blank!*"

I said, "*That was the finish, wasn't it?*"

He goes, "*Yeah, yeah! You blankety-blank, blank-blank!*"

I thought, "*Are these guys crazy?" (laughs)* Then Don grabs me. I asked him, "*That was the finish, wasn't it?*"

"Yeah, yeah, good! You blankety-blank, blank-blank!"

I even went to Red Roberts. "*Red, wasn't that the finish?*"

"Yeah, kid. Great!"

Lee and Don grab me again. Oh, the people were hot, too. "*Get the referee!*"

I was working for the railroad from four in the morning until noon. One day, I didn't go to bed when I got home. Well, Herb called me and wanted me to come to Dyersburg. I was dead tired. When I got there, all the guys are going, "*Come on, let's shoot.*"

I said, "*No, man! I'm dead tired. Just pin me. I ain't fightin' you.*"

Sam Platania tried something one time. For years, I thought Sam Platania could wrestle. Everybody told me how good he could wrestle. Well, we went to Dyersburg one night. I got up there and they told me to go over in three falls. Woody Burnett was the referee, so he took the message to Sam about the finish. He came back and Herb said, "*What did he say?*"

Woody says, "*He said he isn't gonna do it.*"

Herb said, "*What does he mean he isn't gonna do it?*"

"He said he isn't gonna put him over."

Herb said, "*What!?*" He asked me, "*Are you two having any problems?*"

I said, "*No. We even rode up together.*"

Herb said, "*Go back over and see if he's joking.*" Woody came back and said, "*No.*"

Woody said Sam told him that he wrestled Rip Tyler in Jonesboro one night when I was helping book the town. Rip was wrestling as Jerry Dean at the time. I was trying to do something with Jerry, so I had to tell Sam to let him go over. Sam said, "*Why can't I win?*"

I said, "*Shit, Sam! You don't mean nothin'. Jerry's the guy we're tryin' to build.*"

Now it's a year later and he decides he wasn't gonna put me over because I said he didn't mean shit. (laughs) So, for the first two falls, we basically worked. It was the dead of the summer, so it was real hot. I weighed about 215 at the time. I was in real good shape. I made up my mind that I wasn't gonna lay down. He was gonna have to beat me. In the dressing room after the second fall, I told Woody Burnett, "*If I shoot his arm up, and drop down and go behind and cradle him, you give him a fast count.*"

We wrestled a while and he kept tryin' to beat me. I kept getting away and finally made my move. Zip! I went down there and pinned him. One, two, three!

On the way home, he never said a word about nothin'. All those years, I thought he could wrestle, but if he couldn't beat me, he couldn't wrestle.

(laughs) I think he was one of those deals where you get your reputation in the back seat of a car.

I've had several people tell me that Sam could wrestle.

I tell you he couldn't. Either that or I'm an awful good one. Corsica Joe was there, and Herb. I asked Joe, "*Was he trying to beat me, Joe?*"

"Hell, yes, he was, but he couldn't do it, though, could he? You didn't lay down for him."

I said, "*No! I was gonna make him beat me.*"

You started your career in West Tennessee. What was the first outside territory you went to?

Bill Golden was booking out of the Dyersburg office, which was a subsidiary of Nashville. He called me and said he had a couple of bookings if I wanted to drive down to Mobile, Alabama. I got to Mobile and they said, "*Sonny Myers needs a ride over to Pensacola,*" so Sonny, Scotty Thompson [Frank Thompson] and somebody else and myself drove over to Pensacola. I carried them down to the San Carlos Hotel and they got out. I had the money to stay in a motel, but I didn't really want to. I went to an all-night filling station and pulled over to the side to sleep for a little while. It was summertime. The next morning, I picked up Sonny and he said, "*Where'd you stay?*"

I said, "*I stayed at a little place up the highway.*" *(laughs)*

Scotty Thompson and I stayed at the YMCA in Mobile. There wasn't a lot of hotels back then. That was on Monday night. On Tuesday, we wrestled in Mobile. We stayed on the beach all day, and while we were there, a couple girls from Memphis came walking by. They said, "*Hey, what are you doing here?*"

"I'm wrestling."

Memphis TN • June 15, 1959

They said, "*We saved all year to come down here for a week.*"

Sonny says, "*See what I mean, Gabe?*" He called everybody Gabe. "*They saved all year to stay here. We're down here and they're payin' us.*"

I thought, "*Boy, what a great life!*" (laughs) I was about eighteen.

What a coincidence that you ran into wrestling fans from Memphis all the way down there.

Oh, yeah. That happened a lot. I stopped to get gas on my way to Tucson, Arizona, one time. This guy walks up and says, "*Hey, what are you doing out here?*"

I said, "*Where do I know you from?*" I just got in there that weekend and hadn't been on TV but one time. What it was, he was from Jackson,

Tennessee. He said he used to watch wrestling every Saturday night on ... well, it was WDXI or something back then. He had moved to Arizona.

I left Mobile and came back to Memphis. There was a place over in West Memphis called Danny's Club. Mario told me, *"Go over and see them and tell them I sent you."* He had worked there years before. It was an after-hours club. Man, it was great! There was a lot of girls there. Danny asked me if I could work on weekends when I was in town. It paid $7.50 a night, which was a lot of money back in 1953. That was great, but I just wanted to meet all them girls. It was a gold mine.

What did your parents think about your ambition to be a wrestler?

Daddy was real proud. Mother probably was, but she was more scared about me getting hurt.

Did they ever go watch you wrestle live?

Oh, yeah. Whenever we had a big feud, a blood-and-guts type deal, she'd be standin' and crying at the ring. I thought, *"Oh, I wish she wasn't here tonight!"* Daddy didn't say nothin'. He'd just watch, but Mother would actually be crying.

Did you begin wrestling as Dwayne Peal?

Yes.

Did you wrestle under any other names?

Well, I forgot to tell you this. I went in the Army. I was in Special Services working the gym. I was going through the file cabinet and found a letter from the general that said he didn't care if professional wrestling was held on the post. They were gonna try to have wrestling on the post. They *did* object to military personnel wrestling professionally.

Before I got drafted, I was supposed to go to Georgia. I called Don McIntyre, who was the booker, and told him I'd be there. He told me to get ahold of Bibber McCoy. I went down on a Monday night and told Bibber, *"The only problem I have is that I can't use my real name,"* because of that letter I found.

He says, *"We'll think of something. How about Jack Burns?"*

Where he came up with that name, I don't know. The next morning, I went into Lieutenant Thibeaux's office and he said, *"How are you doing, Jack Burns?"* (laughs) They really didn't care. I was actually a celebrity on the post. He watched TV every Saturday.

I wrestled as Jack Burns the whole time I was down there. We'd do live TV on Tuesday in Savannah, then another live TV in Augusta on Wednesday. The house shows were on Monday in Augusta and Thursday in Savannah. Atlanta TV was on Saturday morning and the house show was Friday night. I didn't go to Columbus because it was a little too far for me, but after I got out of the Army, I wrestled in Columbus.

Where were you stationed?

Fort Gordon, Georgia.

What year was that?

I went into the service in 1957. I had already been wrestling for a couple of years. I was in the Army for two years before I got out.

What were your regular duties in the Army?

Really nothing. I could have stayed there a hundred years. We took care of the baseball field, the swimming pools. I was just there, really. At times, we had to clean the gym up, but that wasn't nothin'. All you did was take the big dust mops and run over the floor. Normally, I'd get there about 8:30 in the morning and we'd drink coffee for about an hour. I'd mess around until eleven or so, then go eat and come back at one. I'd go to the back, lay down and sleep until 3:30 or four, then go home.

What a life.

(laughs) We had a driving range. They asked me to go over and run it one day. I was complaining. *"Oh, man!"* I got over there and they had buckets of balls for ... well, it amounted to a penny a ball. Twenty-five cents for a bucket of 25. Everybody had to sign in when they got a bucket. Well, there was so many guys there, they'd hit a bucket of balls, lay their money down and walk off, without taking time to sign in. At the end of the day, when I balanced the books, I had almost twenty dollars extra with no other names. I put it in a fund. (laughs)

No doubt it went to the Buddy Wayne fund.

(laughs) The next day, Frank says, "*I need somebody to run the range. Dwayne, you did it yesterday. Let me get somebody else.*"

"No, no! I'll do it!" (laughs) I wasn't gonna lose that deal.

We had a detail of men to pick the balls up. The post commander was a full colonel. He came down one day to drive some golf balls. When we got through, he says, "*How do you get those picked up?*"

I said, "*Normally we have a detail of men here, but today we don't have anybody. Me and Willie are going to pick them up.*" Willie was a black, civilian guy, an older man. "*We have a machine, but it doesn't work, so we have to pick them up by hand.*"

He said, "*Are you two going to do it by yourselves?*"

I said, "*Yes, sir. It's just us.*"

He said, "*Me and my driver will help.*" (laughs) He said, "*Come on, Jimmy. Let's get these balls picked up.*"

We're out there pickin' up golf balls and the captain of the Special Services looked out his window. He calls over to the gym and says, "*Frank, you aren't gonna believe what Peal's doin'.*"

Frank says, "*What's he doing now?*"

"*He's got the post commander out there picking up golf balls.*"

That was a big joke on the post for a long time. He said he really enjoyed it. It was a beautiful, sunny March afternoon in Georgia.

I wrestled all over Georgia, but they used a lot of real big guys in Georgia. I was one of the smallest guys there, so for the first few months, I refereed. Then smaller guys came in ... Wild Red Berry, Marco Polo, Al Galento, Bennie Matta. They were more my size, so I actually started wrestling. The reason I got away with wrestling when I was in the Army is that I didn't ask permission. That way, they couldn't say I violated orders. I never was ordered not to.

In fact, when I went to basic at Fort Chaffee [in northwest Arkansas], the Field First and our platoon sergeant were all big wrestling fans. They went down to Fort Smith, Arkansas, which was about 20 miles away. They had matches on Wednesday night down there and they all went. We had a mail

Buddy Wayne, 18 years old

clerk named Riviera. He was a little Puerto Rican guy. He'd bring me my mail every day at noon. It made the rest of the guys mad. *"Oh, yeah. You get your mail hand-delivered and we have to wait until tonight and get it at mail call."* (laughs)

We had to march out to the rifle range one day, then march back in. It was probably three or four miles. Riviera came out and picked me up. He said, *"They need you back at the company."*

When I got in the truck, I said, *"What's wrong,"* and he said, *"Nothin'. I just figured you didn't wanna walk back."* (laughs)

When I was stationed at Fort Sam Houston in San Antonio, I went to medic school. I was the acting sergeant, so I didn't pull KP there, either. That's where Brooks Army Medical Center is. San Antonio is beautiful. I loved it. I would have stayed in the Army if I had some assurance that I'd do what I was doing for the entire twenty years.

When did you start wrestling as Buddy Wayne and what was the reason for the name change?

1968. There was two reasons for doing it. One, Nick called and wanted me to wrestle on the Birmingham end of the territory. He said, *"The only thing is ... Dwayne Peal is a flat-sounding name."* Second, Lee, Don and Bobby Fields were well known in that area, so a lot of people assumed we were brothers. Fields and Peal sound a lot alike, so they'd get us confused. To this day, people in Arkansas come up and want to know how my brothers are doing. (laughs) I just tell them, *"Oh, they're doin' good."*

Nick and I came up with the name Buddy Wayne. Very few people now, Scott, even know my real name. I don't hide it, but I don't use it much. If someone comes up and calls me Dwayne, I know they knew me years ago.

Who actually came up with the name Buddy Wayne?

Nick Gulas.

You wrestled as Buddy Wayne in most places, but when you wrestled in Memphis, you still used the name Dwayne Peal, correct?

Yeah, but we started using Buddy Wayne Peal. We had to do that because the [Memphis] tape would go into Nashville or Huntsville and I'd be introduced as Dwayne Peal. It was confusing the people, so we eased into it by using Buddy Wayne Peal, and eventually dropped the Peal.

I only think of you as Buddy Wayne. I never knew you when you were Dwayne Peal.

They used to show the Memphis tapes around. I was always Dwayne Peal there. This girl came up one night in Huntsville, wanting to know if I knew Wayne Fields. I said, "*Yeah, I know Wayne! Where do you know him from?*" Believe it or not, Wayne Fields was a friend of mine here in Memphis. (laughs) She said she saw him on TV. Well, she didn't see him, she saw me. She thought they said Wayne Fields. I told Nick, "*We need to do something,*" so what we did, we used Buddy Wayne Peal.

Gorgeous George was one of the first wrestlers to use music, but a guy named Cowboy Wayne did it up in Toledo, Ohio.

Cowboy Wayne. Was that you?

Yes. Don Fargo and I was up there in 1955. Cliff Maupin was the promoter and it was a real good territory — Indianapolis, Chicago, Detroit, Fort Wayne. I don't remember where I came up with the name, but I wore a buckskin shirt and cowboy hat. Anyway, Eddie Arnold's new song *Cattle Call* had just come out. Don said, "*You need to get that and have it playing when you walk to the ring.*"

I said, "*I don't know, Don.*"

He said, "*I'm tellin' ya. Do it!*"

I did it and it got over. People crowded around with their cameras. Kids were asking for autographs. I still have some ads from where I used that name in Missouri.

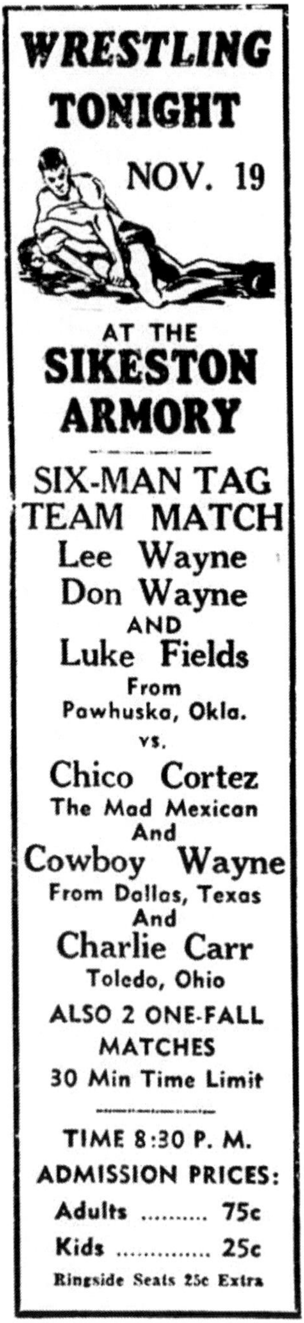

Sikeston MO • Nov. 19, 1955

We stayed at the Waldorf Hotel in Toledo. I came in one night when I was back in Tennessee. I said "*Bill* [Golden], *you ain't gonna believe what happened to me up in Toledo a few weeks ago. I went back to the hotel after the matches and there seemed to be a convention going on. That lobby was packed. There was people everywhere. I had on my blue jeans, cowboy hat, boots. When I walked in, somebody hollered,* 'Hey, look everybody! Cowboy Wayne just came in!'" I said, "*Bill, everybody starting lookin' and pointing. I was so embarrassed. I kind of wish I hadn't yelled it.*" (laughs) Bill told that story everywhere.

Was Herb Welch promoting the Missouri end of the territory?

No. Lee Fields' daddy, Virgil Hatfield, was the promoter. Virgil promoted Jonesboro on Tuesday night. Sikeston, Missouri ran on Saturdays. Jack Welch [one of the four original Welch brothers] ran Poplar Bluff, Missouri. Later on, he promoted Huntsville and that area. Mike Meroney ran Blytheville. He actually promoted the town, but it was through the Nashville office, of course. Meroney had something wrong with his throat. He was always pullin' at his collar … "*Acchh, eccch, aaahchh.*" Did you ever hear the story about Chico Cortez? I know you did. The story about the guy who was gonna challenge a wrestler?

Yeah. That's a classic. George Grant told me the story. I printed it in an issue of WHT.

That's a true story.

Chico the Shooter

by George Grant

One night in Blytheville, Arkansas, all of us got in the ring for a battle royal. There was a guy in the audience who was working on the pipeline … big arms, beefy build, the typical small-town tough guy. He jumped up and yelled, *"You bunch of phony wrestlers. I can beat any of you bums!"*

Now, the promoter was a guy named Mike Meroney. He was in his seventies, half his face was eaten up with cancer, and he didn't weigh a hundred pounds. He said, *"I'll tell you what you do, punk. Get up in the ring. If you can beat any of my boys, I'll give you a hundred dollars."*

That guy jumped in and we all started getting out of the ring. We figured on leaving him in the ring with Lester [Welch]. Lester could get in there and work with him the best he could and still half kill him. I'm just kidding. Actually, to be honest, Lester was the best worker of all the Welch boys.

Anyway, the guy says, *"No, no. I get to choose my opponent."*

Meroney said, *"Alright, anyone you want."*

The punk says, *"I'll take Chico Cortez."*

Now, Chico's sitting there thinking, *"What am I gonna do?"* He got in the ring and said, *"The guy has to take those big boots off."*

So, while the guy is unlacing those big boots, Chico is psychologically blowing him up. He's saying to the crowd, *"Hey, everybody. I'm gonna take his left arm off and stick it* [where the sun don't shine]. *I'm gonna tear his right arm off and stick in in his left ear."* So, by the time that guy started unlacing that second boot, he's slowin' down a little. He's starting to think about this stuff.

Come time to ring the bell, that guy's standing in the corner with his hands up on the ropes, lookin' at Chico, who's acting like a man possessed. Chico was blind in one eye. He had an artificial eye for many years, and he used to wear his hair just like Buster Brown … bangs down to his eyebrows. You ask

Lester Welch. He was there and will tell you this is the truth. Chico came running out of the corner, jumped straight up in the air, screamed as loud as he could, pulled that black hair straight down over his face, and the guy fainted … dead fainted! Now little old Mike Maroney got up there with his shoes on and said, *"Why, you SOB. You mess with one of my wrestlers. I'll kick you right out of here."* He kicked the guy right out of the ring onto the floor, cussing him and calling him all kinds of names. The funny thing was, Mike forgot the microphone was still turned on.

Chico is another one who helped me a lot. In fact, he's the one who got me in Ohio as Cowboy Wayne. He had been up there as Chico Garcia. Mario Galento was wrestling up there as Aztec Garcia, so Chico went up as Chico Garcia. We were coming back from a town in Missouri and he asked if I wanted to go up there. I said, *"I don't know."*

He said, *"Well, when we get to Memphis, we'll send a night letter."*

What's a night letter?

It's like a telegram, except now, instead of delivering it in the middle of the night, they deliver it the next day. In other words, years ago, they'd bring it to you at three o'clock in the morning. They had guys in Memphis that rode bicycles and did that.

Wait a minute! I forgot all about that! That's where I got the name Cowboy Wayne. Chico said, *"We need to come up with a name other than Dwayne Peal. I know! We'll call you Cowboy Wayne."* Chico and I were coming back from Poplar Bluff [MO]. Chico was gonna catch the bus to Dyersburg from Memphis. Of course, I could have went through Dyersburg, but back then, there wasn't a bridge. I wasn't gonna cross on the ferry because I was scared of it, especially in the middle of the night. He asked if I would like to go to Ohio. I said, *"Yeah, I'd like to."*

He said, *"When we get back, I'll send a night letter to Martino Angelo."*

Do you remember Herb Langston? He promoted Jackson, Tennessee.

(laughs) Oh, yeah! Herb "The Snake" Langston. He always dressed nice, but they called him "The Snake." That's all I remember about him.

They were all part of what was known at the time as the Mid-South Booking Office, which was run by Roy Welch and Nick Gulas. What towns did Herb Welch promote?

At that time, Herb wasn't promoting anything.

I'm surprised that Herb wasn't running any towns.

I don't believe he was, but if he was, I wasn't aware of it.

He didn't promote Dyersburg?

No. Bill Golden run that back then and did the booking. Bill was married to Buddy Fuller's sister … Roy Welch's daughter.

There was a lot of Welch kin around there.

Oh, yeah. We wrestled in Canton, Mississippi, a few weeks ago. I don't know if you remember Jack Curtis, but he says, *"Are all these people kin to you?"* There was Ken, Aubrey, my son Greg, my daughter-in-law Vickie. (laughs)

Instead of the Welch clan, it's the Wayne clan.

(laughs) That's right. It's a family affair. Vickie is married to my son, Greg, who referees for me. A few years ago, we did a little thing with her as Vicious Vickie. She wrestled Jackie [Miss Texas].

What other towns did Bill Golden run?

Bill Golden did the booking for this end up here, then he went down and opened Sheffield, Alabama, on Mondays. Then he started running Florence on Fridays. Bill also ran Decatur. He had his own little territory down there and drew some money. They're pretty good-size towns now. Muscle Shoals, Florence, Tuscumbia and Sheffield are like one big city now.

I helped Bill Golden a lot, but it's really funny. I went to Louisiana. Lee [Fields] was promoting, but Bill was running it. Tuesday night, after the matches in Baton Rouge, we'd do our TV. I'd give Bill ideas. Then I went to Montgomery when he was promoting that. Bill goes, *"Buddy Wayne, let me tell you something. I came down here and dug this out on my own. Everybody that comes in tries to book my towns."*

"Well, Bill! I've always helped you before."

"Well, I don't want your help!"

After that, I noticed that when Jerry Myatt told Bill to do something, Bill would do it, so I started tellin' Jerry what we needed to do. Jerry would tell Bill and he'd do it. Years later, me and Bill were talking. *"You know, Jerry Myatt used to have some good ideas down in Montgomery."*

I said, *"Bill, every one of them was mine, but you wouldn't listen to me."* (laughs)

What towns did Roy Welch take care of personally?

Memphis. Of course, they had the whole territory, but on Mondays, Roy handled Memphis and Nick took care of Birmingham. Nick also ran Huntsville, Chattanooga, Nashville. John Cazana ran Knoxville, Morristown. His brother George promoted when John was younger. Mickey Baarns took care of Kingsport, Johnson City, and all that area. Nick and Roy booked them, but they had promoters for each of the towns.

What was it like working for Herb Welch?

Herb was very, very fair. In fact, he would overpay you. He was a good business person, but he was one of the boys, you might say, so he knew both sides of it.

Jack Welch promoted Poplar Bluff. I used to work there when I first started. Roy said to Jack, *"If I start booking this boy, would you use him?"*

Jack said, *"Yeah! I'll use him every night."*

He also ran Huntsville, but they took the town away from him. He had a wife named Grace. That was Joann Phillips' sister. Do you remember Joann Phillips?

I sure do.

Joann Moore was her name. Grace was a little on the heavy side. She'd get up in the ring and announce, but Roy didn't like it. (laughs) He'd tell Jack, *"Don't let that big, fat whore up in the ring!"* (laughs) That's the way Roy talked. Jack would say, *"Well, that's my wife and she wants to do it."* They took the town away from him [Jack]. They sure did! On his last night there, he got up in the ring and told the people they took the town away from him. He asked them to please not come any more. (laughs)

I never will forget. He was wrestling in a tag match with Bobby Fields or somebody as his partner. Whoever it was did a flying scissors. Me and Virgil Hatfield were standing on the stage. When he tagged Jack, Jack went in to do a flying scissors, but he didn't get knee high. Virgil says, *"Dammit! I knew that son-of-a-bitch was gonna do that!"* (laughs)

When did you start promoting Jonesboro?

In 1962, Buddy Fuller left Memphis and went to Arizona. Arizona was deader than a doornail, just like Memphis was when Fuller came there. Buddy came in here [Memphis] on Thanksgiving Day of '58 and they had about two or 300 people. When I got out of the Army in March, they had about 3,500.

Anyway, we run Phoenix on Monday, Mesa on Wednesday, and back in Phoenix in the same building on Friday. Chandler, Tucson, Yuma ... they were all packed. I went to Florida for Fuller for two weeks, come back, and they sold out for the next year. That was when Buddy had the Mobile office. I came back in May and that's when I opened up Jonesboro.

Who did Buddy use in Arizona?

A lot of the same ones who worked in Memphis. Sputnik [Monroe]. Ken Lucas lived there and was just starting. Tex Riley, Len Rossi, Rube Wright, Greg Peterson, George Harris, Dick Dunn, myself. They had a good crew. He was out there about a year or so, then he sold to Clint Starr.

What exactly did Clint Starr have to do with Memphis? I never did figure that out.

He just did the programs. When Fuller got through there in Arizona, I think he went to Australia with Barnett. He was wanting me to come down there, but I really didn't want to go. Now I wish I had. I didn't go because I was making money here. Steve Clements tried to get me to go to England in '69. His daddy was the promoter over there. Steve told me that, being a foreigner, I would make good money. We got a $400-minimum guarantee, but Steve said I'd probably make that much in one night. I kicked myself for not going. At that time, though, you couldn't go over there and stay just a week or two. Because of the air expense, you had to go for a three-month period.

If I'm not mistaken, Scott, you couldn't wrestle in England more than eight weeks each year. What you did was go in there in November. November and December was eight weeks. Then you stay through January and February, which is another eight weeks, but in the next year.

That's another thing about the name Peal. Peal is a common name over there. Robert Peel was the founder of Scotland Yard. Bobby Peel, or Robert Peel, is where they got the term "bobbies" for the policemen over there.

Who promoted Jonesboro before you started running it?

Clint Starr. In fact, me and Clint went out to Phoenix together. We carried two rings out there.

Did Starr just shut down Jonesboro when he left for Arizona?

Yeah. Fuller sold Clint a piece of Arizona. When I came back, it [Jonesboro] wasn't running, so I called Nick [Gulas] and asked about running it. He said, "*Yeah, go ahead.*" We opened up on a Tuesday night. We had Jesse James and Red Roberts on the card. I remember that. We did around $310. Our tickets were fifty-cents, one dollar and a dollar fifty cents. The next week, we came back and did $360. I moved to Friday night and we did about four-and-a-half, then we went to Saturday and I did five and six. The best house I had in there at that time, I brought in Mighty Jumbo. He weighed 500-plus pounds. We did real good, somewhere between 600 and $700. Then I brought in Happy Humphrey against Jumbo. Nine hundred pounds against 600 pounds. Before the match, we got sawhorses put up under the ring to brace the ring up. We had a packed house. We drew over 900 people.

Was that the biggest house you ever had there?

No. We drew 1,486 — which was the most I ever had there — but we turned over 2,000 away. It was unreal.

Who was headlining?

Lou Thesz and Tim Tyler. They wrestled for the [NWA world heavyweight] title. I'm not exaggerating. We got there at five o'clock, Scott. At six o'clock, we quit sellin' tickets, and the matches didn't start until eight-thirty. We turned at least 2,000 away. I couldn't believe it! People sat there from six until eight-thirty, waiting for the matches to begin.

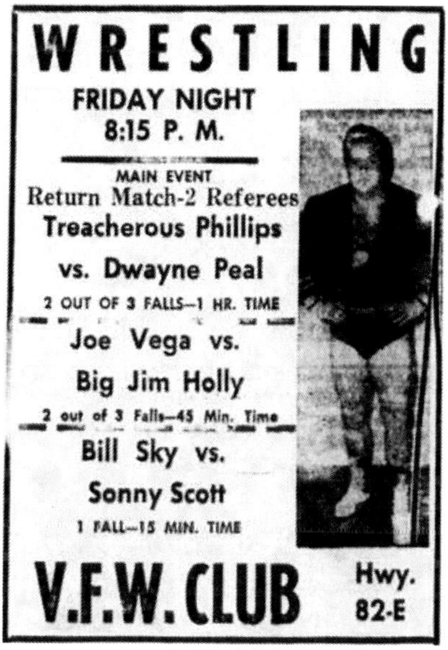

Greenwood MS • April 7, 1967

Did you have trouble with fire marshals back then?

Well, yes and no. If we were at a school, naturally, they'd let everyone in. Now in Jonesboro, there was a local guy who came in the dressing room with the commissioner. He always wanted me to stop selling tickets. He had a badge about as big as your thumb. He'd say, "*This is where I get my authority.*" The problem was, I had a deal with the [American] Legion. They got a $50 minimum, a $150-dollar maximum, and in-between was 25 percent.

Explain how that worked.

For instance, in Jonesboro, if we didn't have anybody there, they still got $50. Then I gave them 25 percent, with a maximum of $150. In other words, they could make $150 or they could make $85, but no less than 50. Well, once they reached their $150, they didn't really care if any more people came in or not. In fact, they felt that if it was jam-packed, people wouldn't get up and buy concessions. They wanted room for people to move around.

You once told me a story about you and Jim Holly being the only two guys who showed up to wrestle one night.

Oh, yeah. (laughs) It was a live show. As a rule, I didn't want to wrestle because I was the promoter. I didn't think it looked good. A few weeks before that, somebody wasn't there, so I wrestled. The week after that, I had to wrestle again. On that night, there was ice and snow everywhere, but we had a decent crowd. It was me, Big Jim Holly, and the ring man. I couldn't begin to tell you how I got there. I said, "*Jim, we're gonna have to wrestle three falls and fill the whole time.*" My ring man didn't know anything about wrestling and I didn't tell him nothing, but I asked him to referee.

He wasn't wise to the business?

No. I said, "*If my shoulders are down, you count me out. If his are down, count him out. If somebody says,* 'He pulled my hair' *and you don't see it, don't break it.*"

I don't remember how I took the first fall. The second fall, he would slam me, then he'd get behind me and reach over me and take my head like an upside-down facelock. My face would be like in his armpit. He'd pull me up and take his right forearm and bang! He'd hit me across the chest. He'd do that three or four times, then cover me. In the third fall, he did it twice, but I hooked his head, turned a flip, went over him and pinned him. One, two three.

Except for Lou Thesz, I was the only guy to beat Jim Holly. The only reason I beat him was because I was afraid the people would be disgusted because there was only one match.

He was so strong in that area that you never beat him?

Oh, yeah. Jim drew me some money. He had a match with Lou Thesz. We had the stipulation that if he didn't beat Lou, he'd lose his hair. Lou put up his title. Back then, a haircut meant something, and the place was jam-packed. Lou used that Greco-Roman backdrop to win the first fall. Jim lost the second fall when he couldn't continue. Lou got on the microphone and said, "*Look! The man is one of the toughest men I've ever wrestled. I don't think we ought to cut his hair because I didn't beat him twice by pinfall. So let's not cut his hair.*"

The audience went nuts! "*CUT HIS HAIR!! CUT HIS HAIR!!*" (laughs)

Lou looked over at me and said, "*Well, I tried,*" so we had to cut his hair.

That's when that [NWA world title] belt meant something. Before that night, Fargo told me, "*Oh, man! You made a mistake. Lou don't like those kind of matches.*" Lou never said a word. Lou is a great guy ... one of the best I ever met. He is my idol. I say that with all sincerity.

Jim Holly weighed around 325 pounds. I weighed 200, 210 at the most. One night, I forgot how big he was and I went to slam him. I got him up in the air and I thought, "*Oh, shit! What am I doin'?*" I have a picture of it. My face is straining, but he went up like a feather. The people at ringside had their mouths open, like "*Good Lord!*" Then he slammed me a couple of times. Then ... BOOM! I'd slam him. Those people would go crazy. Jim made a lot of money for me in those little towns.

Why didn't Jim go anywhere else? I don't think he ever wrestled in Nashville.

For one thing, he had an air-conditioning business. I really don't think he wanted to travel.

As the local promoter, what did you do each week to promote the shows?

I put posters out and placed ads in the newspaper. On the night of the matches, I carried the tickets over and got the box office set up. I got with the boys and gave them the finishes. When the show was over, I collected the money, checked it, put the money in envelopes, and paid the guys, paid the American Legion. Whatever was left after I paid the booking fee to the Nashville office was mine.

You paid Nick Gulas and Roy Welch a booking fee to use their talent. Do you remember what your agreement was?

Yeah. I paid more than I should have. In '62, I had just started promoting, so I wasn't familiar with things. When I promoted a town, I paid Nick fifteen percent of the house. I found out later that it should have been ten, but I paid fifteen. Treach Phillips asked me one time, *"How much did you pay for the booking?"*

I said, *"A hundred twenty-five dollars."*

He said, *"Don't you hate to send that?"*

I said, *"No, Treach! I'd be happy to send $500. If I did, then I had one heck of a house."*

I never thought about it when I sent it. I could call Nina [Bond, the wrestling office manager] on Tuesday and say, *"Nina, I need a picture of Jackie Fargo, Len Rossi, and Tojo."* The next day, I'd have four or five pictures of those guys.

Did you have an agreement for Nick and Roy to send a certain number of wrestlers?

Yeah. I'd call Nick and say, *"I have a town runnin'."*

He'd say, *"Okay, here's the men I have available."*

He'd tell me who was available and I'd say, *"Let me have this guy, this guy and that guy."*

There were times when he'd book the card. He'd say, *"Here's the card I have booked for you."* I might want to change parts of it, or I might not. The card he booked was probably okay because he followed his TV pretty good.

Now, when I had my own TV in Jonesboro, I did all that myself. He would send me guys, but most of them were guys that wrestled underneath. He'd send me Lou Thesz. Danny Hodge wrestled four weeks in a row for me and we packed it every night. One of the best matches on the card was Danny against Billy Wicks. What a match they had! The people just sat there. They weren't yellin' and hollerin'. Scott, they were lookin' at the match. I remember Joe Moore. He was a referee. He said, *"This ain't gettin' over."*

I said, *"What are you talkin' about?"*

He says, *"They're not yellin' and hollerin'."*

I said, *"Look at these people! They're on the edge of their seat."*

Today, the guys think if they ain't yellin' or screamin', they ain't gettin' over. In fact, go back and look at the Andy Kaufman and Jerry Lawler tapes. They show it a lot on Comedy Central. Watch when they pan the crowd. There's two things you'll notice in particular. This one woman is yelling, *"You son-of-a-bitch!"* You can't hear her, but you can read her lips. And they're *all* mad! Later that night, I'm watching WWF and it's a completely different mindset. Everybody's sitting there laughing, waving the big foam fingers, holding signs up. It's nothing like it was years ago. We wrestled and people came to see wrestling. We could schedule a card, but we didn't have to hype ... say, for instance, Jerry Lawler versus Bill Dundee. You could just say "wrestling" and people came out.

When you get right down to it, they didn't come to see individuals. They didn't come to see Buddy Wayne or Jerry Lawler or Billy Wicks or Sputnik Monroe. They came to see wrestling. When you did have a guy on the card like Lawler or Tojo [Yamamoto] or [Jackie] Fargo, you drew better, but you could draw three or 400 people with absolutely nobody.

If you put "wrestling" on the marquee, people would show up.

Yeah! We'd run Helena, Arkansas, at the Catholic Club. About 500 people is all the little building would hold. It was like a gym with bleachers on one side. We'd draw three or 400 people every Wednesday night. Then, if I got a couple of guys that were involved in a hot deal, we'd pack the place. I'm talking about having just six men on the card, not fourteen to twenty. We drew people week after week after week in all the towns.

So *you* handled the payoffs to the boys for the towns you ran.

Yes. Later on, when I started working more closely with Jarrett, I started out making the payoffs myself. As time went on, we figured it was a lot simpler if I sent the money to them. That way, I didn't have to keep a set of books and they didn't have to keep another set of books. I didn't have to file the 1099s and all that. Jerry asked me if it would be easier. I said, "*Actually, it would.*"

When Jerry broke away from Nick and took over the western end of the territory, what percentage did you pay?

Ten percent. Let me tell you. I made more money with Jerry Jarrett than with anybody. If I had listened to Jerry and put my money away like I should have, I would be well off right now. You think it's gonna keep coming in, but it don't.

Even 30 years ago, a lot of the boys were making money. All of a sudden, you got older, or hurt. For instance, look at Buddy Colt. He's a good example. He was making tons of money, then he had the airplane crash. Don Fields ... he was in a car accident and broke his leg. Fortunately, he was in a position with his brothers where he could make money with the promotion. You couldn't ask for any better people than the Fields boys.

Did John Regus take over the promotion work in Memphis while you were there?

Yeah, but he didn't do anything. He was nothing but a front-man. He had no more to do with it than you did. They just needed him to get on TV and act as the promoter. Roy couldn't be there every week and neither could Nick. Roy and Nick were pretty ... well, Nick wasn't as bad, but Roy wouldn't get out in front of that camera. Neither did Buddy Fuller.

Nick loved being in front of the camera.

Oh, yeah. He couldn't be at Memphis TV, though, because of Birmingham and Nashville TV.

Who actually took care of Memphis as far as taking care of the house shows?

Roy. Nick took care of Birmingham. Roy would be on that stage at the old Ellis Auditorium when the matches started, just like Nick would in Birmingham.

The only difference between 'em was, if you messed up your match or did something Roy didn't like, he didn't say nothin' to you. He just wrote a little note and put it in his vest pocket. Nick would meet you at the door, cussin'. It would be over with in no time. But Roy would talk to Nick the next day and say, "*Nick, where's Joe Smith booked next week? Where is he Monday?*"

"*Oh, he's in Memphis. He'll pick up a hundred and a quarter.*"

That was 25, 30 years ago. That was a lot of money. It's a lot of money now, but even more then. Roy would say, "*What else do we have running on Monday?*"

"*Well, we have Birmingham, Owensboro, Itta Bena, Mississippi, and Bluefield, West Virginia.*"

"*Send him to Itta Bena, Mississippi, instead of Memphis.*"

The guy just went from a hundred and a quarter to a ten- or $15 payoff. The same thing on Tuesday. "*Louisville.*"

"*What else have we got?*"

Nick would tell him. When the boy got through, he went from a seven or $800 week to maybe an $85 week. That's the way Roy worked. But, they ran a business. The only thing is, Roy would go behind your back and Nick did it to your face. Nick was cast as the bad guy, but most of the boys didn't know what Roy was doing to them.

I never met Roy, but several people with close ties to that office have told me that.

It's real funny. Nick was the no-good, son-of-a-bitch to everybody ... and Roy was the nice guy. Actually, Roy was the son-of-a-bitch and Nick was the nice guy. Roy was a cold-hearted son-of-a-bitch. He really was. Years and years ago, Lord Littlebrook came into the territory. He wrestled three times and made $45 ... but he spent sixty. He goes to Nick and says, "*Mr. Gulas, I wrestled three times last week and only made forty-five dollars. My expenses came to sixty.*"

Nick said, "*What did you say?*"

He told him again and Nick said, "*Wait a minute.*" Nick got Roy to come out and said, "*This is my partner, Roy Welch. Tell him what you just told me.*"

He told him the story. Roy said, "*Huh. You wrestled three times, made forty-five dollars, and it cost you sixty?*"

"*Yes, sir.*"

Roy said, "*Well, ain't you glad you didn't wrestle six times?*"

He turned around and walked off. That was when Littlebrook was just getting started. He was like a lot of guys. He didn't know what to say.

Everybody thought Roy was a real nice guy. One of the boys came in one morning and said, "*Mr. Gulas. I'm not making any money. I need better bookings.*"

You know how Nick talked, with that tough-guy voice. "*I don't know. We'll see what we can do.*"

Roy was sitting there. He said, "*Wait a minute, Nick. This is a good ol' boy. He don't complain about the trips. He don't complain about anything we ask him to do. He don't bitch about the money. You need to take care of this boy and make him some money.*"

"*Okay! All right, all right! I'll see what I can do.*"

The guy walked out thinking he had it made. As soon as the door closed, Roy says, "*Hey, Nick. Starve that son-of-a-bitch until he has to leave.*" That's the kind of guy Roy was.

Everybody knocked Nick's payoffs. Nick paid fair, but what he did was exaggerate the houses to the boys. When he'd pay them, he paid them on what the house really *was*, which was less than what it should have been based on what he told everyone the house was. We were in Chattanooga one night and he walks in the dressing room and says, "*Damn, boy! The house is ten thousand dollars!*"

I said, "*Nick, you said it was eighty-one hundred!*"

"*Well, that's close enough.*"

He told everyone it was $10,000, then when he paid 'em, he paid 'em on $8,100, which is what it should have been.

He put his foot in his mouth by exaggerating the house.

Yeah. Nick was bad about that, always exaggerating. In Huntsville, Alabama, we never got paid what we should have because Nick's brother was stealing. We tried to tell Nick and he wouldn't believe it. Me and Rip Collins went to the old Armory, before it burned, and counted the seats. We figured it at around 1,050 people. That night, we sold out, and it was a $600 house. Well, shit! At just a dollar apiece, it would have been $1,100. We tried to tell Nick. "*That can't be. My brother sits right there and so does the commission.*" They were the ones stealing! Jerry Jarrett and I used to talk about it. They'd run at the [Madison County] Coliseum and had a packed house. That was four or $5,000. They'd send back $1,800.

What was your understanding of the relationship between Nick and Roy? Did they split things down the middle?

As far as I know, and from what I've always heard, it was a 50-50 deal.

Earlier, when Buddy mentioned Itta Bena, it sounded like Eat a Beana. I thought it was something he had made up.

Itta Bena? You made that one up, right?

No, there is an Itta Bena. In fact, Johnny Cash got into some trouble when he mentioned Itta Bena one time. He was talking about how, years ago, he didn't draw real well in the big towns, but he was real big in Itta Bena, Mississippi. The people in Itta Bena got up in arms and wrote to him. "*Hey, don't make fun of our town.*" (laughs)

Years ago, I ran a town called Peach Orchard, Arkansas. Nick Gulas said, "*Where are you gettin' these towns?*"

I called Nick another time and said I had booked Evening Shade [AR]. He says, "*Are you makin' these towns up?*" (laughs)

I said, "*No, these are real towns, Nick.*"

I had TV on Channel 8 and it covered all those little towns in Northeast Arkansas. We packed those little places. Back then, there wasn't cable or nothin', so people were looking for entertainment.

What about your relationship with the boys? Did their interaction with you change when you began promoting?

As far as I know, it didn't. The one thing about it ... when I first went to work for Jerry, we didn't have problems with anybody because we were making so much money. Nobody really had anything to complain about. In fact, that's another reason that Jerry started making payouts. If we had a house, and the boys thought they had more coming than they did — because everybody thinks the house is always bigger than it is — he said the boys wouldn't argue with him, but with me, they wanted to complain. And that was true.

The promoters you worked for — whether it was Nick, Roy or Jerry — had a big town running almost every night of the week. They obviously wanted their best drawing talent in their big towns. Did that make it hard for you to get the better talent in your own towns?

Okay. That's a good question there, Scott. When Nick was doing the booking, you didn't get the top boys all the time. You'd get them occasionally, but you still made decent money. But then, in 1975, when they were going to split the territory, Nick was going to handle one end and Jerry was going to handle the other. There was all kinds of good towns around Memphis, Louisville and Evansville that hadn't been run in years. They put the top names in those smaller towns, gave me good publicity, plugged it on TV, and so forth. They said, "*Here's the deal we'll make.*"

I said, "*That sounds good to me.*"

We talked one time and you mentioned having your own TV show for your towns.

Yeah. It was like, all of a sudden, the crowds dropped to nothing. I couldn't figure it out. There was a new TV station in town [Jonesboro] ... Channel 8, KAIT. Someone told me that they were airing a wrestling show from Texas, so Nick told me, "*Go work a deal with them for TV.*"

I said, "*Nick, we won't have the same guys they have in Memphis.*"

He told me, "*Make your own stars.*"

So I went to the station and set up a local program at 6:30 on Thursday night. We had live studio matches and worked a hot angle between Red Roberts and Slim the Hillbilly. We turned people away. From then on, I had my own TV program.

That was unusual for a station back then to air wrestling in prime time.

Yeah. At the time, we didn't think it was a good time-slot, but it really was. We ran live from 6:30 to 7:30 p.m. Later, they got a tape machine and started taping it on Tuesday, then showed it on Thursday at 6:30 and repeated it at 11:30 that night.

Who hosted the show?

We used a local announcer.

Did you smarten him up?

No! I didn't smarten anybody up at the TV station. I told the boys, "*Don't talk in the ring. If you do, and I hear you, you're gonna be gone. I don't care who you are.*"

It was different back then from what it is today. If you told a guy to do something, he'd do it. Now they want to argue with you. I remember Jerry Jarrett giving guys a finish. The guy would start bitchin'. Jerry would say,

"*Wait a minute! All week long, I've been thinking about this. You heard it less than three seconds ago and you're complaining.*" Jerry was a smart person. I never argued when a promoter told me to do something because I don't know what he had planned down the road. It might not make a bit of sense tonight, but two weeks down the road ... "*Ah, that's the reason.*" Now that ain't true in every case, but ... and a lot of 'em don't know what they're doing. I'm not callin' any names, but they don't have a clue.

Who were some of the guys you used on your TV?

I used a lot of local boys. Rip Tyler, Treach Phillips. Red Roberts wasn't local, but he was one of them. Slim the Hillbilly. We had a guy named Gordo Chihuahua, a little Mexican. He didn't speak English. I asked Nick if I could have him. He said, "*What the hell do you want him for, boy?*"

"*I wanna make money!*"

Roy Welch said, "*If you made a nickel with him, you'd be the luckiest man in the world.*"

We sold out every little town in Northeast Arkansas and the boot heel [of Missouri].

The boot heel consists of what towns?

Kennett, Mauldin.

Mauldin is the town that Henry Rogers promoted later on.

Yeah. Henry used to come to the matches in Jonesboro. I'm the one that got him started in it. At that time, you had to be a resident of Missouri to get a promoter's license. (laughs) There was a guy they called Sarge Freeman. He was a friend of Henry's that refereed. He didn't know what was going on. He was just a good man. I got the license in Sarge's name, then that asshole started running towns on that license. There wasn't nothin' I could do about it because it was his license.

He started running shows on his own?

He was running his own towns! There was nothin' I could do about it because the license was in his name, even though I paid for it. At that time, you had to be a resident to get a license.

Did Nick send him talent?

No, he used his own guys. Henry Rogers was another one who used his own guys. He ran up in Malden for years and years. In fact, a lot of the guys worked for him ... Larry Latham, Wayne Farris.

Eddie Gilbert got his start with Henry.

That's right. One of Buddy Colt's first matches was in Jonesboro. That was when he was still wrestling as Ron Reed. I don't remember who he was wrestling with, but he's in the dressing room. I said, "*Let me see, Ron. Your match is one-fall, no time limit. Just go through.*" I turned around and walked off. (laughs) If you go through [to a draw] with no time limit, the match would just go on forever and ever and ever. (laughs) I looked over my shoulder and he had a real puzzled look on his face. I was kiddin' him about it at the reunion one year. He told me, "*I didn't know what to say.*"

I didn't catch on right away, either. I thought you were going to tell me that he didn't know what "go through" meant.

No, but that reminds me of another funny story. I had someone ask me one time, *"Are we gonna do a Hollywood?"*

I thought, *"A Hollywood?"*

(laughs) Instead of a Broadway.

(laughs) I said, *"Do you mean Broadway?"*

"Yeah, that's it. Broadway!"

Tell me about the deal with Gordo.

What we did was, I had wrestled on TV two or three weeks before. He couldn't understand English and he came out there during my interview. I was wearing a suit and sitting at the commentator's desk. When he walked out, I picked up the chair and threatened him with it. Well, the chair hung in the curtain, so I gave it a good, hard yank. It came loose at the same time that he stepped forward. It caught him dead center on his head. The funny thing about it was, he didn't even go to his knees. He staggered back, his eyes crossed, and the announcer goes, *"Good Lord! He didn't even go to his knees. Get a shot of that chair!"* The metal chair was actually bent.

The next night, we were in Newport, Arkansas. We expected three or 400 people. We couldn't get all the people in the building. They all wanted to see that Mexican. They had never seen anything like that! If I had knocked him down, or if he went to his knees, it wouldn't have meant anything.

We went to a little town called Doniphan, Missouri. Snow was everywhere and the ice on the power lines was as thick as a baseball bat, but the roads were good. This was in 1964. The reason I remember that is I had just bought a '64 Ford Convertible. The further north we went, the worse it looked. We got up there and had a $1,055 house. That was 1,055 people and we couldn't get any more in. Betty Boucher was on that card.

On the way home, I got stopped by the highway patrol. There was a guy with us from South America. He had just opened a beer. When they saw we had beer, they checked us for DWI. Of course, I wasn't drinking, but they left my car on the side of the road and carried us all the way back to Jonesboro. I had about a thousand dollars in the car, which was a lot of money then. As far as that goes, it's a lot of money now. I said, *"I need to get my bag out of the trunk."*

He said, *"What's in it?"*

I said, *"Money. We just had wrestling over at Doniphan."*

He said, *"Let me see."* I opened it and he said, *"Okay, that's good."*

Did they leave your car sitting there?

Oh, yeah! That idiot drove 90 miles an hour on those little roads. We walk into the police station and there was a lot of people that knew me. *"Hey, what are you doin' in here?"*

"This guy says we're drunk."

A few months later, he stopped me in a regular routine road check. They had road blocks up. I had a little bag that contained three fifths of whiskey. He said, *"Does that thing have money in it?"*

He remembered that bag of money. I said, *"Well, it's got some good stuff,"* and that's all I said because it was a dry county. (laughs) It wasn't a problem, though.

Here's a funny story about Bill Lewis, who used to promote in Richmond, Virginia. Bill's nickname was "Big Blue." Bill had a little boy that looked just like him that everyone called "Little Blue." Things weren't drawing too good in Richmond, so Bill decided to give a Shetland pony away. It was probably worth a thousand dollars. He ran the contest over a six- to eight-week period. On the night of the drawing, the place was jam-packed. Bill gets in the ring and says, "*Okay, we're gonna give away this Shetland pony. Come on up here, Little Blue, and let's draw this name!*"

Little Blue jumps in the ring, runs over, and they shake those names up. Bill says, "*Okay, Little Blue. Let's see who won this Shetland pony.*"

Little Blue reaches his hand down in the bowl and hands his daddy a piece of paper. Bill looks at it and goes, "*Well, well, well, folks. What do you know? Little Blue done went and won a Shetland pony.*" (laughs)

(laughs) He really did that?

Oh, yeah. "*Little Blue done went and won a Shetland pony.*" The next week, there wasn't nobody there. (laughs)

Buddy Fuller did something similar to that in Mobile. He gave away a stereo system. It was on the up and up, though. He said, "*I don't want anyone from the office or any of the boys to buy a ticket.*" Well, one of the guys who worked in the office did buy a ticket and won it. Buddy had to go around in the crowd showing everybody that the guy had really won it. (laughs) Buddy said, "*Damn! I'd have bought him one. I didn't want him to win it.*"

How long did you promote Jonesboro?

From 1962 to 1967. I left there and went to Lafayette, Louisiana, for Lee Fields. He opened up New Orleans, Morgan City, and Lake Charles.

Joe Gunther used to promote New Orleans. What happened to him?

I don't know if he just quit, died, or what. New Orleans had a real corrupt athletic commission. It was *real* corrupt. It was a payoff-type deal. That's how Lee lost Southern Louisiana. They was wanting a big payoff and he didn't want to do it. I'm trying to remember the name of the guy who was head of the commission down there. It was an Italian guy. He was as crooked as a barrel of snakes.

I haven't heard the story about Lee and New Orleans.

I went down there just before that happened. He was trying to get Northern Louisiana. I can't remember the commissioner's name, but it seems like it was an Italian name. What it amounted to was, whoever paid him the most money got the territory. So, instead of Lee getting Northern Louisiana, LeRoy [McGuirk] ended up getting Northern Louisiana *and* Southern Louisiana. It was a real corrupt commission.

Roy Welch is the one that had the commissions put in here [TN] years ago. They'd keep you out. In other words, if you wanted to promote in Nashville, they'd say, "*I'm sorry. Nick Gulas and Roy Welch are promoting there.*" They kept the outlaw groups out.

What actually happened to Jonesboro? Did Roy and Nick decide to take the town back?

That's a long story. Rip Tyler had just started wrestling. Tim Tyler, who was Marvin Hickman ... he wanted to go in partners with me. After thinking about it, I felt like it would be a big mistake, so I didn't want to do it. I was fixin' to open Jackson, Mississippi. I had the Jonesboro TV and started sending tapes out to places like Jackson, Tennessee. Then we went to Greenville and Greenwood on Channel 6. Then I talked to a guy in Jackson, Mississippi, and he was going to do it. It was going to be on at midnight on a Saturday night, which is still good. Then a guy named Butterworth, who owned a TV station in Biloxi, called me and wanted to run my tape on his station.

It all just blew up. When I told Tim I wasn't interested in doing a partnership, him and Rip went and told Roy I was gonna run opposition to him. Rip Tyler went along with Tim, but he didn't know what was going on. He was just getting into the business, so he didn't know any better. He apologized years later. He said, "*Dwayne, I didn't know what they were doing.*"

Anyway, Treach [Phillips] went over there, too. Treach is a no-good rat. I don't care if he's dead. He's a no-good, dead rat! He said, "*Listen, if you want to run opposition against Nick, I'll help you. I'll be your manipulator.*"

I said, "*Treach, I don't want to run opposition. I'm makin' money with Nick. Why would I want to do that? We've had Danny Hodge four weeks in a row. If I went opposition, do you think they're gonna send people like Danny in to work for me?*"

The next day, I find out later, he's down talking to Nick and Roy, tellin' them I was gonna run opposition to them. He sure did! Nick called me and wanted me to come to Nashville to talk to them. I didn't know any of this was going on, so I didn't go. I called him and he said, "*Can you come up tomorrow?*"

I said, "*No, Nick. I have to go ...*" somewhere.

"*Well, boy! We need to talk to you.*"

"*Talk about what?*"

That's where I made a mistake. I didn't go. I was telling [Buddy] Fuller later ... he always called Roy "Bag Ears." He said, "*Well, where you made a mistake is, old Bag Ears only heard what* they *were saying. You didn't go defend yourself. They wanted you to come in. Even though you didn't know what they wanted, you should have went.*" He said, "*When you didn't go, they thought,* 'These guys must be right.'"

Then I added fuel to the fire when I told Nick I was goin' to Florida for a week on vacation. Tyler had already told 'em I was goin' down to see Lee [Fields] to work on plans to run opposition against them. And none of that was happening! Me and my girlfriend were going for a week's vacation. That's all it was. Tyler told Roy that I was going down to Florida to get with Lee and make a little deal. Nick says, "*Boy, don't you get with Stud* [Lee Fields] *and get your heads together, now.*"

I said, "*What are you talkin' about?*"

After all that, he tells me what was going on. I wrestled in Pensacola and Mobile while I was there. I did talk to Rocky

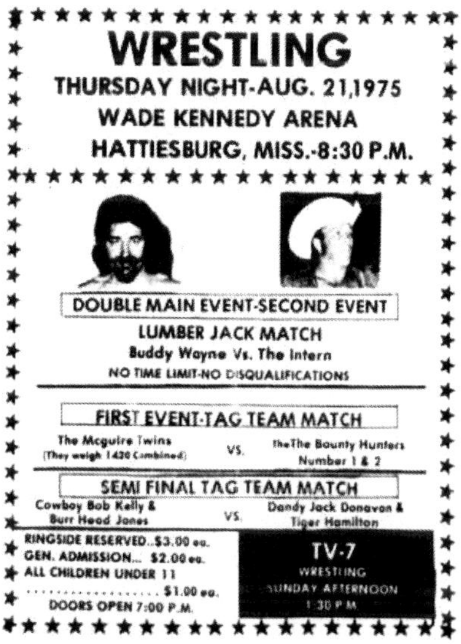

Hattiesburg MS • Aug. 21, 1975

McGuire, who was doin' the booking down there, but we didn't even talk about running towns. And then, where I got my real heat with Roy, was (pause) ... Bob Hamby. He was a little guy, about 5-foot-6 — *maybe* — but a heck of a little wrestler. We were doin' a little business with him. Well, Herb [Welch] was promoting. He was white-headed at that time. He was old. I put Hamby over.

(laughs) You had him beat Herb?

Yeah. Herb kind of looked at me, but didn't say nothin'. Well, on Monday night, I saw Roy, and he looked at me real disgusted. He didn't even speak. A few weeks went by and I told Bobby Whitlock, "*There's something wrong with Roy. I don't know what I've done, but he's hot about something.*"

Whitlock called me one Sunday and said, "*I've found out what's wrong with Roy.*"

I said, "*What?*"

He said, "*Did Herb wrestle over in Jonesboro a few months ago?*"

I said, "*Yeah.*"

"*Who did he wrestle?*"

I said, "*Shit! I don't remember. I think it was Bob Hamby.*"

He said, "*What did you do?*"

I said, "*Bob did the little deal where he comes off the top rope and nails him.*"

Bobby said, "*Well, that's the problem.*"

I said, "*What are you talkin' about?*"

He said, "*Herb was up in the Log Cabin,*" which is a little restaurant there in Frayser. That's right here in Memphis. "*His windshield wipers quit working and he sat there for two or three hours, talking. He said he had worked some of the West Memphis spots and he wasn't on the main event. He said Dwayne Peal did a little deal in Jonesboro a few weeks ago and old Bag Ears didn't like it.*"

That's where I got my heat. If it's a Welch, he had to have his hand in the air. It doesn't matter if that's the right thing to do or not. It was the right thing because the name was Welch. [Jackie] Fargo told me, "*Nick fought for you tooth and nail. He finally just told Roy,* 'The hell with it. Just do what you want to do.'"

What it amounted to was, they didn't want to send me no talent. Unfortunately, at that particular time, I didn't have a lot of cash. I had a friend who was a millionaire, but I couldn't get ahold of him. He was in Florida. He owned a big neon sign company in Memphis. Then Lee called me and wanted me to come down there.

So you just gave up Jonesboro?

Yeah, I just left. John Regus took it over. Scott, if that hadn't happened, I guarantee you that today, I'd be worth several million dollars. It happened at a time when I didn't have any cash.

I have to say it did look suspicious because you went to Mobile, then returned to Nashville just a few weeks later to work for Lee Fields, who had just opened up in Nashville in opposition to Nick. What was the story behind that?

Jack Pfefer had a contract with Nick on Jackie Fargo. He got a percentage of Fargo's earnings.

Actually, Nick paid Pfefer for the rights to book Fargo, but it was over and above what Fargo made.

Oh, I didn't know that. Everybody was scared to death of Pfefer. He killed territories. He would kill 'em, man! He'd go into a territory and handbill 'em. For instance, he'd print "*Wayne Steele won so-and-so title in so-and-so town, and lost it somewhere.*" That was before the Internet and newspapers reported that kind of thing. He'd pass out handbills telling people that the guy had lost the title the night before. (laughs) I'll never forget a poster of his that I saw. He had "BOBO" in real big letters. Real big letters! Then in small letters, he had "from." Then he had big letters again ... "BRAZIL." When you looked at that poster, all you saw was Bobo Brazil. You go to the matches to see Bobo Brazil, but it wasn't him. It was just another black guy that Pfefer was booking. He had one guy he called Lou Khesz ... K-H-E-S-Z. (laughs) Another one was George Valentine.

That was Buddy Fuller.

Right! (laughs) Bobby Whitlock went up north and they were booking him as a Jap! (big laugh) Anyway, back to the other story. Pfefer called Lee Fields and wanted him to come up to Nashville. Well, Lee and Nick never did get along, anyway. Pfefer put up the money for Lee to come up and run Nashville. By golly! I'll tell you what, Scott. We did good! The first week was so-so. The second was better. By the fourth week, Lee said, "*We can make money now.*" Then Pfefer and Nick got their differences settled and Pfefer pulled out, so Lee said, "*Well, I'm going back to Mobile.*"

Lee only ran for six weeks.

That's right, and the last two weeks, he made money.

Don Fargo and Frank Dalton were wrestling in Mobile at the time as Jack and Frank Dalton. They came into Nashville, of course, as Don and Frank Fargo.

(laughs) Ken Lucas was working as a babyface and he couldn't get over. (laughs) No matter what the Fargos did, the people cheered them, so they ended up switching during their match. They each went the other way.

I never saw Lucas work as a heel. He was usually a babyface, but I know he worked in Phoenix as a heel.

Oh, yeah. He was one heck of a heel!

I always enjoyed listening to Nick rant and rave when opposition would come in. He'd say, "*Anyone who works for that outlaw bunch will never work for me again!*" Of course, he never followed through. You were a good example of that. You were booked back in Nashville four months after Lee closed up shop.

(laughs) I left Mobile and came back up here in February 1968.

I said, "*Nick. I'd like to work.*"

Nick says, "*Oh, hell! I thought you and Lee Fields were gonna break me?*"

"*Oh, Nick. You know better than that.*"

Nick said, "*Well, can you be in Birmingham on Monday? I have a little thing planned for you.*"

I went down there and he put me over a hundred percent. Rip Collins [one of the Scufflin' Hillbillies] got hot about it. He said, "*Yeah, all these guys work opposition to Nick. Now he has them on top!*" *(laughs)* The funny thing was, it was the truth.

(laughs) Rip and Tim Tyler were back working for Nick before you were. They were back in December. Eddie Sullivan started back in April.

Saul Weingeroff ran opposition to Nick one time. Nick said, "*If I* ever *use him again, I hope I die from cancer!*"

A few months later ... here comes ol' Saul. [Jackie] Fargo says, "*Nick! You said if you ever use him again, you hope you die from cancer.*"

"*Hell, Jackie! I had my fingers crossed.*" (laughs) He was real serious. "*I had my fingers crossed.*"

(laughs) Did I understand correctly that John Regus took over Jonesboro when you left?

Right.

He just did the legwork. He didn't do any booking, did he?

He wasn't nothin' period. John was a real con man. He had Nick and Roy thinkin' that he was real strong politically. They also let Bert Bates buy into it. Bert wasn't that strong, either, but at one time he was. Bert was a leg man for E.H. Crump, but E.H. Crump had died.

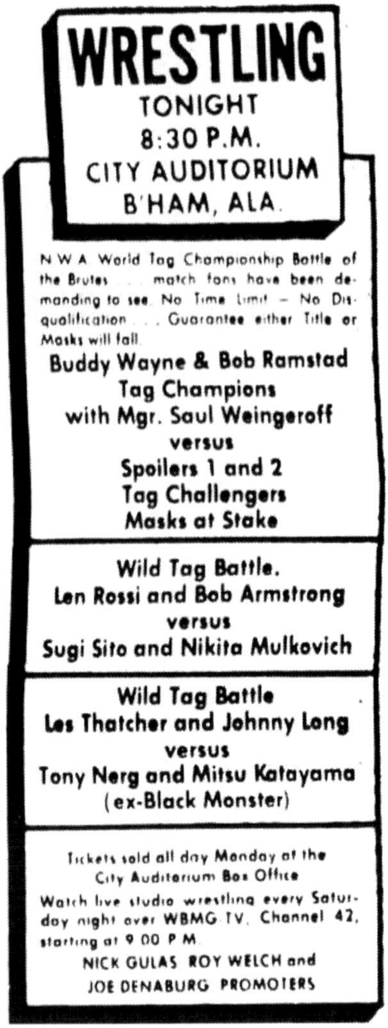

Birmingham AL • Jan. 19, 1970

I'm not familiar with E.H. Crump.

E.H. Crump was a big political figure in Memphis ... Edward Hull Crump. They called him "Boss." Crump was a politician, even though he wasn't an elected official. They called him the "King Maker." He put the mayors in office. He *was* the mayor at one time [1910-1915], but he preferred to work behind the scenes. He elected governors and everything else. He was real strong. They called it the Crump Machine. After he died, of course, Bert didn't mean nothin'. Bert worked over at Chuck Hutton Chevrolet. Regus had them conned into thinking he was really strong politically, but Regus didn't have the connections they thought he did. I think they paid him $250 a week, which again, was good money back in the '60s.

Was that Bert Bates' only political connection?

As far as I know. He might have had some local politicians.

What do you remember about the series of events that took place resulting in Jerry Jarrett actually taking control of Memphis?

I'll tell you the whole story on Jerry. Christine told me he lost his job at the bank, so he went to work at the wrestling office, putting money in envelopes, going to the bank ... whatever they needed. They decided to let him come to Memphis to referee, then they began to teach him about booking. They let him open up some towns, so he opened up Lexington. Well, that did real good. From there, he went to Louisville and opened that up. We figured it would do at least 5,000, maybe ten. I ran Florence, Alabama, at the time, on the same night as Louisville. He came into the office the next morning and looked real discouraged. I thought he was just puttin' me on. I said, "*What's wrong?*"

He said, "*Oh, man! It was a disaster.*"

I said, "*Come on. What did it do, about fifteen?*"

He said, "*No. Twenty-five hundred, but we just knew it would do five, and maybe ten. We spent over five thousand.*"

Where did Jerry run in Lexington?

It was at the Catholic High School. That's where Lawler drew the picture.

What picture?

Oh, you haven't heard that story?

I don't think so.

(laughs) Well, Jerry Lawler was around nineteen years old and he was one heck of an artist, as you know. He draws a picture of a naked woman on the door with a magic marker, but when he drew the — the private parts we call it — instead of drawing the female parts, he drew a man's. The next day, the priest calls Christine Jarrett and says, "*Miss Jarrett. Do you have any men that are artistically inclined?*"

She said, "*Oohh, yes we do! We have one man who does wonderful work. You should see some of the things he's done!*"

He said, "*I think I have.*" (laughs) He says, "*I'm gonna save it and let you see it next week.*" Christine walks in the next week and here's this picture. (laughs)

(laughs) How long did it take Jerry Jarrett to pop Lexington?

One week! The next week, it did 5,000. It jumped again the next Tuesday, and from then on, it was money all the way. Eventually, they let him promote Memphis. He came to me in 1975. We were in Chattanooga. It was Christmas. He wanted to ride back to Memphis with me. He asked me if I wanted to run some towns around Memphis. I had just come back from Alabama. I had been wrestling in Montgomery for Bill Golden for three or four years. He told me Nick would be running one end of the territory, and he'd run the other. I said, "*I guess I could.*"

At the time, I was broke. Scott, I was broke! I had a 1970 Oldsmobile Convertible ... which I still have, incidentally. I didn't have a phone in my house. I had to have it cut off because I couldn't pay the bill when I came back from Alabama. I had a worn-out 14-inch black-and-white TV, my icebox was wore out, and my washer wouldn't work. I mean, I was in bad shape.

This was in January 1976. I ran Forest City, Arkansas, about 50 miles from Memphis. We drew $1,500. I couldn't believe it. That was fantastic! That was a fantastic house, especially considering we charged a dollar, two dollars, and three dollars ... about 750 people. So Jerry called Nick from Channel 13. He said, "*Nick, you won't believe what Buddy did over in Forest City last night.*" Now remember, Scott. I didn't have any money. I even borrowed money from my mother to get gas to go open towns ... and I used her telephone. That's how broke I was.

I ran Gadsden, Tennessee and did $1,600. Savannah, Tennessee, $2,200. Marianna, Arkansas — that's right outside of Humboldt — we did $2,200. That was like $10,000 now at those prices. By March, I bought a brand-new icebox (pause) ... refrigerator — Aubrey's kidding me about calling it an icebox — a new washer, a new Continental Town Coupe, a color TV, plus I had American Express and Diner's Club credit cards, and money in the bank.

So you promoted five or six semi-regular spot shows?

Yeah. You asked earlier about getting the top names. At this point, I did get the top names. I'd run something on Tuesday, Thursday, Friday and Saturday. I ran them every month. As I said, we ran Forest City and did $1,500. The next week, I had [Jerry] Lawler on the card and did $2,200. Sam Bass came in and said, "*Buddy! Jerry ain't gonna be here.*"

Man, there was people everywhere. I thought he was ribbing me. "*Yeah, sure, Sam!*" As we got closer to the main event, I went looking for Lawler. I said, "*Sam, where's Jerry? He's not here!*"

Sam said, "*Buddy, I told you when I got here that Jerry had the flu.*"

"*Oh, no! Sam, I thought you were kiddin'.*"

Well, we went out and announced that Lawler was sick. I don't remember who Lawler was gonna wrestle, but Sam went out and made a challenge, then he wrestled. A month later, I came back with Lawler booked again. We did $2,800. We couldn't even get 'em all in. They made me quit sellin' tickets. On average, that would be around 1,400 people.

I hate to break the flow, but you mentioned working for Bill Golden a short time before this. Jim Lancaster mentioned being in Montgomery when you and Dennis Hall ran it. What were the circumstances behind Golden giving up the town?

He just let the territory go, then sold it to Dennis Hall. Dennis called me and asked me to book it. Bill used to have a saying that stuck with me. It made a lot of sense. "*You can't plow a field if you don't have a mule.*" We didn't have any mules. We had the Bounty Hunters and pushed them hard. Me and Joe Turner put them over two straight. Me and Burrhead [Jones] put them over two straight. Burrhead and Joe put them over two straight. In other words, all three of us all the way around. Then we teamed Dennis Hall with Tony Ladue, who only weighed about 190 pounds. Well, if we couldn't beat 'em, *they* sure couldn't. That's the way people looked at it. I say that because it didn't draw, and we did one heck of an angle with them. The reason it didn't was the people thought, "*What can Dennis Hall and Tony Ladue do against those two big guys?*" One of the Bounty Hunters was a pretty good-size guy.

Jerry Novak.

Right. The other one [David Novak] kind of reminded me of the guy here they call Spellbinder [Harry Del Rios], but Jerry could work. Spellbinder can't work.

Jim Lancaster said the towns weren't drawing and payoffs were pretty bad.

Twenty dollars.

I think he said it was twenty-five.

Well, we started with a $25 payoff, then Bill Golden gets talking to Dennis Hall. "*Nick Gulas doesn't pay twenty-five. I wouldn't pay but twenty!*" But the thing about it is, with Nick, you might make a hundred the night before somewhere, or the next night. Twenty would be okay, but in Montgomery, it was twenty every night. Then, after it went on a week or two, Bill got in the dressing room, "*Boys, when I was here, I paid twenty-five to everybody.*"

I thought, "*God, Bill! Why'd you say that?*"

It wasn't the fault of the Bounty Hunters or Jim Lancaster that it didn't draw. The reason it didn't draw was because Dennis Hall and Tony Ladue didn't get over. Dennis is a great guy. I think the world of Dennis, but we didn't make any money. I left and came back up here, then Dennis went out of business. Nick called me and wanted me to go back and take it over. I went back down there and Bill Golden thought he was still involved. I told Nick and he said, "*Hell, I don't care. Do whatever you think is best.*"

I said, "*Well, the people know him.*"

Every night, we'd run a town and Bill would say, "*I'm gonna sell this damn territory. I ain't gonna lose my ass. I'm gonna sell it.*" Then we drew some money and made four or 500. "*Buddy Wayne, I think we can make it.*" The next night, we might not make any money. "*I'm gonna sell it.*" No matter what I did, it was the same thing. Then he sold it to Lee [Fields] and I worked for Lee for a while. I just wasn't making any money. I was trying to run some towns on the Montgomery end, but the territory had been hurt real bad. Lee thought we could put some talent in there and we'd really make some money. It just never did do anything. I finally told Lee that I had to go home.

I never knew all that.

Montgomery AL • June 23, 1975

I booked a show in Helena, Arkansas, at Phillips College. I thought we'd do 2,500, maybe $3,000. David Shultz and I had to go to Kiel Auditorium that night. Ken was only seventeen or so, but he and my wife took care of it. I called and said, "*How did it do?*" It did $4,600. It was absolutely amazing, especially when you remember what the prices were. There was about 2,200 people. Today, that would be roughly a $22,000 house. It was just unreal what we did back in those days. In fact, Jill — you know, Jeff's wife — we were all talking at Christine's funeral. She said, "*Jerry* [Jarrett], *did ya'll make much money years ago?*"

He said, "*Jill, you wouldn't believe the money we made. I'll tell you what Buddy did.*" And I forgot all about this.

He said, "*We went to a little town called Marianna, Arkansas. It was on a Saturday night and I asked him how things were.*" *He said,* 'Come on out here.' *Buddy had just bought a new Lincoln Continental from me.*" Jerry had a real nice car lot up there at the time. The car was only nine months old and a banker had it. He let me have it for $7,100. They sold for $13,000.

Anyway, Jerry said, "*Buddy opened his trunk and he had two paper sacks full of money. Not the little sandwich bags, but the regular-size grocery sacks.*" Now, this was ones, fives and tens. It wasn't twenties and hundreds, but there had to be $10,000 there. Today, that would be $60,000, and those were just our spot shows. (pause) What I did with that money, I don't know. (laughs) We made money. We sure did.

Were you still paying Jerry a booking fee on your towns, or were you doing some kind of a split?

I gave him a percentage, a booking fee. Jerry was always real honest with me, and he helped me a lot. He gave me a lot of good advice. I'm older than him, but that don't mean nothin'. We were just talking one day and he said, "*If you ever have a bill, don't wait 'til it's due. If you don't think you're gonna have it, try to get the money to pay it about three weeks before it's due. Don't ever wait until they call you because that hurts your credit.*" I've never forgot that.

What was your best town?

(pause) Well, Owensboro was good. The first time we went in there was when Elvis was buried. I remember because we watched it on TV that afternoon. We thought that might hurt us, but it didn't. We held it in the Sports Center and drew $6,800 that night. I don't know if you've ever been up there, Scott, but when we got up there, the people were lined up to the end of the building, about a block down. It was so big that the manager called the newspaper and they came down to make pictures. They said they never had an event draw like that.

I called Jerry Jarrett. Back then, in my towns, I paid the guys that night, right after the show. I said, "*Jerry, I don't know how much to pay these guys.*"

He said, "*What was the house?*"

I said, "*Take a guess.*"

He said, "*Twenty-five hundred?*" (laughs)

I told him, "*I'll pay your booking fee on that, but it did sixty-eight hundred dollars.*"

He said, "*Good, Lord! We never had a spot show that did that.*"

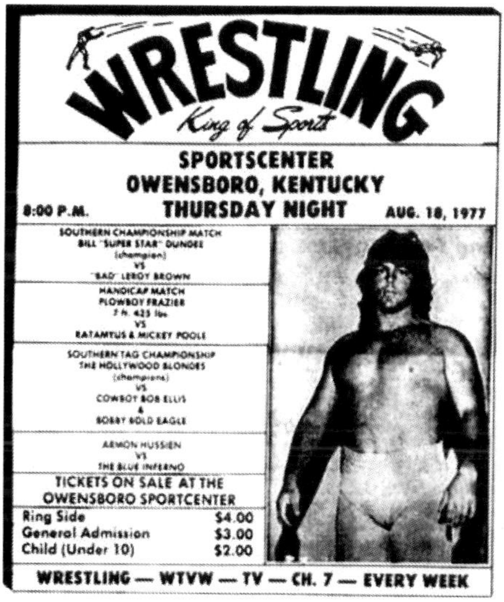

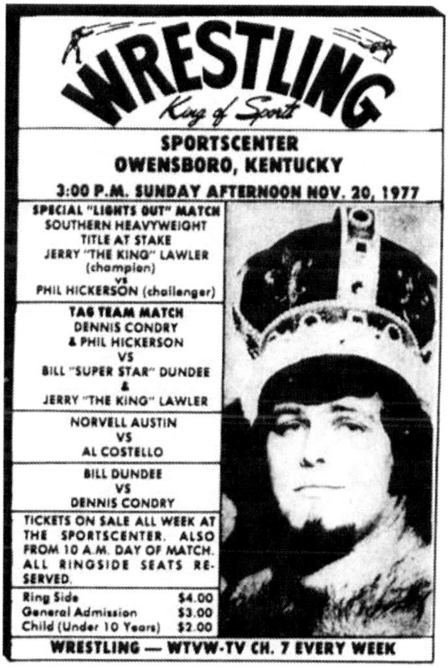

(above) Aug. 18, 1977 (right) Nov. 20, 1977

I went up there one night and nobody wanted to go. The only time I could get it was Sunday afternoon. Me and Lawler sat there at TV doing interviews. He said, "*Well, let's just book it.*"

I'll tell you what we put in there. Dennis Condrey against Bill Dundee. Norvel Austin against Al Costello. They came back in a tag match and the main event was Lawler against Phil Hickerson in a "Lights Out Match" for the Southern title belt. We did over $6,000 with six men on the card. The next night, we went to the [Memphis] Coliseum. Both Steve Kyle and Dickie Steinborn ... "*Why didn't you put me on the card?*"

"*You didn't want to go.*"

"*Well, we didn't think it would draw that!*"

"*I didn't know what it would draw, either, but I gambled.*"

A lot of the towns were good, but it wasn't the town that was good. It was who you had in it. If I'd run a town that would draw real good, somebody would say, "*Oh, Buddy! You drew good last night.*"

I said, "*No, I didn't draw nothin'. The boys did.*" They didn't come to see Buddy Wayne. Most of the time, Buddy Wayne didn't even wrestle on the card. They didn't come to see me.

Ken used to kid me about a sellout house because I'd be down, real serious. But if there was nobody there, I'd be laughin' and carryin' on a bunch of crap. He'd say, "*Daddy, I've never seen nobody like you. If there ain't nobody here, you're laughin' and kiddin' around.*"

I said, "*Ken, let me tell you something. When it's down, it's gotta come up. There ain't no sense in me going in and tellin' all the boys how bad it is. All that does is put them in a down mood. I go in there happy.*" If I lost money, I never went in and said, "*Boys, I lost two hundred dollars tonight,*" or a hundred, or a thousand, whatever.

How long did you promote for Jerry?

Up until Larry Burton and them came in. I just couldn't handle Burton. He didn't know nothin'.

I was working for Nick when the split took place between Jerry and Nick. I really don't remember things being as hostile as a lot of people make it out to be. Did Nick pretty much relinquish control over Memphis to Jerry before the actual split?

Here's what happened. We were at TV one Saturday morning and Jerry was all down. We were makin' money, though. I said, "*Jerry, what's wrong?*"

He said, "*Buddy, I haven't made any money out of this business in the last six weeks.*"

I said, "*Jerry, what are you talkin' about? We've been packin' the houses.*"

He said, "*Yeah, but Nick's towns aren't drawing, so it's takin' everything we're making and going back into Nick's.*" I think Jerry had some stock in it and Nick was tryin' to screw him on it. I'm not sure of this now, but it was something like that. Jerry said, "*I don't know what I'm gonna do.*"

I said, "*Jerry, if you wanna go on your own, let me know and I'll be with you.*"

And that's exactly what happened. He went to Channel 5 and got that. In fact, we were on that station in 1959. It was the first TV station to come into Memphis. They ran wrestling direct from Ellis Auditorium. I picked Jerry Lawler and Jerry Jarrett up at the airport. Lawler was living in Nashville at the time. I carried them over to the TV station and they said, "*Well, wish us luck. This will be where we make it or not.*" They got the TV. Nick was gonna sue him and so was Bert Bates (pause) ... or it was Guy Bates at that time. They were gonna sue him for conspiracy and all that crap. Fortunately, Channel 5 went with us.

What happened to Channel 13?

Channel 13 said, "*We don't want Nick* or *Jerry.*"

Why didn't Channel 13 want either one of them?

Because Nick was gonna sue Jerry *and* the TV station [Channel 5]. They just didn't want to be in the middle of it, so they took them both off. The first night we ran Memphis at the Cook Convention Center downtown, we drew $16,000.

George [Gulas] is really what hurt Nick. Nick was just like a lot of fathers. They think their son is great, but they're not. Ken's first match was against Gorgeous George Jr. in Springfield, Kentucky. Somebody didn't show up, so George suggested we let Ken wrestle because Ken worked out a lot. I told Jerry about it and asked about working him in. Jerry said, "*The only thing you have to remember, Buddy, is that everybody thinks their son is great. Nick thinks George is great. A lot of guys think their sons are great, but the fact is that they're the shits. I just want you to accept the fact that if I think Ken is the shits, don't let that interfere in our relationship and hurt* our *business.*"

I said, "*It won't, Jerry. Business is business, but I think you're gonna be surprised.*"

He kind of grinned and said, "*Yeah, I know. I've heard this before.*"

Ken is booked to wrestle in Jackson, Tennessee. He watches Ken wrestle and says, "*You know, Buddy? These guys are gonna be the future of our business.*" He was talking about Ken, Eddie Gilbert, and some others. There's another guy I met that I'd like to tell you about. You may have met him. It's David Flair.

I've never met him.

Ric Flair's son. He's a super-nice guy. It shocked me. Everything was "*Yes, sir,*" "*No, sir,*" "*Thank you, Mr. Wayne.*"

I told him, "*David, I want to tell you something. Everybody is always quick to knock everybody else, but nobody compliments the good things. I really appreciate the respect you're showing me.*"

He said, "*Mr. Wayne. I've been raised and taught to respect the wrestling legends.*"

I said, "*I sure do appreciate it.*"

Then you have other guys, like Brian Christopher. He's the biggest little prick there is. Oh, he's a Class-A asshole. Now, Jeff Jarrett's a nice kid. He's always real polite.

Most people don't teach their kids respect these days. I seldom hear teenagers say "Yes, sir" or "No, sir."

Jerry Jarrett told me one time ... this was when my youngest son, Aubrey, was about ten. We were in the Memphis Coliseum up on Critic Row. Do you remember Critic Row?

I don't think so.

(laughs) I'll tell you how that got started. They weren't using all the balcony. Me and Jerry would go sit up there to watch the matches and we'd criticize the matches. We got to callin' it Critic Row. (laughs)

Anyway, we were sitting up there one night. Jerry says, "*Buddy, I meant to tell you. You've got the nicest son I've ever talked to on the phone. He always says,* 'May I ask who's calling' and 'Would you hold on, please?' 'Yes, sir.' 'No, sir.' *I just wanted to tell you that.*" I told him I appreciated it and that I tried to teach that to all of my kids. It makes you feel good when people recognize your kids for doing something good.

I'll be honest and blunt with you. I'm really impressed by all this. You worked the west end of the territory, while I was primarily involved with the middle part. I suppose that's why I never realized how big a part you played in the promotion. All I ever knew of you is that you'd come into Nashville to do jobs. That's all I ever saw you do. Of course, I didn't move to Nashville until '74 and we didn't meet until '76.

You see, by that time, I wasn't doing anything but promoting. I only wrestled once in a while. I didn't want to wrestle. We were making a lot of money in the promotion. Why would I want to go somewhere and wrestle and make a hundred dollars when I can run a town and make 1,500?

I agree. I just never heard anything about you promoting until the '80s, and that's about the time I got out of the business.

I remember wrestling with Big Bad John one night. We just had a few minutes on TV, so before you knew it, it was over. Jerry apologized. "*Buddy, I hated to do that to you, but we didn't have but two minutes of air time.*"

"I don't care! I'm not an ego. Let's make money. Who cares? As long as I'm makin' money, who cares how long it goes, whether it's thirty minutes or an hour?"

I knew guys who were more concerned about being featured in the main event than making money.

To give you an example of how things have changed … me, Dennis Hall and Len Rossi were wrestling Tojo [Yamamoto], Johnny Long and somebody else in Huntsville. Joe Louis was the special referee. The place was jam-packed. Back then, we didn't start until 8:30. Joe and I had been together all week. He was laying down in one of the dressing rooms. Nick comes into the room we're in and says, "*Boys, they're lined up out there for four miles!*" (laughs) It wasn't four miles, but they *were* lined up at all doors. Nick says, "*I want to start the matches right away! Buddy Wayne!*"

Huntsville AL • Dec. 13, 1968

Now remember. I'm on the main event. He says, "*Do you mind going out there and having a warm-up match with so-and-so? Just go ten minutes.*"

I said, "*No, I don't mind, Nick.*"

We were killing time until they got all the people in. He didn't want to start the scheduled matches. I started getting my ring jacket on and Joe wakes up. He says, "*What are you doin'?*"

I said, "*I'm fixin' to go to work, Joe.*"

He says, "*Is it that time already?*"

I said, "*No, no, no! This is just the opening match.*"

He looked real puzzled and said, "*Wait a minute! I thought you was in that main event that I was refereeing.*"

I said, "*I am.*"

He looked even more puzzled. He said, "*Wait a minute. You're in the main event* and *the opening match?*"

I said, "*Yeah!*"

He didn't know we were killin' time. He just shook his head and went, "*Uh, uh, uh. Sho must be a low-budget show.*" (laughs)

He must have thought it was so low budget that they didn't have enough money to pay a couple of other guys. That's the humorous part, but to relate that to today, if you asked a main-event guy that was going to wrestle in the main event with Mike Tyson as the special referee — if you asked him to do a warm up match — he'd tell you, "*Hell, no! I ain't doin' that! I'm on the main event!*" But it didn't matter to me whether I wrestled three times a night, once, or eight times. I was there to wrestle. After I drove 200 miles, it didn't matter to me if I wrestled another ten minutes.

Ron Sexton came into TV one Saturday morning. He looked wore out. I said, "*Did you have a long trip, Ron?*"

He said, "*No, Buddy, but I am dead. I had to wrestle three times last night.*"

I said, "*Oh, really? How long was your first match?*"

"*Six or seven minutes.*"

"*What happened in the second?*"

"*Well, so-and-so didn't show up, so I took his place.*"

"*How long did that go?*"

"*Probably five or six minutes.*"

"*And the third match?*"

"*It was a battle royal.*"

I said, "*Did you win it?*"

He says, "*Nah, I was about the second man out.*"

I said, "*In other words, you wrestle* maybe *fifteen minutes ... and you're tired? We used to wrestle an hour or more.*" What's fifteen minutes?

Nick tried to build me and Bob Ramstead up. We had 60 matches with no losses. Then we got up to a hundred, but we didn't get over. We just weren't drawin'. He switched us heel and then we drew money. Back years ago, though, Nick and Roy wouldn't use anybody in their own hometown. Fargo and I had talked about this. Fargo said, "*Dwayne, they'll never use you here because they're afraid if you get too big, you'll take the town away from 'em.*"

They knew you had the contacts and possible political connections.

Exactly. Bob Ramstead and I had the Southern tag title and the world tag. We were the only ones that ever had 'em at the same time. Of course, Lawler and Dundee came along later and said they was the first, but they wasn't. I also held the Mid-America tag with one of the Dominoes when [J.C.] Dykes was managing them. We won the belts in Birmingham. When Bob and I came to Memphis, though, they didn't advertise us as world champions. They did everywhere else ... Birmingham, Knoxville, Chattanooga. But in Memphis, they didn't give us that recognition.

Joe Louis refereed quite a few matches for me. I have a picture of me and Joe on my wall. One time, he refereed a match with me and Eddie Sullivan. The first punch I threw, I accidentally split Eddie's eye. Then he threw a punch and busted my nose. Joe said, "*Mmm-mm-mm. I seen amateurs that didn't fight this hard.*"

Who do you feel were some of the better referees in this area?

That would be hard to say. There were a lot of good ones. One of the best was Bud Clardy. Jerry Calhoun was a good referee. You know you've got a good referee when you go back to the dressing room and you can't remember him being in the ring. A guy might come up and say, "*How'd I do?*"

I'd say, "*Well, I guess you did alright because I don't remember you being there.*" They didn't get in your way at all.

It wasn't that big of a deal back then, but when I look back on how things were in those days, it's amazing to think that promoters drew thousands of people every single week of the year.

When Vince started running his stuff, they should have ignored him and stuck with what we were doing. We were drawing money. Why do you want to change something that's working? I mean, we can't run things like Vince was running it. I tried to tell them that. When I go out now [in public], nobody even talks to me about wrestling. It used to be, everywhere I'd go, especially if I was on TV that day, people would come up and talk. Now, nobody even mentions it, period. Sure, they *might* mention the local wrestling, but that's only to say how bad it is and how they don't watch it anymore.

I know the WWF sold out here. I ain't gonna say they didn't, but 20,000 people when you've got over a million to draw from? That's not a big ratio. And that's only once or twice a year. You can draw anything once or twice, but let them try it week after week. They ain't gonna do it. I'm not knockin' what they're doing as far as selling tickets. What I'm talking about is what Vince has done to wrestling as a whole. We used to run 30 to 40 towns a week, and sometimes 50. That's every week, Scott.

I know.

On Monday, we had Memphis, Birmingham, Owensboro, and usually two spot shows. On Saturday, we had six or seven live TVs. You never worked just once on Saturday.

I remember going to three TVs and a house show in one day.

I worked four times. I sure have. Most of the time you worked three. I'd make Huntsville [TV], then go to Chattanooga [TV], then to the house show, then jump in the car and go to Birmingham for TV.

That's when they filmed live TV in Birmingham late on Saturday night.

That's right. Years ago, it was at 10:30 p.m. The station was way up on that mountain, where you could just go up one car at a time. Then they moved to another location. I remember having to go up there one Saturday. I left here at three in the morning. Dadgummit! There was two guys from Memphis and they did the same thing. Gil Shelby and that ol' boy that called himself Rufus Jones who got shot.

I heard that story years ago, but I don't recall the details.

Rufus Jones. Arthur Williams was his real name. This wasn't the Rufus R. Jones from the Carolinas. He was from Memphis. He was killed by a jealous boyfriend. Gil Shelby was a policeman there and showed me the photographs. "*Look here, Buddy.*"

"*Oh, shit! I didn't want to see them.*"

You couldn't tell who it was. He got shot in the face with a shotgun.

Let me tell you a funny story about Rufus. We came back from Alabama and got into Memphis. I'm drinkin' beer and had to pee bad. I said, "*Pull over, man.*" He pulled over and I did my business. We drive off and the blue lights hit us. This is about six o'clock in the morning. The cop says, "*What are you doing in this neighborhood this time of night?*"

I said, "*We've been wrestling in Alabama. We're just getting back into town.*" (laughs)

He shined his light on Rufus and said, "*Oh, are you his chauffeur?*"

Rufus said, "*No, man! I'm his tag partner.*" (laughs)

I said, "*The only reason you stopped him is because he's black. If he had been a white man, you wouldn't have stopped him.*" (laughs)

Rufus is going, "*Shut up, Buddy! It's okay, man!*"

They let us go. (laughs) I remember when we were in Montgomery, they asked us to not call Burrhead a shoeshine boy on the interviews. They had a lot of racial problems at the time.

Anyway, we got to the TV in Birmingham and I said, "*Well, dang! I wish I'd known you were both coming. We could have all rode together.*" Nick didn't tell us. I think Gil or Rufus one had to go on back to Memphis. Me and the other had to go to Cherokee, Alabama. I thought, "*Man, I'd just rather be off than go to Cherokee.*" We didn't draw nothin'. And the reason … and I know this sounds crazy, but some prominent woman died and they just stopped everything. Everybody in this little town was at the funeral home.

Nick Bockwinkel and I were talking several years ago when the WWF started doin' their TV in our arenas. He said, "*Buddy, we give them a good show to watch at home for free, but we don't give them anything to come out and pay their five dollars for.*"

The WWF does all their bullshit. When they come to town, it's a big thing. "*Hey! It's the WWF!*" That's the in-thing to do now. Let 'em try to come back five weeks in a row. I guarantee you, they wouldn't have nobody there the sixth week. I'm not knockin' what they're doing from the standpoint of making a lot of money. I am knocking them from the standpoint of putting a lot of the boys out of work. Years ago, we all made money. We didn't have the big $25,000 payoffs that some of the guys are getting for one nights' work, but we made money.

Plus, you had a place for the young guys to learn their trade.

That's right. Now they don't. They put guys in the ring that shouldn't even be in there. The thing about it, Scott ... I know they're drawin' tremendous amounts of money. I'm not arguing that point one bit. But they couldn't do what we did every week in little towns like Wynne, Arkansas, or even a small town like Jackson, Tennessee. We went in there week after week and packed it week after week, but we did it with wrestling. Now you see the hoopla, the fireworks, the pretty girls. How many times can you shoot fireworks off? I saw Mick Jagger and the [Rolling] Stones. I thought, "*The WWF had more stuff than Mick Jagger did.*" (laughs) Ken went to a Mick Jagger concert at the Liberty Bowl. A few days later, we were talking and he said, "*That Mick Jagger concert was great!*"

I said, "*I didn't get to see a lot of it.*"

He said, "*What are you talkin' about?*"

I said, "*One of the guys from Channel 5 went to do an interview, so he asked me to go with him. We were backstage and in the dressing room with Mick most of the time, so I didn't get to see much of the concert.*"

"*Oh, Daddy! You've gotta be kiddin'! I paid big money for seats way up in the bleachers and you're back there with Jagger.*" (laughs)

Take the Pyramid, for instance. They might draw $20,000 twice a year. Divide that by 26 weeks and see how many they average. It's less than a thousand people. We'd average 9,000 a week. Multiply that times 26 and you see what we averaged. People say, "*Oh, you can't compare it that way.*" What do you mean you can't? Sure you can!

That was the average or the high-end?

Memphis averaged about nine to 10,000 people a week. A lot of times, it would do more than that. The most the building would hold was 11,600 and it was full almost every week. There were times when we turned people away, too. If we had a bad house, we'd still have 7,500 to 8,500.

Things changed, though, and they started to rush angles and storylines. It's like the Baron Leone-Lou Thesz match that drew a record crowd in the '50s. They worked that deal for a long time. They don't do that anymore. I'd say, "*Jerry, why don't we do this?*"

"*Buddy, we don't have time.*"

"*What do you mean we don't have time?*" How can we do something on Saturday and expect to draw something on Monday? You can do that if both guys are over real good, but it takes time to get guys like that over.

If you've got the money, you should take time to build things up. If you don't have the money, you shouldn't be tryin' to do it. Take two guys ... Lawler and Jim White were a good example. Jerry Jarrett brought them in here and I'll bet he put them over every week for six months. There was this girl named Ann up in Millington. I can still remember her saying, "*I'll tell you one thing. I keep telling Jerry Jarrett that if he'd put Lawler and White in there against Tojo and Fargo, they'd beat 'em!*" Blah-blah-blah. She proved that Jerry knew what he was doing. They were building 'em. When they did put 'em in there, this girl called me, "*Well, Jerry Jarrett finally listened to me.*"

I told her, "*Yeah, he liked your advice.*"

When you get right down to it, Jerry *did* listen to her, but he waited for the right time to put those four together ... for a time when the fans were demanding a match between those four.

Exactly! And they packed the arenas! They built it, and continued to build it even *after* people were asking for the match. If people started saying, "*Oh, I wish they'd put that Buddy Wayne in there against Scott Teal. He'd kick his ass!*" If you wait until they start sayin' it, then let 'em sit for a few more weeks, *then* do it ... you've got a sell-out house.

Now you have fifteen matches on a card and they're all the same thing. Grab a headlock, throw him off, duck down, miss an elbow ... it's the same old thing over and over.

That's another thing that's changed. I wrestled many guys that I never saw in my life until we got in the ring. Guys today want to get together before a match and talk for 30 minutes. Why? The promoter should be able to say, "*You're wrestling so-and-so. Go over with an abdominal stretch.*" That's all you've gotta tell me. Tony Williams and Derrick King ... they must have wrestled each other here in Memphis 50 times, then on Saturday morning, they'd talk for 30 minutes about what they were gonna do! I go, "*God! How many times are ya'll gonna have to wrestle each other before you know what you're doin'?*"

I wrestled Frank Hickey in 1955 in Zollner Stadium in Fort Wayne, Indiana. I never saw him in my life. I never knew who he was. Bozo Brown was the name he was using. He was in the ring before me and turned around when I got in. I went, "*Oh, my Lord! What have I got myself into?*" He was a mean-lookin' old guy.

In fact, last Saturday night, Bert Prentice called me at the last minute to carry the ring to Savannah. I didn't talk to any of the guys. It was all the New

York boys and I didn't know them. I mean, I know them, but I have nothing in common to talk about with 'em. If I tried to tell to them about anything, they look at me like I don't know what I'm talkin' about. Tracy Smothers was there and I talked to him a few minutes.

I went in the dressing room at TV not long ago and this guy was sittin' there. I asked, "*Who is that guy?*"

"*Oh, he's okay. That's Todd Morton's daddy.*"

"*So what! He doesn't have any business in here.*"

Today, if the janitor walks in, they keep going over the finish and don't even lower their voices. On TV last Saturday morning, a guy walked in while they were talking over the finish. When he left, I said, "*Didn't you see that guy over at the Coke machine?*"

"*Oh, he's okay. He works in the newsroom.*"

What's that got to do with it?! If Herb Welch had seen that kind of stuff, he'd have taken that cane and beat the devil out of them.

Daddy went to the matches in Huntsville with me one time. I didn't let him go in the dressing room. There ain't no way I'd let him go in the dressing room. None of my family is smart. I did a little deal with Mick Tierney a few years ago and my mother worried to death. He's a big monster from Ireland who weighs about 280. He could go! He was in here with the WWF developmental talent when Randy had the deal. Anyway, we had this little deal goin' where he had to beat me two times in five minutes. She says, "*Oh, son! What if he hits you in the throat and that cancer comes back?*" I'm sure she cried, but I never told her anything.

They don't hide *anything* anymore. It's like The Rock on Jay Leno the other night. He told Leno, "*Yeah, we know who's gonna win.*" He said, "*Let me tell ya who.*" He leans over and whispers in Leno's ear. Jay Leno says, "*Madeline Albright?*"

Did you witness much steroid use during the past decade?

Yeah. Even back in '73, some of the guys were using Dianabol. Steve Kyle did. By the late '80s, a lot of the guys were doing it. Jeff Jarrett said he never used it, and I believe him because he looks different from most of the guys. Jeff worked out hard. We used to go to Jonesboro later in the afternoon after we did the TV. I remember hearing Jerry [Jarrett] say, "*Are you going to the motel?*"

Jeff said, "*No, daddy. I'm going to work out.*"

He'd go to the gym and work out, rather than go back to the motel and lay around watching TV. I have a lot of respect for Jeff.

What was your average weight?

When I first started, I stayed around 210. It was that way for a year. When I went to Birmingham in '68 or so, I was up to 235. Then, of course, later on, I got up way too heavy.

I was always in good shape. I didn't look like I was in good shape, but I was. I was looking at some tapes the other night from 1978. I was fat, but I was still in good shape. One thing I noticed. I always looked like I was about to have a heart attack. My tongue would be hangin' out like I just couldn't go anymore. I think that's why I got so much heat. They'd yell, "*You fat son-of-a-bitch!*" That tickled me to death when they said that. If you're workin' that

style and they ain't cussin' you, you ain't doin' too good of a job. I've heard heels brag about getting more cheers than their opponent. I'd say, "*You dumb son-of-a-bitch! You ain't very over then, are you?*"

Which leads me to another topic. There's no clear distinction between the heels and the babyfaces anymore.

No, there's not. It's because of the way they work. Everybody works the same. Years ago, Len Rossi used the sleeper for his finish. I used the abdominal stretch. Fargo used the atomic drop. Everybody had a special move they used for a finish. Now guys go out and use an atomic drop for a highspot. And how long has it been since you saw the sleeper hold put on someone and the guy went to sleep? It's the same old thing. The referee holds the hand up, he drops it. He holds the hand up, he drops it. The third time, the guy starts shaking and comes up. They've killed the sleeper. We used to sell that sleep hold, and it got over.

When I went over to referee those matches for the AWA, Jon Stewart got in the ring with this girl. It was some silly shit they were doing. He puts the sleep hold on her ... and dang if she don't do the same thing. I said, "*Oohh, Jon! What are ya'll doing?*" A 125-pound girl and a 240-pound man and he can't put her out? She comes up and hits him in the gut with her elbow. He bends over, she kicks him in the balls and DDTs him. Then she pins him.

This is in a live match?

Yeah, and he's the AWA champion! That's when Dale Gagne was running it. Then he comes back and works with Road Warrior Hawk in the main event. I mean, if he can't beat that girl, how can he possibly beat this man? The first thing they did was go out of the ring and start fighting on the floor. I didn't leave the ring. I just stood there. I didn't start counting because I knew they weren't gonna get back in. Somebody hollered out, "*Why ain't you countin' 'em out?*" (laughs) Fortunately, somebody said, "*It's a 'Fight Anywhere match'. It wouldn't count, anyway.*"

"*Thank you, fella. I appreciate that.*"

I only remember you as a heel. Did you do that for the majority of your career?

At the beginning, no, but later on, yeah. I'd rather work that way. It was a lot easier. I always knew that if me and you were wrestling, Scott, and I was a heel and I got tired, I could go out on the floor and take a break. *You* can't! The people would be going, "*What's he running for?*" (laughs) The heel can jump out to get a breather and still keep the heat because the people are all yelling, "*Get him back in there, referee!*" If you're workin' the other way, you can't do that.

Not only that, but a babyface has to work a lot harder in the ring. A heel can get over in one match at times, but the other guy can't because he has to prove that he can do something. I can prove real quick that I'm a no-good son-of-a-bitch, but it's hard to prove that I can really wrestle. You have to do a lot of matches before the people realize, "*Hey, this guy really can wrestle!*"

What were some of the security and fan-control measures you took in your towns?

Fortunately, we always had good police protection. When I'd run a town, I'd tell the guys, "*I have police here. If somebody takes a poke at you, let them handle it. If you run out into the crowd, they can't always protect you.*"

In Montgomery, Alabama, I'd walk to the ring with Jerry Myatt. We called him Golden Hawk. We'd have four or five policemen surround us all the way to the ring and all the way back. I've had guys hit me as I walked by, but I always tried to act like I didn't even feel it. That bothered the guy even more than if I'd turned around and cussed him, or took a swing at him. They'd be like, "*Damn, I hit him as hard as I could and he didn't even feel it!*"

That's another thing I never did when I was in the ring. I never picked out one person and agitated them. I worked the whole crowd. That way, if a guy *did* jump in the ring, they couldn't say I baited him to get in there. It's like guys that would point to a big, fat girl at ringside. You shouldn't do that. The girl knows she's fat. Why do you want to call attention to it? She probably won't be back the next week. Or some guy sittin' at ringside with two or three kids. "*Where'd you get those clothes? Salvation Army? Look at these welfare people!*" Well, maybe they did go to Salvation Army.

And they might have spent their last five dollars to get into the matches.

Exactly! Karol Krauser and I were talking in Jonesboro one night. We had some people there that were just poor, old farmers. They were good people and hard workers. I told Karl, "*You know, this one old man comes with his wife and three or four kids. I almost feel bad taking his money.*"

Karl said, "*Just remember, they probably work all week to save up the three or four dollars to come to the wrestling. If they didn't get to come, it would be a real loss to them because they look forward to it all week long.*" I never forgot that.

I was wrestling one night and an old man came up to me. It was in that town I mentioned earlier … Doniphan, Missouri. When I came out of the ring, this man walked up to me. He was 70, 80 years old, wore bib overalls, looked like a farmer. He took my hand and said, "*I want you to have this.*" It was a dollar bill.

I said, "*What? I don't want this.*"

If I had slapped him, it wouldn't have hurt him any more. He said, "*That's all I've got. I don't have any more.*" Oohh! I didn't want his money, but he said, "*That's all I've got and I wanted you to have it.*" I tried to give it back, but he kept telling me he wanted me to keep it. I felt so bad about that.

I was in Atlanta at the Ponce de Leon ballpark on May 27, 1961. Argentina Rocca was there, Yukon Eric, Dick the Bruiser. Me and Bruiser were in the dugout. That's when he was hot as a firecracker. This little girl, maybe four or five years old, eased over and said in a shy voice, "*Mr. Bruiser. Can I have your autograph?*" He looks all around, reaches over for the paper, writes on it, hands it back to her. "*Thank you,*" and she walks off. Dick looks all around again and goes, "*I don't guess nobody saw that, did they? I couldn't tell a pretty little girl like that no.*" (laughs)

The fans ... I don't use the word "marks." To the fans that come to the matches, the heels are celebrities to them, also. People say, "*The heels shouldn't sign autographs.*" Why not? That doesn't take anything away from their character. If it does, they probably don't have any heat to start with, anyway. There are different situations, like the Moondogs. They killed themselves off. They did all that crazy stuff, like they were nuts. Later on, they're sittin' at the table selling their photos. "*How are you doing?*" "*What's your name?*" That *did* kill their gimmick, but that's a different situation.

What were some of the worst arenas in terms of fans getting out of control.

I always had good security, but we had some "Hey, Rubes." Florence, Alabama, was a rough place. We were in there one night. I wasn't wrestling, but I looked up and there must have been 30 people in the ring. One guy had gone in and it was a chain reaction. They hit the ring from all sides. I thought, "*What in the hell?*" When I went into the ring to get them out, there was this one guy I knew. I said, "*Get your ass out of here!*"

He looked around him, like he just woke up. He said, "*Oh, shit, Buddy! What am I doin' in here?*" He just got carried away.

The next week, I got some clothesline and ran it from the dressing room to the ring, making an aisle, then around the ring and back to the dressing room. That rope wouldn't actually stop anybody, but for some reason, they'd go as far as the rope, but they wouldn't go across it.

Pedro Zapata got stabbed there one night and liked to have died. This guy stood up, climbed in the ring, and stabbed him. He was real nonchalant. He wasn't yellin' or screamin' or nothin'. They thought Pedro was gonna die, and he almost did.

I think Phoenix was one of the worst. We had at least twelve security people around us. We had four city police, four deputies, and four private security ... but people still tried to get to us. One night, a guy got in the dressing room. He wanted old Bunk Harris, the Baby Blimp. Sputnik said, "*Hey, do you want him? Here he is!*"

The guy looked around like, "*What am I doin'?*"

Sputnik took him down and was gonna bust him the hard way, but the guy kept jerkin' his head away. Greg Peterson walks over and says to Sputnik, "*Uh, fella? Why don't you let him up?*" (laughs)

Another night, me and Len Rossi was wrestling the Mighty Yankees. If we lost, we'd throw a hundred dollars out to the crowd. It was one of those real scary finishes. I told the Yankees, "*When it's over, boys, you're gonna have about fifteen seconds to get out of there and back to the dressing room. Don't hang around. One-two-three, get your hand in the air, and get out.*"

Me and Len did the deal. Boom, boom, boom! We look around ... and they're still in the ring. I thought, "*Oh, shit!*" They started to get out, but they had waited too long and had to get back in the ring. People were all around that ring and I'm thinking, "*Oh, my Lord!*" I said to Len, "*Let's run around to that side and throw the money out. When everybody runs around here, that will leave it open to where they can get out.*"

We threw the money out real slow. You know, two or three dollar bills at a time. We finally got rid of it all, looked around ... and they're still in the ring. "*Oh, man!*" I said, "*The only thing I know to do is you and me leave. Once the people see that nothin' else is gonna happen, they'll leave."* We did and that worked. We were fortunate the people didn't go into the ring that night.

Scott, we used to have matches like that a lot! People would come in the ring on you all the time! Now it's all a big joke. I was watching the deal between [Jerry] Lawler and [Andy] Kaufman on the Comedy Channel. You know, the thing they've run a million times. The fans are all screamin' and cussin' Kaufman. On Monday night, I'm watching WWF and everybody out there's laughing and holding the big, foam fingers in the air. I think I mentioned this already, but it's nothin' like it used to be.

We were in Selma, Alabama, one night [1974] when somebody threw a chair. The heel was in the ring, so he picks it up. What does that goofy Burrhead Jones do? He throws one in. When he did, the chairs rained on us. I'm not kiddin' you. Ask Jack Donovan. He was there. I'll bet there was 50 to a hundred chairs in that ring. That was when Lee was just takin' that territory over from Bill Golden. We had to go see one of the captains on the police department. Bill says, "*Well, we'll guarantee you that it won't happen again.*"

Lee says, "*Hold on, Bill. We can't guarantee that. We'll do all we can to keep it from happening, but we can't guarantee it'll never happen.*"

That captain came in one night when Bob Kelly was handling things for Lee down there. He says, "*Boys, if anyone* [fans] *goes in that ring tonight, I'm closin' this thing down!*"

Bob says, "*What did you say?*"

He says, "*I'm tellin' ya. If anybody runs in that ring, I'm closin' it down. There won't be any more wrestling.*"

Bob says, "*You don't have to do that. Boys! Get your stuff. Let's go home.*"

The captain said, "*What?*"

Bob says, "*You aren't gonna tell us what to do. We'll just go home. My boss will be happy with me because we were gonna lose money. This way, we won't lose any money.*"

"*No, no, no! Hold on a minute!*"

You see, Bill [Golden] would tell them every week what we were gonna do in the matches. They'd go tell all the other policeman, then I'm sure they went and told their wives and kids.

Not too long ago, Randy [Hales] did a deal with Spellbinder, Jeff Gaylord, and someone else. They did a deal where they had to take him to the hospital. Dadgummit! A security guard sat there and watched while they drove to the corner and the guy got out. The guard was tellin' people later, "*Oh, don't worry about it. He ain't hurt. They took him down to the corner in the car, then he got out and left.*" I couldn't believe it. If you're gonna do it, do it right. Carry the man to the hospital.

Roy Welch killed a wrestler [Eddie Baker] in Corinth, Mississippi, years ago. [May 15, 1937] He picked the guy up and gave him a bodyslam. The guy had a heart attack and died, right there in the ring. And Pat Malone cut a guy's throat one night in Brownsville. A fan got in the ring with a knife. Pat chased him out of the ring, down the street, took the knife away from him, and cut his throat. (laughs)

No kidding?

He sure did. (laughs) They didn't have wrestling there for years after that. Years later, I talked with the mayor, Joe Taylor, about it. He said, "*Oh, yeah. I remember that real well!*" Back then, if they [fans] got in the ring, it was their ass on the line. It ain't that way no more, but it used to be.

Rocky Smith and I were both getting started at the same time. Rocky could wrestle a little bit. We were in Dyersburg one night. This skinny, little kid was telling everybody that he could beat any wrestler on the card. He was playing to the crowd, so a lot of the wrestlers got hot. Mario [Galento] was gonna go out and bust the kid's eyes. Bill Golden was promoting it at the time. He said, "*No, hell, no! We'll get Rocky to do it.*"

He got on the microphone and said this kid had challenged, so there would be a match afterwards. About half the people stayed. Rocky went in there and just ate that boy up. In fact, Bill jumped in the ring and said, "*Dammit, Rocky! I told you not to hurt this kid.*"

What about the wrestling bears? They used a lot of them in West Tennessee.

(laughs) There was an old boy named Billy Walker from up in Missouri. He called himself Rip Tyler.

Yeah, I knew him. There wasn't any love lost on the guy by our Rip Tyler ... Jerry Dean. Rip didn't like him using his name.

He brought his bear to Montgomery. The poor, old bear was sick. I felt sorry for him. Billy just didn't take care of him. I wrestled him one night, but he wouldn't do anything, so I kicked him in the butt, trying to get him stirred up. He just laid down.

Another night, Burrhead [Jones] wrestled Gentleman Ben in Anniston, Alabama. Burrhead used the headbutt, so he used it on the bear. Burrhead staggered back, like it stunned him, but the bear fell down. (laughs) That got Burrhead's headbutt over. (laughs) That old bear died shortly after that. In fact, Billy's wife is the reason they couldn't use the bear in Mississippi for a while. She was menstruating and got in the ring with the bear. The bear got behind her and a lot of people complained.

Nick Adams had a real good one. That was Gentleman Ben. Speedy Hatfield had a good bear. That bear could wrestle. He'd leg-dive you, flying mare you. He could do a lot of stuff.

Did you ever have any embarrassing moments?

I always worried about going to the ring and falling. If you were heeling, it wasn't a big deal, but if you were a babyface, that was bad. We were in Jackson, Tennessee. I was in a tag match and I tagged in. Boy, I was comin' in smokin'. Just as I went through the ropes, my toe

Anniston AL • Jan. 10, 1974

hooked on the second rope and I felt myself falling. "*Oh, no!*" I fell right out in the middle of that ring. Somebody hollered out, "*It didn't do much good to tag, did it?*"

Another time, when me and Kimala was doing the deal. The first time I went out with him, I put grease paint on my hands to make it look like I was black. I put the mask deal on, but you could see my eyes, so I put on a pair of those mirrored sunglasses. As we walked into the Coliseum, that air conditioning hit the lenses and they fogged over. I couldn't see three feet in front of me. I could see a policeman in front of me, so I followed him. The spotlight came on, so Kimala couldn't see anything, either. He's following me. We wind up walking up into the bleachers. Somebody grabbed us and said, "*It's that way.*" Oh, that was so embarrassing.

We get to the ring and I still can't see. I hold the ropes open so Kimala can get in. As I start to go in, I felt myself falling. The Coliseum was packed, so I'm thinking, "*Oh, noooo!*" I threw the attaché case into the ring, grabbed the top rope with the crook of my arm, and hooked the second rope in the crook of my knee. Jerry Calhoun says, "*Damn! You almost fell, Buddy!*" I didn't fall, though. (laughs)

Was your character called Friday?

No, they never did call me Friday. They called me Keeper. Bill Dundee used to call me the Beekeeper because that's what I looked like in that outfit. The Friday thing started in Louisiana. Frank Dalton was the one that got the name Friday.

He wore the mask, didn't he?

Yeah. I wore a black hood, more like a hangman's hood.

Did anyone in Memphis recognize you?

No, they didn't! That's what was so amazing. Scott, people had no idea who I was. There's a girl in Memphis named Sheila. She walked right past me in Blytheville and looked me right in the face. I knew she knew who I was. At TV that week, she said, "*Oh, Buddy! You should have been in Blytheville last night. It was the biggest crowd they've ever had! You wouldn't believe it!*"

I thought, "*She's right. I can't believe she didn't realize it was me.*" I just knew she knew who I was.

I told one of the little black kids that worked for me that it was me. He said, "*Ah, I don't believe it.*"

I said, "*Okay, when I come to the ring, I'll look at you and clap my hands in front of me.*" He's standing there, so I look at him and clap my hands. He kind of grins. A week or two later, we're gettin' ready to go out of town. I needed help with the ring, you know. He comes over to the house and saw my stuff hangin' up. He looked at it, then looked back at me. "*That really was you, wasn't it?*"

I said, "*Yeah. I told you I'd clap my hands.*"

He says, "*I just thought you got the guy to do that.*"

Another night, when I went up to the ring, I heard people yell, "*Tojo!*" I'd turn around real quick and look at them, then turn away, like, "*Oh, shit! You caught me.*" I'd do it on purpose. I was bigger than Tojo, but I heard someone say, "*He's wearing padding. He ain't really that big.*"

Kimala and I were in Jeffersonville, across the river from Louisville. This guy walks up to us and goes, "*Are you guys professional wrestlers?*"

I said, "*Professional wrestlers? Lord, no! We drive a truck for Allied Van Lines.*"

He says, "*Well, you're big enough.*"

I said, "*I wish we was wrestlers. We wouldn't be driving those big rigs up and down the road.*"

A day or two later, Kimala is driving and he starts beeping the horn and waving. I said, "*What are you doing?*"

He says, "*I'm just waving at a couple of my buddies.*"

I look back out the window and there's an Allied Van Line going the other way. (laughs)

You trained Bobby Whitlock, didn't you?

Yeah. I used to kick the shit out of Bobby Whitlock at the YMCA when I was training him. I didn't tell him nothin'. Several years ago, he told me, "*I remember those days when we worked out. The next day, I was so sore that I couldn't get out of bed.*" He said, "*You called me about three o'clock and wanted to know if I wanted to work out. There wasn't any way I was gonna let you know how bad I hurt.*" He came down and we worked out, but I still didn't tell him nothin' about the business.

Well, several months after the workouts, he called me one Sunday night. He was mad! "*You son-of-a-bitch!*"

I said, "*What?*"

He said, "*I just found out about wrestling!*"

I said, "*What are you talking about?*"

He said, "*It's all a work.*"

I said, "*Work? What are you talkin' about, Bobby?*"

He says, "*Don Sharpe and William Koch! We were at the VFW club.*"

Don Sharpe was a local boy here in Memphis. He was a good, little wrestler who later went to work for the fire department. He became real bitter about wrestling because he never really made it in the business. The problem was that he was too little. Don was all pissed off because they weren't using him, so he told Bobby everything. I said, "*That son-of-a-bitch!*" I still hadn't told Bobby anything. (laughs)

And you were beating him to death during the workouts.

(laughs) That's right. That's the way you should break a guy in. At least, back then that's how it was done.

Nick called me one time and wanted to know if I could get a guy to come work with Don and Al Greene in Nashville. I said, "*Yeah, Nick. I have a boy named Bobby Whitlock that I've been training.*"

"*Do you think he can do it?*"

"*Oh, yeah!*"

I never will forget. It was on top of a mountain in Nashville and the dressing room was real narrow and long. (laughs) Bobby was standing at the end of it with his belly stickin' out. Here comes Nick. "*Where's that boy you brought, Dwayne Peal?*"

"*He's right down there, Nick.*" Nick looks down to where Bobby was standing ... and Bobby's standing there with his belly stickin' out, poppin' a big pimple on it. That was the first impression Nick got of Bobby Whitlock. (laughs) I'm thinking, "*Oh, God!*"

Nick goes, "*Good God!*"

I said, "*It's alright, Nick. He's okay.*" (laughs)

Anyway, we had the match and Nick was real happy with Bobby. That was the night they told Al Greene (pause) ... there was a kid in town who was going to medical school. This kid could wrestle. Buddy Fuller had a deal where people could challenge a professional. If they won, they'd get a hundred dollars.

That was Carlton Hazelwood.

Yeah, that's right. They put him in there with Sam Platania. Of course, I told you the story about Sam. That should have smartened me up then. Sam couldn't beat him. Then they put the kid in with Al Galento. Al hit him in the nose and got disqualified. Finally, they put him in with Charlie Carr. Of course, Charlie beat him ... no, they didn't. Charlie went with him and the people started booing. "*Get this over with! We wanna see rasslin'!*"

That happened in Forest City with Billy Robinson, too, when he wrestled the boy from Wales, Tony Charles. They had a fantastic match! Man, I was eatin' it up. They were makin' moves and counters that I hadn't ever seen. They were working, but they were wrestling. An old woman come up to me and said, "*When're ya'll gonna have some real rasslin'?*"

I thought, "*Oh, shit! I can't believe this.*" (laughs) There was no punches being thrown, no hair pulling. It was straight working, or as Lou Thesz says, performing. Anyway, I remember thinking, "*Can't Charlie beat this guy?*" Me and Charlie talked about that years later. I asked him, "*Charlie, could you have beat that boy?*"

He said, "*I could have beat him, but Fuller didn't want me to.*" He said, "*What Fuller wanted me to do was go out there and make it stink so bad that the people started booing, then we wouldn't do it* [amateur challenges] *anymore.*" They were wanting to end it because everybody was comin' up, wantin' to wrestle.

Two days later, we go to Nashville and Jack Welch goes over to Al [Greene]. (laughs) and says, "*Al, do you know that boy there?*" Al didn't know who I was.

He said, "*No.*"

Jack said, "*That's the kid from Memphis that Edward had so much trouble with. Nobody could beat him.*"

Edward was Buddy Fuller's real name. Al said, "*Really?*"

They told me what Jack did, so Jack comes up later, when Al was in the room with us, and says to me, "*Did you wrestle anywhere while you were in the Army, Dwayne?*"

I said, "*Yeah, I did. I wrestled in Texas. I won the Fourth Army tournament. Then I went to Third Army and won that. They sent me to Europe and I won All Europe.*" (laughs)

Al's sittin' there lookin' at me, you know. He walked out a few minutes later. When he was coming back in, Don [Greene] said, "*Dwayne! Start doing deep knee bends."* (laughs) I start doin' deep knee bends. Al walks in and Don goes, "*196, 197, 198, 199, 200."* Then I started running in place, and I'm barely breathing. Don tells Al, "*Watch that son-of-a-bitch when you get in the ring. He'll hook your ass and ride you."* (laughs) Poor old Al. He didn't know shit about me. (laughs) Don and I started the match and wrestled for a while, then I tagged Bobby. I tag back in and Don tags Al. You can see that he's apprehensive. We locked up and I'm just loose as a goose. Al goes, "*Son-of-a-bitch!"* He immediately knew what we had done. (laughs) He looked over at Don and cursed him.

Back to Memphis, they were talkin' about bringing Danny Hodge in, but Danny had boils real bad and couldn't make it. They smartened Carlton up later. He said, "*I knew something was up when they mentioned Danny Hodge,"* because Carlton knew who Danny was.

Did you get tired of the traveling over the years?

Not really. I hated making a lot of the trips by myself, but I figured it was what I had to do. It was my business, so I had to take care of it. I would get tired from the standpoint of being physically tired. When the speed limit was 75 miles an hour, I'd drive from Knoxville to Memphis and get home and not be tired. When they dropped it down to 50 — and they were real strict then — I'd get home and be dead beat. Sometimes, I'd have to stop in Jackson, only 70 miles from home.

Did you ever have any problems with guys on your shows who refused to do what you asked?

I don't know if you remember Mark Starr or not.

Sure. He was a short guy. Ricki Starr's brother.

No, that's a different one. This one was Chris Champion's brother. We were in Charleston, Missouri. I thought we were gonna have a heck of a house. I thought we'd do five or $6,000. We did $360 or $390. We didn't draw shit! Somebody didn't show up, so I was gonna have to work. I went in the dressing room and Mark said, "*Buddy, I'm not gonna wrestle tonight. There isn't enough people out there."*

I said, "*I don't give a fuck if you work or not!"* And I said, "*Does anybody else not want to work? How about you,* [Billy] *Travis?"*

Billy said, "*Hey, I'm here to work, Buddy."*

I said, "*If you wrestle, you get paid. If you don't, you don't get paid."*

Mark said, "*I'll bet I do."*

I said, "*I bet you don't because I'm the man that pays you."*

He came up later and said he'd work. (laughs)

About a year or so later, Ken [Wayne] was out in Kansas City and met Mark. Mark said, "*Yeah, I met your daddy one night. Let me tell you what he did the first time I ever saw him. It wasn't a big crowd, so I thought if I told him I wasn't gonna wrestle, he'd give me some extra money. He looked at me and said,* 'I don't give a fuck if you wrestle or not. Your name's on the card, not mine. Evidently, they don't want to see your ass.'"

Ken said, "*Yeah, that's my daddy."*

That's something ... I never argued with anybody. If I told somebody to do something, and they said, "*I ain't gonna put him over,"* I'd just tell them, "*You don't have to. Ken, go out to the car and get my bag."* Or Aubrey, or whoever. I never had to wrestle. They'd always back down.

How did you meet your first wife?

A friend owned a bar in West Memphis. This was the Cotton Club, not Danny's. I worked there some, too. This old woman come in with this pretty, little girl. It was Faye. She was seventeen, blond, and the prettiest little thing you've ever seen. I got her number and we started going out.

Faye was Ken's mom, right?

That's right. Ken will be 42 in January.

Your other son, Aubrey. You had him with your second wife, right?

Yeah, with Terry.

Did Ken travel with you much?

He went everywhere with me. When he was five, he'd go to St. Louis with me to the Khorassan Ballroom [at the Chase Park Plaza]. That place was fantastic! They had big tubs of beer in the dressing room. Anheuser-Busch would send it down. Bobby Bruns was running things. When the show was over, Bobby would say, "*Boys, don't leave this beer. If we have a case left over, then next week, they'll short us a case. We may have a bunch of guys next week that drink beer.*"

Whitlock went up there with me a lot. When we went to St. Louis, we'd carry a big suitcase because we knew we were gonna get beer. It wasn't all the time, but there were many times when I'd leave with a whole case of beer in my suitcase. We weren't stealing it, you know. They wanted us to take it.

Ken would go in there, get a can of beer, and smoke a cigar. He wasn't barely five years old. (laughs) Sam Muchnick would come in and go, "*Ken, come out here and sit with me.*"

Later on, Ken said, "*Daddy, Sam gave me a dollar to stop smoking. Here, let's buy some more.*" (laughs)

When Terry Funk first started, Dory Funk Jr. came in. "*Dwayne, Dwayne! Is Ken here?*"

I said, "*No.*"

Dory says, "*Oh, hell! Terry's with me. I've been tellin' Terry about Ken. He wants to see him.*"

How did the cigar smoking get started?

When he was three or four years old, I bought a cigar. He said, "*Dane, get me one.*" He called me Dane. He couldn't say Dwayne. I thought, "*I'll stop this shit real quick.*" I lit the cigar, puffed on it, got it burnin' real good, then said, "*Okay, smoke it.*" We're walkin' down the sidewalks, right there in downtown Memphis, with little Ken smokin' that cigar. That little rascal never did get sick. That's how he got started smoking cigars. I have a picture of him when he was little. He's wearing a little suit and is holding a cigar. It was made at Olan Mills. (laughs)

Did it ever bother Ken to see you getting beat up?

(laughs) That night in Huntsville with Joe Louis as the referee ... the night before, I got bloodied up. Well, during the match, the Band-Aid came off. I said, "*Johnny, whack my eye.*"

Johnny says, "*Why?*"

I said, "*Just whack my eye.*"

He said, "*Okay.*"

Well, he proceeds to bust me the hard way. I said, "*Not that way, Johnny! I just wanted to get it bleeding!*" (laughs)

We're walking back to the dressing room from the ring and Ken's walkin' beside us. "*Daddy, you're bleedin', you're bleeding!*"

He was cryin' and hollerin'. Dennis Hall is going, "*Buddy, I thought he was smart! I thought he was smart.*"

I said, "*Shut up, Dennis!*"

Just as we walked through the dressing room door, where nobody could see us, Ken stops his cryin' and goes, "*Man, that looked good!*"

Dennis goes, "*I'm a son-of-a-bitch!!*" (laughs)

(laughs) We had to walk down a long hall to get to the ring. As we were walking back for the next fall, I asked Jerry Jarrett, "*Jerry, how does it look?*"

He went, "*Oh, don't, man! Don't!*"

I said, "*No, really! Look!*"

He almost got sick. (laughs) Jerry was just starting to referee and wasn't used to seeing it up close. I wasn't doing it on purpose, though. I just wanted to know how it looked. (laughs)

What did you think about your son Ken's interview on 1wrestling.com with Jess McGrath?

It was good. Randy Hales wrote a letter because Jess had asked him [Ken] why he wasn't involved with wrestling in Memphis. Basically, Ken said it was garbage, low-class, and he didn't want to be associated with it. Randy was hot about it and e-mailed Jess back. (laughs) But it's true! How much heat do you think I'll get for doing this interview?

(laughs) You won't have any heat from me. Nobody else matters.

(laughs) The reason I'm saying that is because after Jess McGrath did one with Ken, David Jett posted a photo of Ken on Lawler's deal [website]. It has Ken with a headlock on a bear. The caption says, "*Ken Wayne demonstrates how he captivates the audience for twenty-five minutes by holding a headlock on his dad, Buddy.*" David makes little comments like, "*Randy Hales probably learned more in the last four years than in Buddy's lifetime, but he'll go down in the history books as a mid-card wrestler who sells inedible hot dogs.*" You know ... knocking me. In the first place, Scott ... I'm not bitter. I'm not bitter one bit. And I wasn't necessarily a mid-carder. Everybody had to be on the opener some time, but I was on a lot of main events.

I've been on both sides, so I always tried to do what was right. The one thing I can say, Scott, with all sincerity, and not have to worry about ever answering to God about it, is I never stole no money. Like saying the house was one thing when it wasn't. I never told Nick the house was smaller than it was. If I misreported a hundred dollars, I really wasn't stealin' much. I was stealing 30 from the boys, ten from the booking, and ten from taxes. The other 40 or 50 would have been mine, anyway. I'd be making a thief out of myself for $40. I don't want anybody to ever say, "*Don't work for Buddy because he'll sure screw ya.*" They might have said that, but it wasn't because of anything *I* did. It was just a lot of guys always thought the house was better than it really was.

Your mother lives with you now, doesn't she?

My mother is 90 years old. She fell and hurt herself a few months ago, so I moved her up here. At the time, she weighed 98 pounds and could hardly get up out of a chair. I said, "*Mother, there's nothing wrong with you.*" For breakfast, all she was eating was half a packet of grits, then half a TV dinner for supper. I said, "*You're starving to death. It's nothing but malnutrition.*"

Then she fell and broke her pelvis. She spent three days in the hospital and two weeks in a nursing home. I brought her back home and quit selling cars so I could take care of her. I'd like to go back to work eventually because I need to make some money. Right now, I'm doing alright, but I'm getting older and might not physically be able to work five years from now.

I make her do fifteen sit-ups every morning, then 25 leg raises with the left leg, 25 with the right, and 25 with both. After that, it's sit down in the chair, get up, sit down, get up ... fifteen times. I help her do deep knee bends and have her walk in place while holding onto her walker. Six weeks ago, she weighed 98 pounds. I weighed her this morning and she weighed 117.

She argues with me and I literally have to get firm with her. "*You* are *gonna eat! When I stand up here and cook, you don't tell me that you aren't gonna eat!*" It's like taking care of a little kid. (laughs) The other day, I said, "*I'll be back soon. Don't you go get in that bed.*"

I walked away and she said, "*Well, I will.*" (laughs)

I turned around and said, "*What did you say to me?*"

She grinned and said, "*I just wanted to see what you'd say.*"

My son Aubrey says, "*Daddy, it sounds like you're the dad and she's the kid.*" (laughs)

When was your last match?

I wrestled Mick Tierney about 18 months ago. [Memphis, June 11, 1999]

Have you put up the tights for good?

Uh, I could wrestle if I wanted to, Scott. I don't really want to wrestle because there's nobody that can do what I do. Oh, sure. I could work with Dundee or somebody, but some of these young boys have no idea. If I put a hold on them, I'd have to let them go because they'd have no idea of how to get out of it. If you put a short-arm scissors on a guy, he wouldn't know what to do. It would be a stinkin' ass match.

Does it bother you that you can't get in the ring and do what you used to do?

Not really. Mainly because I don't want to. If I wanted to and couldn't, then it might bother me. When I watch the matches today, I just thank God that I'm not in it.

Did you ever get tired of the business?

No, no. I always said that if I did, I'd quit. When it quit being fun, that's when I was gonna quit. I loved wrestling. I really did. I was reading a book last night by Jeffrey Mayer, "*Success is a Journey.*" It said, "*If you ever want a job, and don't want to work, always get a job that you love.*" I read a lot of those type books.

You don't regret not going into another line of work, like being a veterinarian, which you really seemed to enjoy?

No. I had a job with the railroad that I quit, but I don't regret it at all. Before I had cancer, I worked selling cars. I had called Sonny Myers and asked him what he was doing. He was 71 years old, but he was selling cars. He said, "*It's a hell of a job, Dwayne. You'd really like it.*" That was about five years ago. I called a friend and sold cars for about a year. It wasn't long after that that I got cancer.

Do you mind telling us a little about that?

No. A knot came up under my left ear. I knew it was a tumor. The doctor ran a light down my throat and found a cancerous growth on the base of my tongue. He suggested we use chemicals and high radiation to treat it, so I agreed to it. He said, "*The first thing we have to do is pull your teeth.*"

I said, "*For what?*"

He said, "*The radiation is so strong that if you got one infected, we'd have to take your whole jawbone out.*" Then they told me that with the chemotherapy, I could go blind or lose my hearing, have a stroke, be paralyzed, or die.

In the first week, I felt fine, like nothing was wrong. After the second week, it hit me. I lost a little of my hearing, but it came back. I was real, real weak and stayed in bed all the time, but I never got sick. Later on, they operated and removed the dead glands.

You lost a lot of weight. I almost didn't recognize you in Mobile that year.

One hundred five pounds in five weeks. Nobody knew who I was. (laughs) I still weighed 200 pounds, though. If I hadn't been that heavy, I would have died. I go back for a checkup every three or four months.

Are you happy with what you're doing now?

Yeah. I just have too much free time. I went back to selling cars about a month ago. I can't sit around here all day. It's like I told my sister. Right now, I'm in good shape physically. Three years from now, I may not be. I can work now, but I may not be able to in three years, and I might need the money then, so I need to put as much away as I can. It doesn't take long before your savings is gone.

Do you have cauliflower ears?

I wish I did. (laughs) They're a little bit thick, but not much. Oh, I wanted one. That was a big deal, having ears. When I was a 19-year-old kid, I would have given a thousand dollars for one. That was the sign of being a wrestler. Mine just wouldn't do it. Mario Galento tried to do it. Treach tried. Red Roberts. They just wouldn't bust. They were soft, so they'd bend. They wouldn't bust.

Do you ever run into any of the older fans who still recognize you?

Scott, I'm not saying this as a way of bragging, but a guy will come up and say, "*You're Buddy Wayne, aren't you?*"

I say, "*Yeah.*"

He'll say, "*Can I shake your hand. Man, you're a legend.*" That makes me feel so good. We were in Corinth, Mississippi, recently. I was kidding around with Aubrey's girlfriend. I said, "*Yeah, you're sittin' here with a legend.*"

I hadn't barely gotten that out of my mouth when an old man comes up and says, "*Buddy, let me shake your hand. Man, you're a legend!*" (laughs)

I looked over at her and I said, "*See?*" (laughs) It was like I had planned it.

It's a shame. Our era is over. Wrestling will never be the same as it used to be. They'll never have the big territories. The boys are only interested in themselves, not the business. How many times did I leave the house to wrestle, knowing full well that I wasn't gonna make a nickel. Many times, I went to Bowling Green [250 miles each way] for fifteen to twenty dollars, knowing when I left here that I was barely going to break even. To make it worse, I had to drive through Jackson, where I could have made $75 to $80 that same night if I was just on the opening match. Then I turned around and came back that same night. But I was a professional and I loved the business.

I can't think of a better way to end this interview than with what you just said. Thanks for taking so much time to share your story with me, Buddy. I thought I knew a lot about the old Tennessee territory, but I learned a *lot* of things from you that I never knew. I'd love to talk with you again in the future and record some more of the stories and history that you can remember.

I'd love to. Feel free to call me anytime you want, Scott. I'm home most of the time.

Buddy passed away on Dec. 31, 2015, after a long battle with pulmonary fibrosis.

TITLES

World tag (TN/AL 1970 w/Bob Ramstead)
Tri-State tag (AL 1975 w/Burrhead Jones)

Buddy in the dressing room with Len Rossi & Johnny Walker

DAVE LEVIN

George Wenzel
"The Jamaica Butcher Boy"

his interview, conducted by Scott Teal in Dec. 1993, was originally published in issue #4 of *Whatever Happened to ...?*

Tell us a little bit about your background.

I quit school when I was sixteen to work full time at a meat market. I started working there on Saturdays when I was 14. That's why they called me the Butcher Boy. I decided I'd better learn a trade instead of spending the next four years in high school and coming out to get nothing. During the Depression, jobs were hard to find. Jim McMillen, Joe Savoldi, and many others got out of college and couldn't find a job. That's why they got into wrestling.

You worked out with them while you were still an amateur, didn't you?

We all worked out at the YMCA and Bothner's Gym in New York. When I first went up there, they bounced me around like a rubber ball and I was always covered with bruises. I'd also go to the matches all the time in my hometown of Ridgewood Grove, because I wanted to improve myself. I figured I could make big money wrestling and get out of the meat business.

Who gave you your first break in the pros?

Jack Pfefer, who was the promoter in New York back then. I saw him at a card one night and asked him what I had to do to become a wrestler. He told me to bring my tights to Bothner's on Sunday for a tryout. I didn't know what was going to happen, but I showed up. He tried me out with Herbie Freeman and Tony Morelli. I had seen these guys work in the ring and I almost turned around and went back to the meat market.

Pfefer gave me to big, heavy Herbie first. I knew it would be foolish to try to beat him, so I just went on the defensive. I just bridged and kept my shoulders off the mat. Pfefer figured I'd eventually make a wrong move and be pinned, but I stayed with him. So he put Tony on me. Tony was one tough cookie and was all over me like a bed of ants. He was faster and quicker than Herbie. I just tried to keep him from pinning me, and that was pretty good if you could keep Tony from doing it.

Pfefer said he liked the way I handled myself. He said there were no big Jewish champions around there and he wanted to know if I'd mind taking a Jewish name. I told him to put down any name he wanted, just give me a job. He gave me the name Dave Levin.

It's a funny thing. Pfefer had to change the names of anybody that came into his territory. See, my real name is George Wenzel. It wasn't two weeks after I came in that a guy comes in and Pfefer gives him the name George

Winchell. Isn't that something? I thought if he wanted a George Winchell, he could have given it to me.

I started working out daily at Bothner's with McMillen, Orville Brown, Cliff Olsen, Freeman and Morelli. My mother kept trying to get me to quit. You know how mothers are. She couldn't stand to see her son come home limping every night.

Where was your first match and who did you wrestle?

My first match was on Nov. 1, 1934, in the Jamaica Arena on Long island. I wrestled ... I can't remember names like I used to. I think I took one too many bumps on my head.

Dave was scheduled to debut against Dick Griffin, an Australian wrestler. His opponent wound up being Sammy Gold, one of Jack Pfefer's fall guys during the first half of the 1934-35 season in New York. Dave, who weighed 182 pounds at the time, won the match in a scant 24 seconds. In fact, he each of his first three matches in less than one minute.

Newspaper reports referred to him as "a Jamaica butcher boy." The nickname stuck and he was referred to as the Jamaica Butcher Boy throughout his career. In the *Times Union* report on the day following match, he was said to be "a miniature of the old Russian Lion, George Hackenschmidt. After the bout, Jack Pfefer, the chief mahout of the light heavy grapplers, was lavish in his praise of Levin."

Photo of Dave used in the Nov. 8, 1934 edition of the *Brooklyn Times Union*

There are conflicting reports of the events following your June 12, 1936, win over world champion Ali Baba in Newark, NJ. Some records state that the state commission didn't recognize the title change. Another says Dean Detton won the title from Strangler Ed Lewis in a Philadelphia tournament after you became champion. What was the real story?

I never wrestled in Jersey after that, so I guess it doesn't matter what they decided since I was recognized in the other states. In regards to the Detton-Lewis situation, Detton beat me for the title in Philly. In Philadelphia, the rules were for two out of three falls, but if the first fall exceeded one hour, it was converted to a one-fall match. Whoever won that fall was the winner. We went 2 hours and 5 minutes and I lost that one. I remember Pfefer telling me to be sure and get my money from Ray Fabiani, the promoter, before I left, or I probably wouldn't get it.

You remember Hans Steinke, of course. He came up to get his payoff from Pfefer one time, and this was the tenth story of the Times Building in New York. That's where Pfefer's office was. He didn't like the payoff Pfefer gave

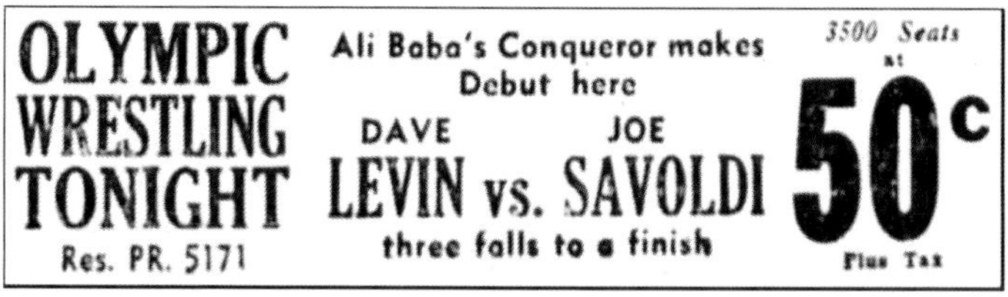

Los Angeles CA • July 15, 1936

him, so he took Pfefer by the ankles and hung him out the tenth-story window. That's a true story. At that point, Pfefer was ready to give him anything. Needless to say, Steinke got what he wanted.

Two months later, you beat Vincent Lopez in Los Angeles for another version of the world title. How did that title come into existence?

There's another thing. Lopez was never a real champion. He was Lou Daro's champion in California. Lou Daro ran a tournament that lasted several months, which Lopez won. Lopez didn't beat a champion to win it. He was just declared the champion.

And what about your win over Orville Brown in Kansas City, Missouri on May 4, 1944? Wasn't he claiming the world title then?

That was the Kansas City title. It wasn't really a world title like the other one was. It was their version of it. He took it back later on. We wrestled once more and went to a half-hour draw.

Levin won the first and third falls from Brown. He was presented with the MWA title belt in the ring before more than 4,000 fans, the largest crowd to attend a mat card in the history of the Memorial Hall arena.

When did you retire?

I left in 1954. I had just turned 42 and felt like I was getting a little bit old. I had some problems that had been bothering me since 1937. In January of that year, right after I lost the title to Detton, I got a rope burn. You have to remember, ropes were ropes in those days. There wasn't any velvet covering back then. It was just a friction burn, but it got infected and I fell over when I got out of bed the next morning. The doctors took care of it, but I had a stiff ankle from then on. I was laid up and unable to wrestle for over a year.

On Jan. 21, 1937, Levin wrestled Robert (Bobby) Bruns at the Brooklyn Hippodrome and suffered a rope burn on the back of one of his legs. A few days later, he was taken to Wyckoff Heights Hospital in Brooklyn for treatment of an infection that had spread into his blood stream. Levin's condition was diagnosed as hemoletic streptococcus, which is blood poisoning at its most vicious stage. Dave was ruled to be in critical condition and doctors said he wouldn't live. Ten wrestlers, including Bobby Bruns, visited the hospital as blood donors. It was touch and go. Strangely enough, Bruns, whom Levin had wrestled in the match in which he had been injured, was selected for the blood transfusions, Levin began to improve. His stay in the hospital, though, was a lengthy one. The last report found said he had been in the hospital for three months and would be out of wrestling for up to a year. By the time he was released, much of his 195 pounds had burnt away until he resembled a thin skeleton of a man.

Levin began making his comeback in late May 1938. His last match appears to have been against Hans Schwartz on Feb. 22, 1940, at Ridgewood Grove in Brooklyn.

What line of work did you pursue?

In '54, I did some ring announcing at the Long Beach arena. While there, I got a letter from a fellow in the liquor business who wanted me to work for him. He figured I was known and could be an asset. Bars were a big thing in those days. They had wrestling posters in the windows and would broadcast the matches in the bar, so many of their customers were wrestling fans and knew who I was. I had a route and called on accounts for about eight years. When the place went broke, one of my customers asked me to manage his store, Joseph's Liquors, in Santa Monica. I stayed there for another eight years. I retired after that and that was the end of my working days and I've been retired ever since. I couldn't do much more, because my legs were going bad on me.

Tell us about your life now.

There's more leisure here than anything else. We have dances here almost every Saturday night. That's what I like about this place. If we didn't live here ... and Ginger and I just went out on a Saturday night. I can't dance, you know. I'm lucky I can walk with a walker, but here, we know all our neighbors. They come up and ask her for a dance and she loves it. We enjoy it. Virginia is the best thing I got out of wrestling. We've been married 55 years. Isn't that great? We got married in January of '39. We've got our 55th anniversary coming up on January 19th.

I'm from New York, and when we met, instead of saying Ginger, like they say out here, I called her Ginja. So when I got a letter from her one day, she signed it Ginja. I wrote back and said that was a pretty fancy name ... where'd you get that? She said that's what I called her. She's gone by that ever since. We just got back from taking our daughter, son-in-law and two grandchildren on a cruise down to Mexico on the Nordic Prince Cruise Lines.

Little additional information is known about Dave's after this interview was conducted, other than the fact that he died on Aug. 25, 2004.

TITLES

World (CA '36)
World heavyweight (Toots Mondt, Ray Fabiani, '36)
World junior heavyweight (CT '39)
Midwest (Kansas City '44)
Texas ('45, '46)
Midwest (Fred Kohler '47)
World heavyweight
(Jack Pfefer '49 (2x), '50

Dave Levin

WORLD'S CHAMPION
JOE "TOOTS" MONDT Manager
DAVE LEVIN
BERT'S STUDIO K.C.

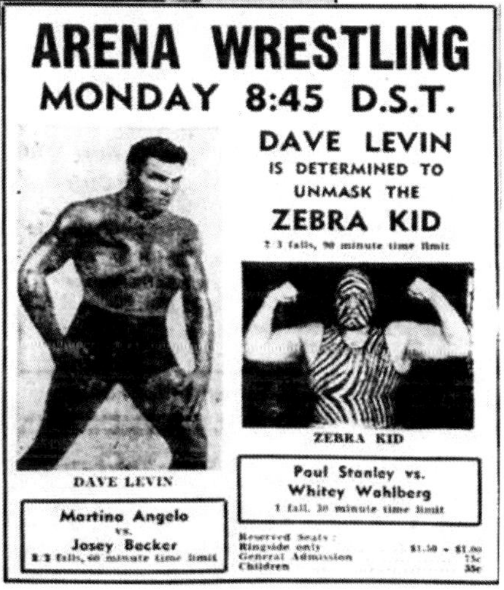
ARENA WRESTLING
MONDAY 8:45 D.S.T.
DAVE LEVIN IS DETERMINED TO UNMASK THE ZEBRA KID
2-3 falls, 90 minute time limit
DAVE LEVIN
ZEBRA KID
Martino Angelo vs. Josey Becker
2-3 falls, 60 minute time limit
Paul Stanley vs. Whitey Wahlberg
1 fall, 30 minute time limit
Reserved Seats:
Ringside only $1.50 - $1.00
General Admission 75c
Children 35c

AL COSTELLO

Giacomo Costa
"The Man of 1,001 Holds"

This interview, conducted by Scott Teal on July 9 and Aug. 19, 1993, was originally published in issue #3 of *Whatever Happened to ...?*

The Fabulous Kangaroos have been recognized as the best tag team during the Golden Age of pro wrestling. During their reign, they acquired most major and regional tag team titles and their effect on the popularity of tag team wrestling is significant.

Born Dec. 14, 1919, Al Costello was the mastermind behind this successful team, and from 1956 to 1974, campaigned with more than eight different wrestlers as *The Fabulous Kangaroos*. Roy Heffernan, Ray St. Clair, Don Kent, Tony Charles, Mickey Doyle, Jack Carter, Dennis Kass, and Bruce Swayze were all part of this prestigious team at one time.

How did you get started in wrestling?

Actually, I was an amateur boxer at age 16, two years before I started to wrestle. One night, after I'd finished boxing, this fellow named Basher Bonas walks up to me and asks if I'd like to try wrestling. At the time, Basher was the middleweight champion wrestler of Australia. You see, after the boxing matches were over, they'd put the mats down and the amateur wrestling would start. Basher convinced me to hang around and see what I thought. I knew nothing about wrestling, but I waited around and watched. To make a long story short, I decided to give it a try. It was tough. The featherweights, middleweights, and everyone were beating the heck out of me because I had no concept of balance. But I persevered, and within a month, I was beating everybody. I had that natural aptitude. I became fanatical about wrestling and soon won the Australian Junior heavyweight amateur wrestling title. From then on, that was it. That's all I've ever done.

What made you decide to enter the pro ranks?

I was training very hard at the time. I'd get six or seven guys together and wrestle them, one after the other, and it was all amateur wrestling. That's how I trained. The person who inspired me to do that was a fellow named Dr. Len Hall. He was a claimant to the world title against Lou Thesz way back in the early '20s and '30s. He was the one who convinced me to do a little exhibition one night. It wasn't what I expected. At the same time, I used to go down to the gym with him and train with him, amateur style, because he was good.

Sydney, NSW, Australia • Sept. 27, 1947

Where was your first professional match?

My first match was in 1938 against a fellow named Johnny Gilday in Sydney, near Rockdale where I lived. At that time, I was studying to be an opera singer. My father didn't even know I was wrestling. My second match was a young man called Frank Hurley.

What brought you to the United States?

In 1952, Ed "Strangler" Lewis arranged for me to come over. My first match in the U.S. — at the Winterland Arena in San Francisco for promoter Joe Malcewicz — was against Warren Bockwinkel. From there, I went to Texas. The big names I wrestled during those years included Gorgeous George, Danny McShain, Duke Keomuka, Ray Gunkel, Baron Leone, and Lou Thesz. From there, I went to Buffalo for Ed Don George and into Toronto for Frank Tunney.

How did the Fabulous Kangaroos get started?

I always had that thing in my mind. I kept thinking of kangaroos, bush hats, boomerangs ... things pertaining to Australia. Well, I used to coach Roy Heffernan when he was about 17 or 18. I was wrestling at the time. He'd come to Rockdale where I lived and I'd take him down to the mat and show him some stuff. In 1952, when Strangler Lewis brought me to the states, I lost track of Roy. In '56, I happened to be in Honolulu and Lord Blears and Joe Blanchard were there. I'm telling them about my ideas and Joe suggested I get ahold of Roy, who was in Calgary with Stu Hart. So, I contacted him and told him about my ideas. He loved the idea.

Madison Square Garden
Aug. 30, 1958

Where did you and Roy first wrestle as the Kangaroos?

Right there in Calgary. Stu Hart was a great promoter and a prince of a guy. He used to carry an extra two guys on the payroll in case somebody got hurt, and even though they weren't working, they were still paid. That's the sort of promoter he was. How many promoters do you know would do that? And that's where we got started! We got over fantastic together and went from there to Toronto. Then we called Vince McMahon Sr. and wrestled in Madison Square Garden. We had turnaway crowds all over the East Coast.

How long were you together as the Kangaroos?

We were together almost eight years ... from '56 until '64. He went back to Australia. We had planned on going back together. I had told him years before that Australia was a gold mine. In the meantime, he got together with Jim Barnett and that was the end of that. They said, *"You stay in the States and we'll send for you."* They never sent for me. When Roy quit wrestling, they agreed to have me there for a month and that's all. Under no conditions would they let me stay any longer. So that ruined our situation in Australia. Later, Roy sent me a tape and talked about the possibilities of us getting back together and do all these great things. But it was too late. The Golden Era was gone. Once it's down, it's down. You can build, but it takes a lot of work.

Tell me a little about your first manager, Wild Red Berry.

Red Berry was a five-time holder of the world light heavyweight title in the early '40s. Red made a lasting impression on my life, as a teacher and philosopher, and was a real source of inspiration to me during the three and a half years we were together.

The Kangaroos were his first venture as a manager and I'll never forget it. At the time, Roy and I were working for Morris Siegel and Paul Boesch in Houston. Danny McShain, Roy and I were driving up to Fort Worth when we heard Red plugging the wrestling matches on the radio. I told Roy right then that Red was going to be our manager. Roy thought I was crazy. He didn't like the idea, and in the years to come, he tried his level best to get rid of him, but I always felt that Red was an asset to the team.

Roy's animosity towards Red finally came to a head in Florida. We were wrestling Don Curtis and Eddie Graham in Jacksonville on a Saturday night. Roy gave me an ultimatum ... either I retain Roy or Red. I chose Red. Red and I went back to New Jersey, where we lived at the time, for a two-week vacation. In the meantime, I called Vince McMahon Sr. and told him that Roy and I had split up. We told Vince that Red and I had decided to ask a fellow named Jacob Grobbe [Hans Mortier], who had wrestled as The Great Zorro in Florida, to join us as the new Kangaroo. Vince gave his approval.

So, we returned to Washington, D.C. where I wrestled on the television tapings as a single at the Capitol Arena. Red gave a great spiel that we had booked Jacob Grobbe to further add to the Fabulous Kangaroos, as a bigger and better combination. In the meantime, Roy called Vince McMahon, told him about our split, and asked to come in and wrestle as a single. Vince told him that he had me booked with someone else and couldn't use him.

Red and I returned to Jacksonville, as Roy and I were booked for two more weeks against the Von

St. Petersburg FL
Nov. 10, 1962

Brauners. When I got there, Roy pulled me aside, apologized for his outburst, and asked if we could keep working together. I looked him in the eye, we shook hands, and the original Kangaroos were back together.

I called Vince McMahon and gave him the news, which he was happy to hear. Vince decided to bring Grobbe in as a single and billed him as Hans Mortier. Red managed Roy and I as a team and Mortier as a single. As a matter of fact, when Roy and I left New York, Red stayed on to manage Mortier, Gorilla Monsoon, and others. It wasn't too many years later that Red passed on.

You had several tag team partners after you and Roy went your separate ways. Tell me about a few of them.

I soloed for a while and went to Atlanta in 1965, where Louie Tillet and I teamed up as The Globetrotters. We didn't see eye to eye and I left for Nashville, Tennessee, in 1966, where I met up with Karl von Brauner. With Playboy Gary Hart as our manager, Karl and I wrestled as The Internationals in Texas and Detroit.

Wasn't it about this time that you reactivated the Kangaroos?

That's right. My second choice for a Kangaroo was Ray St. Clair. I had seen Ray wrestle in England many years before under the name of Tinker Todd. We got together in 1967 and he got over fantastic, but he didn't have staying power. Two months of tough campaigning and traveling, three tapings per day, flying all over the place, must have taken its toll on Ray. One day, he just took off and returned to England.

In the meantime, Francis Fleser, who co-promoted in Detroit with the Sheik, asked me to select another Kangaroo. This was back in late 1967. One evening, while waiting in the wings at the Cobo Arena, I was watching the matches. On the card was a young man called Joe Smith. Fred Blassie, who was on loan from Vince McMahon, was standing there with me and mentioned that Smith had good potential. I later learned that Joe had been the booker in Phoenix, Arizona, and obviously knew his wrestling. I waited until the following week and approached Joe with the idea of being a Kangaroo, and he loved the idea. Nick Gulas had billed Joe as Don Kent in Tennessee during the late '50s, so we decided to use that name. Don and I wrestled together until 1974.

While wrestling in Rochester in 1973, a riot broke out in the Rochester, New York, War Memorial. A fan threw a fire extinguisher from the balcony and it hit Costello in the hip. The hip was broken and Costello had to undergo hip replacement surgery, which led to severe arthritis.

Al had a hip replacement in 1974 and curtailed active competition as a wrestler. He kept active as a manager for The Love Brothers (IWA '75), The Spoiler (Frank Morrell) and Bruce Swayze (TN '76), Dennis Condrey and Phil Hickerson (TN '78), and Don Kent and Bob Della Serra in Puerto Rico ('82). In 1983, after 45 years of constant traveling, Al gave up wrestling to begin working as a security chief in Detroit. In 1989, he moved to Clearwater, Florida, and took over as head of security at College Harbor in St. Petersburg. He retired in 1992 and went back to doing what he really loved ... teaching wrestling. At the time of this interview, at age 73, and despite two hip replacements, Al was in great shape and maintained his well-being with daily workouts, swimming, and a myriad of exercises.

In 1966, during a stopover in Detroit and on his way back to Australia, Al met Cleo Wilson, and they were happily married for 25 years. Al had three daughters from a previous marriage who lived in Australia, and one daughter who was an artist and owned a health food store. Besides working out, he enjoyed a relaxing game of golf and playing the piano.

By the late '90s, Al was suffering from both heart problems and Alzheimer's disease. In Dec. 1999, he contracted pneumonia and passed away on Jan. 22, 2000, at the age of 80.

TITLES

South African Trophy ('49)
British Empire (South Africa '49)
World tag (TX '58 w/Roy Heffernan)
Rocky Mountain tag
(Albuquerque '59 w/Roy Heffernan)
Brass Knucks tag
(Albuquerque '59 w/Roy Heffernan)
International tag
(Amarillo '59 w/Roy Heffernan)
International tag
(Los Angeles '60 w/Roy Heffernan)
U.S. tag
(New York '60 w/Roy Heffernan, 3x)
U.S. tag (Florida '61 w/Roy Heffernan)
World tag (FL '62 w/Roy Heffernan)
WWA world tag
(Los Angeles '64 w/Roy Heffernan)
Pacific Coast tag
(WA '64 w/Roy Heffernan)
International tag (Winnipeg '64, 2x)
World tag (TX '58 w/Roy Heffernan;
'66 w/Karl Von Brauner)
Southern junior (TN '66)
World tag (Atlanta '66 w/Louie Tillet)
World tag (TN '66 w/Herb Welch;
'73 w/Don Kent)
TWWA tag (Japan '68 w/Don Kent)
WWA world tag
(IN '70 & '71 w/Don Kent)
World tag (Detroit '67 w/Ray St. Clair;
'71 w/Don Kent; '76 w/Tony Charles)
WWC world tag
(Puerto Rico '77 w/Don Kent)

ALIAS

The Fabulous Kangaroos

ROY HEFFERNAN

Roy Heffernan

After he died, Roy Heffernan was featured in the "Finishes" column of *Whatever Happened to ...?* #3. Shortly after that issue was published, we received a copy of an Australian newsletter called *Piledriver* magazine from publisher Lazarus Dobelsky. Two of the issues had lengthy interviews with Heffernan, which Lazarus allowed us to reprint.

Early years — I started when I was ten years of age, lifting weights and wrestling around in the back yard. I joined the Police Boys Club when I was fourteen. I spent six years in the Woolloomooloo Police Boys Club, and then turned pro at twenty. I had twenty seven years as a professional wrestler and sixteen years promoting.

... My father was a professional fighter at one stage, then he was on the Tivoli circuit as a strongman.

Dirty Dick Raines — Funny thing. Dirty Dick Raines was kind of my idol. I used to hang around the Leichardt Stadium when I was a kid. If you got to carry in a wrestler's bag for him, you got in for free. So, you had to be pretty tough. There was a big fight on out the front there every Saturday night ... kids trying to grab the wrestler's bags. (laughs) One night, I missed out and there was this guy standing there. I said, *"Are you a wrestler?"*

And he said, *"Yeah."*

I said, *"Who are you?"*

And he said, *"Dirty Dick Raines."*

And I said, *"Never heard of you!"* (laughs) But he became my idol.

... One of my first bouts when I went to Texas was with Dick Raines. He was more or less over the hill by then, but he was a booker in San Antonio.

Stadiums — There was the Leichardt Stadium and the old Sydney Stadium. But they're all gone now, all pulled down. Used to be a Cobram Stadium and a Carlton Stadium. They're all gone now, too.

Promoters — In Leichardt, it was Herb McKeogh. And Sydney Stadium was Harry Miller.

WRESTLING—LEICHHARDT—TO-NIGHT

8 ROUNDS: AL COSTELLO (Aust.) v LEO JENSEN (U.S.A.)

Supported by Wrestling (4 rds.), Roy Heffernan v Snowy Dowton, Ken Hawthorne v Alf Greer: and BOXING and VAUDEVILLE. First event at 8. Ladies and Children Half-price to Ringside and centre terraces. Bookings: Millard's, Mick Simmons, and LM4323.

Sydney, NSW, Australia • Dec. 23, 1950

(The shows) were all run through Dick Lean in those days, in Melbourne. They controlled all of the stadiums, all of the festival halls in Melbourne, Adelaide, Brisbane, and so on.

Harry Miller — (Harry) started working at the Sydney Stadium when he was only fourteen. Just an office boy, but he became stadium manager and it was all that he knew. And when they pulled the stadium down — afterwards, he tried to promote a few other little shows at different places, but he was drinking all the time — anyhow, he blew his brains out.

Leichardt Stadium — was the greatest Saturday night's entertainment around. You had two boxing bouts to start off with. Between the bouts, you had vaudeville, juggling, or whatever, then you had two wrestling bouts. It was like vaudeville, the whole thing. It was a hell of a night. If you were lousy, the crowd used to count you out. Oh, they were cruel.

Johnny Doyle — He became a partner with Jim Barnett, but I don't know how they got teamed up, because Barnett was the brains and Doyle couldn't even handle the guys in the dressing room. One night, Johnny said to Jim, *"Jim, tell the guys, they won't listen to me."* They had no respect for him. Barnett got things done. He knew how to handle people and Doyle couldn't do it.

America — I left here in '53. I went to India first, then Ceylon — Sri Lanka it's called now — and Pakistan, Singapore, Europe, then a year in South Africa. I went to Canada, then finally to America.

Roy made his U.S. debut on May 10, 1955, in Edmonton, Alberta, Canada, against Firpo Zbyszko.

Al Costello; The Fabulous Kangaroos — I had a couple of bouts with him in the early days, when I was twenty. He was in America and I was in Canada when he phoned me and said, *"Come on up here."*

... We made our debut in New York in '57.

Roy and Al wrestled as the "Australian Kangaroos" in Western Canada in Sept. 1957, and were only referred to as the "Fabulous Kangaroos" a few times. It was more of a passing reference than the nickname they would later adopt. They didn't wrestle in New York until March 1958. For their first appearance in Madison Square Garden — March 17 — they wrestled in singles matches. Their first "team" match in the Garden was June 14, 1958, against Skull Murphy and Larry Hamilton. Newspapers writeups and ads referred to as either the "Fabulous Kangaroos," the "Australian Kangaroos," or simply "Kangaroos Al Costello and Roy Heffernan." The "Fabulous Kangaroos" nickname didn't really take off until 1959.

... We had little boomerangs that we threw to the crowds, and we had our manager with us. We had a big banner with "The Fabulous Kangaroos" on it, and a recording of "Waltzing Matilda" that we'd march down to the ring to.

... I remember the first time carrying the banner. It was a low ceiling and the top of the banner hit it. Then our manager, Red Berry, starts to fall. Al Costello tries to catch him, and he starts to fall. So, I try to catch them both. And suddenly, all three of us fall down! And this is our grand opening! Our debut! All three ofus are floundering around, our hats are all twisted, and we look just like the Three Stooges! We never lived that down. (laughs) It was awful.

Pat O'Connor — We were up in Edmonton, in Canada, and the promoter up there had a backyard zoo. We went there to get some publicity shots taken and there was a cheetah roaming around in the back yard ... and we've got these quivers on our backs. Only we had our boomerangs in them.

So, we were making out that we were going to go hunting bear with our boomerangs and our pet cheetah for a publicity shot. Later on, we saw a bear stuffed in a museum, and it was nine feet tall. (laughs) And we were going to hunt them with our little boomerangs!

Anyway, in the best publicity shot, the cheetah's sitting up — a beautiful animal. Al and I are crouched down there, one on each side, and Pat O'Connor's behind us. We're all trying to get our heads close together for a nice shot. The promoter had all these big hedges around his yard, about six feet high ... the cheetah suddenly spotted an insect, and took a big bite at it! I ran this way, Al ran that way, and Pat O'Connor tried to jump the hedge! He got stuck in the top of the hedge. (laughs) So, when you talk about these tough guys ... but, it was a great shot.

Lou Thesz — When I first met him, I used to call him Mr. Thesz, but he had this thing. He didn't like guys like Gorgeous George or Baron Leone, guys with a strut, Buddy Rogers. He didn't like all that. He just wanted to wrestle. He'd get them on the ropes and give them a slap across the face

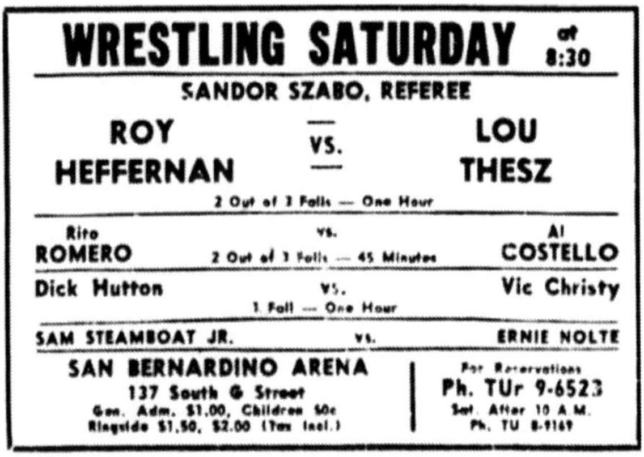

San Bernardino CA • June 11, 1960

that could be heard all around the arena. That was just to say, now wrestle, don't fool around. Don't be a bloody clown. I never liked it when he slapped my face, so when I first wrestled him, I said, *"Now, Mr. Thesz, there's no need to slap my face."*

He said, *"Well, I've got some good reports about you. Have we got a match?"*

I said, *"Alright, but just don't slap my face."*

Anyhow, we became good friends. I've got his boots from the last match I had with him, on Victoria Island, across from Vancouver.

He said, *"Are you going home to Australia?"*

I said, *"I've been away for fifteen years. I've got to go home sometime."*

So he said, *"Well, it's sad to see you go. Let's go out there and we'll wrestle for the whole hour, and show them what wrestling's all about."*

Now, I had to catch the ferry. The last ferry was at eleven o'clock, and it was a two-hour ride across. If we wrestled for an hour, I'd miss my ferry, and then I'd have to drive sixty miles to another place called Nanaimo and get a four o'clock ferry. I said, *"That's no good, Lou. Beat me when you're ready, so I can catch the eleven o'clock ferry."*

And he said, *"Nope. We wrestle an hour."*

We earned our money. We wrestled for an hour, and I got his boots. He still doesn't know. He said, *"They've seen better days."* He just threw them in a corner. I thought I'd keep them for a souvenir. There's a hole in the toe, but I got them bronzed.

Dick Hutton — You get a few who do that. (shoot) Some of these guys, they cheese you off. Dick Hutton ... he was one of the greatest. He was a Big Ten champion ... college champion. Even the Olympics. They wanted to make him world's champion, but they were hesitant, because if they made him champion, if they ever wanted to change it, who was going to beat him? He was the greatest in the country. Anyhow, Al and I had the job of teaching him holds, some little high spots and different things. We became good friends, but he had no sense of humor.

I wrestled him somewhere, in Canberra, I think. Some woman in the front row had a cheque for $200, and she said, *"Roy, you beat Hutton and I'll sign this."* So, I took the cheque down to the dressing room and showed it to the guys. I showed it to Dick, too, and we were laughing amongst ourselves. So, I'm in this match with Hutton, and I got him in a little manoeuvre when he was down. It was like — it's like when you're playing chess. This was check, the next move would be checkmate. But there's this little manoeuvre you put on — it's nothing great, but they can't go forward or backward. They can't get out of it. A wrestler would never get in that position, but I got Dick in it. I tied him up a bit, and he's on his side, and he can't go this way, can't go back there. And when he moves around, I've got hold of his tights, so I move around with him. He looks up at me like, *"What's going on?"*

I said, *"I'm going for the $200."* (laughs) Hell, he couldn't get up, but he fought so hard we bounced. We bounced over to the ropes and the referee made us break. And then I was fighting for my life. (laughs) No sense of humor.

Johnny Valentine — This was in Washington. The Alaskan [Jay York] had asthma, bad breathing, and Valentine put some lighter fluid in his medicine. Gee, it nearly killed him. But he was a little crazy, too. You should hear the stories about him. Now, Valentine had a big bag in the dressing room. The Alaskan went out to his car, got his shotgun, and POW! ... blew this big hole through his bag. Then he said to Valentine, "Next time, it won't be your bag." (laughs) He was a crazy guy. He used to carry hand grenades.

Riots — I remember one time, we came out one night after a match through a side door which came down on to English Avenue. We tried to sneak out this side door, but there were still about 2,000 people out there, hanging around. It was one of those big metal doors. You know, with a heavy metal bar? I said to Al, *"Come on. I'll peep around."* Anyhow, Al's behind me, and we're peeping around, and CLUNK! The bloody door closes. And now we're locked out. All these people start to see us. I said to Al, *"There a little shop, a juice bar, across the street there. Let's try and get in there. But,"* I said, *"Don't touch anybody! Don't say anything! Don't even look at them!"*

So, we just tried to make it to the other side of the street. And they're kicking us in the arse, kicking our bags, pulling at our hats, grabbing the flag. We just kept going. Didn't say a word. We went into the juice bar and all these faces in the window are looking at us. Al got eight stitches in one side of his face and six in the other side.

Stan Stasiak — We had a six-man tag match in Winnipeg, and what a riot we had. We gave Stan a slouch hat, too. Made him an honorary member, and he carried our banner in. It was a six-man tag ... and the crowd started throwing chairs. I said, *"Listen, let's get under the ring because we can't make it to the dressing rooms."* They folded the chairs up and threw them at us under the ring. They threw in so many chairs that it made like a wall around us. I could see Karl Gotch's legs from under there, and he said, *"Come on, get out of there!"*

I said, *"Are you crazy? I'm staying right here."*

He said, *"Come on, come on."* He was fighting them off for us, and knocking people down. He's a rugged guy, too. Anyhow, we finally got back to the dressing room. Al got cuts on both sides of his face and Stan got six stitches. And the promoter, he says, *"Fan-tas-tic!"*

His words exactly. He said, *"Do you want to do it in Vancouver?"* (laughs) I never answered him. I just looked at him, but the look was enough. He said, *"No, well, I guess not."*

Do you know what else the crowd did? They pulled the drape off the ring and were trying to light it, to burn us out. Later, we said to Stan Stasiak, *"Did you like being the third Kangaroo?"*

He said, *"You can shove your Kangaroos. You can shove your banner. You can shove the lot. Get stuffed!"*

I thought he was going to hit me. (laughs)

Promoting — In Korumburra, there was this couple. The girl sold the tickets and he took them at the door. Now, I used to stand around and watch things, you know. I finally woke up when they got married and went on their honeymoon. They wanted to come back early to do the show. I said, *"Oh-oh, here we go."* I put Joyce selling the tickets, someone else on the door, and we took an extra $1,800. They'd been skimming off the top. They were going to break off their honeymoon to come back, so I knew they'd been up to something.

Commercials — (Mario Milano) and I went down to the Channel 9 studios. I told the receptionist, *"This morning, we're doing a commercial for Kolatron pants."* Now, Mario's wearing the Kolatron pants and I've got on the ordinary pants. Jack Little's refereeing. They ring the bell and we get out there all dressed. He's slamming me, we're throwing each other around, taking bumps. Then he gives me a big slam, dives on me, and BAM! He stands up like he's the winner. They had a special belt made … the Kolatron belt. They're like the "Champion Pants." (laughs) Mario held the belt up … and it was upside down. They yelled, *"Cut! You've got the belt upside down!"* We ran through it all again, and he held the belt upside down again! You know the funny part about it? My pants looked better than Kolatron's. Oh, the things you do in this funny business. All we got out of it were three pairs of pants each.

Roy retired from wrestling in 1971. In early 1992, he broke his back and his health took a downturn. He died on Sept. 24, 1992, at the age of 67.

TITLES

Southwest (Amarillo '55)
Pacific Northwest tag
(Portland '56 w/Red Bastien)
World tag (TX '58 w/Al Costello)
Rocky Mountain tag
(Albuquerque '59 w/Al Costello)
Brass Knucks tag
(Albuquerque '59 w/Al Costello)
International tag
(Amarillo '59 w/Al Costello)
International tag
(Los Angeles '60 w/Al Costello)
U.S. tag
(New York '60 w/Al Costello, 3x)
U.S. tag (Florida '61 w/Al Costello)
World tag (FL '62 w/Al Costello)
International tag (Winnipeg '64, 2x)
WWA world tag
(Los Angeles '64 w/Al Costello)
Canadian tag (Vancouver '64, 3x)
Pacific Coast tag (WA '64 w/Al Costello)
International tag
(Toronto '64 & '65 w/Al Costello)

The Fabulous Kangaroos
Al Costello & Roy Heffernan

GUS RAAP

Gustave Raap

This interview, conducted by Scott Teal in Oct. 1997, was originally published in issue #36 of *Whatever Happened to ...?*

I was born in Hamburg, Germany on Jan. 9, 1911, to Fritz and Henrietta Raap. My dad worked with telephones. I went to Realschule [secondary school] in Hamburg and competed in wrestling and soccer. My parents wanted me to go to school and study, but I didn't think that was the thing for me, so I moved to the United States when I was 16 years old. I wrote an uncle of mine who lived in the Bronx and he sent me the papers and a ticket. It was an 11-day trip by ship. My uncle owned an ice cream parlor, so I went to work for him for a couple of years. That was when I started wrestling at the YMCA.

Did you wrestle competitive as an amateur?

No, but all the wrestlers at the YMCA were amateurs. Through the YMCA, we used to put on exhibitions for the Masonic Order, the Catholic schools. It was a show, but when they had kids fighting, we used to take them aside and give them five dollars to knock their opponents block off. Then we'd give the other guy five dollars to knock his block off. That sure stirred up the action.

I used to see wrestling at the Coliseum in the Bronx. Jack Pfefer was the promoter. "Halitosis" Pfefer. He promoted the light heavyweights ... Georgie Becker, Maurice Lachappelle, Pat Malone. I was introduced to different people and started wrestling professionally around '37, 38. We used to go to George Bothner's Gym down on 42nd Street. George was a terrific wrestler. He wrestled with Ivan the Terrible for eight hours at Union Square on 14th Street. The cops had to take 'em apart. George did the strongman stunts, like putting his hands together and having two horses try to pull them apart. We didn't make much money on the house shows, though. I'll give you one example. I worked on the main bout in Reading, Pennsylvania. We got $12.

I wrestled in carnivals for a number of years, wrestling all-comers. This was in the '40s and '50s. I worked for All-American Shows, Coleman Brothers Shows, Colonial Shows. I had my own show with a partner, Joe Ricco. He was a real showman. His brother, "Terrible" Tony Ricco, had glaucoma. When Joe got sick, I took the show over. I ran it for fifteen years or so.

The state police used to come after us, because the state athletic commission wanted you to have a doctor, a referee, and two judges ... which you didn't do. We didn't have fighters, except for one black guy. Kayo Smith from Jersey City. All I had to do was say, "*That's it,*" and he'd knock 'em out. He took on guys from the audience. He went to war and I never heard from him again.

Nine out of ten matches were shows. We had a couple of sticks working in the crowd, but most of the time, the sticks were locals ... amateur wrestlers. Today it would be tougher, because every school has a wrestling team. In them days, they didn't. Father and mother were scared to let 'em wrestle, because they figure the kid is gonna get killed. But there were times when you had guys with a little experience and they were interested in a few dollars. The rest of them got a dollar a minute. If you thought you could draw with them two or three times, you let 'em stand five minutes and give 'em five dollars. You'd come right back for seven minutes, but get the guy hot enough that people would come back and pay another quarter. That's what we used to charge. We'd gross eighteen to fifteen hundred dollars a day working twenty shows.

The travel wasn't bad. We slept in the ring some of the time, but had to stay in a hotel a few times a week, because we had to do laundry. We paid 30 percent of the gate to the house for the privilege of putting up. The stick got 20 to 25 percent. When I worked the inside, whatever came in was mine, except a percentage for the show. If I used a stick, I paid him. You could get about 400 people in the tent. It was a 30 by 40 tent. The center poles were 12 feet apart, so you get a ring that was 12 by 12 by 12. You get 'em in and out, in and out, in and out. Each time they go out, then come back in, that's another quarter.

I used to work the bally. I'd say, "*There must be one woman out there that's married to a man.*" There was a guy in upstate New York. He was bigger than Primo Carnera. He came up and says, "*I'll wrestle you.*"

I looked at him and said, "*If I was as big as you, I'd want to wrestle, too.*"

To make a long story short, it was the son of the captain of the police department. Now what do I do? You can't knock him off. I let him stand twice. At that point, I had to go over to his father to tell him what was happening, because the old man was hotter than a pistol. He didn't want his son to be a carnival bum, so I went back, beat his son, and discouraged him.

A wrestling coach from one of the local colleges wanted me to wrestle the team, from top to bottom, one at a time. I said, "*You pick 'em, I'll punish 'em.*" What do you do to get out of a situation like that? Very simple. I took the YMCA, the high school, and Cornell University ... and I matched the guys against each other on the show. They worked, and I was collecting. I wasn't paying nobody. We had an agreement that the top man was gonna get a nice wristwatch, but Saturday night it rained, so we left. We didn't have a winner, so we didn't have to give away the wristwatch.

Did you have any police protection?

No. We were at a fair in Massachusetts that was about 80 percent drunks. When we opened up, we had about ten guys, all drunk and wanting to wrestle. I went over to a cop and said, "*You'd better come over and give us a hand.*"

He said, "*If you can't handle 'em, then close up your show. We're not paid to protect you guys.*"

Did you make much money?

That's hard to say. No. You made a living. But there were days when you had fifteen hundred dollars.

Did you have problems with tough guys outside the ring?

On the carnival, they know that you can't go getting tough on the carnival lot, because of the "*Hey, Rube!*" Then the whole show is on you. You didn't have to worry about that. The average bum knows you keep your hands to yourself, or you'd get hit by a stake, or a Ford axle. Very, very rarely did you have to get tough with someone. They know if they hurt one of you, they'd have the rest of them to deal with. There were some, later on, when I was working the house shows. One guy came from Mexico and Jack Pfefer had spent quite a bit of money merchandising him. He had a nice body, but when I wrestled him on WPIX Channel 11, he tried to be "it." So I put him across my knee and tanned his ass. Jack Pfefer said, "*Do you know that cost me ten thousand dollars?*"

I said, "*That's too bad.*"

Did anyone ever offer you money to put them over, or make them look good?

Oh, sure. That's what you call invitation money. You don't mind. He don't get no money, so you've got it coming from two sides. A guy comes to me and says, "*Look, I want to wrestle you, but I can't afford to lose.*"

"*Okay, give me ten dollars and you won't.*"

So you let him stand five minutes and then he wins. You don't pin him ... just let him stay five minutes.

We had a black stick working with us, so I got him up on the bally. I said, "*You see this arm?*"

He said, "*Yeah.*"

I said, "*Let's see your arm. Is that the same color?*"

He said, "*No.*"

I said, "*Well, I ain't wrestling no nigger.*"

I wasn't racist. He was part of the show. Well, that was the start of the fun. The crowd was hotter than a pistol. I went on to say, (hollers) "*I'm a member of the master race. I'm German. I was with Hitler and I ain't takin' none of these guys! I'll take this guy, break him in half, and make mincemeat out of him.*"

If you were cooking, you could fry an egg on the tent. I said, "*The entrance for this show is one dollar, because I know nobody out there wants to spend a dollar for this show, so please don't buy no tickets. I'll wrestle this guy without an audience.*"

We sold four hundred tickets.

I had a "G" on the ring. A "G" is a fix. We had two by fours underneath the mat. We turn two of them over, so the knots are facing down, instead of up. If I take a bodyslam, them knots is gonna give. After the second body slam, I come up with a couple boards. I tell them, "*Look what the guy did. He broke my ring. What am I gonna do?*"

The people were happy. They carried him out of the ring. That was important. You get 'em fired up, then you cool 'em off. If you can't cool 'em off, then you'd better not start.

I worked some pro [house show] matches during the time I was with the AT show. I was in Florida for a few weeks [1946' and worked for [C.P.] Cowboy Luttrall. Tommy Ward was there. He was promoter later in Atlanta, Georgia.

That's right. He was known as Fred Ward.

Yeah. Mostly, I worked in the Northeast.

Lou Albano tells me you worked with him in his first match.

That's correct. I know Albano very well.

How did you get the nickname "The Lion Man"?

Al Haft.

Lebanon PA • Oct. 9, 1951

What happened to your athletic show?

I just put it in winter quarters and left it there. I left mine in Middletown, Connecticut, with the Coleman winter quarters. That was in 1953, right after I got back from Europe. I had been wrestling in Germany. I left the wrestling business completely. I wanted to go into full-time floor scraping and floor laying. My wife says, "*If you go back to wrestling, then I won't go into business with you.*" So I had a choice to make. I left wrestling behind. I took the tights off and never put them back on.

There were other reasons. The pay was getting bigger and bigger, but the rides were longer and longer. You had to do too much traveling. I made one trip in a snowstorm. I came to the tollbooth and the guy says, "*Where did you come from?*"

I says, "*From Pennsylvania.*"

He says, "*You got through?*"

I said, "*Yeah.*"

He says, "*Well, you're the first one through in a half an hour.*"

I said, "*Oh, that's all right.*"

When we got through wrestling, I got paid twelve dollars. We had something to eat, which left us with nine dollars. Now the gas ... (laughs) It didn't pay. Plus, I had three girls and a boy. I didn't want to be away from home as much. My son is a pastor and my girls are registered nurses ... one in Detroit and one up here. My oldest daughter is gone. She passed away when she was 61.

It sounds like you raised some good kids.

Well, it was the battleax that did that. That was to Mary's credit. We met in my uncle's store while I was working there ... 64 years ago. (laughs) I'm trying to trade her in now, but nobody wants me. (laughs) I retired five years ago after selling the business. We have a nice place in the country now. My hobby is taking care of my garden and my house. I have an apartment in the Bronx, so if I want to go down there for a day or two, I have a place to go.

This was the first of a series of first-person interviews conducted by Phil Willon, Sunday Press staff writer.

Press and Sun-Bulletin (Binghamton, NY): Sunday, Sept. 11, 1949

Character Study

Cracked Ribs, 87 Stitches, Cauliflower Ears, Target for Hatpin-Jabbers – But He Loves It

Wrestler Gus Raap Takes on All Comers, Curries Fans' Venom, Calls His Job Fun

In Conversation with Phil Willon

I'm going to stay in wrestling another 20 years. To me as an individual, I can't think of any better way to earn a living. It's the sport that I love. It's the life that I like to lead. I got 87 stitches in the stomach; three hernias; two internal abscesses. I had all the ribs broken, had the right shoulder broken twice, the left once, both cartilages torn in both knees, and both heels fractured.

We don't worry about getting punchy like fighters. We have two hazards that is the most common. That's glaucoma — in the eyes we get blind. And another is strep, where we might lose an arm or a leg through mat burns and we have to watch it very carefully.

CAULIFLOWER EARS

I carry 300,000 units of penicillin with me at all times. As soon as I see an infection of any kind, I give myself an injection.

Ear drums, I haven't got. And cauliflower ears, they're pretty well on their way. They're turned around, but the hearing isn't too bad.

Some people hate us; some like us. Some people curse us out, and others invite us to dinner. I mean, the contrast is so great and the difference is so great, that it's really funny. And to watch reaction of the people, there's no other business where you'll find it like wrestling.

The people come for excitement. It makes no difference what you do to make excitement. Like my hair. I wear it long on purpose. It causes commotion. Somebody always comes up and says, "What's the matter, can't you afford a haircut?"

THEY HATE ME

I tell them, "Whaddya care? What business is it of yours? You the sheriff or something?" Right away they hate me. That's important. Like we had Hatpin Mary down in New York. I mean, she used to get so excited that she actually did take a hatpin and jab the fellows with it. She was going to the extent that the New York State Athletic Commission barred her from any further arenas.

I was lucky, she never jabbed me. I tried to kick her in the face one time, but I also was lucky that I didn't catch her because I would have went to jail if I did.

Once I got hit with a chair ... seven cops standing alongside of me and I still got hit with a chair. That was in Reading, Pa. I just took a local boy and I heaved him over the top rope into the audience, and when he came back, I gave him a shot in the belly, so he flew out again and he didn't come back. And the people somehow didn't like it. In Asbury Park, I got cut with a knife by a sailor. In Washington, D.C., I got hit with a Coca-Cola bottle on the head. In these fairs, I got hit with two-by-fours, shoes, whatever there was handy, I got hit with.

But, I mean, you get hit, you get mad, and in a couple of minutes you laugh about it. That's all there is to it. It's fun.

Television has helped. Today, if you look at the audience, you'll see you have 60 to 75 percent women, which prior to television wouldn't dare come near them because they thought it was awful.

THE FAIR CIRCUIT

This is the third year we've been hitting the summer fairs. It's a lot of fun. You get a lot of good boys on the road, and we get a lot of bums. They get $100 if they pin me, and if they stay for five minutes they get a dollar a minute.

Last year we played the Ithaca Fair. So the first day we came in, everything is pretty quiet. We had a couple of nice little shows and it was going along swell. The second day, a coupl'a boys came in and they was getting pretty spry. The third day come the revolution. The whole team [wrestling] come down from Cornell one day, the next day Ithaca High, and the next day the Ithaca Y. So I had my hands full, and I mean, I had them full.

OLYMPIC WRESTLER

Glen Stafford was the biggest. He was the trainer of Cornell University a few years ago and he was an Olympic heavyweight wrestler. I just kept away from him as much as possible and hoped that the five minutes go out quick. I ran, and I mean I ran for dear life. All I actually was interested in was staying away from him. Never mind the $5. I rather give him $5 more.

Originally, I'm born and raised in Hamburg. Germany. I came to this country in 1927 by my lonesome. Wrestling in Germany is more or less of a national sport, like baseball is over here, but it's scientific.

Here, in wrestling, there is a lot of showmanship, there's no question about it, and I'm not going to insult anybody's intelligence. But the American people more or less ask for it.

Originally, I came over to get out of school. My father had quite a bit of money and he wanted me to study. He was the second highest man on the telephone in the German government. Over there, the telephone is run by the government.

When I first landed, I worked in a store for an uncle of mine, an ice-cream parlor up in the Bronx. I was working seven days a week, 18 hours a day, for $25 a month and twice a week I got a licking. I started wrestling as soon as I got here for the Bronx Union YMCA.

I worked for my uncle just long enough that I could speak English and get out on my own. Then I saw America. I took off. Freight cars, buses, anything that could go faster than I could walk. In seven months I saw 48 states. Then I settled in the Bronx again and started wrestling again. I started working for a carpenter, a floor-layer.

I turned pro in 1933. I had a fellow out in San Antonio, Tex. He was wrestling amateur and he saw possibilities in me, so he approached me and said to make me a little money. So during the day I was wrestling amateur, and at night pro under another name, and an organization was paying for my amateur status and expenses, so between the two of us we did excellent.

Then the amateur union found out about it, and, of course, I got booted out, and then I had no choice of the matter and I stood pro and I've been wrestling pro ever since.

I'm not sorry.

The last match in my records for Gus was the Oct. 16, 1954, match in Reading that he mentioned earlier in the interview.

Gus was living at 4585 Park Avenue in the Bronx in 1951. At the time of this interview, he lived at 315 Meyers Corner Road in Wappingers Falls, New York.

I have been unable to find any newspaper reports about his death, but Tim Hornbaker pegs it at Sept. 5, 2002. The SSDI has a "Gustave Raap" born in 1911 who died on that date.

ALL STAR
WORLD'S
CHAMPIONSHIP
WRESTLING
at the
MUNICIPAL FIELD
Millville, N. J.
Thursday, Oct. 1st
8:30 P.M.
For the
JR. HEAVYWEIGHT
CHAMPIONSHIP OF
THE WORLD!
MARVIN
(Atomic)
MERCER
The Jr. Heavyweight Champion and holder of the JIM LONDOS BELT.
VS.
GUS RAAP
Champion of Germany
In the Semi-Finals
Sid Dorenberg
Champion of Belgium
vs.
Comacho Cortez
Champion of Mexico
Australian
Tag Team Match
New Jersey vs. New York
PRICES:
$1.30 General Admission
tax included
RESERVED SEATS
$2.25 tax included
Tickets on sale at Millville Bus Terminal
Phone 292 or the
SPORT SPOT
Millville 2074-W

MARVIN MERCER

WRESTLING
Reading Armory
SAT. NITE 8:45, Oct. 16
Bert Bertolini Promotion
Main Event 2 Out of 3 Falls
Marvin Mercer
vs.
Gus Raap
TAG TEAM
TEDDY BREUR and
BARBRA La ROSA
VS.
LENNY SCHAEFFER and
ED CLINCH
Roy Wayne vs Siol Doernberg
Tickets now on Sale at Kagen's
641 Penn St. Adms. $1.25 - $2.50

WRESTLING
Blytheville Legion Arena
Monday, July 15, 8:15 p. m.
Adults, 36c, Tax 9c—Total 45c. Reserved Seats 12c, Tax 3c—Total, 15c. Children's Seats 12c, Tax 3c, Total, 15c.
Reserved Seats on Sale at the Legion Arena Every Monday From 6 p. m. on
TAG MATCH
Tex Riley and Tommy Ward
vs.
Barefoot Ballard and
Gus Raap
Also 2 One-Fall 30-Minute Matches
TEX RILEY vs. BAREFOOT BALLARD
TOMMY WARD vs. GUS RAAP

(above) Millville NJ • Oct. 1, 1953
(top r.) Reading PA • Oct. 16, 1954
(bottom r.) Blytheville AR • July 15, 1946

High Spots

EVERYTHING EXCEPT PINK ELEPHANTS

by Dano McDonald

(reprinted from Dean Silverstone's reunion program)

I don't know first-hand about this story, but it went around the Midwest for a long time, so I'm sure it is in part true.

Lou Klein was the booker for the wrestling midgets. In fact, I think he was the founder. As you probably know, there were several groups on the road at all times. Most years, they would all gather at Christmas at the booking office in Detroit, Michigan, to review the coming season. Well, it seems that some social club nearby wanted a battle royal with as many midgets as available. Lou put it to the group as a good easy payoff and all agreed.

He loaded them all in a van and headed out for the shot. It was a cold, icy evening. On the old two-lane road they were on, up in front of them was a drunk who was driving all over the road and eventually ended up in a ditch in the snow. They stopped the van and could see that the driver was okay.

Lou suggested to the group, we could have some fun with this guy. He told them to put on as much of their gimmick clothes as they could and help him out of the ditch. Well, I guess it was a nightmare to the drunk to see little Indians, cowboys, little black chiefs, arabs, a little gentleman in a beautiful suit and fedora, a little Englishman in a derby, and others, all climbing in and out and over this man's car, and Lou telling him it was all in his mind — that there was only Lou and him there.

They got the car on the road and made him promise to sleep it off. Lou left his jewelry business card in the drunk's car. One year later, he got a letter from this person thanking him for his help and to say he has had nothing to drink in a year.

HOMEMADE COOKIES

by Rocket Monroe

When we were in Quincy [FL] one night, Flash [Monroe] and Ken Ramey hid my bag. I thought somebody had stolen it, because they had the police in on the rib. I was riding with them, and when I got home, I caught them trying to sneak it in my car. Well, Flash had a weakness for chocolate, so I waited a couple of weeks. I melted a 49-cent package of Ex-Lax over a bunch of homemade cookies. I planned to get Flash and Ramey both, but Ramey didn't ride with us that night. When we got to Mobile, Flash was grinning from ear to ear. I knew he was up to something, but I wasn't sure what he was up to, and I had forgotten about the cookies. I found out that while we were driving, he had snuck into the cookies ... and ate every last one. He had a real problem in the ring that night.

LEO GARIBALDI

This interview was conducted by Scott Teal in April 2005.

Your dad, Gino Garibaldi, got into wrestling sometime around 1928. The earliest mention I can find in newspaper of your dad is an article in the *Philadelphia Inquirer* that said he was "a newcomer here from sunny Italy" and the article indicated that he had wrestled before coming to the States.

Yes and no. My dad *was* an Italian immigrant, but he never said anything about wrestling professionally in Italy. What I do know is that he was working out in a St. Louis gym and met some professional wrestlers. They were looking for an Italian hero because there were a lot of Italian people in St. Louis. At the time, the world champion was Jimmy Londos. The two of them had some classic matches, including a main event at Madison Square Garden on November 17, 1930.

Londos defeated Gino on that night to retain the world heavyweight title. The pair drew a reported 22,000 fans and set an all-time indoor attendance record of $46,800. However, Jack Curley, the promoter, was an outrageous liar, well-known for inflating attendance figures, so it's likely that the claimed 22,000 wasn't legitimate. In fact, two New York newspapers, The *Daily News* and The *Standard Union*, reported the crowd as 18,000, the *St. Louis Post-Dispatch* said it was 20,000 (which filled every seat in the Garden), while other newspapers reported attendance at 16,000. Vince McMahon did the same thing in the '70s when he slowed nudged up crowd numbers to "set" records.

Because of his success, he created opportunities for his brothers to wrestle — Chick, whose real name was Charles, Ralph, Tony, and Joe. So, I was born into what you might call a wrestling family, but Gino was the only big star. Chick died in the ring. [Feb. 18, 1961] He had a heart attack after a match with Bruno Sammartino.

Ralph did pretty good. He wrestled for at least ten years, maybe longer. Joe didn't make it at all. I talked with him recently. He said he had one match and threw up in the ring. That was it for him. Tony didn't last too long in the business ... maybe ten years, if that. It was kind of rough then.

Ralph's career seems to have begun in 1934 and extended into the mid-'50s. Prior to that, from 1929 through 1930, he was an amateur wrestler at the

North Side YMCA in St. Louis. In Feb. 1957, shortly after his in-ring career ended, he received a referee's license for the state of Missouri and worked occasionally as a referee for Sam Muchnick in St. Louis.

Do you know much about what Gino did before he got into wrestling?

He was a coal miner, but he gave that up after a cave-in.

Tell me a little about your childhood.

I was born on July 19, 1929, in St. Louis, the Mecca for wrestling at that time. I spent my childhood there and in Long Island, New York. I had to go to school and I couldn't follow my dad around, so they parked me in New York Military Academy in Cornwall-on-Hudson, New York. That was in '43, so I must have been fourteen. I was 16 when they diagnosed it [polio]. Fortunately, I came out of it unscathed. I had some weakness in my back, but it went away. I was very lucky. It was tough being a kid and laying around, thinking you're gonna be a cripple.

Did your classmates know your dad was Gino Garibaldi?

Oh, yeah. My dad's friends were always showing me moves, like I was their favorite kid. As the son of a guy who was a big-time wrestler, other boys would want to take me on, so I had to uphold the Garibaldi name. I felt that I couldn't possibly lose one match or I would disgrace my father's name. That sounds kind of silly now, but that's how I felt.

So you were bullied because your dad was a pro wrestler?

Early on, yes, before I got into the amateurs. When I was just a kid-kid, the bullies used to single me out because I was the son of a wrestler. I think the turning point in my life might have been when I started amateur wrestling. When I came home on vacation, the same kids would try to take me on and I just handled them like they were children. (laughs) I kind of liked that. (laughs)

Leo was captain of the wrestling team at the military academy and wrestled in the 196-pound class.

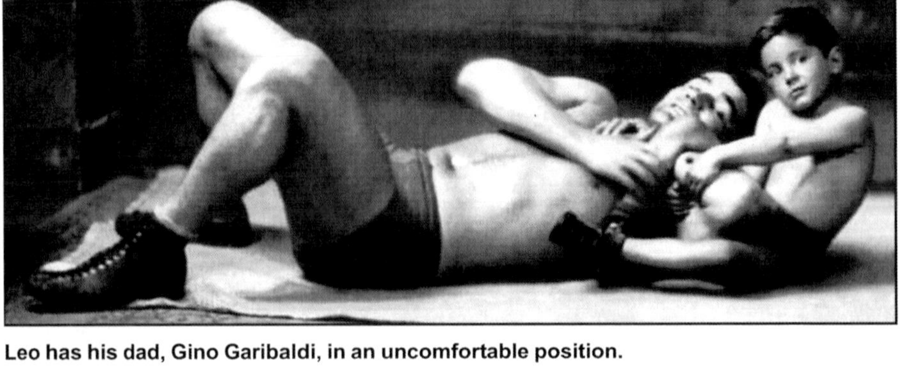

Leo has his dad, Gino Garibaldi, in an uncomfortable position.

When you were a child, did you travel with your dad often?

I didn't get to travel with my dad much, but I went with him during summer vacations. I went with him to Canada in the summer of 1946, just before my senior year. That's when I had my very first match. We went to a little French-Canadian town [pause] ... I forget the name of it now. Somebody didn't show up, so they whipped out some shoes and tights and gave them to me. *"The kid wrestles in school, so he can wrestle here."* It was the opening match and I went the distance. That pleased my dad ... and me, too. (laughs) I was hooked.

WRESTLING
ARENA 46th & Market | Friday Nite MARCH 1
ED (Strangler) Lewis vs. Gino Garibaldi
The UPRISING ITALIAN SENSATION
H. CANTOWINE vs. CAPT. SMITH
PAT McGILL vs JOE STENGLE
MAIN TICKET OFFICE 41 S. 15th St.
Prices $1, $2, $3; Locust 4200—1540-41

Philadelphia PA • March 1, 1929

Did you always think you'd wind up in the wrestling business?

I always felt that, somehow, I'd end up in wrestling. I never could see myself doing anything else. My dad didn't think it was a good idea. He wanted me to be a doctor or lawyer. Once I established myself, though, he was there to help me. I had a lot of help that most people never got. I was made aware of many of the pitfalls, such as guys who tried to stretch me out of jealousy.

Do you remember any of the wrestlers who came to your house to see your father when you were a kid?

Lou Thesz, for one. Ray Steele, Paul Jones. Once I got into the business, I had so many of the great, great old-timers sharing their intimate secrets.

So you started wrestling as soon as you graduated from high school. Did you ever work a civilian job after that?

No. I was hooked after that first match. That was it for me. That's what I wanted to do. I got paid for it, too.

Do you remember how much your payoff was for that match in Canada?

Yeah, it was $140. (laughs) Fifty years ago, that was like a thousand dollars to a teenage kid.

Actually, 50 years ago, that was like a thousand dollars to a grownup. I would imagine the money also helped spark your interest in pursuing a career in wrestling.

Oh, absolutely. Of course, I'd have done it for free. The money was just a big bonus. The telecaster at the time in Jamaica, New York, was Dennis James. When I went to California, Steve Allen was the ring announcer.

What training did you have?

My dad built a ring in the back yard. (laughs) Believe it or not, he didn't have any ropes, so he made them out of chain link. We lived in a country town ... Lindenhurst, Long Island. People would drive by and see this big wrestling ring ... and my dad training me.

Who promoted New York at the time?

Milo Steinborn, Rudy Dusek.

What did your mother think about you following in your dad's footsteps?

I really don't know. I guess she must have (pause) ... that's a good question. (laughs) I never asked her.

How long was it, from the time you graduated from high school, that you actually began a full-time career in wrestling?

About a year.

Do you remember where you had your first official match?

Jamaica, Long Island.

Who did you wrestle?

I swore I'd never forget his name (pause, laughs) ... uh, I guess I forgot. It was nobody of any note.

The first newspaper report found for Leo in a professional match was found in the July 18, 1947, edition of the Wilmington, Delaware, *Morning News*. Leo, billed at 190 pounds from St. Louis, wrestled to a 30-minute draw with Olaf Erickson. In the main event on that card, Marvin Mercer and Joe Montana scored an upset victory over Gino and Chick Garibaldi.

It appears that, for two months, Leo was billed as Gino's youngest brother. The Sept. 5, 1947, *Evening News* in Harrisburg, Pennsylvania, reported "*Three brothers, Gino, Chick and Leo Garibaldi, will be in featured matches ... The oldest of the St. Louis triumvirate, Gino, will take on George Macricostas ... Leo, youngest of the battling Garibaldi clan, will meet another Greek grappler, Mano Mellas.*"

During that same time, other newspapers listed Leo as "the 18-year-old son of Chick and nephew of Gino". By mid-September, newspapers were accurately reporting that Leo was Gino's son.

You worked with Dave Levin in one of my earliest records of your career.

Oh, yes. He was one of my idols. He had polio as a kid, too. That's why he wore those long tights. His legs were kind of shriveled up, but he had a great upper body. I had a lot of respect for him.

In 1949, we moved to Los Angeles. My dad was wrestling there and it was the era of wrestling on TV. We were billed as "the only father-and-son wrestling team in the business". Due to the exposure on TV, I became what you might call the teenage idol of California. I became very popular and made so much money it was insane. I did things on the TV show like play the accordion, and promote vitamins. My interviews at the time went something like, "*Leo, you're wrestling so-and-so tonight.*"

"*Yes, I am, and you know, I feel real good about this because I'm taking my Orvita Vitamins. They give me a lot of strength and I feel real good. And, you know ... after the matches, I'll be making a personal appearance out at yak-yak place, giving out my pictures and orchids to the ladies. I'd like to see my fans out there. This Sunday, I'll be at the Hudson automobile dealership on Manchester. I'll be driving my new Hudson over and will be glad to sign autographs.*"

You had a fan club called Leo's Loverettes, who were based out of Long Beach.

That's right. Billy Darnell once told me that he had a fan club in Baltimore called Billy Darnell's Darnell Darlings.

The Teen Set
by Betty Betz

I was quite astonished to learn Hollywood fans are passing the drool cup to Leo Garibaldi, the 22-year-old "junior wrestling king of America". I watched several thousands screaming dollies mob this muscle man at a department store autograph party, and then asked what had become of the screen heroes they used to idolize … before I left for Korea. "We all like the wrestlers on TV!" some girls sighed. When I asked if there were lady wrestlers for the boys, I learned that "in California, they're illegal"! So, the fellas there have to settle for Ava Gardner! Tough!

— *Honolulu* (HI) *Advertiser*: Monday, Dec. 3, 1951

Dr. Lee Grable had a fan club called the Grable-ettes in San Diego.

I didn't know that. I had three brand-new cars given to me ... one for my dad, one for me, and one for our business manager. We had a business manager who did nothing but book non-wrestling gigs for us. There were so many people who wanted to equate themselves with wrestling as sponsors. I ran into one guy who said he saw me playing the accordion on TV. He said, "*I have a band that will be doing some rehearsing this Sunday. Would you like to come and play your accordion?*"

"*Oh, sure. I'd love to.*" I went there and found out I'd been tricked. They were making a record, but didn't let me know until they did it. I sat in and played, then I found out that they'd been recording me. They asked my permission to use the material, so I said, "*Hell, yes. Why not?*" (laughs) I still have the record.

They sold all kinds of stuff in the arenas. (laughs) They had salt and pepper shakers made of me and my dad, which I still have a pair here. I appeared on a lot of TV shows. It was wild! We made appearances and wrestled seven nights a week, stuffing money in the bank the whole time. My dad, being Italian … he'd come up the hard way.

That's how I got started, so you can see how guys would be jealous of me. And they ought to be, but it was just one of those things. I had the background, I was a teenager, (laughs) and I was a good bullshitter, too.

Did you use your given name in the early years?

Good question. We moved to California in January '49, but they didn't want to use me under the Garibaldi name. They said if I bombed out, it would make my dad look bad, so I took a Mexican name ... Frankie Garza. There was a wrestler in California before me named Manuel Garza, so they brought me in as his brother. I wrestled for five months before they revealed who I really was.

I was pretty successful as Frankie Garza, so they decided to reveal my true identity on TV. They told the people that I didn't want to disgrace my dad's name and wanted to make it on my own, so I wrestled under an assumed name ... and the fans liked that. Basically, it was true. At that time, there was a wrestler named Stanley Pinto. His son was starting out, too. His son broke his back and never wrestled again. His name was Jack Pinto.

I never knew that Stanley Pinto had a son who wrestled.

Yeah, when you're gone, nobody ever heard of you. (laughs) They didn't want anybody to know. The last thing they wanted anybody to know is that somebody got hurt. It kind of takes away from the glamour of it.

You won the world junior heavyweight title from Red Berry in Los Angeles on March 8, 1950. At the time, you were the youngest wrestler to ever hold that title.

That's right. I had to give it up when I went into the service.

On Oct. 27, 1951, Leo weighed in at 210 pounds and was inducted into the U.S. Air Force as a private first-class in the 921st Reserve Training Wing, Long Beach Air Force Base. The Second Photographic Squadron based at the base filmed Leo's induction into the service.

A few weeks before that, on Oct. 3, Leo dropped the belt to Red Berry. Rube Samuelsen, a columnist for the *Los Angeles Evening Citizen News*, picked up on the fact that Leo was going into the service when he wrote: "*Leo Garibaldi, the rassler, is Army-bound, which may account for his recent defeats, and also his dethronement as junior heavyweight titlist. Wrestling, of course, is like that, and yet, the DA pays a call when such things happen in other sports.*"

In November, he was transferred to Lackland Air Base in San Antonio. At that time, a newspaper reported that he was hoping the Air Force would allow him to wrestle occasionally.

On March 15, 1952, a letter to the editor in the *Los Angeles Mirror* asked the question, "*Why is it, demands a mat fan, that sailors and marines were allowed to box on a CBS-TV program, but Leo Garibaldi is not allowed to wrestle? Who makes the rules? A commanding officer can do what he pleases in matters of this nature. It's entirely up to him and how he feels about the extracurricular activities of his men in his command in their off-duty hours.*"

Leo was released from the service in 1955 while he was stationed at Bergstrom Air Force Base, where he was a U.S. Army physical training instructor at March Field, Riverside.

I got hurt a lot. In fact, after I had my last match, which was in the Olympic Auditorium in November 1961, that's when I became a promoter because nobody else would give me a job. I mean, who could I work for? I had no skills at anything except wrestling.

Leo's last full-time match was in Los Angeles on Nov. 15 when he wrestled Ramon Torres. He broke his shoulder during the match, and under advice from his doctor, he made the decision to quit wrestling in Jan. 1962. At the time, he lived in San Bernardino and served as the announcer of the matches at the 137 S.G. St. Arena.

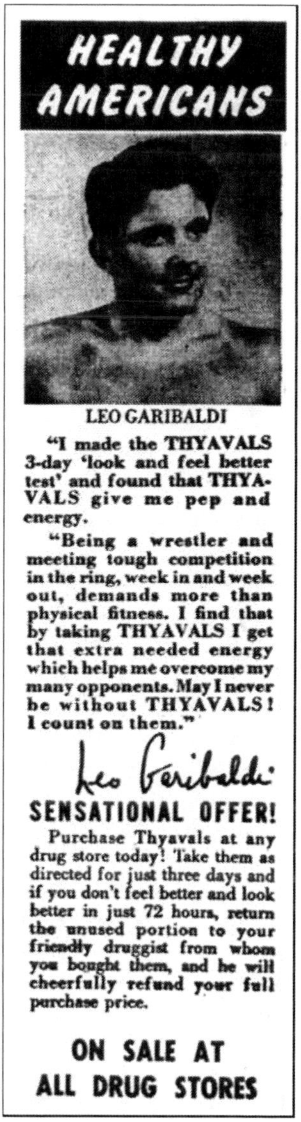

(above)
Los Angeles Times
Monday, April 2, 1951

(top l.) Asbury Park NJ
Sept. 19, 1947

(left) Fresno CA
July 8, 1949

Where did you first start promoting?

Actually, it was in Tyler, Texas. Tyler was just a little, shit town, but it was so successful. When I was promoting Tyler, it was out-drawing some of the bigger cities. Paul Boesch asked me to go into Austin, which was a dead town. That must have been '61.

Leo first card as a promoter took place at the Mayfair Arena in Tyler on March 13, 1962. The *Kilgore News Herald* reported that "the fact that countless attempts to promote here have long since gone sour doesn't discourage Leo, who claims he can give the public big-enough shows to put Tyler back on the grappling mat." It was a resounding success with approximately 700 paid fans attending to see Al Torres defeated the Zebra Kid in the main event. Leo promoted matches in Tyler every Tuesday night.

What did you do that was different from what had been done before?

Well, the first thing you've gotta do is get the boys on your side ... and pay 'em. (laughs) I gave 'em fantastic payoffs. They'd bust their ass for you, then ... and rightfully so. That's the way it should be.

It's funny, but even with the big money they're making now, the promoters are still screwin' 'em to the limit. Sure, they're getting a thousand instead of a hundred dollars, but the promoters are raking in millions. I have great empathy for the boys. I understand that they love the game so much that they'd eat shit rather than quit, which is how it's always been. Not only that, but what would they do?

Going back in time a little, after you were injured in Los Angeles, why did you choose to move to Texas?

My wife, Sammy, was from Texas. I met her while she was on vacation in California. We thought we'd look for a job in Texas ... something to get by on for a while. I got a job working in a 7-Eleven, stacking groceries. I was up on a ladder putting groceries up when Paul Boesch walked in to get some stuff. Oh, I was humiliated.

So he knew you?

Oh, yeah. He asked me to come up and see him. He said, "*Why don't you think about promoting wrestling?*"

I told him, "*I don't have any money to start the towns.*"

He said, "*Well, it wouldn't take much to open up someplace like Tyler. We've never done any good there.*"

(ad at right) Leo's first promotion • Tyler TX • March 13, 1962

I said, "*Well, maybe I'll give it a try.*" And I did. My wife was from Rusk [40 miles from Tyler]. I went up to Tyler and I liked the venue and everything. What I learned is that no one actually promoted the town. They paid some kid to put up some window posters, but that's not enough. I knew it would take more, and I was willing to do whatever it took, especially when my only option was to go back to the grocery store. (laughs)

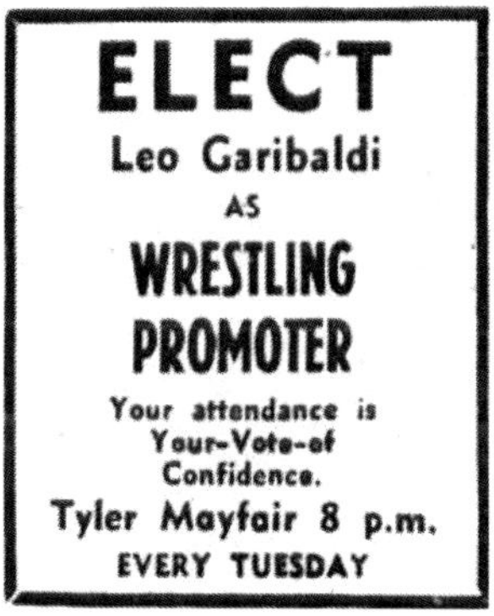

Tyler Morning Telegraph
May 2, 1962

I took posters around and was a one-man publicity campaign for wrestling. You get two or 300 posters, then go into places like barbershops and talk to people. You ask if they'll put a poster in the window. Sometimes, they'd say they didn't want to. You say, "*Hey, look. If you'll do it, I'll give you these four complimentary tickets to see the wrestling.*"

"*Well, I don't like wrestling.*"

"*Well, how about some of your customers? They do, don't they? Wouldn't they be pleased? You'd probably get a big tip if you give them some wrestling tickets.*"

"*Yeah, that sounds okay.*"

Then you go to the newspaper guy and they don't want nothing to do with wrestling. I'd say, "*I know you like to pitch basketball, football, and so on, but wrestling is coming here whether you like it or not. If you ignore it, and it becomes real popular, and you haven't even mentioned it, how will that look? I guarantee you it's gonna become popular. I'm not gonna let it flop. I'll tell you what. I'll buy some nice ads in the paper. If you'll play ball and give me a hand, I'll take out an ad right now.*"

So, you do these kind of things. You buy ads and beg whatever you can for free ... and, of course, then you have to have enough sense to know what's gonna draw and what's not. You could do all the preliminary legwork and still go right down if you book shit. You have to get some talent there ...

So, did you actually book that first show, or did Paul tell you who he was going to send and what the lineup would be?

No, I had to fight for the talent, just like you do anything else. "*This is who I'd like to have.*" He had to be finagled just like anybody else. I'd say, "*I know that so-and-so doesn't like to work these small towns, but this is the strength of the game. We've all been through this. You set me up here, so now, if you want it to succeed, you have to help me out. I don't have to have your big stars. Just give me some guys that can wrestle. Give me some guys that will bust their ass and become local stars. I can make my own stars. I just need some people to do the job.*"

Do you remember who you booked on that first show?

I think Jerry Kozak was there. (pause) Later, I brought in Tuffy Truesdale's wrestling bear, Victor, and his alligator. I booked Joe Christie, Tosh Togo, Danny McShain. Those are the only ones that ring a bell. Oh, yeah. Ivan the Terrible was a great draw. He wrestled later as Pampero Firpo.

What kind of money deal did Paul work with you?

The split is always the same. The booking office takes ten percent off the top, which is their charge for booking. The wrestlers get 50 to 60 percent and the promotion gets 40 to 50 percent. All the expenses come out of your percentage (laughs) ... and the office gets their money whether or not there's people there.

It sounds like you actually worked hard to promote your events, as opposed to guys who just put up a few posters and expect people to hear about it by word of mouth. Did you study other promoters during the years you wrestled to learn the secrets of successful promoting?

(pause) Yes, it was my background, but the secret wasn't in studying the promoters. When I was a kid, I'd sit in the dressing room and listen to the boys talk. You had to have motivated men. When they get in the ring, they had to get the job done. I knew when they were dogging it ... and they knew I knew.

You'd been there.

That's it (laughs) ... and they also know when you're fucking them on the payoff. Then they *will* dog it. It was a lot of things. Number one, you have to go around and talk to the people who can help you, and show them where it helps them.

Did you father have any experience as a booker or promoter?

No, not a bit. For those old-timers, the business became a completely different ballgame. The focus of everything began to revolve around TV, so you had to get those people on your side. When I went to [promote] Austin next, there was only one TV station. Lyndon Johnson owned it, and he wasn't about to have me on there. It was beneath his dignity and he was lookin' to be the President. So, I bought time. I couldn't afford it, but I bought it anyway, because I had to have it. I had to have TV more than anything else.

Did you use Paul Boesch's tapes?

No. His tapes weren't what I wanted. I was trying to teach people wrestling, and they were doing stuff they had been doing for hundreds of years. It wouldn't help me. The thing was, if I was paying for it, I wanted the time for myself. I could only afford fifteen minutes, but that was fifteen minutes to get my message across, brother.

What did you do, have two short matches and a couple of interviews?

That's it ... interviews of what's comin' up. Two short matches, but those matches were great, hard-fought matches. I also donated my time to the YMCA in Tyler, teaching kids to wrestle. I enjoyed working with those kids because they picked things up quickly.

Did the boys treat you any differently when you became their quote-unquote boss?

The boys loved me because I paid them. That was the main thing. If you did everything else right and screwed the boys, you would not get a hundred percent. I took it to this point. When it was time for a guy to leave ... well, let's say a promoter came to me when I was the booker. He'd say, "*Leo, we've gotta get rid of this guy. He's been here too long. Give him his notice.*" Two weeks, you know. What I would do is call all the different territories and build this guy up. I'd try to book him somewhere. When I'd get a booking for him, I'd tell the promoter, "*I'm gonna have to call you back and confirm this because this is one of my best people. I just need to get him out of here for a while, then bring him back in about six months when he'll be fresh again, but he'll do wonders for your territory.*" I'd confirm the date and tell them I'd call back.

I'd call this guy into my office and say, "*Jack, we're so pleased with what you've done here, but as you know, you can't stay here forever.*" You pause ... and he begins to look nervous. "*So-and-so in El Paso has called me and he'd like you to come in there. He heard about your work and thinks you'd do a lot for him. It'll give you a rest from here and help you for when you come back. I really think you should do it. Here's his phone number. Why don't you give him a call? He's waiting to hear from me, but it would be even better if you'd call.*"

The guy calls and the promoter says, "*Oh, yeah! We'd like you to come in on so-and-so date.*"

The guys hangs up and says, "*Oh, Leo! How can I thank you for giving me this opportunity? I have a family to support and I had nowhere to go from here.*" I'd been there myself and knew how it was.

There are so many of the guys, though, who later became promoters, and forgot all about taking care of the boys.

Oh, I know. There's a big difference when you're actually raised in the business. It's more than a place to earn some money. I know how I would feel if somebody told me, "*Get the hell out.*"

I'd estimate that out of ten responses I get to a question of who the boys consider to have been one of the most creative bookers in the business, seven will mention your name.

Oh, I'm so pleased to hear that. That's great to hear.

What kind of money did Tyler do?

A thousand or two, which was tremendous because I only charged a dollar for general admission and $1.50 for ringside. We had many, many sellouts. I think my biggest was 1,300, which was the most Mayfair Arena could hold. On average, though, we drew a little more than a thousand each week.

Did the first show sell out?

Almost ... but, my God! I worked so hard on it. I had cards up everywhere. Half the auditorium was comped because I was determined to have people there the first night. We wanted people to see what we had to offer.

The Texas promoters needed more towns for the boys to work in, too. Since it did so well, I was able to pick and choose who I wanted. I wouldn't necessarily ask for the big stars. When those guys are booked in a little shit town, they're not gonna bust their butt. The boys told me they loved to work for me because I paid them right. They said they made as much money working for me in this little shit town as they did in Dallas. It gives me a good feeling to know that I took care of the boys and treated them with respect.

What night of the week did it run?

Let's see. They ran Houston on Friday, Saturday was Beaumont.

They ran Fort Worth on Monday and Dallas on Tuesday.

That's right. It was Tuesday. I got the guys they didn't use in Dallas. When I started to promote Austin, I couldn't devote as much time to Tyler, so it fell by the wayside. People lost interest. I had people putting up posters, but that's not enough. Somebody had to be there and take advantage of every opportunity.

Leo's promoted his last card in Tyler on Oct. 30, 1962. A *Tyler Morning Telegraph* article the next morning quoted him as saying, "*Due to failing attendance, this is my last night of scheduled wrestling in Tyler,*" which falls in line with what Leo said in the previous paragraph.

On July 12, 1962, the Austin city council approved a 13-week lease of the City Coliseum for Leo's Thursday night shows for $100 a week. Leo's first show, scheduled for Aug. 9, was delayed one week due to a conflict with the Aqua Festival being held at the Coliseum. His debut card drew almost 2,000 fans to see Nick and Jerry Kozak retain their world tag team title against the challenge of the Mummy and Cyclops.

On Jan. 9, 1964, Leo packed 3,400 fans into the Coliseum to see Lou Thesz defend his NWA world heavyweight title against Danny Hodge.

Austin American
Jan. 16, 1964

My method of promotion was not the usual. The only way I knew to promote was to get the guys out there and let 'em go at each other. I had a funny experience. When I was promoting in Austin, I had the Harlem Stars against former University of Texas basketball stars. As promoter, you had to supply the team to play the Stars. Basically, everybody feels like the team that plays these guys is supposed to kind of lay back and let them do their stuff. These college boys were All-State champions in basketball. They said, "*Mr. Garibaldi. What are we supposed to do?*"

I said, "*Well, hell! Go out there and whip their ass.*"

Those guys [Harlem Stars] were really, really surprised ... because they were doing their little dipsy-doodle, and one of those Texas boys got the ball, run up the court, and boom! Dunk! All of a sudden, they were ahead ten or fifteen points. The Stars called a timeout and got together. I can imagine what they said. "*We're gonna have to show these guys some respect.*" It turned into a really tough basketball game with no bullshit or showmanship. Those kids had their tongues hangin' out. They just didn't have the conditioning of the younger guys. After everyone got that out of their system, they went back to their razzle-dazzle style and finished the game. First, though, they had to learn their lesson about who the boss was. (laughs)

The basketball exhibition, which ended with a score of 53-52 in favor of the Harlem Stars, took place on Feb. 5, 1965. One year earlier, on Jan. 17, 1964, Leo brought the Harlem Stars in to play former University of Texas alumni, ich he called "Garibaldi's Grapplers". The Stars won the game 98-46.

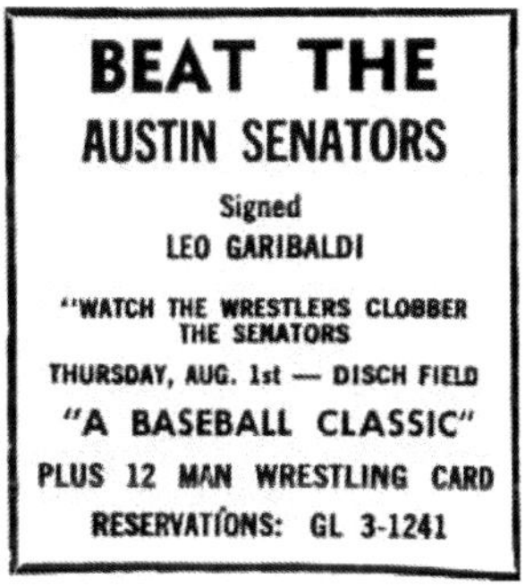

Austin American
Aug. 1, 1963

I also promoted a baseball game. Pro baseball wasn't doing too good in Austin, so I made a match with the Austin Senators against the wrestlers. My team had Jack and Jim Dalton, Mark Lewin, Ricki Starr, Tiger Conway, Nick Kozak, Bob Ellis. We did some interviews. "*Yeah, we watched these guys play and they're the shits. We're gonna show them just how bad they are.*" It drew really well. Before the game, the baseball players came to see me and said, "*You know, we appreciate this. It's really giving us a boost in our gate, but do you want us to do something special with these guys?*"

I said, "*No, just make them look as bad as you can. And I'll tell you what ... when we look so bad that the people can't believe it, we're just gonna knock the shit out of you guys.*" (laughs) That's what we did. They looked like the best team, then they got the shit knocked out of 'em. (laughs) You know, you have to do things in small towns. There was only one TV station, and it was owned by Lyndon Johnson. When you don't even have TV, you have to be imaginative.

(laughs) I brought in Victor the Bear ... Tuffy Truesdale's bear. [Nov. 22, 1962] Texas A&M had a big rivalry with the Longhorns. They had this one big game every year. When the Texas Aggies came to play, they brought all the Aggies and all their support and had a big parade right through the heart of Austin. No one would give me permission to drive in the parade because it was an Aggie parade, not a Texas parade. I put ribbons with Texas colors all over this red Pontiac convertible that I had, and then put Victor the Bear in the back seat of the car, up high, like he was a celebrity. I had signs on the side of the car that said, "See Victor the wrestling bear wrestle Tony Borne tonight at the Auditorium." Fifty thousand people attended that parade. I sat in the car on a side street until I saw an opening and snuck right in. (laughs) That's promotion! (laughs)

One of the things I'm proudest of is a benefit show that I ran. A cop named Don Carpenter got killed in a liquor store robbery. Everybody knew him at the matches. He took care of things at the wrestling all the time I'd been there. I was asked to run a show to help his widow. I thought about it and thought about it. It would serve two purposes. It would be great publicity for my shows and would help her financially. You won't believe what I learned.

I decided that I had to be careful of repercussions that would surely come ... that I stole money or made money on the deal. I knew how these so-called charity shows worked. They keep most of the money. I talked to my wife about it and told her that "*I will have the first honest, legitimate wrestling show ever. Every dime will go to the widow.*" The cost of the tickets ... the cost of the ads. Even the press will have to buy a ticket if they want to get in.

I found out that it was a tough nut. When I went to the ticket printers, I laid it out to 'em. I said, "*I'm going to have a charity show and I want you to print the tickets.*"

He said, "*Okay, that's gonna be seventy-five dollars.*"

I said, "*This is a charity show. We'd like you to contribute the tickets.*"

"*Oh, we don't do that.*"

I said, "*I also need you to do my program for me. I want you to print a full-page ad saying that all the tickets and programs were printed and donated by you to the trust fund.*"

The more I talked about what a big thing it was going to be in Austin, the more they liked it. The newspaper was next. "*Blah, blah, blah.*" The same thing. "*You know we don't like to fool with wrestling, Leo, but we're gonna get behind you on this one.*"

I said, "*Well, what I want is free ads for the show.*"

"*Oh, no! We don't do that!*"

I said, "*I know you don't, but at the bottom of the ad, you print* 'This advertisement paid for by the Austin newspaper in honor of the Don Carpenter Trust Fund.' *What wonderful publicity for your newspaper.*"

You have to force it down their throat. What can they say, though? They can argue about it. They can say they have to go to someone else about it. Eventually, if you're really set on doing it, you can do it. I had to go to the radio and TV station and do the same thing. But I made it real clear to everyone. "*I don't make a dime off of this.*"

This wasn't a wrestling show. I hired local acts to come in and do this thing. It was the same with them. They wanted to get paid.

It was more of a variety show.

That's right. The crying started when I wouldn't let the press in. They had to buy a ticket. That's when they realized that I was serious about it being a benefit. There was a group of ladies who were married to the police and had regular meetings. I put them in charge of selling the tickets, to be sure none of the money was diverted away from the trust fund. So, I kept myself clean. They couldn't say nothin' about me. It drew a lot of money, but also a lot of hatred and bad talk ... but what the hell.

Even with all the precautions you took?

Well, everyone who donated did so grudgingly. They had never heard of such shit. It had probably never been done before (laughs) ... but a charity show should be a charity show. (laughs) We even made the widow buy a ticket. (laughs)

Did it bring her some good money?

Oh, yeah. We did about ten thousand, which was big money then, and wrote her a check for the full amount. It's enough to know that you did the right thing.

I'm surprised Boesch didn't bring you into the main office to book.

Oh, they had their deal. I had never been a booker. How I got started booking [other territories] is a story in itself. Texas began to taper off due to circumstances beyond my control.

Austin American • **Saturday, May 8, 1965**

Leo first closed up after his Dec. 10, 1964, card. He had promoted Austin for 28 months and was quoted as saying *"there is only a slight chance that I might resume operations in the future."* Despite that, he returned on March 9, 1965, with 700 mat fans in attendance. Leo promoted cards on March 23 and 30 before wrestling disappeared once again. On May 8, Leo promoted a studio wrestling show on KHFI Channel 42 at 3:00 p.m. on Saturdays with Paul Boesch doing the commentary. Live wrestling at the Coliseum started up once again on May 19 and ran through June 2, but on May 30, Leo broke his leg while roller skating at a local skating rink and was hospitalized for six days. He suffered two broken bones and had to wear a cast for six months. Part of that time was spent in a wheelchair. His wife, June, acted as the promoter while he was recuperating, but only promoted two shows, June 2 and 9. June, a singer in night clubs, didn't have the time to devote to the wrestling business, so wrestling went dark once again ... this time for good until San Antonio promoter Frank Brown re-opened the town in Sept. 1966.

I had the chance to get a job in Tulsa as a maitre'd in a nice night club. I thought it would be steady money, so we moved to Tulsa and I began working as a maitre'd. I noticed that Leroy McGuirk had a shit program ... the printed [arena] programs. I said, "*Why don't you let me do that program?"*

He said, "*Let me see what you've got."*

I was famous for the programs I did in Austin, so he let me publish his.

Leo and his wife, June, took a job at the Camelot Motor Hotel in Tulsa — Leo as manager and June as a singer. They were there only a short time before packing up in Aug. 1966 and taking a booking job in Atlanta.

You said you had never booked matches. Didn't you book the matches for Tyler and Austin?

Well, I did, but it was still within their guidelines with the people they gave me. I could only do certain things with certain guys. At any rate, the biggest success I had as a booker in wrestling was in Atlanta. I got a phone call from Ray Gunkel, who asked me to come and book Atlanta ... which to me, was like being asked to book Madison Square Garden. I took it, of course, but I remember thinking, "*Why would they hire me?*" I was just a guy who had booked Tyler, and then Austin. I didn't have the experience of booking a whole territory. But, I took it, and we moved lock, stock and barrel to Atlanta.

The mystery was ... why would Gunkel call me? When I got there, I discovered that they had a problem. A lot of the boys were in charge and there was a lot of disorder. Oohhh! There was a lot of jealousy. Not only that, but Atlanta was the only town doing good. They gave me a free hand. "*Do whatever you want.*" So, I took that like, "*If I die, I'm gonna die with my own shit ... not with what they've been doing here.*"

There were guys that I saw something in that had just been hanging around, so I pushed them. If there were guys that I thought didn't have it, I wouldn't push 'em. I started bringing in my own guys ... guys that had never really had a break in their lives, like Tim Woods. He was an AAU champion wrestler out of New York, but he had no color at all. He was colorless, but when he wrestled under a hood as Mr. Wrestling, the people got with him. I took guys like that who could move and tried to educate the people in wrestling.

(laughs) Ray Gunkel, Buddy Fuller and Lester Welch were partners. I eventually found out that Gunkel wanted to buy the interest from the other two, so he was trying to run the territory down. (laughs) If the territory was on its ass, he could buy them out cheap. That's why he called me in there. He wanted somebody that would run the thing down. (laughs) So, what happened was ... instead of going to hell, it came to life. Now you know the reason why they hired a small-town promoter from Texas to book the big city of Atlanta.

(laughs) Did anyone actually verify that to you?

Well, they hinted at it. (laughs) Here' a good one. Nick Bockwinkel is coming in to wrestle in Atlanta. For six weeks, every show is a sellout. Ray Gunkel gets me alone in my office and says, "*Leo, I'm tired of you hot-shottin' this territory.*"

"*What do you mean hot-shotting?*"

"*The shows are selling out and you're turning people away.*" (laughs) Can you believe that? He says, "*If those people can't buy tickets, they'll probably never come back.*"

I say, "*Well, what do you want me to do?*"

He tells me, "*I don't want to turn people away.*"

I said, "*Well, would a hundred people short of a sellout make you feel better?*" (laughs) I said, "*You realize that it's sort of tough getting it to where everyone who comes to the arena has a ticket, and then* 'Boom!' *... there's nobody left when the last ticket is sold.*"

"*I don't care how you do it ... JUST DO IT!*"

Atlanta GA • June 16, 1967

I had heard the rumors about this ... now I was believing them. I got a hold of Nick and I said, "*Nick, I can't explain this to you. There are some things you don't need to know, but what I want you to do is, on your interview, talk about anything but wrestling.*"

"*What the hell ...?*"

I said, "*Nick, take my word for it. Talk about anything you want, but don't talk about wrestling. Don't talk about your match with El Mongol for the title.*"

Then I went to Ed Capral, the TV announcer, and said, "*Ed, Nick has a habit of rambling on and on, and getting off the point. This match with El Mongol is really important, so keep him talking about wrestling.*" (laughs)

As long as my hands were tied, I wanted to cheat every wrestling fan out of what always happens. I wanted them to see the system going crazy. I wanted them to think, "*What in the hell is going on?*" Who else had ever done that?

So here comes Ed Capral. "*Okay, ladies and gentlemen. You've just seen him in the ring ... the greatest champion in the history of wrestling ... Nick Bockwinkel. And here he is. He's all prepped. He's all ready for his big match with El Mongol! How do you feel about that match, Nick?*"

"*Ah, Ed. It's good to be here in Atlanta. You know, I just came from Hawaii, and the surf is wonderful out there. I took my surfboard out and ...*"

"*Yeah, but what about the match!?*"

"*I was out there with all these beautiful girls and I told myself,* 'Nick Bockwinkel. You must be the luckiest man in the world.'"

"*But what about the title match?*"

I'm up in the control room, motioning for Ed to get him talking about wrestling. (laughs) Nick went on about nothing until time was about to run out, then says, "*Oh, about that match. May the best man win!*" (laughs) It still sold out. That's the way wrestling should be.

Did Gunkel finally concede and let you do your thing?

No. Gunkel put so much pressure on me that I finally left him. I went to Florida. They were going strong there, but they were running out of ideas and needed an idea man. The problem was, when I began booking, they wanted to change those ideas to suit themselves. That was the problem with most promoters. They pay a booker, then want to change their ideas. They bring you in and say, "*What should we do, Leo?*"

"*We'll do this, do this, do this.*"

"Well, that's not the way we do it."

Were you still booking when Mike Graham was breaking in?

Yeah.

Was there a lot of pressure on you to give him the big push?

Well, it wasn't so much a situation of giving him a big push. Eddie wanted his son just not to lose. (laughs) It really wasn't a problem because Mike could beat anybody anyway. (laughs) He had the credentials.

What were the differences between working for Graham and Gunkel?

Graham was one of the greatest promoters that I ever worked for. He was a great worker himself, so he knew what was going on. Graham was always knocking the shit out of the spectators, though, which I don't agree with ... especially now, when they all say it's only entertainment.

I've always wanted to ask how you feel about the bookers wrestling. That seems to have been the downfall of many good bookers because, instead of concentrating on what was good for the business, they were constantly thinking about what they could do to make themselves look good.

You're actually right. The booker has to be neutral. I didn't have any choice because I couldn't wrestle anymore (pause) ... but I probably would have done it if I could have. (laughs) It's a disease that gets you.

You also booked for the Charlotte office.

I went in to try and do some booking, but they had a lot of other guys doing it. They pushed me right out.

What did you think the first time you read an interview with a wrestler in which they opened up and talked honestly about the working of the sport?

It seems like all the wrestlers that are being interviewed are spilling their guts, but they're not really. The people doing the interviews are masters at editing. Gene Kiniski might say something like, "*Oh, yes. There's lots of showmanship in wrestling. You really have to be a good showman.*" They clip that out, then put it after them saying something like, "*We've talked about wrestling being fake and here's former world heavyweight champion Gene Kiniski.*"

"*Oh, yes. There's lots of showmanship in wrestling. You really have to be a good showman.*"

It sounds like he's agreeing to their statement. They interviewed Lou Thesz, my lifetime idol, and he made a statement. I know that statement wasn't, "*It's all fake, isn't it, Lou.*" He'd have knocked them on their ass. (laughs) But they edit those statements to suit their own purpose.

Do you follow wrestling today?

I don't know how to describe what I think of today (pause) ... well, here's what I think. In our time, instead of two people owning all the wrestlers, which would be [Vince] McMahon and the geek with the movie-star wife (pause) ... what's his name?

Ted Turner. His wife is Jane Fonda.

Yeah. (laughs) Those two guys own wrestling and are fighting for control. I mean, they literally own the wrestlers. Those guys can't wrestle and make a living without going through them. It wasn't like that when we left.

In the old days, there were rogue promoters who would gladly go against the establishment. You didn't have to do a damn thing you didn't want to. If somebody told you, "*Hey, you should lose to Lou Thesz tonight,*" who's gonna argue with that? He's gonna beat you, anyway. Now, it's a complete travesty. I watched Vince's show and they had a guy with a big rubber dick hanging out of his tights.

I recently read that Jim Barnett was back with WCW.

Well, that's bad news for wrestling. I drafted an answer to the A&E special [The Unreal Story of Professional Wrestling (1998)] that I've been sending around to some of the guys. I need to send it to you.

What about injuries? A back injury put you out of the business. Were there others that have bothered you?

I'm like all the boys. We all have terrible arthritis, new knees, and new hips. I have two totally new hips. I have a knee that needs doing, an ankle that needs fusing ... all this from wrestling. The body takes tremendous punishment. You're able to absorb it when you're a kid, but you reap the bitter harvest later on.

We've all become friends again. This time, there is no jealousy, nothing about who's the better wrestler. We've all been through the thing and have weathered the worst. We know how lucky we are that we aren't like Jack Pinto ... like my uncle who died in the ring. We're lucky we made it.

Do you miss being a part of the wrestling business?

It's hard to be a big star all of your life, then all of a sudden, you're out of the limelight. No one even calls you. The people you looked at as your dearest friends and close associates ... you never hear from them.

I'll tell you a funny story. I was being honored by the Cauliflower Alley Club in Sherman Oaks, California. My wife and I were watching these movies stars being recognized. The wrestlers seemed to be afraid to come out and say anything controversial because they wanted to be hoity-toity. I told Red Bastien, "*Red, this is boring. These guys are getting trophies and they're saying* 'Thank you very much. I appreciate this.'" Yak-yak. That's all anybody ever said. I said, "*The people here are used to seeing these guys on TV, screaming and hollering, saying ridiculous things. We have to jazz it up.*" I gave him the plan, then executed it when they brought me up for the award.

I had a legal pad of paper and took it up with me. Now, mind you ... the people who were there were the old, old timers, who were 30 or 40 when I broke into the game. These are guys that I was in deadly fear of. I thought they could squash me (pause, laughs) ... a lot of them did and thought it was funny. (laughs) I was like 55 at the time, but these guys were 75 and 80. Some were in wheelchairs, on crutches, had people helping them around. They were guys, though, who had been ferocious in their day. They had horrible reputations for knocking the shit out of people.

My speech went something like this. "*I thank you. It took me a long time to make the Hall of Fame. I'm looking around at so many people who deserve this honor, too. I'm sorry about that, but only one person can get it. Looking out at you, I see so many familiar faces of guys that I wrestled. I thought I'd make a list of the people that I could beat right now, today.*"

There was a grumbling that began at that point. Guys started to stir around. I said, "*When I started out, I was the teenage idol of California. In fact, that's how they introduced me. I knew guys who had twenty and thirty years of experience, and could beat my ass to a pulp. They felt like I was under my dad's protection and that got me easy matches.*"

I said, "*Most of the guys could, but it's different now. Some of you guys out there don't look so tough.*"

They were stirring around in their chairs, trying to get up on their crutches. You could feel the tension in the room. Lou Thesz is on the podium, looking at me like, "*Oh, my God!*" I never cracked a smile. I said, "*Many of you might not think it's gracious of me to make a list of people I could beat now, but why not? If they thought it was okay to beat me when I was a kid, then it's okay for me now that I'm a grown man to beat these old men.*"

I raised the yellow pad up and said, "*I have a yellow pad on every table with the names of the guys I can beat. You might want to look at them.*"

They were all looking around for them. There weren't any, except for Red ... he has one. Red jumps up with his yellow pad and says, "*Hey, wait a minute! You've got me on this yellow pad. You can't beat Red Bastien, asshole!*"

I told him, "*Sit down. This is my ceremony.*" He comes walkin' down the aisle. The people are trying to hold him back. They bought it completely. Red comes up and Thesz is even buying into it.

Red says, "*You've got me on this list, but you couldn't beat me then, and you can't beat me now!*" He's shaking the pad at me.

I says, "*You really don't think I can beat you, huh?*"

He says, "*You'll never see the day!*"

I said, "*Well, okay.*" I took a pencil out and erased his name. I said, "*I'm gonna scratch your name off this list, Red.*"

They all burst out into laughter. (laugh) That loosened the atmosphere up. It was like a good TV interview.

Leo passed away on May 12, 2008, at his home in Las Vegas from complications of Alzheimer's Disease.

TITLES

Texas junior ('55)
Southwest tag
(West Texas '56 w/Enrique Romero)
Pacific Coast tag
(CA '51 w/Gino Garibaldi)
Southern tag
(NC '56 w/Chick Garibaldi)
Texas tag ('59 w/Cyclone Anaya)

Memories of Leo Garibaldi

by J Michael Kenyon
Nov. 30, 1999

I don't keep much of anything, including programs. Haven't had any Austin programs for years, although Leo even let me write a few things for those at the time (I was in the service, using my given name of Mike Glover).

I can tell you a little about the spirit of his promotions, however.

The program was typewritten WITH LOTS OF CAPITAL LETTERS FOR EMPHASIS and he would underline a lot of stuff. It was a style that was quite unique for the time and which I later adopted for my own use with boxing and wrestling programs for years afterward. You might ask him whether he did it for reasons of style, or whether it was just a way to save money by not having to get any type set. He did all his own programs, I think, clipping headlines and stories out of other programs and pasting them up in his. They were as good as any programs I ever saw, anywhere in the country. As I noted, he let me do a few things for his programs — and I shamelessly copied that style for the next 25 years I did programs for wrestling, boxing, drag racing, soccer, boat racing, poker tournaments, you name it — and I still use it a lot in personal correspondence even today. He was a communications genius.

Austin TX • June 18, 1964

I'm not sure, but you might ask him if there was a stunt (I don't think so) that Paul Boesch had introduced, or used, in Texas that Leo didn't find some use for in Austin, or Tyler. Plus some of his own invention ... tar (molasses) and feather matches, ambulances at ringside, Texas death matches ... you name it and Leo had it. In those days, losers rode donkeys around the ring and losers were painted green on St. Patrick's Day, etc. I did a piece for a Stanley Weston magazine on the time Leo had the wrestlers play a baseball game as part a card held outdoors at the Austin Senators' ballpark. Moolah was there that night, adding plenty of spice to the proceedings; Killer Kox, too.

Leo got miles and miles out of Kox, who was just coming into his own as a top-notch ruffian. Leo and the cops had him put in jail one night so Leo could show a picture of him behind bars for the next week's program. Leo would occasionally hold shows in the opera house in Austin, not his regular building (which was fairly spacious, but not as toney as the opera house), with the ring up on the stage. Kox tossed Tito Carreon into the orchestra pit one night. It must have been a 15-foot drop. I don't think I ever saw a wilder bump in those days.

Leo always had big matches when Thesz came to town with the belt. I saw him defend against Ernie Ladd, Danny Hodge, and Bill Miller, among others. The shows were on Thursday nights in Austin, after Wednesday in San Antonio and before Friday in Houston.

Bill Watts was still a babyface in those days, but Mark Lewin came in just as he began his career heel turn. Duke Keomuka, Danny McShain, Tony Borne (and loveable old Leo the Lion Newman, his manager) were staples on the cards. Otto Kuss and Marvin Jones did the refereeing. Boesch would occasionally show up to work a special program. The [Morris' Sigel office always had top-notch old pros working as refs. Dick Raines was around in those days; later years saw Danny Plechas, Bronco Lubich and McShain take their places.

Ricki Starr came through Texas in the early '60s when Leo had Austin. Naturally, he was always a big draw. Dick Steinborn was in at that time, too.

One thing, for sure, you ought to quiz Louie Tillet on is HIS side of the coin when the two of them, he and Garibaldi, were booking Atlanta at the same time. Louie had some of the best matches in his career, I would wager, while working for Leo ... and I'd love to learn whatever he remembers of their times together in the 1960s.

Leo always had boundless enthusiasm and bounced around pretty good, even though it was because of a back injury that he had quit wrestling and gone into promoting at that time. He later came back to more or less fulltime wrestling, at least for a while. He was so energetic, though, that you got the impression that he could go on forever, just like his dad.

I saw Gino near the end of his career, in 1960, and then a year later saw Leo for the first time, working with Gorgeous George in Seattle. They were, of course, the first father-son tag team in history, dating back to Leo's early days in the ring after World War II (1947, I think, was when he started working with Gino back east). He lost some time during the Korean War (both he and Bastien were in the Air Force in North Africa during that time) and then got hurt in the early '60s, occasioning his promotional turn. Afterwards, of course, he became a top booker for different promotions, e.g., Atlanta, Tulsa, Los Angeles, etc.

The last time we talked, you mentioned the concession-stand fracas in Tupelo staged by the USWA promotion. I told you that Leo did it long before they did. It took place in Tyler. To my mind, the match between Colonel Stu Gibson and Dangerous Danny McShain was one of the great moments in wrestling history. They wound up fighting outside the ring and atop the concession stand, with Gibson stuffing hot dogs, buns and mustard down the throat of McShain as they were counted out. Leo brought them back the next week with, not a "no holds barred match," but a "no mustard allowed" match and condiments were banned from the concession stand.

The work between Leo & Red at the CAC is a classic little story. Turning the old pros into marks was pretty easy, it seems.

— JMK

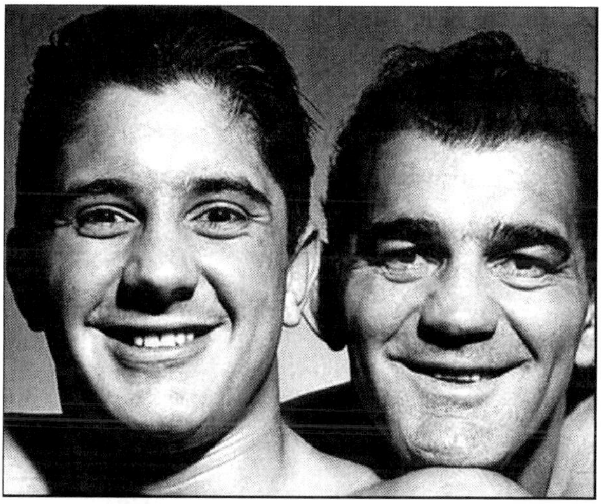

(from top left, clockwise) Leo at West Point Military Academy; Leo & Gino; Leo's montage publicity picture; Gino & little Leo; Leo publicity photo; Leo as a heel in Atlanta; Leo plays the accordion.

(below) Los Angeles CA • Oct. 3, 1951 • The night Leo lost the light heavyweight title.

WRESTLING TONIGHT—OLYMPIC AUDITORIUM

LEO GARIBALDI vs. WILD RED BERRY

18th & Grand World's Junior Heavyweight Title PR-5171

THE
OX

OX BAKER

Douglas Baker

This interview, conducted by Scott Teal in Sept. 1995, was originally published in issue #16 of *Whatever Happened to …?*

Tell me about your childhood, Ox.

I was born in Waterloo, Iowa, on April 19, 1934. I graduated from West [Waterloo] High School in '53. It was a good thing, too because I had gotten too big for the desks, so I got out of there. At the time, we were the greatest wrestling school in the country. I was on the All-State teams and wrestled in the heavyweight class. In fact, West High won the state title nineteen out of 20 years. Several guys made the Olympic team.

From there, I went to Iowa Teachers College [Cedar Falls] for one semester. I tried out for football, but wasn't quite fast enough. I made the wrestling team, until one day when the coach got on me pretty hard. I got angry, threw one punch, and I was out of college. At that time, I was about 300 pounds and thought I knew it all. You don't realize how smart your folks are until you're 30 years old.

Iowa Teacher's College hosted an annual tournament for high-school kids with more than 250 entrants competing. During his senior year at Waterloo, the future Ox Baker then Doug Baker — reached the finals of the heavyweight division on Dec. 14, 1952, only to be pinned in 4:42 by Bob Kroeger of nearby Independence, Missouri.

***The Courier*, Jan. 8, 1953 • West High School team, Ox on far left**

What's the saying ... by the time we realize our parents were right, we have children who think we're wrong.

That's right. After that, I wrestled in a few invitational meets. I wasn't great or anything, but I was fair. Then, I went into the Army as a medic down in Fort Sam Houston, Texas. They sent me over to Germany and I was attached to a Field Artillery, where we took care of the walking wounded during field training. Whenever anyone asked me why I wasn't in the Infantry, I said I wasn't geared for that. I enjoyed myself, even though I didn't make any rank. I played football as a defensive end over there for two years. We were the 34th Blackhawks ... Black Warriors, or some damn thing. [Black Dragons] We're talking over 30 years ago, right? Anyway, we were from the 34th Infantry group. It was a good team and we rated second-best of the service teams. I wasn't the fastest, but I could run a 60-second 440 at 300 pounds. The worst thing was, I banged my knees up pretty good.

I came back home and worked as a butcher for about six years at Rath Packing Company in Waterloo. Rath bacon was some of the most famous bacon in the country at that time. It was a decent job, but every time I saved up a little bit of money, they'd have a strike, or walk out, and I'd be dead broke again. In fact, when I got into wrestling at age 24, I hadn't even owned my own car yet. I didn't even get my license until I was 24. I drove my brother's car quite a bit, but the first car I bought was after I started wrestling ... a 1965 Ford. A year later, through wrestling, I had lost the car because I couldn't make the payments.

What was your involvement in pro wrestling at that time in your life?

I hadn't paid much attention to professional wrestling until I got out of the service and got a job. They started running pro wrestling on Channel 7 in Waterloo, the show out of Kansas City. Several of the guys that I had wrestled in high school and college were wrestling pro. Some of them, I thought at the time, were making great money. We're talking about the days of working for a dollar an hour, or make three or $400 a week in wrestling. It would be nothing nowadays, but it was great back then.

One day, I walked into the arena right after the guy who set the rings up got fired. They wanted some jabroni, some goof, to set the rings up and take coffee and cigarettes to the wrestlers. So, I started to work for Pat O'Connor and [Bob] Geigel. For two years, that's all I did. I'd set the ring up and drive 200 miles

Waterloo • Oct. 30, 1965

for twelve dollars. I sold programs, brought coffee to the wrestlers. There wasn't the dope like we have now, but there were a few boys who drank pretty heavy. They'd come around and say, "*Hey, do you want to learn a hold, kid?*" Then they'd slap you around. They found out that I could wrestle a little bit, and I had been around long enough that I could understand the terminology, even though they never let me in on anything. I think they had me timekeep a couple of times and referee once, and I didn't even know what the hell was going on. I'm in there as a referee and I suddenly realize they're talking to one another. It's a different ballgame today. They smarten you up overnight.

It was a great background for someone breaking into the business, though. I started wrestling in Kansas City at about 340 pounds. After eight months, I was down to about 290. I was on a great diet plan. You tried to get by on one meal a day.

Right away, they decided to come up with a gimmick for me. They said, "*We need to come up with a gimmick so we can keep you halfway decent. We won't give you wins over the big superstars, but we'll make you look good.*"

I was so big that whenever I walked into some place, everyone always said, "*Hey, look at the Ox.*" So, I wrestled as the Ox. I wore a big hat, glasses, an army trench coat, and tennis shoes. I wasn't supposed to know how to wrestle. They wanted me to portray a stumblebum fresh off of the farm.

In 1965, I headed down to Nashville for Nick [Gulas] and Roy [Welch]. I spent $190 a week to make 150. Nick had a rundown hotel there where you could stay for $25 a week. For the next five years, I was on the same diet plan as in Kansas City. The only reason I made it there was that I was a bouncer in a night club on Broadway for a year, right by Tootsies. On Sunday, they used to have a card game, and I carried sandwiches. I was assured of a hundred bucks on the weekend. Everybody said, "*You make the same as us, yet you've always got money in your pocket.*" In fact, I had a couple of weeks where I made as much as two or $300 on the weekend. They had some real big games.

One thing about Nick, though. If a guy had the desire to wrestle, he gave them a chance to prove themselves. Oh, yeah. Don't get me wrong. The fact is, I really liked Nick. He let me wrestle every night and I learned a lot from him. That's the problem today. There's nowhere to work. I could name a ton of guys who would have never made it in the business if it weren't for Nick Gulas. He had his faults, but he gave a lot of guys a chance.

That's like Eddie Graham in Florida. He said, "*Ox, I don't really like you, but you can wrestle forty minutes a night for six weeks with no winner.*"

He did me a favor because, up to that time, I had been wrestling six to ten minutes and getting real tired. I told him, "*My longest match up to now is six minutes. How in the hell can I go forty minutes?*"

He said, "*You put a hold on and you sell it. The other guy counters and puts a hold on you, and you sell it.*" After wrestling for Eddie Graham, I never got tired in the ring again.

I remember telling one of the guys I admired, "*I'm gonna beat you with the abdominal stretch.*"

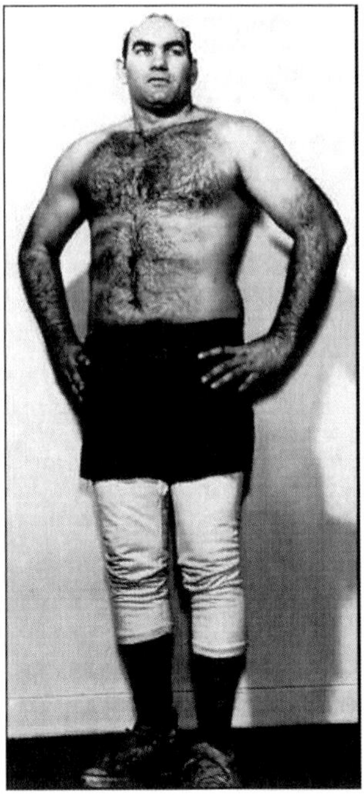

He said, "*Nobody beats anybody with the abdominal stretch.*"

That was true in some cases. Nobody sells it if you don't put it on properly. You have to convince people it can hurt your opponent. I remember the first time I seen a suplex. I was terrified. Done properly, a suplex is an awesome move. Now they do a suplex off the damn top rope and kick out of it. I tell my students, "*We don't do any of that. We do basics and you guys ...*" It's almost like the Poffos. Angelo had the Macho Man and Lanny lose matches for a whole year before he'd let them win. He told 'em, "*Until you learn how to lose, you can't learn how to win.*" Nowadays, nobody wants to sell anything. I mean, I seen a guy the other night who jumped over the top rope, did a back flip, and kicked somebody in the face. (laughs) I can't even jump over the top rope.

Then I got a real good break when I got booked into Pensacola, Florida. Rocky McGuire, the promoter, took one look at me and sent me to the gym with Ken Lucas, figuring he'd teach me how to wrestle. I surprised him when I pinned him about 30 times, wrestling amateur. Ken said, "*My God. I had no idea you knew how to wrestle.*" So, I told him about my wrestling background and he went back and told Rocky.

Rocky called me in and said, "*Throw all that stuff away. You're going to buy trunks and shoes.*" He changed my name over to Ox Baker. They had figured that because of my gimmick, I didn't know anything about wrestling. It wasn't too long before they had Bobby Fields drop the strap [Gulf Coast heavyweight title] to me. I was shocked. My head was so big that night. I won a few belts over the years, but I think that was the most impressive because I felt that I really didn't deserve it.

While I was in Mobile, Ole Anderson was wrestling at the time as Rock Rogowski for Joe Dusek in Omaha. Rock had the tag belts with Tom Andrews, who was wrestling as the Claw. When Tom broke his leg or something, this left Rock without a partner. So, they sent me from Mobile up to Omaha and put the belts on me and Rock. It was a bad move in a way because Bill Watts was going to send me up to Verne [Gagne] because Verne wanted to try me out.

As it turned out, though, it was a move that would result in getting you some notoriety with promoters and the fans.

Yes, that's when the accident happened. However, it didn't happen anything like it was reported later. Joe came into the dressing room one night and said that Alberto [Torres] had gone to the hospital. Me and Rogowski had wrestled him and Cowboy [Bob] Ellis one Sunday night in some small town. [Verdigree, Nebraska on June 13, 1971] Believe me, they kicked the living hell out of us. Joe didn't like to beat his babyfaces and put them over every night.

What it was, he [Alberto] had a yearly checkup because he had cracked his pancreas as a kid. He had mentioned that week to Joe something like "*I have to get a checkup because I think somebody kicked me too hard last week.*" He wasn't even sure who it was. He wasn't bitchin. He was just saying that he needed to have an examination. The last time I saw him he seemed to be fine. He was hugging and kissing all the fans because he was the fan's favorite.

The story told was that Ox hit Torres with the heart punch. Torres dropped to the mat and failed to get back to his feet. He was rushed to a hospital in Omaha and died on Thursday, June 17, 1971. An autopsy showed that he died of a ruptured pancreas. Joe Dusek, the promoter, made the announcement and told the Associated Press that Torres was "about thirty" years old. His actual date of birth, per the Social Security Death Index, was Jan. 2, 1934, so he was 37 years old at the time of his death.

They were going to work something off of it — a hell of a big angle — and say it was my heart punch that did it. We got on TV and said we held him down, put the boots to him, and held him while I clobbered him with that big heart punch. Of course, I was goofy and said that I hoped he never gets out of the hospital. Three days later, Alberto rolled over in bed and died.

I felt bad about the whole thing for a while, but was told later that we probably had nothing to do with it. His pancreas had just split open.

Did the tragedy hurt business in Omaha for a while?

Well, Omaha was such a friendly, friendly place, and Joe Dusek fit right in. He was a happy-go-lucky, go-hunting-every-weekend, put-the-babyfaces-over type of guy ... but he was actually strangling the territory, killing it with kindness. Right away, here in wrestling, there was a tragedy, and probably for the first time, the people — the naysayers — began to believe that it was halfway real. Someone was dead in the ring. How can you overlook a death? Someone hit a guy and he's dead!

And we did great business for the next eight months. I remember when [Tarzan] Tyler was around. He was full of ideas. For a year, everything that Joe did, he did through Tyler. In a three to $500 a week territory, where I was making 325 bucks a week, Tarzan was making 550. Their biggest house was like 3,300 people … him and Verne Gagne in a championship match at the Auditorium. With Ramon Torres, we drew 9,000 people. Ramon didn't like to wrestle. He didn't like anything about it, and really didn't know how to wrestle. In fact, he pounded on me for real for about five or six matches. I was like ... give me Danny Hodge. But the people loved him!

I'm jumping around a little bit, but, anyway, Cowboy Ellis had swung back through, and he was Alberto's partner. He sat down with me one night and said, "*Ox, let's start a 'whip versus saddle' match.*" At the time, I carried a little whip with me. Ellis liked gimmick matches, like "loser wears a saddle and the winner rides him." We got a big spur and sharpened one end of it up because he liked to blade every night. We had a run you couldn't believe for months, and I passed what Tyler had made, but it still wasn't getting me a thousand dollars. Tyler told me later that he never thought someone could make $750 or $800 a week in Omaha.

That summer was good in Omaha because they had fairs and I had the reputation surrounding Alberto's death. That's when I started using my famous saying: "*I love to hurt people.*" We had a great run for nearly a year after the ... accident, or whatever you want to call it. But, for that eight months, Joe wouldn't give in, and I never won a match. I lost a lot of credibility.

Omaha never was a strong wrestling territory again after that, was it?

By that time, it was dead on its feet, but I was getting a lot of offers. I went from being a jabroni to a point where people were calling me up and saying, "*Hey, do you want to make five hundred dollars a week?.*" Finally, unbelievably, Ray Gunkel called me up and said, "*How would you like to make a thousand dollars a week.*"

So, I went to Atlanta. Ray Gunkel had just made Tom Renesto, one of the Assassins, the booker in Atlanta. Renesto was probably one of the greatest brains in the business. Eddie Graham was number one, by the way. I met them all, but Eddie had great ideas. What a great finish man. A lot of guys thought I hated Eddie Graham, but I don't know why they thought that. I always admired the man. A couple of years ago, I had the opportunity to talk to Mike Graham and I said, "*Mike, I always admired your dad. I don't know where that came from.*" Another great idea man was Jerry Lawler. I was right there when he painted the ring around the eyes of Jim Harris, handed him a spear, and made him Kamala. Here was a guy who, four or five years before, was mugging people to make money.

I had three marvelous years there in Atlanta. I thought I was gonna live there forever. Tom Renesto brought me into Atlanta because Alberto Torres had been a star down there, and I was supposed to have killed him in the ring. For three years — if you can, look it up — I never won one match. Tom never beat me on TV, but I got my rear end kicked at the house shows.

Ox *did* lose more house matches than he won, but he did win some. For the first eight months, he wrestled for Ray Gunkel and Buddy Fuller's NWA promotion. When Ray died and Ann Gunkel formed All-South Wrestling Alliance, Ox Baker made the jump to All-South and was with them until they closed up shop in late 1974.

At the end of that time, the policemen still had to pull people off of me. Ernie Ladd put me upside down in a garbage can and everybody laughed for about 30 seconds, until I bent the garbage can over his head. It's all about getting your heat back by doing something afterwards.

Ray [Gunkel] would wrestle about twice a year. I have no idea why because he was a millionaire, but he always drew a sellout whenever he wrestled. He was as tough as Danny Hodge ... not wrestling-wise, but physically wise. He booked a Texas death match with me in Savannah [Aug. 1, 1972]. He broke my wrist that night, blacked my eye. What he did was overexert himself and his heart just burst. Dickie Steinborn told me later that Ray had eaten nine or ten pieces of chicken that afternoon out at the beach. He had baked himself. He was one of the first guys with a great tan.

In the dressing room after the match, Gunkel suffered a massive heart attack and dropped dead. The results of an autopsy revealed that Gunkel suffered from arteriosclerosis and had died of heart trauma. The death was an accident, but a blow to Ray's chest by Ox caused a gumball-sized hematoma to form. The hematoma swelled, broke off, and turned into a blood clot, which went to his heart and caused his death.

The last time I saw Ray, I was trying to straighten my wrist out, catch my breath, and my eye was swelling up. I went to the dressing room to soak my wrist when a policeman came in with a sawed-off shotgun. He said, *"Better get your ass out of here. Ray just dropped dead in the dressing room."* Was that ever a kick in the rear end.

Of course, that was the beginnings of the first wrestling war down there. You see, Ray Gunkel was so tough that none of the guys could move in on him. Somehow or another, Buddy Fuller actually owned more of the territory than Ray did, but when Ray died, Ann [Gunkel] thought she could take the whole territory over. The boys that stuck with her thought she owned it and everybody was trying to steal it from her. At the time, me, Jody Hamilton, and Rock Hunter were the hottest thing going in Georgia — especially *me* with Ray being dead.

Atlanta GA • June 16, 1972

[Buddy] Fuller and his crew started bringing all these superstars in, but we were outdrawing them. The key to the whole thing was that we had Savannah, Augusta, and Atlanta. You could make money even if the rest of the week was down. We thought Fred Ward was with us at first, but he decided to go out on his own. If Fred Ward had stayed with us, we'd have beaten them hands down, but unbeknownst to us, he had hated Gunkel for years, but was scared to death of him while he was alive. If we would have had Macon, it would have helped. As it was, when they found out they couldn't beat us with talent, they started making deals with guys and shutting us out of buildings. Then [Jim] Barnett got in with his millions and started taking one town after another, and squeezed us dry. Ann Gunkel was a pretty nice person, but she wasn't a wrestling promoter. And Renesto — he never shot me down by the way — but what he did was sell out to Barnett. He did right by me, though, and made sure he got me booked with Dick [the Bruiser] before everything collapsed.

I left Atlanta to work for Dick in Indianapolis. I did very good with Dick, but he only wanted to run a couple of nights a week. He had millions and millions of dollars, and didn't need it. He treated me real good. I made four or five hundred a week, but I never had a $600 week. We only wrestled two nights a week. We filled up the Amphitheatre in Chicago eight straight times, but in three years, that was probably the eight best payoffs that I had. So, after a while, I said, "*Bruiser, I have rent and a family in Missouri. I can't do it on just five hundred dollars a week.*"

Dick started sending me to other places, but by the time I drove around, I was eating up what extra money I was making. I worked a few times with Ernie Ladd in Buffalo for Pedro Martinez. Martinez made me some big money, but he wouldn't pay me. He'd say, "*Ox, you got six hundred dollars coming. Here's a hundred, I owe you five.*" He did that all the time, but he'd have you there the next week and do the same thing all over again. He was the first one to realize the market for wrestling tapes. Now, [Mario] Savoldi is doing the same thing today, making tapes two or three times a year. Anytime someone wants a wrestling show, he has one ready.

Then Eddie Einhorn and the I.W.A. came along, challenging the major promotions.

Eddie Einhorn started a little war and I made the mistake of my life. I had left Renesto, Bruiser wasn't treating me right, and I was flim-flamming around. Einhorn offered all these stars ... twelve, fifteen hundred a week to help him start his wrestling promotion. He offered me a thousand, right? Well, I was the first guy to quit him. It turned out to be a very, very bad mistake, but I felt with Bruiser, I was a main eventer. Bruiser used a lot of guys who weren't going anywhere. Einhorn made a mistake, also. He made those big payoffs and the guys bled him dry. Yeah, he had a year-run, but it cost him a couple million. He ended up buying a ball club. [Chicago White Sox, 1981]

How did you get booked in Florida?

I think Eddie Graham and Dusty Rhodes first saw me during the war in Atlanta, then my interviews on the Einhorn tapes. Eddie loved interviews, you know, and I was gifted as a great talker. I don't think I was ever a world-beating wrestler, but as an interview, I couldn't be topped. That's not a brag, but I could put myself up against anybody, except for King Curtis. He was better than I was, but he had a different kind of rap ... a mysterious type of interview. I have a pretty good imagination and, to tell you the truth, I'd write stuff because I wanted to see my name in print. I always saved everything my name was on. For instance, even if I was only on the opening match, I'd save the poster from the card.

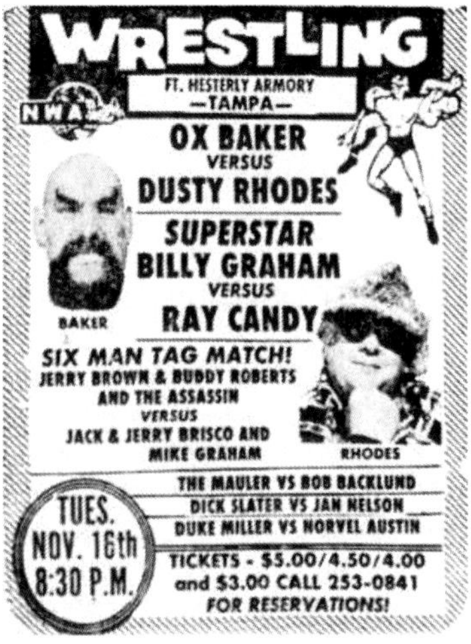

Tampa FL • Nov. 16, 1976

In one of the great breaks of my lifetime, three or four of the top heels quit Eddie [Graham] over pay. And here I was, in six months, making an average of fifteen hundred dollars a week. At the same time, I didn't think about the fact that, because Dusty was an insatiable monster, he was beating me every night. Ernie Ladd probably beat me twenty times in Atlanta, but Tom Renesto would do things after you get pinned. I'd break a chair over his head, and that would leave the heat. If you lose with style, it doesn't make any difference.

Dick the Bruiser taught me that all you had to do was argue that your shoulder was raised up on three — argue with the old fat woman in the front row — and you got your heat right back. I see all these prima donnas today ... "*I can't get beat. People would hate me.*" And that's probably true because they don't know how to use that psychology, and that thinking. Dick told me once, "*Put a stick in your trunks at the start of the match, and the whole match, reach for that stick. Plan never to take that stick out of your trunks.*" He got more heat out of that then if he took the stick out and wiped out six people. You and I both know, the audience wants to participate and anticipate. They want to be part of the action. That's why tag team matches are so popular. The guy didn't tag in. He cheated behind the referee's back. If you can get the audience involved, yelling and frothing at the mouth, they stay with you.

Even so, Dusty and I had such a great run in Florida, but I felt like they should have given me the Florida belt. Dusty's the one that really pushed me at that time, but they wouldn't put the strap on me. When Superstar [Billy Graham] came in, they switched everything to him, but he quit them and went with Vince [McMahon]. Superstar left without ever losing the belt. He just gave it back to them. If they had worked an angle with me to where I had won that belt, I would have had two or three more years in Florida. Instead, they threw me a bone and gave me the Southern belt, the "nothing" belt. That was one of the disappointments in my life.

Ox's self promotional flyer

That was one thing that always ... well, I could never break into any of the cliques. For instance, I went back and forth for Geigel and O'Connor quite a few times. They'd go up and downhill. They'd bring in Cowboy Ellis, the Mongolian Stomper [Archie Gouldie], and they drew great money with me. But, I always overheard guys in the background, "*That goof.*" You know, in those days, if a promoter or someone cheated you, you were a goof. Nick Gulas was the only promoter that didn't say that about anybody because he cheated everybody.

That's another thing. For a big part of my career, I didn't realize how much jealousy there was in the business. I was a big guy, especially when I was up around 340 pounds, and behind my back, guys were going, "*Hey, he's a big goof. We don't want to put him over.*" One thing I never worried about was the other guy. If you got a break, I was happy for you. I don't think I ever said one time, "*Why in the hell did they push that guy?*" I wanted the belt in Florida, and I'd be the first guy to say I did, but I wanted it because I wanted to last ... for longevity. I didn't want it as an ego thing ... just to see it around my waist.

I think some of my trouble was that I didn't portray out of the ring what I was in the ring. I was just an Iowa farm boy in a big business, who didn't realize or understand the politics going on. My philosophy was always to try to be nice to the guys who weren't made. I think if I had been one of these tough guys, I'd have gone to Eddie Graham and said, "*Hey, Eddie. I sold out eight weeks with Dusty Rhodes. Give me one win over the fat SOB and I'll sell out another ten weeks. You bring in Ernie Ladd for a big angle. Why don't you work the big angle with me?*" I was already there, already over.

See, I couldn't compete with that. Dusty had the promoter's ear. Dusty says, "*Well, you're not sinkin' the blade in.*"

"*Hey, you get a lot of blood, I get a little blood. What's the difference?*"

When I was in Texas, I couldn't wrestle Fritz' boys. They never beat me, but I never got to beat his boys, either. I worked a lot of Toronto matches and anything [Frank] Tunney wanted me to do, I'd do. These guys would say, "*Why in the hell are you putting over Bulldog Brower? You'll never wrestle up here again.*"

I'd say, "*I'll put him over, but I'll make myself so strong that they'll want me back.*"

I'd go out there and get in an argument with some woman ... "*Get in the ring and I'll beat your ass*" or "*Wait up, fat boy. I'll be there in a minute.*" Just some of the psychology that I learned from the older wrestlers. Even when Brower beat me, the people were yelling and screaming at me. I'd yell back at 'em, "*Sit down. You just want to take me out for a meal.*" I never lost my heat.

Back to Florida, I got my notice when they hired Buddy Rogers as the booker. He said he didn't like my style or my loudness. Fritz [von Erich] had lost a couple of heels in Dallas, so his booker — one of my good friends — Gary "Playboy" Hart, brought me in. Paul Boesch was a force there because Houston sold out all the time. If a guy wanted to make it in Texas, he had to make it in Houston, not just Dallas. Paul fell in love with my interviews, so he took a liking to me and wouldn't let anyone beat me there. He had the reputation as the greatest payoff man in wrestling.

I was there about a year and that's about all you could last in Texas because of Fritz and his sons. Gary really helped me out because he [Gary] wouldn't let his [Fritz's] sons wrestle me. He [Fritz] had a standing order that when you wrestled his sons, you got beat. So, after a year, I was through. I went over to Australia to take Bruiser Brody's spot, who was finishing up there.

I went to California and North Carolina, but I knew that my career was winding down. The legs just wouldn't hold up and there were times that I fell into the ring. I went to New Zealand twice, and even went back to Mobile, when Louie Tillet was the booker. He gave Hulk Hogan a break, who was making his start as Sterling Golden. Puerto Rico was at the end of my run.

I got a decent break when the Savoldis started an independent group. At the time, though, [Kevin] Sullivan and Mark Lewin moved in and I got pushed aside. They brought Abdullah the Butcher and Bruiser Brody in and I saw the handwriting on the wall. They wanted me to put all these guys over, which I wouldn't have minded if it was working into programs or main events, but it was just to get them over.

You worked with a guy in California named Enforcer Luciano. Who was that?

Ah-haaa! Somebody you don't know, right? That was Guillotine Gordon. His real name was Charles Valentine. He was one of the first guys who got into making long-distance calls on someone else's number, so the law started looking for him. He was about 330 pounds, so he knocked off about a hundred pounds of weight. He let his hair grow out and wore an eye patch.

One of the reasons for my success is that I loved every fan I met. It didn't matter if they blew snot out of their nose, coughed, scratched their ass ... I never judged anybody. I'd hear guys in the dressing room, *"Those goofy fans."*

I'd say, *"That guy paid four or five dollars to come see your ass ... and you can't even wrestle that good."*

They came to see me, so I love every one of them. Well, I hated the Puerto Ricans over there. They thought I was invincible and my heart punch terrified them. Those guys would knife you, punch you, kick you. All I did was raise the fist up. In all those years, Ox never hit one fan. I let 'em push and shove, kick me in the rear end, but they'd be swingin' knives at other guys. What's the difference? I'd walk through them Puerto Ricans and they wouldn't get near because they thought I could knock 'em out with that heart punch. I had many a promoter say, "*Ox, you went out with that old woman you called a douche bag.*"

"*Yeah. I wanted a free sandwich, so I sat down with her.*"

He said, "*Wait a second. You chewed her out, then ate a sandwich with her?*"

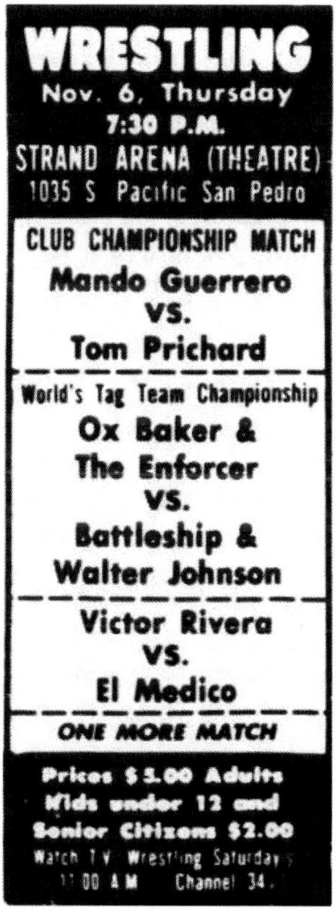

San Pedro CA • Nov. 6, 1980

I said, "*You don't pay me outside of the ring.*"

I realized that from day one. The only guys I ignored. A lot of guys would take a hundred pictures. I'd ask, *"Could I have one for my scrapbook?"*

They'd say, *"I don't give these things away. I sell them."*

I'd say, *"Don't ever take any more of me."*

You know yourself. You'd send me stuff, and I never belittled you. We might have laughed a little bit. I don't know. I just loved the fans.

Why did you move to Connecticut?

My first wife got killed in a tragic accident. I met a lady from Connecticut, so I came up here. Just like a love story.

What are you doing now?

I'm training a couple of guys. The Russian Brute [George Petroski] and I have been working on some ideas. George had a millionaire to back him, but the guy didn't know nothing about wrestling. He had his own ideas and he wouldn't follow George. The guy wanted to try some other avenue, so George is trying to do things on his own. Just watch for "The Man in the Golden Wheelchair."

Do you have any plans for more movie or television work?

I did a tape for some movie people the other day. It's just a bit part, if I can get it. I had starred in several movies, including *Escape from New York* with

Kurt Russell and Ernest Borgnine. John Carpenter, the director, originally chose Bruiser Brody for the role, but I got the part for some reason. I did *The Price Is Right* and some other television stuff.

I need two knee replacements, but I still walk around good. I walk around funny, you know. The toughest thing to accept is that I'll never wrestle again.

Little has been reported on Baker's boxing career, which began on an amateur boxing card in Des Moines on Dec. 14, 1957. His trainer, Gene Miller, hyped him in newspapers during the weeks leading up to the event as one of the up-and-coming heavyweights. Doug won a three-round decision in his debut match against Sam Montjoy, another Waterloo heavyweight. A return match on Jan. 11, 1958, saw Doug repeat the accomplishment.

On Feb. 11, Doug faced University of Iowa's Frank Davis for the open heavyweight title in a Golden Gloves tournament, only to lose by a decision in Cedar Rapids. As reported in The *Gazette*:

> "The most disgusted loser was Doug Baker, Waterloo giant who dropped a close decision to Frank Davis in the heavyweight final. Handed the runner-up's bronze belt buckle by referee Alex Fidler, Baker flung it angrily over the ropes. He thought he deserved to win, although all three judges voted for Davis, who landed the most damaging punches."

The Feb. 12 *Des Moines Tribune* reported that Baker wanted to be a professional wrestler, but had turned to boxing to gain a reputation and was said to have entered the Golden Gloves tournament solely to attract attention. The article also noted that he wasn't a poor sport, but that he and his cornermen all thought he deserved the decision. The protest was based on Davis not being penalized for a low blow, even though the referee stopped the fight to give Baker time to recover.

The scenario drew so much attention that Baker and Davis were scheduled to fight on an amateur boxing show at the Waterloo Hippodrome on March 4, with former NBA, NYSAC, and *The Ring*, world middleweight champion Tony Zale as the referee. Davis failed to show, claiming he thought the card was to take place on Wednesday. Baker won a decision over replacement Lee Schrege. The two mixed it up quite evenly for three rounds, but towards the end of the third, Schrege walked into one of Baker's wild swings and went to the canvas for an eight-count. The bout ended as Schrege regained his feet.

Baker and Davis were scheduled to meet once again nine months later, but Davis "failed to appear because of illness" and Doug was awarded a forfeit.

It's noteworthy that, during this time, newspapers began referring to Doug as "The Cardiff Giant from Waterloo."

Newspapers began to report the possibility of a Baker-Davis rematch, but a narrow loss by Baker to Tate Wilson on Feb. 18, 1959, ended the hope that Baker had of revenge. Wilson was slotted to face Davis the following week in the Cedar Rapids Golden Gloves tournament and defeated him with an uppercut that send Davis reeling into the ropes.

On Feb. 15, 1964, Ox won a Golden Gloves title as a heavyweight at a tournament in Des Moines. In newspaper reports, he was said to be 6-foot-4, "balding," and weighed 284 pounds. Baker was said to have won the match "by bulldozing his way past Eli Strand, Iowa State football lineman."

AMATEUR BOXING
Waterloo Hippodrome
TUESDAY, MARCH 4 at 8 P.M.
10 3-Round Bouts Featuring
TONY ZALE, Referee
Former World 160-Lb. Champion
MAIN EVENT
BIG DOUG BAKER VS. FRANK DAVIS
RINGSIDE $1.50 GENERAL ADMISSION 90c
For Reservations Dial AD 4-3437
Tickets on Sale at Hummel's

The first pro wrestling match I could find for Doug was an Oct. 30, 1965, card in Waterloo. I'm uncertain as to whether that was his debut match, but if it wasn't, it was one of the earliest.

On Feb. 12, 1981, Ox appeared on *The Price is Right*, hosted at the time by the legendary Bob Barker. His movie credits include *Battle Creek Brawl* (1980), *Escape from New York* (1981), *Blood Circus* (1987), *Chilling Visions: 5 Senses of Fear* (2013), and *Pinwheel* (2017). In 2011, he self-published a cookbook with his favorite recipes.

Ox was one of the legitimately scary men in the wrestling business. His bald head and bushy eyebrows, along with the fact that he stood 6-foot-4, gave him a menacing, intimidating look that made wrestling fans think twice before approaching him. On the flip side, he was one of the most congenial, friendly people in the wrestling business that you could hope to meet.

Ox passed away from kidney failure on Oct. 20, 2014, at the age of 80. He had recovered from a heart attack earlier that year and was suffering from diabetes.

TITLES

Gulf Coast (AL '67)
Midwest tag (NB)
'71 w/Rock Rogowski (Ole Anderson)
'71 w/The Claw aka Tom Andrews
'71 w/The Great Kusatsu
NWA Georgia tag
('72 w/Skandor Akbar)
ASWA Georgia TV ('73)
ASWA U.S. ('73)
NWF North American
(NY/Pedro Martinez '74)
WWA World (IN '74)
IWA North American
(Eddie Einhorn '75)
WWA tag (IN '76 w/Chuck O'Connor)
Southern (FL '76)
Florida tag ('77 w/Billy Graham)
American (TX '77, '80)
Texas ('77)
Austra-asian tag
(Australia '78 w/Butcher Brannigan)
WWC Puerto Rican ('78)
America's tag
(CA '80 w/Enforcer Luciano
World tag (CA '80 w/Enforcer Luciano)
Mid-Atlantic tag (NC '81 w/Carl Fergie)
British Empire (New Zealand '82)
Australasian tag
(New Zealand '82 w/King Kamaka)
WWC world (Puerto Rico '83)
ACW tag ('84 w/Purple Haze)
MCW International (Iowa '85)

ALIAS

Doug Baker
The Spectator (Amarillo '66)
Bob Baker (St. Louis '67)
The Friendly Ox (WWWF '67)
The Ox

PAT BARRETT

Ivor Patrick Barrett

This interview, conducted by Scott Teal in June 2000, was originally published in issue #45 of *Whatever Happened to ...?*

When and where were you born?

I was born in Ireland.

What was the date?

I'm not gonna tell you that! (laughs)

You sound like a woman. Give me the date.

No. (laughs) March 11th (long pause) ... 1964.

(laughs) Oh, yeah. Right!

(laughs)

What were your parents' names?

Barrett. (silence)

I mean ... first and last names.

My parent's name was Barrett. Mr. and Mrs. Barrett. (laughs)

(laughs) **I can tell already that this is going to be a challenge.**

(laughs) My father died before I was born. I think it was the shock of me coming. (laughs) My mother brought me up ... myself and my sister.

In what part of Ireland did you grow up?

Dublin. I went to Wesley College.

Did you play any sports?

I played a little rugby and a very small amount of cricket. I used to fall asleep on the line, so they put me right in front of where the batsman normally whacks the ball. I wrestled, put the shot, running. Other than wrestling, though, cycling was the major sport. I raced all over Ireland.

I just read a recent study they did. Every time a boxer dies, they talk about stopping boxing in England. Well, they did a six-year study on the number of boxers who die compared to other sports in England. Nine cricket players died in that time. I don't know how many horse riders died, but quite a few died in England during that timeframe. Then, of course, you have guys falling off mountains and walkers getting lost and dying of hypothermia. It was amazing! I forget how many people died in car racing, but it was the cricket that got me. You don't expect that.

How many boxers died during that time?

One. It just shows you. It's a morality thing. That's what annoys me. It's not that they're trying to save lives. They *say* they're trying to save lives, but what they're doing is (pause) ... the upper-class people are saying, "*These brutes shouldn't be allowed to do this to each other.*"

That's where wrestling is way ahead of boxing. The promoters are pretty smart about it. They give people non-violent violence. In the old days, when you watched wrestling at two o'clock in the morning, you saw everything ... fighting fans, blood. They've scaled it back so they can entice more women and children to watch. They want them to say, "*Oh, they're not really getting hurt. Let 'em watch it.*" Anyway, I played a little rugby in school, but I was never a team player. I liked individual sports.

How many years did you wrestle amateur?

From age twelve to twenty.

How did you get into pro wrestling.

Well, I knew of it, but I didn't know anything about it. I went into the wrong gymnasium in Brixton, in London. Brixton Prison is where they chopped that policeman's head off in one of the riots. Anyway, I was looking to work out someplace in the morning. I went to this gym and it was closed. Most amateur gyms in Ireland and England are open on Sunday morning. For guys that work, Sunday morning was an ideal time, so I couldn't understand why this particular gym wasn't open.

What gym was it?

It was Martin's gym. Dale and Martin were the promoters. [The promotion was run by Les Martin, Jack Dale, Johnny Dale, and Billy Dale. The Dale's real last name was actually Abby.] They had a gym there for the boys to work out in. I mean, it was filthy dirty and they only had a few weights. It was the old-style weights with the big, thick bars and round balls, the unusual things that strongmen used to use years ago.

There was a man standing outside washing his car. His name was Les Martin, one of the partners of Dale and Martin. He had a Jaguar that was his pride and joy. I didn't know him then, but he was an obnoxious bastard. Of course, he probably thought I was an obnoxious bastard. I was banging on the door of the gym and he said, "*What do you want?*"

I said, "*I want to get in and work out.*"

He said, "*I don't know who you are.*"

I looked him in the eye and said, "*I don't know who you are, either.*" (laughs)

He said, "*Are you a wrestler?*" and I said, "*Yes.*"

He said, "*I've never seen you ... a pro wrestler?*"

I said, "*No, no!*" I wasn't really sure what he was talking about. As I said, I knew about pro wrestling, insofar as I'd seen magazines, but other than that, I didn't know a darn thing about it. He said, "*You're an amateur. What title have you won? Did you ever think about turning pro?*"

I said, "*I won the welter and mid-heavy divisions.*"

I was actually a welterweight moving into the middleweights. When I was middleweight, I went for the light heavy because I beat the guy in the gym. I figured if I beat him in the gym, I could beat him in competition. In other words, I moved out of my weight division. The guy said, "*Do you want to try out for the pros?*"

I said, "*No,*" and walked away. As I did, he said, "*What, are you afraid?*" (laughs) Of course, I didn't have enough sense to say, "*Yes." (laughs)* I turned around and said, "*Hell, no!*"

He says, "*Then come on down tomorrow about ten o'clock and we'll see if we've got a pro around to work out with you.*"

They put me in with (pause) ... probably one of the top shooters there, from Wigan. His name was Arthur Beaumont, the only guy to beat Billy Joyce [Joe Robinson] when he was in his prime. Arthur had trained with his brothers, Cliff and Jack. It was a promoter's match behind closed doors. It was a money shoot. Billy was, by far, the better wrestler. Billy used a crossface and top ride and would slowly submit the guys, but he had a very kind streak running through him.

Do you know any details of the match?

The story I heard was that Arthur trained for months with his brother Jack before the match ... riding on him, hooking in on him, stretching him. He concentrated on the front facelock, which was Billy Joyce's favorite way of submitting guys. Billy Joyce was good at that top ride. In the end, when Arthur fought Billy Joyce, Billy got the top ride on him.

Billy's only weakness was, he was actually a nice man ... a very nice man. He rode him and rode him and was really damaging him, but Arthur had a lot of guts. He held on, even when he was bleeding, and Billy urged him, "*Give up, lad!*"

Arthur said, "*No.*"

The story is that Billy went to stretch Arthur, where you hook the leg across the thighs and the arm up across the face. Arthur got up to his hands and knees. When Billy shifted his weight around to get his legs in further, that was the opening that Arthur was waiting for. Arthur reached down and grabbed the toe, half stood up, and threw his weight back, tearing Billy's knee out as he went back. Actually, Billy's knee was never the same after that.

They both sound like they were pretty tough.

They were. Arthur was tough, but he was a nice guy. His brothers — they were all shooters — very, very good. Jack, the one in the middle, was the middleweight. He was the meanest. He put the fear of God in all the middleweights. He was a nasty fucker and used to do all kinds of things. He was like a miniature [Bert] Assirati, except he was a better wrestler than Assirati was. He didn't have the power, but he was a mean bastard.

"Mr. Perpetual Motion" is what they called Cliff. He never stopped in a match. And it didn't matter how you threw him up in the air; the bastard landed on his feet. He was an acrobat and gymnast, as well, but also a terrific shooter.

It was very interesting. They had promoter shoots. In fact, Bert Assirati had a promoter's shoot with a boxer. I wasn't there, but there was an old guy who came from Canada called Charlie Mascall. He had been a reporter, but he was also a historian. He loved the history of wrestling. He did the programs for Dale and Martin. I love history, so he and I were good friends. Actually, he was a fabulous guy. (laughs) He had big buck teeth and looked like a rabbit. I used to love the stories he'd tell about Farmer Burns, Doc Roller, and [Ed] Strangler Lewis. He knew about all the things that went on. We used to talk non-stop because I loved all that.

We were riding back in the coaches. He told me about a match between Assirati and a young, up-and-coming heavyweight boxer. The boxing promoter said he could beat the shit out of any wrestler, so they get behind the closed doors of a London gym. When the bell rang, the guy turned around, and Assirati (pause) ... now, you have to remember that Assirati had been in a circus act and could move with unbelievable speed. This was when he was in his prime. He ran across the ring and leaped into the air, smashing this guy in the face with his head. The guy went down. Assirati picked him up, slammed him, then went up in the air and dropped on his chest. The guy was totally fucked. Assirati got up and said, "*They don't make those fuckin' boxers like they used to.*" (laughs)

What always amazed me about Assirati was his short legs. He wasn't very tall, probably around 5-foot-6, 5-7, but he had unbelievably long arms. In a way, for the power he had, he had the perfect build. You couldn't get under him because of his short legs, but he could reach you from a long way away. He had arms that were long enough for a guy that was about 6-foot-4. I used to think, "*What is it about him?*" It was only when I looked at a photograph of him that I realized, "*That's it!*" He taught me respect for (pause) ... well, you should never underestimate anyone. You never know what you're up against because, if you saw Assirati dressed, you'd think he was a little, fat man. When he stripped off, he was definitely awesome. And the closer you got to him (laughs) ... especially when you wrestled him, he got more awesome all the time. When I saw him in the dressing room before my match, I looked at his milky eye and thought, "*Ah, he looks a little old.*" His hair was thinned out. When the bell rang and I turned around ... well, he looked a lot more awesome than he did twenty minutes before.

So you had to face Arthur Beaumont in that initial workout?

Yes. I got in there with him and it took him ... oh, I don't know. I think it was a matter of (pause) ... 30 seconds or so. I'm not sure, but it was a very short time. (laughs) He front facelocked me as I was sitting through. He was a decent guy, though. He let me go. He was hurting me, but the problem was that I didn't even know how to give up. I didn't even know about tapping or anything like that.

Did you go in expecting more of an amateur contest?

Yeah! I didn't know about submissions or hooking or anything like that. It was a totally different world to me.

What did you say when he hooked you?

Well, after he let me go, I said, "*Jeez, what was that?*" (laughs)

He said, "*It's a grovit.*"

I've never heard of a grovit.

That's what they called it up there in Wigan ... a grovit. It's a northern expression. It's a front facelock with a bar. I said, "*Oh.*"

He said, "*Want to try again?*"

I said, "*Yeah, okay.*"

We went down and he did it again (laughs) ... from a different position.

There was a man that had come in wearing a suit and tie ... very well-dressed, big cauliflower ears, short. He was definitely the ex-wrestler type. It was Jack Dale. He said, "*Bloody hell! Try him amateur style. Leave out the hooks."* Arthur and I locked up again and we went quite a few minutes. Jack Dale said to Arthur, "*What do you think?"*

Arthur said, "*Yeah, he's good."*

Jack said, "*Let me try him."* Jack took his jacket off and got down in his good suit. I couldn't believe it because the gym wasn't the cleanest in the world. We pulled around, but Jack was a smaller man than Arthur. Not only that, but I was a bit wary, so I was able to hold him off. He wasn't in the same class as Arthur Beaumont. Jack liked me, so he asked me if I wanted to come down and work out. I said, "*Sure."*

Then he said, "*Come up to the office."* I did and he said, "*Would you like to turn pro?"*

I said, "*No."*

He asked me, "*What are you doing over here in England?"*

I told him, "*Well, I'm gonna go around the world, working different jobs."*

"*Well-lll,"* he said. "*This is the best business in the world for traveling. You'll get paid well."*

Of course, money was always very important to me. (laughs) I said, "*How much?"* When he told me, I said, "*That doesn't sound too bad,"* but I tried to up the ante. He gave me a match just three days later. He put me on with a guy named Johnny Czeslaw, a Polish wrestler.

A working match?

It was supposed to be, but I didn't know anything about working.

Did the promoter tell you anything at all before that first match?

When Jack Dale came in, I said, "*What do I do?"*

He said, "*Oh, just do an amateur match, only don't try to beat him. Go fifteen minutes with him."* Well, hell ... I was goin' hammer and tongs all around the place. Oh, the poor guy. (laughs) That's all. Johnny was doing his best to defend himself ... and not screw the match up in the process. He was trying to work and I was doing amateur moves on him and taking him down.

I had seen, in an earlier match, a guy do the move where you get your opponent on his back, split the legs, and stomp on his stomach. (laughs) Unfortunately for Johnny, I hadn't seen where the guy stomped him. (laughs) I stomped poor 'ol Johnny dead center and he never forgave me. (laughs) Ohhh! When I stomped on his balls, you should have heard him. He was cursing in both Polish and English. (laughs) We laughed about it later.

Johnny was wrestling a fellow named Spencer Churchill one night. Spencer was one of the famous bodybuilders. You've heard of Reg Park?

Sure. He won the Mr. Universe several times in the late '50s, early '60s, and played the lead in several old Hercules movies.

Spencer was second to Reg Park. [Note: In the 1951 NABBA Mr. Universe contest, Churchill placed fourth in the medium class, while Park won the tall class.] He wasn't a big man. He was small-boned ... probably only a middleweight, but he had this very small waist and had an awesome body. But he was a very cold-blooded bastard. Spencer stepped aside when Johnny charged him and Johnny went through the ropes into the ringside seats. His head was cut open and it knocked him out. He was talking to me when

Czeslaw was being carried out on the stretcher. He had this very precise English accent. He said, "*That was wonderful, John. Thank you very much.*" (laughs)

Did anyone start working with you at that point, teaching you more about working?

No. Actually, I used to go down to the gym and pull around with some of the fellows that came down from the north ... Wigan and the northern places. A lot of people don't know this, but there were two rival schools; Wigan and the Yorkshire. There were some good wrestlers come out of Yorkshire. I loved training. I used to enjoy it. To this day, I wish I could train. I can't train like I used to because of joint trouble and everything else, but that got me over with Jack [Dale]. Not that I was trying to, but (pause) ... he'd come down and take his jacket off. It always amazed me that he didn't give a crap about how dirty or grovely he looked. He'd be down there with the boys. He was different that way. He was a good promoter in that sense. (laughs) No, he didn't worry about explaining the concept of working. He just let me pick it up as I went along.

Do you remember how much your first payoff was?

Oh, I don't even want to talk about that. It was, uh ... six pounds, I think. That would be about fourteen bucks.

That's not too much out of line from what you would have received here in America.

No, but they had a structured scale there. In other words, you got so much for a preliminary and so much as you moved up the ranks.

Regardless of the house?

Oh, yeah ... very much. They kept great control over it. That's the way it was. I thought it was terrific when I went to America and found out, if you drew a house, that you hopefully got a percentage.

Did any of the boys try to discourage you?

Oh, I had a few, but you know ... that's just grist for the mill. I enjoyed competition and learned pretty quickly how to at least defend myself.

Were you still in school at this point?

No. I was over twenty. I was gonna go back to university when I came back, but then I got hooked in the wrestling business. I was taking a sabbatical, as they say, going around the world. I was going to work jobs here and there. I was an electrician and had my ... what they call "card," so I could have worked anywhere. Once I started wrestling, I really couldn't do both, though. At that time, Dale and Martin were probably the biggest promoters in the world. They had something like five or six shows running a night, so you had all kinds of work. The [Royal] Albert Hall was the premiere [venue]. It was the flagship. That is THE venue for artists, operas, stuff like that. They feature high class stuff there, so when wrestling made it to the Albert Hall, it arrived, if you know what I mean.

What part of England did the Dale-Martin territory cover?

South of England, basically, up as far as a place called Coventry [95 miles northwest of central London and 19 miles east-southeast of Birmingham]. One of the wrestlers, Johnny Yearsley, was part-time. He was a Welshman who did some strong-arm things. He said to me, "*Why don't you come and stay at my place? I'll get you a job at the swimming pool."* I gave notice to where I was staying. I was in a small (pause) ... I was in a room, actually. I had arrived in London with twelve pounds in my pocket; about 25 dollars. That's all I had. I didn't have much money. (laughs)

What did your mother think about your travels through Europe?

Well, at fifteen, I had hitchhiked all around France, England and Germany, so she was used to me disappearing. She knew I had wrestled amateur, so I wrote and told her I was wrestling pro. She didn't know what that was, actually. Of course, she never liked me [amateur] wrestling, anyway. I boxed before that, but I found I wasn't built for boxing. My arms were too short. I boxed in the National Stadium in the juniors, but boxing wasn't (pause, laughs) ... I just preferred wrestling. It was more natural to me.

So prior to your first pro match, you had never even been a show?

No, no. No, I didn't know what they were. As I said, my first match was when I showed up at Beckenham Baths. Baths Hall ... a public bath. The bath halls were very popular in England. The Beckenham Baths was always full. It's in Kent. A lot of the older houses in England didn't have bathrooms. The toilet was outside and there was no bath, or they had a tin bath, so they set up a lot of these bath halls. Many of them had a balcony running around the top and a café. You might say they were much like the Roman baths. The Baths people would rent out the hall for wrestling. They would put boards across (pause) ... they'd drain the bath, I guess. That's funny. Now that I think of it, I don't know if they did drain it, but the boards went over it and the ring went on top of that.

Did you wrestle that first night as Pat Barrett?

No. My given name was Ivor [pronounced eye-ver]. It's a Welsh name, actually. When I came to America, no one understood it and they had difficulty with the pronunciation. They'd used to call me Ivor [pronounced ee-vor], or Igor. (laughs) In the end, I just told them to use Pat, which is my middle name. Pat was easier, so I used it. A promoter called me Paddy, so that stuck for a while.

Were any of the guys helpful in terms of pitching in to teach you things about the business?

Not too many. They were very (pause) ... ah, especially the older ones. (laughs) For instance, I wrestled a guy called Charlie Fischer. For some

Peterborough, Cambridgeshire, England • May 19, 1960

reason, they pushed him in certain places and he got over a little bit, but he was a horrible worker. His wrestling was stiff. I don't mean stiff in the manner of a tough wrestler (pause) ... it's hard to explain. He was like a robot. He did a preemptive strike and busted me in the nose. When I came into the dressing room, he came over and said, "*Bloody hell! You hurt my elbow.*" My face is covered in blood and he says, "*Oh! How did you do that?*" No, they weren't that helpful. (laughs) You know, life was hard. It was hard making money because England was not in great shape then. Money was hard to come by, so every new face was a competitor.

Back to Johnny Yearsley ... I got off the train with my two cases and walked about two miles to his house. There were no cabs, but I probably couldn't have afforded a cab then, anyway. When I arrived, Johnny wasn't there. His wife answered the door and said, "*Who are you?*"

I said, "*I'm Ivor Barrett. Johnny told me I could stay here.*"

She says, "*You're not staying here. I've just gotten rid of one. I'm not bringing in another.*"

I said, "*What do you mean you've gotten rid of one?*"

Lee Edwards, who was a Canadian wrestler ... Johnny had him staying there, and the wife didn't want anybody staying there. Johnny didn't tell anybody that. He was a real con artist. (laughs) We almost had a fight on the doorstep. I said, "*Johnny told me I could stay here.*" Because, to me, John was the man of the house. (laughs) I didn't realize that the power wasn't Johnny.

I talked my way in, but she insisted, "*Well, you're not staying very long.*" When Johnny got back ... oh, they had the damndest row. She showed me to a back room and I was sitting there having a cup of tea. I could hear them ... "*He's not staying here!*"

Johnny says, "*Just give him until Monday. He's leaving Monday!*" I think that was a Friday. Anyway, he came back to me and said, "*Okay, your room will be upstairs. You pay me so much a week for bed and board. We'll go for the job tomorrow.*"

I looked at him and I said, "*What about Monday?*"

He said, "*Oh, that's nothing. She'll be all right.*" (laughs)

Well, she wasn't all right for about a month. Ohhh, she made things painful ... but she was okay. I didn't blame her once I knew the situation. Lee Edwards had been with them for about four months. Johnny was a bit frugal with the food, but I learned to get my own and eat it fast before he got to it. (laughs)

We went for the job and it turned out it was as a lifeguard (laughs) ... but I couldn't swim. When I came out, I was wearing a t-shirt and shorts, and I was in pretty good shape. He said to me, "*You're a fine-looking, young man. What sports do you play ... cricket, rugby?*"

I said, "*Yeah, I've played both.*"

He said, "*What is your major sport?*"

I said, "*Well, I wrestle.*"

He said, "*Jolly interesting.*" We must have talked for about 45 minutes about the sports I was in and what I had done and everything else. Finally, he says, "*Can you swim? Oh, no need to answer! You've got the job!*"

I said, "*What job?*"

He says, "*You're a lifeguard!*"

I thought, "*Oh, crap,*" but I didn't want to say anything because I didn't want to lose the job. I stuttered, "*Well, okay.*"

So, I was a lifeguard, but I couldn't swim eight strokes. I was a lifeguard for three months in the summer. (laughs) What I would do is, as the people came in, if I didn't know them, I made them go down to the shallow end. (laughs) I wanted to be sure they could swim. (laughs) If they couldn't, then I watched them like a hawk to be sure they didn't get in the deep end.

I only had one experience … and thank God, Johnny was there the same day. I happened to be in the pump room when I heard this shouting. I looked out and there was a guy going up and down in the water. He was obviously drowning. I thought, "*Oh, my God! What am I gonna do?*" I was looking for the hook. (laughs) Johnny was looking around for me because he had his clothes on. Of course, I'm hiding. He walked around the pool until he got as close to this guy as he could. He took off his t-shirt (pause) ... now he couldn't help but pose while he was doing this (laughs), but in the meantime, this fellow is drowning. (laughs) Finally, Johnny plops in beside him, grabbed him by the hair, and dragged him in. I picked that moment to materialize out of the pump house. (laughs) What had happened was, this fellow couldn't swim, either, and somebody had bet him that he wouldn't go down the slide in the deep end. (laughs)

I had one real bad experience there. There was a group of teenage kids there who used to hang around. They knew I was sort of semi-pro wrestling. They were always asking me to get in and swim. I said, "*No, no, no, no, no. I can't while I'm on duty.*"

Well, one day, I happened to let it slip that it was my birthday, so they decided to dunk me for my birthday. There must have been ten or twelve of them. They grabbed me, and I tell you ... I was the best wrestler in the world that day. There were guys flyin' all over the place as I got closer to the deep end. (laughs) Nobody would believe I couldn't swim. If I had gone in the deep end, which was probably eight feet, I think ... I'd have drowned. Just before I got to the edge, I broke loose. They couldn't believe it! "*Hey, what's wrong? Why are you so determined to not go in?*"

What could I say? I said, "*Oh, I just didn't feel like being thrown in today.*" (laughs)

You worked that entire three months without ever going in?

No, never. I finally learned to swim in America. There was a fellow called Jack Bence. What happened was, I used to sink, like a stone. I was always told it was because I was not relaxed. Jack was a terrific swimmer. He said, "*Look, I want to show you something.*" He jumped in the deep end and sank to the bottom of the pool, then sat on the bottom. Seemingly, it was muscle and bone density that caused me to sink to the bottom. He took me to the kiddies' pool in Atlanta, Georgia, and we got in together. (laughs) We were getting these strange looks from people while he was showing me how to breathe because anytime my face went under the water, I panicked.

When you finally got into the water, did you find it easier to swim than you thought it would be?

Not really. I never learned to swim well. I could swim just under the surface, but I'd stick my head back up after every third stroke. I could swim for a long time because I was in good shape, but it never was an easy thing for me. The minute I stopped propelling, I sank. Even to this day, and I've got a bit more body fat on, I still have difficulty staying afloat.

To be honest, I'm not familiar with many of the boys from England. Who were some of the wrestlers you watched that impressed you when you were starting out?

Al Hayes. Al Hayes had the best timing in the world. He had the best timing of any wrestler that ever came out of England.

Did Al break into the business at the same time you did?

Oh, no, no. Al was a star when I was starting. I was fascinated by him. (laughs) I don't know whether you're gonna be able to use this story, but it's a story that I like to tell on Al. He was wrestling in Maidstone. It was a terrible town. We wrestled in a big, open shed in a place where they sold cattle. The dressing room was actually behind three wagons that they transported cattle in. It was like you saw in the movies where they were fighting Indians. People used to try and peer through underneath to watch us dressing. When they got mad at us, when there was a riot — and there were riots quite frequently in this town ... it was a bad ass town — they tried to push the wagons over on us. We'd be on the other side trying to keep them up. Ohhh! It was terrible.

Anyway, Al would stand there and, to me, he looked like the epitome of an English gentleman. He was impeccably dressed. I was just standing there watching the matches when this girl came up on the other side of the wagon. She was small, about nineteen ... not bad looking, if I remember right. She said, "*Mr. Hayes, could I have your autograph?*"

He said, *"Certainly."* He signed his autograph, and then says, "*Do you fuck?"*

She said, "*Wh … what?"*

He says, "*Do you fuck?"* (laughs)

She said, "*Sometimes, yes."*

He says, "*Well, I'm going to fuck you tonight. Will you go to my car over there? I'll be over there in five minutes."* (laughs)

I was just a green kid, so I was curious. I followed to see and (laughs) … sure enough, there he was! Oh, my! (laughs) I couldn't believe it! I had just come over from Ireland. I thought, "*How could you talk to anybody as coarse as that?"* (laughs)

Al wouldn't care if you told that, I don't think. I tell it to show how naive I was to the ways of the world. Of all the wrestlers, though, Al was the best. I've always admired him. When I first met him, he was taller than me by an inch or two and he looked so good.

Another story about Al ... he was in the ring with an ex-rugby player who was a pretty tough son-of-a-gun, but the guy wasn't a great worker. I can't remember the name of the wrestler, but he was from the north of England. He had wrestled in the gym in Wigan. He had two cauliflower ears and a broken nose, both of which were gotten from rugby, actually. He had been a pretty good rugby player, so you can imagine that he was pretty salty. He wasn't a class worker, but he was trying to do his best for Al. Al could have a great match with just about anybody. Everything he did always looked so smooth. He was just like a ballet dancer, and the way he used to do his judo stuff was tremendous. That night, though, he had a terrible match with this guy. Afterward, Al said, "*What was the matter with you tonight? I chopped you and chopped you and chopped you ... and you didn't register.* [react] *You did nothing.*"

The guy says, "*I didn't feel 'em!*" (laughs)

Al says, "*You fool! My chops aren't real chops. They're chicken chops. You're not SUPPOSED to feel them!*"

Everybody broke up.

Did Al come over to the States before you?

No, they just about all came after me, except for Timmy Geohagen. I didn't know Timmy over in Europe. I'm not even sure where Timmy came from. I was his partner, but he never really talked about it. I know he was Irish and came from Ireland, but I was just trying to remember where he started. He was in a circus and did the strongman stuff. I liked Timmy. I had a lot of time for him.

There was quite a bit of difference between the style of pro wrestling in England and that of this country.

Oh, yeah. To me, the American style was far superior. The American timing was better, and the pursuit of one hold, and going back to that hold time after time. England was one hold, up and down. When I first went to Georgia, I wrestled in a tag match ... my first tag match. I'd say it was probably the only time I ever really embarrassed myself. (laughs) It was Lenny Montana and his partner against me and somebody else. I came flying into the ring, like over the top rope and charging in. Lenny Montana stood in the middle of the ring and shouted at the top of his voice, "*What is he doing in here? Somebody get him out!" (laughs)* Actually, that was about the fifth time I had come in at the wrong time. (laughs) I was fucking everything up. Of course, Lenny was never behind the bush in voicing his thoughts.

What were the fans like in England? Were they more polite and reserved than in America?

Well, English fans can be, but, of course, knives and guns were not part of the scenario like they were in the States. They were prone to throw bottles and large beer mugs if they happened to be serving them. For instance, in Southampton, you could see the beer mugs coming through the (pause) ... they used spotlights there. It was like being in Vietnam with the mortars coming in. You could hear them whistling through the air, hoping when they land, it wasn't on you.

So they really weren't any more subdued than American fans?

Not really. The little old ladies would carry bricks in their purse. In fact, the first time I was ever in a riot was in Bermondsey Baths in London. It was in East End, which was a very tough area. All the gangsters used to come from East End. Again, there was a salty wrestler from the north of England who also played rugby. A lot of them did both. He was coming out of the ring and he was giving the people the finger. "*Up yours,*" and all that. This little, old lady swung her purse and whacked him in the side of the head ... and it dropped him to his knees. I thought, "*My, God! How could she do that?*" He got up and he hit her! Ohhh! If you looked at her, you'd say she was somebody's grandmother. And, of course, all hell broke loose!

The promoters yelled, "*Come on! Let's go in!*"

I thought, "*Go in where?*" We all bunched together and charged through the crowd. When I walked in the place just an hour or so earlier, people were shouting things like, "*Come on, Paddy!*" "*Hope to see you tonight!*" "*Do good!*" Now the same people were trying to kill me. They're hittin' me with chairs. This was all still new to me. I'm fighting in self-defense. I really didn't know what I was doing there. When we got back to the dressing room, I went over to the guy and the whole side of his face was turning black and blue ... and he was bleeding. I said, "*How could she drop you like that with a purse?*"

The lady was taken off in an ambulance, by the way. In America, there would have been a lawsuit, but there was not a lawsuit. The promoter had grabbed her bag and took a brick out. I was stunned! I said, "*My, God! She had a brick in there!*" It got deathly quiet, and they all turned and looked at me like, "*Where did he come from?*" Then I heard someone say, "*Well, thank God there were no hatpins.*"

I asked one of the guys, "*What did he mean by 'no hatpins'?*"

A fellow said, "*Well, you'll find out soon enough.*" The Londoners used to carry large hatpins. As you walk by, they'd stick them in you. Yes, they could be violent. (laughs)

Was that the only riot you were involved in over there?

Oh, no, but that was the first one. It made me more aware of what could happen. The arenas in the East End of London were pretty bad. Some of the ones up north could be bad ... places like Coventry and King's Lynn. They were big, rough farmers up there and they didn't give a shit. I saw quite a few problems there. Northampton ... that was another town that was pretty aggressive, except Northampton was a lot of Irish at the time building the roads, so I was usually okay. (laughs)

Did they film regular television shows and interviews to promote the house shows like they did here?

No. They did television, but not the interviews. In fact, I think that was tough for a lot of Englishmen when they first went to America. I realized right away that interviews were the way to go, and you had to go with the flow because in England, you didn't. Kent Walton [Kenneth Walton Beckett] was the guy that did the commentary on wrestling in England and you never said a word. That was one of the major things to learn in America. You had to speak to the camera.

How did the promoters compare to those over here?

I find that promoters, generally speaking, were the same. In my opinion, Jack Dale was probably one of the best at the time. He was an ex-wrestler, but he still liked wrestling and liked to see you work out. You could talk to him, too. He had a couple of brothers, one of which didn't know much about the business.

It was Jack Dale, Johnny Dale and Billy Dale. Jack was the guy that had wrestled. He had cauliflower ears and a nose that was a bit banged about. He was a middleweight. Johnny Dale never wrestled a day in his life, and neither had his brother Billy. Billy was the accountant. When Joint Promotions took over all of England, he was an accountant, and he became one of the big powers in it. He never wrestled. I'd say he was fairly ruthless when it came to money and things like that. But you could talk to Jack and say, "*Hey, we've drawn this house,*" and he might say, "*You're right,*" and give you more. Remember now, it was almost a salary-type thing. Jack was one of the first that was flexible when it came to, if not a percentage, then more. Most of the promoters over there didn't think that way. You wrestled in X amount of towns and accepted what they gave you whether you liked it or not.

And Les Martin took care of the politics.

Yeah. Les Martin, because he had gone to Lord Mountevans [Edward Evans, a British naval officer and Antarctic explorer]. Seemingly, he was a partner, although they all hated him. Wrestling had been very, very bad in England back in the '20s and '30s. It had sunk so low that it had been totally barred in England. They weren't allowed because they had broken glass matches and things like that. Bottles were thrown and all kinds of things, so it was illegal.

That sounds like what's going on today.

Well (laughs) ... it finally became barred. Boxing had been banned for a long time before becoming legit. There was a time that you could be arrested if you went to boxing matches ... and people were. So, to make it legitimate, they went to the Marquess of Queensbury and he drew up a set of rules. The rules were given to the government and the government said, "*Yes, if they stick to these rules, we will allow it again.*" It went from the bare knuckle era to ... well, they had to wear gloves again. In England, wrestling seemed to take the same course as boxing.

I guess it was in the late '40s or early '50s that Les Martin came up with an idea, which really was quite smart. In order to get it [wrestling] back on track, Les Martin went to Lord Mountevans and said, "*We want to start wrestling.*"

He knew Lord Mountevans. They asked him, "*Would you consider using the Marquis of Queensbury rules?*" And the Marquis of Queensbury rules are what helped make wrestling legal. The rules let them know what they could or couldn't do. They could make the case that wrestling wasn't like the bad old days. There was no punching or kicking, so for years in England, if you threw an elbow, people would get incensed. They began to sell it as primarily wrestling. And, as I said, I think that's how Les Martin became a partner in Dale-Martin.

Were the referees treated with more reverence over there?

Oh, yeah. You see, in a way, it was very easy to be a heel. All you had to do was throw a sneaky elbow and people would get really mad.

What were the trips like in England?

Well, the trips were longer in America, but easier. The roads were better, especially in the beginning of my career. They didn't have freeways or motorways. [In England], a hundred-mile trip was agony because you were constantly going through small towns. That was the toughest part. The other thing was transportation. Dale and Martin had coaches, which were along the lines of a conversion van. Very few guys could afford cars, so we rode in these banged-up old coaches. They were freezing cold in the winter and roasting hot in the summer. There were times when the whole card rode together. In fact, it was funny because we would arrive in the town where all the people would be lined up to get in. They just stopped the coach and we'd all get out and walk past them. (laughs) And, of course, there was all kinds of things done in the coaches, as well. (pause, laughs) In fact, I think it was a couple of years before I realized that you made love somewhere else other than in the coach. (laughs) Sometimes, we'd leave at mid-morning or noon and just drive all day, then get back home to London around five o'clock in the morning.

One of the names I remember is Mick McManus.

I knew him very well. He became a star because he got into the office. We started a union. In fact, the boys were getting paid a small amount for television. When the TV people and their union discovered how little we were getting paid, the promoters had to up the money to bring it in line with an act.

Like the Screen Actors Guild.

Right. They considered every match an act. Some guys were getting six or seven times more ... maybe more than that, depending on how much they were making before. I've forgotten how much it was. I think it was forty pounds (pause) ... but, anyway, it was a lot more than they were getting. The TV union said they'd shut down the TVs if we weren't given that. It wasn't that they were trying to help us. They were pissed off at how little we were getting.

The promoters did two things to fight it. They targeted the key members in the committee that ran our union and they bought McManus off. I think he was the secretary. They bought him off and, in addition to wrestling, they gave him a job in the office where he could book. Of course, he booked himself on all the top shows.

Was he a good worker?

Mick? Oh, yeah. Mick was a good heel. No doubt about it. Then they sent forms around for everyone to sign that they wouldn't be part of a union. I tore mine up and went to America.

Is that why you came over here?

I was going to go to America, anyway. I wanted to expand my horizons and I wanted to see the world. Of course, wrestling was the best way to do it. [In later years], wrestling in England was eaten up by WCW and the WWF. They just weren't good or exciting enough, especially their TV. It was almost like watching a golf match. It was very slow and lacked the excitement of the American style. I knew once the Americans came in, that would be the end. The Americans have it down to a T. Vince McMahon, Junior, whether you like him or not, has moved wrestling into the 21st century. It's moved on. It's sports entertainment. It had to. People want to be entertained.

Had you wrestled anywhere other than England before leaving for the States?

I had gone to Germany, Austria. There's one story that I think is a classic. It shows how it was in Germany. We got into a fight in the hotel we were staying in. Recklinghausen was a mining town and it was horrible. We were playing cards around the table. It was me, Ski Hi Lee, and Josef Kovacs, the

Hungarian Butcher, plus some others. I had watched a guy in the business called (pause) ... oh, shit!

I never heard of that guy.

(laughs) No, that was a Chinese guy. Les Kellett. He was a short guy that had hands like an orangutan. He was feared by a lot of guys in England. He was a middleweight, but even guys bigger than him were afraid of him. He wasn't a great wrestler, but he used to grab handfuls of flesh and he would just rip. He was a bit crazy. I had seen him, where he'd stick two fingers in a guy's mouth, the forefinger and middle finger, and he'd hook his thumb underneath their chin. He would grab, and he would twist, and guys couldn't do anything. It would paralyze them.

A lot of us stayed in this one hotel. We're downstairs playing cards and Ski had a pile of books beside him. This miner came over and started blowing smoke into his face, and smiling at him. He was trying to antagonize him. Ski just stared at him. Ski was at the end of his career by then, anyway, so he just stood up and said, "*I'm goin' upstairs to read.*" He grabbed his books and he left. Later on, I learned that Ski wasn't a coward. He had just reached the point in his life where he avoided trouble, no matter how cowardly it made him look.

There was a space between Kovacs and me, so the guy got between us. I thought, "*Oh, Christ! Here we go.*" I mean, he was a big bastard. I was watching as he took a deep pull on the cigar. I wasn't playing cards. I was watching. He turned around and he blew it straight into Kovacs' face. Kovacs had obviously been waiting because, no sooner had the smoke got into his face, than he smashed this guy in the mouth. He jumped up, picked him up, and threw him right over the bar. Oohhh! Kovacs had the strength. He was unbelievable. Well, the whole bar broke out into a fight.

There was quite a few miners in the place. This big miner (pause) — well, he looked big to me — came for me and I hit him in the gut. As his mouth opened, I got this super hold on him that Les Kellett used to do. As I did, the guy proceeded to bite my fingers. (laughs) I didn't have the hand strength that Kellett had. Suddenly, I'm in real trouble. The guy's literally biting them off. So I reach down and grab him by the nuts. Right behind me was this glass case, full of cups the miners had won at local football and soccer. I rammed him through that and that's when he let go of my fingers. (laughs) We did some damage and held our own against the miners. There was some pretty tough guys in the German tournament then.

The next night, the promoter came marching in. Gustav Kaiser. He came in like the real Kaiser, real imperious looking. We're all standing at attention while he looked us up and down. We have all these scars from the night before. He says, "*I heard what happened.*"

We thought, "*Oh, shit, here it comes.*" Because, if that was America, one, we'd have to pay for the damage, and there would be a lawsuit. He said, "*My men. You have done very well and I am very happy. And,*" he said, "*the place is packed.*" And it was.

There's a sequel to it all. We went back to the hotel that night and the place was packed with miners. We thought, "*Oh, shit! Here goes.*" They all stood up and gave us applause. (laughs) There was free drinks all around. They admired the courage and fighting ability we had.

I don't know if it's true or not, but Ski Hi Lee told me he went into a restaurant and the owner told him to get out. The fella wasn't gonna serve him because he was a heel. He'd seen him on television or somewhere. Ski said, "*You've got a public restaurant and I'm staying, so serve me.*"

The guy says, "*Okay.*" He put rat poison in Ski's food and nearly killed him. Ski could have been lying to me, but I think it was true. He was a big star, but it's a shame the way he died. He drank himself to death.

What else do you know about Les Kellett.

He was like the Bert Assirati of the middleweights. He wasn't powerful like Assirati, but he had tremendous hand strength. Everyone thought he was slightly mad. The story I heard was they tried to make him serve in the British Army. He did some mad things, so they threw him in solitary for several months. When they took him out, they brought him in front of an officer, who was straddling a chair. The chair was in front of him and he was leaning on the back of it. He says, "*Well, Kellett. I hope you've learned your lesson. We are going to make a soldier of you whether you like it or not. What do you have to say to that?*" Kellett kicked the chair out from under him and then kicked him in the head before they could stop him. They put him back in solitary, then they kicked him out of the Army. But then, I got along with Les. He was okay with me.

What do you remember about "TV" Jackie Pallo?

Jackie Pallo got to be a star because (laughs) ... he used to clean Jack Dale's car or something. (laughs) That's what I tell everyone, anyway. There was more money on TV, so Jack put him on TV more. That's how he became known as "TV" Jackie Pallo. (pause, laughs) He wouldn't like me saying that.

One night, a fellow jumped in the ring on Jackie Pallo at the end of his match and challenged him. The guy was a mark, but if I remember right, he'd done some judo. They asked me if I'd wrestle him.

Jackie wasn't good enough to take him on in a shoot?

No. They didn't want to chance it. Well, let's put it that way. I was a non-entity and nobody really knew me, so they put me in. At the time, I was in very good shape. They told me, "*If you can beat this guy, then we'll put you in later with Pallo,*" and Pallo was a big star then. That's why they didn't want to risk having him get in the ring with the guy. If he had beaten me, he definitely would have beaten the shit out of Pallo.

Kellett was refereeing that match. I took him down. In hindsight, when I thought about it, I think they put Kellett in just in case something went wrong ... in case the guy got the better of me. I don't know what in the hell he would have done, though, but I'm sure they would have come up with something. I was new to the business and they didn't really know how good or how bad I was. I had the guy pinned and bent up like a hoop, with his shoulders on the mat. Kellett says, "*Break his arm.*"

I said, "*Count him.*"

You could hear the guy. He was out of gas, but Kellett wouldn't count him. He said, "*Screw him. Break his arm.*" I let the guy go, and when he got up, I took him down to a sitting position and I put him in a front facelock with a bar. (laughs) I put the ol' grovit on, which I'd learned very well by then. (laughs) I mean, in that position, you are totally fucked. He's sitting down, head forward, and you could hear him scream in the back of the hall. Kellett said, "*What's that you say?" (laughs)* Then he whispers to me, "*Tear his head off!*"

I said, "*If he gives up, I'm letting him go.*"

When I went back to the dressing room, Kellett wouldn't talk at first. He just sat there, hunched over and looking down between his knees. He was like that. He'd sulk. I finally said, "*Les, what the hell's the matter? Come on, tell me. What did I do wrong?*"

He said, "*I told you. You should have damaged him.*"

I said, "*Why? He gave up.*"

He said, "*It would teach him respect.*"

I said, "*Okay, then,*" and didn't think much else about it.

I just finished getting dressed and in the guy comes. He was holding his head to one side. I guess I had hurt his neck or his traps. All I know is that he was hurt. He came over, shook my hand and said, "*Thank you very much. I enjoyed it.*"

I said, "*Okay.*"

He walked to the door, then turned around and said, "*But I'll be back.*" I looked at Kellett, and he looked at me and said, "*I told you.*" He didn't talk to me for a few months, but that's how he was. Of course, he was right, I suppose. Who knows?

I understand the boys speak a different form of carny over in England.

They don't speak carny over there. The Londoners speak (pause) ... I don't remember what they call it. It's apples and pears, a rhyming language.

Adrian Street explained it to me. It's cockney slang.

Yes, that's it. The northerners don't know what the hell they're talking about. The cockneys, who are born within the sound of Bow bells, they speak that. They had their own language, but that was the cockneys, only. That wasn't generally spoken in England.

What are Bow bells?

Bow is a district in London. There's a cathedral or church there with bells. If you were born within the sound of Bow bells, if you can hear the bell, then you were a Cockney. That's the criteria for being classified as cockney. [Note: The Bells of Bow are found in London near Cheapside at the church of St Mary-le-Bow.]

The funniest story I ever heard about kayfabe was up in Calgary. There's an old guy that used to do sweeping in Toronto. I can't remember who told the story, but the guy would sweep out the dressing room. Whoever it was that told me about it, he was watching a match. The old man started sweeping around him and never looked up, but he said, "*Can I ask you something?*"

The guy went, "*What?*"

The man still didn't look at him, but kept on sweeping around him. He said, "*I want to ask you a question. I've been going in and out of that dressing room for twenty years,*" or however long it was that he'd been sweeping in Maple Leaf Gardens. He said, "*Every time I go in, they start shouting at this guy named Kayfabe* (pause) ... *and you know something? They never seem to be able to find him.*" (laughs)

That's a great story. I remember many times in the cars, when we'd be going to a town, when the boys would talk about the wrestling business in England. The common belief was that it was completely controlled by the Mafia. How much truth is there to that?

None. Joint Promotions pooled the talent (pause) ... but what they did was, they had a conglomerate of promoters. That may have been where that came from. The promoters had a meeting once a month, I think it was, and they divvied up the boys. Everyone had a certain demand on different guys. This month, Jack Dale might have a certain number of boys he could pick. I was never quite sure just exactly how it worked. They sort of kept it secret, but it was very effective at keeping the boys in line.

Your promoter had first crack at you. In other words, let's say he only booked you fifteen dates out of the month. They had some type of rotation system worked out where the others could say, "*I want so-and-so for so-and-so dates.*" Now, you could refuse to go ... as I did. I didn't want to go to certain promoters who I had trouble getting money out of. I just said, "*No, I'm not going.*" Some of the boys did that. But, of course, if your own promoter didn't use you very much, it was nice to have other promoters booking you. It was more controlled than it was in America.

Did it hurt you down the road if you refused to work for a promoter?

In other words (pause) ... yeah, it could hurt you. I got screwed by a promoter named Arthur Wright. [Note: Wright promoted Manchester.] He didn't pay my fare and I got into a row with him. I told him to stick it up his ass. I told Jack Dale, "*I don't want to work for him.*" Of course, it created animosity because they'd start putting pressure on Jack, saying "*This guy's a troublemaker.*" I had a couple of fights and rows with promoters over money and things, so Jack said, "*Why don't you get booked in Germany for a while until things cool off?*"

So Joint Promotions could best be described as the British version of the National Wrestling Alliance.

Yes. Joint Promotions was a cartel. You had Arthur Wright, Dale-Martin ... and several others.

What about the use of gimmicks? Was it more reserved than in America?

There were very few gimmicks when I started. They relied much less on gimmicks than they did in the States. As I said, they had just come out of an era of, you might say, horrible wrestling where everything went, and being totally shut down ... so they were treading very carefully. They didn't want the government shutting them down again. I don't think it could have happened in America, but in England, it did.

Did they rely on the use of blood or blades over there?

Well, at the beginning of my career, no. Later on, when I went back to England from America, they had moved into more gimmickry. In the past, one elbow would drive the crowd mad. Bert Assirati got blood his own way. He just whacked you in the nose. In fact, when I wrestled him, he had me down in a headlock. He was kneading my nose with his other hand. I was probably the only one in that hall that didn't know that was gonna happen. He whacked me twice and there was blood everywhere. (laughs) That's how he got it. He didn't bother with blades. He just whacked somebody or head-butted them. If you happened to make the wrong move, you got head-butted.

In your book, you talked about that match with Bert Assirati. Did you ever work with Assirati again?

No, I didn't get the chance.

Would you have welcomed the opportunity?

Yeah-hh. He went opposition and I wasn't working for them, so it never came about. I had mixed feelings about it. I would have liked to wrestle him. I had a lot of respect for the man. You had to have.

Where did you start wrestling when you first came to America?

I flew into New York and then straight down to Georgia. It was funny because nobody knew who I was. I went to the office and said I was a wrestler. I can't remember who was at the counter, but it was a guy with cauliflower ears and a cigar in his mouth. He looked at me and said, "*So, yur a rassler? Who have yuh rassled?*" The only names I knew they would know (pause) ... I said, "*Well, I wrestled [George] Gordienko and Bert Assirati.*"

ALL-STAR BIG-TIME
PROFESSIONAL
WRESTLING
Decatur Recreation Center
Sycamore Street, Decatur
Tonight Sept. 23, 8:15 P.M.
Sponsored by Decatur Recreation Department
TRIPLE MAIN EVENT
INFERNO (MR. FIRE)
VS.
PAT IVOR BARRETT
PLUS OUTSTANDING GIRLS WRESTLING MATCH
MARGIE RAMSEY
VS.
PEGGY ALLEN
PLUS 6-MAN TAG TEAM MATCH
BULL CANNON (325 Pounds)
JOE McCARTHY (Southeastern Heavyweight Champ)
and JACK BENCE
VS.
MARCO POLO
BOB MORROW (Former U.S. Marine Champ)
CRIS OVEROFF
PLUS 1 OTHER BOUT
Get Advance Sale Tickets at DeKalb Sporting Goods; Decatur Sundries; and Decatur Recreation Dept. Phone 377-1704 for Res. Gen. Adm., $1.25; Children, 50¢. Ringside only $2.00.
Fred Ward, Promoter FREE PARKING

Decatur GA • Sept. 23, 1963

He shouted to the back, "*Hey, come here! There's a guy out here that says he's a rassler.*" I had about five of them looking at me like I was some sort of freak, but they gave me a chance. I wrestled Pedro Godoy.

My records show that match taking place on June 8, 1962.

Poor old Pedro. I was working in the European style. I was going up and down his body like a sewing machine. Grab an arm, grab a toe, grab his head, grab anything I could. Every time he got up, I took him back down. (laughs) To make a long story short, he got up and he shouted out to all the guys who were standing at the back, "*Hey, he can wrestle!" (laughs)* I liked Pedro. I had a lot of time for him, too. I was sad when I heard about the bad times he went through before he died. I think he got divorced, he got sick. When I saw him, he wasn't the man he was. He had a good sense of humor and we had a lot of laughs together. (laughs) Actually, we had a lot of laughs about that first match. He was patient with me.

You worked with Jack Bence during that time, too.

Yeah. I became good friends with Jack. Jack became sort of a mentor to me and helped me a lot. Jack was never a big star or such, but he was a globetrotter. We first met in England. In fact, he came up to me and I didn't recognize him. They tried to send me to Louisiana. I asked a couple of guys that came from there what they made. I couldn't believe how little it was. I thought, "*I'm not going there.*"

Jack said, "*Why don't you have a little holiday and come on down with me to Florida.*" He lived in Tampa. I went down with him and he made a few calls. He said, "*How do you fancy going to Arizona?*"

I said, "*Okay, why not?*"

We were in the car a couple days later and he got tired. He said, "*Take over.*"

I said, "*I can't drive.*"

He said, "*You used to ride a motorbike in England.*"

I said, "*Yeah, but I haven't ever driven a car.*"

He said, "*It's the same thing.*" (laughs)

I got behind the wheel and started driving ... and he went to sleep! Oh, it was terrible! I didn't know anything. We drove for two days and I said, "*Where is Arizona?*" I didn't realize how big America was. I mean, I consider myself well educated and knew my geography, but until you drive (pause) ... and I find that, even today, people don't realize how big America is. What I tell people in Europe is, "*Look, from New York to Los Angeles is approximately from London to Moscow and back.*" That gives them an idea of how big it is. They go, "*My God!*" I thought it was a fabulous country.

We didn't stay in Arizona too long. Jack wasn't very happy working that area. I went back to Florida and that's where I met Ken Lucas. He was sort of a star there. I think he was the only one that wanted to work with me because everyone heard that I was European and did all this weird shit.

(laughs) I've never heard it put quite that way.

(laughs) Well, that's the way they considered it. I got feedback later on from different guys. (laughs) Ken was the first one, though, and we had some great matches. He helped break me in to the American style ... which I admired, but just hadn't done before.

In the fall of 1962, there was a guy in Mobile and later in Memphis, who worked as Bobby Barrett. Was that you?

Yes. I don't know who it was, or why, but somebody decided to call me Bobby.

You finished out the year with a couple of shows right here in Tennessee.

That's right, then Nick Gulas came in and called me "boy." I got into a row with him about that. I said, "*I'm not your boy.*"

He said, "*I'm the promoter here and you'll do as I say.*"

I told him, "*Well, you can stick Tennessee up your ass!*" I gave him my notice and said, "*I'm not working here anymore.*"

He said, "*You can't do that.*"

I said, "*Watch me.*" The next morning, I got a call from the office. It was [Jerry] Jarrett's mother, I think.

Christine.

Yeah. She called me and said the boss, the old man [Roy Welch], wanted to see me. I said, "*I have nothing to talk to him about.*"

She said, "*Why don't you come on down. We heard what happened and he'd like to talk to you.*" So, I went to the office and he brought me in. Roy said, "*What happened?*" I told him and he said, "*I told that fucking Gulas.*" He raved on and on about what an asshole Gulas was for treating his boys like that. He said, "*I've heard good things about you. I'd like you to stay. I'm going to fire that no-good Greek son-of-a-bitch!*"

I was looking at him and I said, "*Excuse me, but could I ask you a question?*"

He says, "*Yeah, what is it?*"

I said, "*How long have you two been in the business together?*" (laughs)

He told me whatever it was ... 20, 25 years. I said, "*You're gonna fire him now?*" (laughs)

He started laughing and said, "*That's alright. He won't talk to you that way again.*"

The next town I went to, Gulas walked up, shook my hand, and asked, "*How's the Fighting Irishman?*" From then on, everything was fine. I can't complain. They treated me good.

Gulas and Welch were the original "good cop-bad cop" team of wrestling promoters. There's something else that puzzles me. You worked in Memphis and Nashville as Bobby Barrett, yet in Chattanooga, you worked as Billy Barrett.

I think that was a screw up in the billing. I think the printer fucked up. They left it that way because they didn't want to make the change after the first week. I didn't ask them to call me Billy *or* Bobby. I just went with the flow.

Where did you go from there?

I think I went to New York. Tim Woods, Ron Reed and I were all greenhorns up there. There was an old Irish-American there. Oh, what was his name? I know he used to give Tim Woods an awful time. Not that Tim couldn't have taken him anytime. Tim was that good. The guy was doing a job for him, but he'd go up to Tim and whack him hard, kick him with the boots. (laughs) Tim was trying to get along and get over. The guy liked me and used to talk to me about Ireland. He made me look like a million dollars. (laughs) But he used to give Tim and Ron Reed an awful time.

Tommy O'Toole was up there at the time.

That's it. Tommy O'Toole. He used to do the jobs for those guys, but he made them pay for them. (laughs) They said, "*I don't understand it.*" (laughs) I had nothing but praise for him, and they couldn't understand it. As I said, we talked a lot about Ireland. I believe I went west from there, to California, then up to Vancouver. Roy Shire used me up and down the coast, but he said I came in at the wrong time. Whether that's true or not, I don't know, but he liked my work. That's where I met Ray Stevens and Pat Patterson. I used to watch Ray religiously every time he wrestled ... to gain experience. To me, he was fabulous. He was one of the best. I wrestled in and out of Vancouver for a couple of years. Rod Fenton liked my work and put me on a show as Don Leo Jonathan's partner. Don amazed me that night. (laughs)

He said, "*Paddy, can I start?*"

I said, "*Yeah, okay, Don.*"

We were on the apron and he soared over the corner post. He was doing dropkicks, kip-ups, then he ran along the top rope. I mean, he was running ON the top rope. After about seven minutes, he had done stuff that I could only dream about. (laughs) Then he tags out and he said, "*All right, Paddy. Your turn.*"

I said, "*What's left?*" (laughs)

He started laughing ... but he was a great guy and a terrific partner. I was always grateful for the opportunity to meet him and work with him. He was fabulous. There were nights he wasn't in the mood to do as much as he did other nights, so he'd say, "*Well, Paddy. You go and do your thing.*" But when he was in the mood, Don was awesome! He was awesome! What an athlete!

Vancouver BC • Aug. 9, 1965

I started working with people like Haystack Calhoun. Haystack liked working with me because I never tried to steal his thunder. I did most of the work, then would tag him in at the right time. The guys used to say to me, "*Oh, you're making yourself look like a piece of shit because you're doing all the selling.*" But I looked at it this way; I was making main event money. He was the draw card and I was there to fill in. We got along very well. Anytime he came into town, he always asked to team with me. It did two things. One, it pushed me into main events and it got people used to seeing me in that capacity. Two, I made more money because Rod would appreciate it. Seemingly, some guys would go on with Haystack and they would tag him in at the wrong time. Because he was so huge, he was limited, but he was a big draw at the time.

Rod was a big gambler, you know. You could always tell when Rod lost a lot. I think he was run out of Phoenix because of that. That's the story I heard. That's when he went to Vancouver. Yeah, you could always tell. The payoffs always dropped. I used to say to him, "*Yeah, you've been gambling again, Rod.*" He wasn't a bad promoter, though. He had a pretty fair idea of what he wanted. He ran a nice little territory and it paid reasonably well.

Rod and Stu Hart promoted together, but it didn't last very long. It only lasted a couple of shows, but I don't know why it fell apart. The first time I went to Stu's house, I was sitting in a chair. I had never met Stu before. He was talking about stretching some policeman on the mat earlier that morning. He's going, "*Aaah, yes. I ...*" He was behind me and proceeded to put this hold on me. He got halfway into it and I said, "*Get your hands off me. I've heard all about you from George Gordienko and a few others across the water.*" (laughs)

He said, "*Accch, that's the Great White Stallion.*"

I know George well. In fact, I just saw him last year when I visited him in Vancouver Island. George, you know, beat the shit out of Stu in his own gym. That was when George was at his best. Stu would have had no chance at all. Stu had already tried to hurt Luther Lindsay. Luther had a bad leg and Stu went for it. That's when Luther went bananas. Well, George proceeded to give him an awful shellacking. The wife [Helen] could hear what was

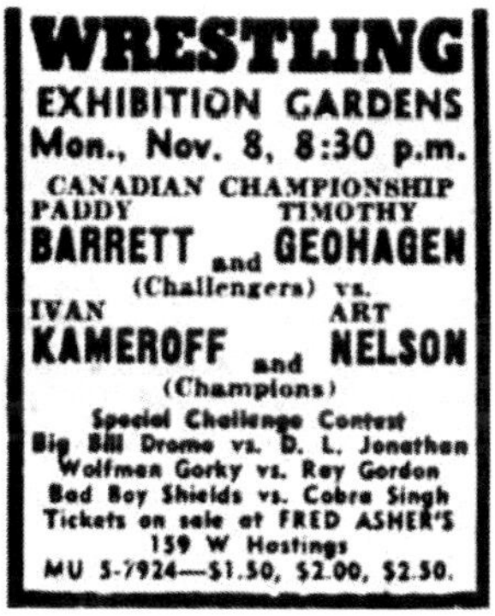
WRESTLING
EXHIBITION GARDENS
Mon., Nov. 8, 8:30 p.m.
CANADIAN CHAMPIONSHIP
PADDY BARRETT and TIMOTHY GEOHAGEN
(Challengers) vs.
IVAN KAMEROFF and ART NELSON
(Champions)
Special Challenge Contest
Big Bill Dromo vs. D. L. Jonathan
Wolfman Gorky vs. Ray Gordon
Bad Boy Shields vs. Cobra Singh
Tickets on sale at FRED ASHER'S
159 W Hastings
MU 5-7924—$1.50, $2.00, $2.50.

Vancouver BC • Nov. 8, 1965

going on because there was a hole in the ceiling. The story I heard was when Stu started hollering, she shouted down, *"Stu, you've got an international call."* George has a pretty droll sense of humor. He shouted back, *"You'd better tell them to call back because they'll be waitin' a long time."* (laughs)

Anyway, I said to Stu, *"You're not puttin' anything on me."* He just went on talking like he hadn't been trying to do anything. Here I was, booked to be in the main event tag match that night, and he's gonna pass me out! He gave no thought that it might screw up his main event. He just couldn't help himself. He's like the scorpion in the old story about the scorpion crossing the river on the back of a rabbit. He just can't help himself.

George Gordienko was, at one time ... if not the top shooter in the world, then darn close to it. You should call George. He said he'd be happy to talk with you. He's up different hours, and he's up late, so don't hesitate to call.

You held the Canadian tag team title with Timmy Geohagen.

Yeah. Rod said something to me about getting an Irish partner. I said, *"I don't really know anybody."*

He said, *"I've heard of a guy named Timmy Geohagen. Do you know him?"*

I said, *"No."*

He said, *"I'll bring him in."* Rod wasn't very happy with Timmy at first. He didn't like his style. I was a fast mover and Rod liked that style. Timmy was not like that. Timmy was totally different ... more the older style of wrestling, and he never really changed that much.

He did have that sleeper hold and the hypnotism. I told Rod, *"Don't worry about it. I don't mind doing the extra work,"* because Timmy could really put that sleeper hold over. It always used to amaze me. We would do a thing where I would invite people up into the ring to be put to sleep by Timmy. What never ceased to amaze me was, we had all these people ... I mean, we had maybe 20 or 30 of them lined up, all waiting to be put to sleep. In the end, you had about fifteen people passed out in the ring, out to the world, laying on the mat with their tongues hanging out. I could never understand it. (laughs) I mean, I wouldn't do that! Not voluntarily, anyway. (laughs) I used to look at them and think, *"What sane person would allow someone to do that to them?"* In Florida, they used to have the guys sign all kinds of contracts saying they wouldn't sue them before one of the boys beat the shit out of them in the ring.

We had to put a stop to that one day on television when Timmy couldn't wake one fellow up for quite a while. He wouldn't come around like he should have and Rod panicked a bit. He almost ate his cigar ... and I don't blame him. It got to the danger time because it cuts off a certain amount of blood to the brain, and at a certain point, it becomes dangerous. I think that's when Rod decided that was enough of that.

Only in the wrestling business would something like that happen. There's no other sport that has the stories that wrestling does. None. In fact, people would freak out. The things that [Mike] Tyson did over here is nothing compared to what went on in wrestling. Like, when Tyson said about the world champion, "*When I meet him, I'm gonna reach in, tear his heart out, and feed it to him.*" Well, everybody freaked out! I sat and thought about what wrestlers have said over the years. They've said an awful lot worse than that.

Before Jim Hady died, he was wrestling Johnny Barend and Magnificent Maurice. They said they'd send him home in a pine box ... then he died after the match. I heard they had to get out. (laughs) Now everyone's on Tyson's case, but the stuff he's done is mild compared with the things that happened in the wrestling business.

I also worked in Oklahoma during the early part of my career in America. That's when I first met Bill Watts. He was just starting in the business and we palled around a bit. In fact, the first time I stayed at his house, I went out partying that night. He tells me, "*Mom says you can stay overnight here.*" When I arrived back about five in the morning, dirty and disheveled after screwing around and drinking all night, I went to bed. His mother woke me up early in the morning and said, "*Get ready for church.*"

I said, "*Church? What are you talking about? Where's Bill?*"

She said, "*Has he not come back?*" That son-of-a-gun. (laughs) He knew the rules. If you stayed over, you had to go to church. (laughs) He never stayed over. (laughs) I was dragged off to church for the first time in years. (laughs) I had about an hour and a half sleep, I think ... but it didn't do me any harm. (laughs) I've been set up a few times, but that's okay. I get them back, usually.

A funny story about Abdullah [the Butcher]. I was leaving Oklahoma and had left my car door open while I paid my bill at the motel. I had all my belongings in it, and like an idiot, I left the door open and the engine running. I looked out and there was a great big, black guy behind the wheel of my car. Ohhh! I thought he was gonna take off with everything I owned. I charged out and leaped in the car. He starts saying, "*Paddy, it's okay, it's okay! It's me!*" After I stopped to think about it, the guy could have had a gun or a knife. All I could think was all my worldly goods were in that car. It wasn't a lot, but everything I owned was in the back of that car.

That was the last time I ever saw Abdullah. I thought he was terrific. We wrestled just before he left Vancouver. Fenton said he didn't want any blood. Christ! Abdullah bled all over the place. (laughs) There was buckets of blood in the ring. He said, "*I just wanted to make you look good, Paddy.*" He was a great guy.

You went to Australia in 1974.

That was the second time. The first time was when Barnett called me up out of the blue. I had been in England for a couple of years and went back to Vancouver. That's when [Gene] Kiniski and Sandor Kovacs had the territory. Barnett called me and made me an offer I couldn't refuse. They wanted me to stay, but I wanted to go to Australia, so we had words about it. I mean, I was giving them plenty of notice. It wasn't like I was gonna leave in a week. I said, "*Look, I'll even come back and do whatever you want.*" But they got very uppity about it.

Then Sandor called me up out of the blue. He goes, "*Ho-ho-ho, hee-hee-hee. You're not goin' to Australia.*"

I said, "*What do you mean?*"

He said, "*You're not going. It's been canceled.*"

I didn't believe them, so I tried to get ahold of Barnett. I couldn't find him, which Barnett was wont to do when he didn't want to talk to you. It was like he was off the planet. I checked my plane ticket and he hadn't canceled it, so I believed they were lying. I went to Australia, anyway. It turned out that he forgot to cancel the ticket. (laughs) I tried to call Barnett, but they said nobody knew where he was. When he finally called me back, I was pretty annoyed about things because we had a verbal contract. He apologized and said, "*I'm sorry. You were supposed to team with Dale Lewis, but he went and got himself kicked in the balls.*" Whether that was true or not, I never found out. He said, "*There no sense in you staying, but I'll get you booked wherever you want.*"

I said, "*Okay, make it Hawaii on my way back.*" I stopped off in Fiji and had a nice vacation before I went to Hawaii, though.

I stayed in Hawaii for about three months. There was some good guys in Hawaii. Ripper Collins ... he was easy to work with. Peter Maivia. I met him in Europe and we became good friends. When I went back to the States, I was told that I was barred all over the States because I didn't go in for Elliott (pause) ... Elliott, the promoter in Washington.

Harry Elliott.

I was supposed to go to a show for him. That was Kovacs' deal, of course. Harry Elliott had gone to the commission and said I hadn't showed up in a town, so they barred me from everywhere in the United States. Can you believe that shit? I went to the commission and explained. "*Look, it's as simple as this. In the United States, you have a law. You can't deprive someone of a living.*"

They said, "*Well, you didn't show up, so yes we can.*"

I said, "*Do you have anything in writing that I was supposed to be at the town?*"

I said, "*No, I don't believe so.*"

I said, "*You tell that to the judge because I'm gonna take you to the highest court in this land. Are you prepared to tell the judge that you're going*

to stop me earning a living in this country, all off of one man's testimony, and he has nothing in writing?"

They said, "*Give us half an hour and we'll let you know something.*" They called me back and said, "*Where are you gonna work?*"

Well, I said I was gonna go down to San Francisco. They said, "*Okay, you're barred here in Washington, but you can work anywhere else.*" I never heard another thing from them. That really annoyed me. It was all bogus bullshit of the highest order.

Luke Graham was there.

That's right ... and Jim Hady. In fact, he died a short while after that. Ray Stevens was there, too. [Mr.] Fuji and Stevens tried to set me up in a bar with a Mickey Finn. I felt myself going, so I slipped out and got in Peter Maivia's car. I had borrowed his car. Fortunately, I knew the amount of alcohol I had had wasn't enough to make me feel the way I was starting to feel. Knowing Stevens ... and I knew Ray very well. I passed out on the floorboard of the car when they came out to look for me. Later, I asked them what they had planned to do. They said they would have stripped me naked and left me there. (laughs)

I left Hawaii and went to California. That was my second time there. I was wrestling in Las Vegas and this man wearing a leather jacket came up to me. He had a heavy French accent and said he'd like to put me in his show. I thought, "*Oh, yeah, sure.*" He gave me his card and said to give him a call. He said he had this casino and wanted me to be in his show. I thought he was a faggot. I thought he was after my body. It turned out that he wasn't.

When I went back to California, I heard that Jay York had been invited to go to a show. I thought, "*Well, maybe this guy's for real.*" I called him up and he asked me to fly out. He wired a ticket, had a limousine pick me up in Las Vegas, wined and dined me. I was told the people who owned the thing were Jewish Mafia. They were in the back with guards all around them. It looked like the old movies. All the producers and directors of the shows in town were there for the dress rehearsal. It was a fabulous show.

Besides me and Jay York, there was a guy named Robert Duranton. He was a big star in France. On the night of the dress rehearsal, he got so mad at one of the little faggot choreographers who was shouting at him. He dropped his pants, spread his cheeks, and told him to kiss his ass. I heard York behind me, "*That's it, Babe. You tell him!" (laughs)* We'd stayed a year. We were supposed to stay two years, but no one knew Duranton [in the States]. Even though the money was good, Jay York and I didn't want to work every night. I enjoyed the time I spent there, though.

I went to Mexico from there. I had been told by Tony Borne that if you made a deal with [Salvador] Lutteroth beforehand, he sticks by everything he tells you. He stopped in Las Vegas on his way back from somewhere and we had dinner together. I told him I didn't want to be traveling all over on buses. I wanted to work the bigger towns and I wanted to be treated right. Consequently, when I went down there, I had no problems. He was very good to me.

Danny Hodge was dying from dysentery there at the time ... Montezuma's revenge. He was in terrible shape. He had made some horrendous bus trips and looked awful. We went out to get some milk shakes. We heard they used raw eggs and milk, so we went down the road to where they made these things. I could speak a little Spanish, but not a lot.

I said, "*Cinco huevos.*" Five eggs, you know. The guy is cracking the eggs into the milk and papaya, and on the fifth egg, I notice a big lump of chicken shit on the shell. The guy cracked the egg and that was the only time he dropped the bloody shell in. Then the guy dove his hand on, which I don't think had been washed for fifty years. He pulled out the eggshell (pause) ... without the shit on it. Here Danny is, feeling like he's dying from Montezuma's revenge, and he's lookin' at this. "*Jeeezz, they're tryin' to kill me!*" He threw the money at the guy and walked away. The guy just stood there, with egg still dripping from his hand, watching Danny walk away.

We had a good time, though. Danny kept screwing the matches up by whacking guys. One guy was really beatin' Danny badly from behind, every time he'd turn his back. I said to Danny, "*Jeez, have you heard of receipts?*" Right then, he walked across and he hit the guy with a short punch, about six inches, and knocked him into the third row. Of course, that killed the match. (laughs) It was a six-man tag. The guy's partners disappeared. They didn't want (laughs) ... I was sittin' on the floor laughing my head off. I couldn't help it. Our partner, the Mexican, was looking around like, "*What's happened?*" He thought we'd gone mad. (laughs) Oh, we had some funny things happen.

Shreveport LA
Sept. 28, 1976

A one-night, round robin tournament was held in Shreveport, Louisiana, on Sept. 28, 1976, to crown a new NWA world junior heavyweight champion. The former champion, Danny Hodge, was forced to relinquish the title after suffering a broken neck in a car accident. Pat defeated Ron Starr in the final match to win the belt. Four other men — Hiro Matsuda, Ken Mantell, Nelson Royal and Buck Robley — were eliminated in earlier matches.

Tell me about your reign as the NWA world junior heavyweight champ. Was it a surprise when they told you about it?

Well, they just needed somebody, I think. To be honest, I wasn't a heavyweight. I was a natural junior heavyweight. We had a bit of a riot that night because of the way I won the title. [LeRoy] McGuirk, who had his arm in a cast at the time, was trying to get in the ring to fight everybody. Oh, I couldn't believe it! LeRoy McGuirk ... cast and blind eyes and everything. He went bananas and was fightin' them all.

He was blind. How did he know what was going on?

He knew what was going on. He was very tuned in. Oh, yeah.

I talked with [Danny] Hodge about the fact that even though LeRoy was blind, he was able to keep a tight reign over his promotion.

He had his people, of course, that were his eyes and ears. He knew everything that was going on. He would listen. I think somebody came up that night and screamed some abuse at him for allowing me to get the title the way I did. I think he took a swing at the guy and away we went. I thought, "*Jeez, there's a lot of fight in the bastard.*"

You dropped the title to Ron Starr just two months later.

It was time and it was what Watts wanted, plus I was making noise about moving on a bit. Watts was promoting and I think he had most of the territory by that time. I could be wrong, though.

The first time I saw you in person was in Florida, when you were teaming with Tony Charles.

I think I had just came back from New Zealand. Before that, Tony was in Mexico and I was going down to team with him. When I got down there [to Mexico], though, he had got off the bus and said, "*I'm gonna go home now.*" They thought he was going back to his hotel. Actually, he was going back to Wales. (laughs) He caught the first plane back and left. He said he walked out on them because he couldn't stand it anymore ... but he told me Lutteroth sent him all his money. Lutteroth sent him every penny that was owed to him.

You also teamed with Norvel Austin for a while.

That was in Tennessee. I enjoyed Norvel. In fact, a funny story about Norvel. I had never met him before and I had that pit bull down there ... Rocky. Rocky didn't like blacks because most of the blacks he met were fans, and since I was a heel, they were all trying to kill me. He had never seen a black person in the dressing room. He used to lay in the shower, or in the dressing room, and he'd never move. When I got ready to go out, I'd get my jacket on, then slip the leash on him, and I'd go out the door. The people waiting outside were predominately black. Rocky used to scare the shit out of people. He was a very tough dog. (laughs)

One night, Norvel came marching in, dressed like a pimp. He had the hat, a feather sticking out of it, high heels. Rocky took one look at him, jumped up, and charged. Norvel jumped behind Superstar Dundee ... and now the two of them are screaming. (laughs) Dundee's in front of Norvel and this dog is right in front of him. I was laughing by now, but I shouted at Rocky to stop. Whenever Norvel came in, Rocky always gave him the bad eye, like he still wasn't sure about him. Finally, Norvel got to pat him on the head one night. Norvel came to me and said, "*Hey, Paddy. Rocky and me ... we're friends now.*"

That's another thing. The first time we wrestled in Memphis, I said to Norvel, "*Hey, all your people are up there. Let's go up and see them.*"

He said, "*Okay!*" I went up and I got the shit beaten out of me by those black women. They were grabbing me and holding me and pinching me. I mean, they were hugging me and kissing me, but at the same time, they were beatin' the crap out of me. I look around ... and there's no Norvel! (laughs) I get back to the dressing room and there he was ... stripped naked, sitting in a chair with his legs up, smoking a joint. I said, "*What happened to you?*"

He said, "*Well, look what happened to you.*"

I said, "*Why didn't you come up with me?*"

He said, "*Hey, look at yourself. Do you think I'm crazy?*" (laughs)

In 1975, Victor Rivera and Dominic DeNucci were the WWWF tag team champs. When Rivera jumped ship and went to work for the IWA, you took his place as Dominic's partner.

That's right. I stepped right into Rivera's shoes, which was a good break for me. It wasn't quite the way I would have had it, but Dominic was a great partner. I was there for about nine or ten months, then decided it was time to move on. Whether that was the right move or not, I'll never know. There are times I think it wasn't, but once I did something, I never had regrets. I went back to Oklahoma.

Did you know Adrian Street or Tony Charles before you came to America?

I knew Tony when we were both in the amateurs. I knew Adrian, but I knew Tony better. Adrian was different. (laughs) Jack Dale almost had a heart attack from some of the stuff he [Adrian] used to do.

Do you mean the gay, effeminate gimmick?

Yeah. You might say he was the first of his kind to do that sort of thing in England. I don't know what went on before the Lord Mountevans, but after that, when the rules came in, Adrian was probably as far out as you could get in England.

Which brings another question to mind. Did you get much harassment from the fans when you wore a kilt?

(laughs) I sure did. When I was a babyface, they asked me what I was wearing under it ... but if I was a heel, I was a faggot. "*Take your dress off,*" and all that bullshit. (laughs)

(laughs) Did you ever work under a hood?

Yes, I did ... in Australia. I went in as Mr. Wrestling. It was for the promoter [Tony Kolonie] that took over after [Jim] Barnett. He came up with this bloody, silly idea that I come in ... I mean, I was well-known in Australia. He gave me a wig to wear. The wig was so bad. I was on the plane and the hostess said, "*Excuse me, sir ... I mean, m'am ... uh, sir?*" She couldn't figure out whether I was a transvestite or what. (laughs) So I get off the plane with this damned, stupid wig on, and

Pittsburgh PA • Aug. 22, 1975

everybody starts shouting, "*How ya doin', Paddy? Welcome back to Australia, Paddy,*" and all the rest.

Then I wore the hood and I worked with Ciclon Negro. He pulled that bloody nose thing out about three feet. All I could see was two little holes in the distance. (laughs) He's whacking me in the head and laughing. "*I'm over here, Paddy!*" I was so mad. I was saying, "*I'll kill you, ya son-of-a-bitch!" (laughs)* I just had to find him first. (laughs) Not that I could, but he was having a good laugh at my expense. Ohhh! It was terrible. It was an awful mask, as well. It was a horrible experience. The promoter had me staying out in the boondocks somewhere, about 30 miles from the town. I think that first night was Melbourne. I was registered under an assumed name. Within half an hour of getting to the motel, the fans were calling me up. "*How are you doing, Paddy?" (laughs)* The whole thing was a fiasco.

So it didn't last long?

No, no. It wasn't for me. That was near the end of my wrestling career. If I had come in under the mask the first time I visited Australia, it would have been different. If they had done the gimmick like [Pat] Patterson did one time, which was a very good gimmick ... he actually put the mask on in the ring.

That was in Northern California.

Yes, it was. It was one hell of a gimmick. Then he'd use something for a finish and get a lot of heat.

Your book talks about a fan being in the dressing room with a mask on. Who was the promoter that asked him who he was?

I believe it was Eddie Graham. He said to his booker, "*Who in the hell is that? I didn't think we had a masked wrestler on tonight.*"

The booker said, "*We don't.*" They walked over to the masked wrestler and asked him, "*Who are you?*"

He said, "*I'm nobody.*"

"What do you mean you're nobody? Who the fuck are you?"

"I'm nobody."

They said, "*Take the mask off.*"

He took the mask off and they didn't know him. He said, "*I'm a fan. I just wanted to come in and sit with the wrestlers." (laughs)* They kicked the shit out of him, then threw him out.

When did you first use a blade?

Louie Tillet did the first blade job on me. They asked me if I'd do it and I said, "*Well, I've never done one. You can knock me in the nose if you want.*"

Tillet said, "*Oh, God, no. I couldn't do that.*" He was like horrified at the idea (laughs) ... at least, that's what he said. I don't think he was, really. (laughs) He said his hand slipped [laughs, pause] ... no, I knocked his hand. There was enough blood there for five matches. After that, I never let anyone do it again. (laughs) It was a good lesson. I learned to do it very quickly after that.

What was your average weight during your career?

In New York, I was probably around 235 pounds. That was my heaviest. I went up for television the first time. When I came out, Lou Albano said to

me, "*You're a good kid. That was a great match. It's a pity you aren't any heavier.*" I started doing heavy squats, bench presses, deadlifts, and was eating and drinking like a pig. Three weeks later, I went back for TV and was the heaviest I had ever been. I was over 235 then, probably a bit too heavy in a way. I knew Lou Albano was sort of a power in there. He came out and said, "*Hey, you're lookin' great, kid!*" That's what they wanted. They were big men there. They said they had plans for me, providing I got over, but then the championship thing came up, so that was even better. It all depends on how you fit in with the clique there and how well they liked you. It was an Irish territory run by the Italians. (laughs) I used to call them "God the Father, God the Son, and God the Holy Ghost." God the Father was Vince [McMahon Senior]. God the Son was Phil Zacko. God the Holy Ghost was the other guy.

Willie Gilzenberg.

That's him. He was on his last legs and looked like he was on death's door. (laughs) I mean, I didn't go around calling them that to their face. That's what I used to call the three of them to myself. (laughs) You have an Irishman, a Jew and an Arab. (laughs) That's like the unholy Trinity. It's (laughs) ... it's hard to believe that combination of personalities could do business together. They're so totally different. (laughs) And old man Vince was like the Godfather. He had that air about him. You had to go through so many people to talk to him. I used to go up and talk to him, but I could see all the frowns I was getting from other guys, like, "*You should have talked to me first to see if it was all right to talk to him.*" He was surrounded by them.

Did you ever have any legit problems with anyone during a match?

Oh, sure. I was teamed with Bobo Brazil in a return match against [Clyde] Steeves and a partner. I got my eye busted when I was sucker punched by Steeves. I don't know the reason, but an old referee up there, an old shooter, told me that it was a deliberate thing. Steeves hit me in the jaw and then on the eye. It opened me up the hardway. The town had been down, but it was a huge crowd that night. I don't know for sure, but I think he was told to do it, to get juice. Anyway, I got him in the dressing room a few months later. He was sitting down and I came up behind him with the shillelagh. I kept tappin' him in the head and told him if he ever did that again, I'd kill him. I said,

"*You'll never know I'm coming until I bury this in your head.*" I kept tapping him because, as I was talking, I was getting madder thinking about it. He apologized. Actually, I got to know him later on and we became good friends.

I had a few other incidents. We were in a six-man tag one night and the Mighty Ursus gave Timmy a problem. He was being very heavy-handed and wasn't selling anything for Timmy. Then he started coming after me. Here's this huge guy. I thought, "*Oh, Christ! Here we go!*" All of a sudden, a voice from the gods came from behind me that said, "*Are we having trouble, Paddy?*" It was Don Leo Jonathan. He saw what was going on.

(laughs) A voice from the gods! That's a good line.

(laughs) Ursus goes, "*Errr, fuck you!*" Then he left. He didn't want to mix it with Don Leo. He was prepared to squash me if he could, or would have, but Don Leo helped me out.

Ursus didn't like me much because I had a German Shepherd puppy. Ursus used to scare the shit out of him, so I told Ursus to leave him alone. I used to train dogs and I owned a lot of dogs. German Shepherds are very intelligent. When they start to get bigger, people get nervous. The dogs figure this out for themselves.

One night, he decided [translated from dog language], "*Okay, I've had enough of Ursus' shit.*" When Mighty Ursus jumped up and growled at him, he jumped and landed on his chest. Now, the dog was quite big by now. Ursus fell back over the bench and he's screaming at the dog. I'm pulling at him, trying to get him off of Ursus. Then again, I'm laughing so hard. I couldn't help it. I finally got the dog off of him. Rod [Fenton] came in and Ursus said, "*You should get that fuckin' dog out of here!*"

Rod said, "*There nothing wrong with the dog. You leave him alone and he won't bother you.*" Then he walked out. (laughs)

So that was that. Mighty Ursus wasn't too happy with me from that day on. Of course, every time he'd come in the dressing room, the dog's hackles would stand up. He had his number from then on. That's a typical German Shepherd. He'd focus on Ursus. (laughs) With everyone else, he'd wag his tail and he was quite friendly with them. And every day, that bloody dog was getting bigger and stronger. He used to pull me around Stanley Park on a bike. I had a leash rigged up around his chest. He used to run five miles or more, pulling me on the bike.

I had dinner with Bill Dromo and Ted Allen last weekend. Bill said they used to call him the Mighty Uterus.

(laughs) That's a good one. (laughs) I used to call Dromo buggy whip. He had arms like buggy whips. He could hit you from three-fourths of the way across the ring. You couldn't get near him. (laughs) I worked with him when he was a heel. I'd be makin' a comeback and he'd flip those hands out ... BANG! (laughs) Of course, Bill was a hell of a wrestler. I think a lot of guys underestimated him. He was that good. He really was. I thought Bill was terrific. I had a great time with him. He was the one that I went shooting with a shotgun. I'd never done it before. He said to me, "*Have you ever fired a shotgun?*"

I said, "*No.*"

He said, "*We're going to a turkey shoot.*"

I asked him, *"Have you done this before?"*

He said, *"Well, a couple of times."*

We get there and he starts takin' out this shotgun, the oil, the grease. I look at it and say, *"What do I do?"*

Anyway, to make a long story short, all these good 'ol boys were there with their own shotguns and what have you. I got a shotgun from the fella that runs the turkey shoot ... and I won the prize. (laughs) Dromo swore I was lying and was an expert with a shotgun ... but I hadn't, actually. I'd never shot. It was beginner's luck. Of course, then I was hooked on it. Every time I saw a turkey shoot, I had to stop. I think I only got the second prize one other time after trying a hundred times.

That's the strangest thing. The same thing happened to me when I was 13 years old. My next-door neighbor took me and I won a ham.

(laughs) The best shoot I ever saw was in England, between a referee and an emcee, the master of ceremonies. The master of ceremonies was a little, round, tubby asshole named Frankie Blake. He was a real loudmouth. The referee was a little guy called Lou Marco. Lou Marco was a real show-stealer. Anyway, they both got drunk, and we used to come back in these vans ... these horrible, miserable, cold vans.

Frankie Blake and Lou Marco had a difference of opinion on who was the star of the match, the main event. Now, forget about the guys who were wrestling. They were talking about who the people liked the most. In the end, Frankie Blake says, *"Fuck you! Do you want to take this argument outside? Stop the bus!" (laughs)* Lou Marco weighed about 80 pounds, soaking wet, and as I said, Frankie Blake was so out of shape and had never fought anyone in his life. Everybody who was asleep woke up. We all wanted to see this.

Frankie Blake got out first, tore off his jacket, and said, *"Come on out, you little bastard! I'll kick you all over the place."* Now, it was pitch dark. There was no lights on in the bus. It was really a piece of junk. When Lou Marco got to the top step of the bus, there was dead silence for a second, then we heard Frankie cursing. *"You bastard! You no good bastard!"* What happened was, Lou Marco had pulled his dick out and pissed all over Frankie from the top of the steps. (laughs) Frankie had no idea what Lou Marco was going to do to him. (laughs) Everybody went hysterical. (laughs) And that was the best shoot I ever saw. (laughs)

(laughs) When did you quit wrestling?

My last hurrah, you might say, was in Jordan. Jerry Monti was a good buddy of mine. He had a little wrestling school and some Arabs got in touch with him. They wanted to promote in Jordan, so he asked me to help him since I had been to so many foreign countries. I took him to Kuwait with me years before. I'll tell you who else was there. [Jimmy] Snuka was there. It turned out to be a semi-disaster. They were screwing around with the money and weren't paying the guys. I think Jimmy and I were the only ones that really got their money because we held out for it. I said I wasn't gonna do anything and I was gonna screw everything up if I didn't get my bloody money.

Anyway, Jerry asked me if I'd be a manager, but it turned out that somebody didn't show up, so he asked me if I'd wrestle. I wrestled this Jordanian guy that had just come back from the States. He was supposed to be the Jordanian champion, but he was an awful worker. He didn't know what in the hell he was doing. And once he got in front of his own people, he went ape-shit. I ended up underneath him, on the ropes. He was strangling me ... and I couldn't get him off me. I'm laying there thinking, "*Well, I'm either gonna die right now, choke to death under this bastard, or I'll take his eye out and die trying to get through the crowd back into the dressing room.*"

I decided I'd take my chance on taking his eye out. Actually, so help me God, I had my finger in his eye and was gonna take it out. I still couldn't get him off me. Fortunately, he ran out of gas and sort of passed out. (laughs) He fell off me. I got up, gave him a shake to make sure he was staying there, and charged through the crowd.

We had a very hairy experience in that town. I don't think people understand how dangerous Arab countries are. We had a couple of girl wrestlers, a couple of midgets, Jerry, myself, and Snuka. We went into this big fairground-type thing. They wanted us to do a walkabout, to let the crowd see us. I had spent time in Arab countries and had told them on the bus that they were making a big mistake, and that we shouldn't go through there, but I was overruled by the local promoter. I had spent time in Arab countries and knew the mindset. "*Oh, no, no, no! It'll be okay.*" Well, it wasn't okay. The only people that were there were males from age seven or eight to up around 30. I didn't see anyone older than that. We were suddenly surrounded by thousands of them. They were pinching the midgets. I had a midget hiding between my legs. I was the tallest guy. (laughs) Can you imagine that? Me being the tallest guy? Then they started to pull at the girls. Of course, the girls are running around in halter tops and shorts, which is a big no-no in Arab countries. I didn't think we were gonna make it back to that bus. If I was asked, I would say, "*Yes, I was frightened.*" I was frightened. Everybody was frightened ... everybody.

Didn't the girls know enough about the local customs to realize they should wear more modest clothing?

Let me tell you about the bloody girls. We got in the bus and I said, "*Keep the bloody windows closed.*" It was after the matches, it was in the dark, and in the back. One of the girls pushed a window wide open. This Arab kid jumped up (pause) ... he must have been an acrobat, I'll tell you ... and he grabbed her by the breast. Three of the fellows jumped off the bus and chased all these kids up this dark lane. I'm shouting at them, "*Come back, come back.*"

They came back about ten minutes later and I said, "*Did you catch them?*"

They said, "*Nah, we couldn't catch the little sons-of-bitches.*"

I said, "*You're very, very lucky you didn't.*"

They said, "*Why is that?*"

I said, "*All these kids carry knives. If you grabbed one of them, the others would pass you, running a hundred miles an hour, and they'd just open you up as they went by.*" I said, "*Two, they've got uncles. They've got fathers, cousins. If you did any damage to them, they'd look us up, wherever we were, and we'd have serious trouble.*" You couldn't tell those guys, or girls, anything. Western people have no idea that the rules are different in other countries ... and life is awful cheap. I said, "*That's it. I am not gonna die.*"

What year was that?

That was about eight years ago, I think.

I didn't know you wrestled that long. I thought you quit in the '80s.

No, I wrestled in England about ten years ago.

Did you have a favorite move or hold?

I didn't really have one in England, but in America, I liked any toe hold.

Did you ever have a part in a motion picture?

Oh, yeah. (laughs) I don't smoke. Years ago, when I was in England, I did a part where I played a bouncer. I came out onto the balcony, smoking a cigarette, and looked up and down. Then I said, "*No, it's gonna be quiet tonight,*" and then go back in. The problem was, they retook the thing about 20 times. Every time, they made me light up another damn cigarette. By the time I was through, if I didn't dislike cigarettes before, I sure as hell did then. I saw the movie on television about two months ago. I did several small bits and parts.

There was another movie where I was being dragged across the canvas by these midgets. I had been knocked out. By the time we did it six times, the canvas was starting to take the skin off my back. I went to the director and said, "*Look, if we do this one more time, I'm gonna drag you across the ring and let you feel what it's like.*" I meant it. I was really pissed off. We did it one more time and he says, "*That's it. Good job!*" Of course, their way of getting around that or getting back at you was to cut it out of the movie. I never saw it, so I don't know if they left it in or not. That movie was on a par with *Attack of the Killer Tomatoes*.

Where do you work now?

I don't work. That's why I was in the wrestling business, so I didn't have to work. I have a hobby where I train rugby players and work them out. I have one guy who plays for one of the top teams. He's gone from being fat and out of shape and on a third division team. He's now in the first division and on the front row. He's in fabulous shape. His brother's in South Africa playing for the under-twenties. I trained him, too. We have a good arrangement. Other than that, I do very little. I don't want to do anything. I spent too many years chasing on the road. I'm quite happy now.

I train troublesome dogs for people, but I don't do it on a regular basis. I have a little rep for training dogs. I have three of my own. I now have a Mastiff named Rocky that's huge. He has a huge head. He can put your head in his mouth. He'd like that, too. (laughs) And, of course, Rip is still with me. He's half Rottweiler and half Great Dane. I bred him. And I've got an Akita. He's a Japanese fighting dog. They're all males, so they do have their moments, but I'm the top dog. (laughs)

I guess what I'm trying to say is that I don't *have* to do anything, so I keep busy with the things I enjoy. I find sitting around all day to be very boring. I think you have to have a certain mindset. I can see where a lot of them become alcoholics. You're sitting there most of the day, twiddling your thumbs.

Are you happy to be home in Ireland?

Yes and no. Ireland's a hell of a country in a lot of ways, but it certainly isn't for the bloody weather. It's gray and cold a lot.

Do you still do any writing?

I thought about getting back into it. I like writing. I've written all kinds of poetry. I write like I'm talking to somebody. Schools ruin people to writing. They make them write essays and things, instead of saying, "*Look, I just want you to pretend you're talking to your friend, and telling them what happened.*" It's like history. I like history and found it very easy to remember once I got over the dates. I thought, "*Crap, the dates aren't important. What's important is what happened.*" If you like it, the dates will come afterwards. You'll pick them right up, or at least the sequence when things happened ... like the Greeks came before the Romans, then after that was the Holy Roman Empire, and so forth. If you like it, then you can start to fit the dates in, but they blind kids with dates, so the kids just walk away from it. And that's a shame, really, because you can learn an awful lot from history.

Look at how popular your magazine is, and basically, you're doing history. If you said to the guys, "*This is a history thing,*" half of them would run away from it. Yet, it is history, of individuals and of what they remember. Just like history, some of it's fact and some of it's fiction, but it's what they remember. Whether it's true or not (laughs) ... but that's the way it works. That's how history is. It's written from the perspective of the person writing it.

You do a good job. I enjoy your articles. I'm sure there's a lot of lies told to you. The only one that probably hasn't lied to you is me. (laughs) Everybody in the world is liar except for me and thee, and sometimes I worry about thee. (laughs)

I've enjoyed this, Pat.

Me, too. Give me a call whenever you have the time.

When Pat retired from wrestling, he was living in Pensacola Beach, Florida. He moved to London, England, in the early '90s, where his mother lived, and a few years later, they moved to Naul, a village at the northern edge of Fingal and the County Dublin in Ireland.

He worked with rugby players as a strength and conditioning coach, but also had a hand in property and land development.

On Aug. 27, 2006, he made an appearance at a pro wrestling event in Balbriggan, Dublin, and presented the Irish Whip Wrestling International heavyweight title belt to Drew Galloway, who beat Sheamus O'Shaunessy that night. That seems to have been his life appearance in a pro wrestling scenario.

In 1990, Pat wrote a book about his life entitled *Everybody Down Here Hates Me: The Traumas and Dramas Inside the Incredible World of Professional Wrestling.*

Pat was diagnosed with multiple sclerosis several years before his death on Nov. 28, 2021, at Beaumont Hospital in Dublin, Ireland, at age 85.

TITLES

Canadian Open tag
(Vancouver '65 w/Timothy Geohagen)
Austra-Asian tag
(Australia '74 w/Tony Kontellis)
NWA world junior heavyweight ('76)
WWWF tag ('75 w/Dominic Denucci)
Southern tag (TN '77 w/Norvel Austin)
America's (CA '79)

ALIAS

Ivor Barrett
Paddy Barrett
Bonecrusher Barrett
Mr. Wrestling (Australia '74)

(r.) Dominic DeNucci & Pat wearing the WWWF tag team title belts

(lower r.) Timothy Geohagen & Pat with the Canadian Open tag team trophy

(below) Publicity photo

RIP TYLER

Wallace Dean Vaughn

This interview, conducted by Scott Teal in Nov. 1997, was originally published in issue #36 of *Whatever Happened to ...?*

Rip, why not start by giving us a little background on your childhood.

I was born in Coffeeville, Mississippi, Sept. 28, 1940. My dad was William H. Vaughn and my mom was Francis Bernice Vaughn. I have two sisters and we lived on a farm. My dad served in World War II, so when he came back out of the war, he went to Mississippi State [University] on the G.I. Bill and became a tool-and-die maker. When I was in the fifth grade, we moved to the outskirts of Memphis. I can't think of the little town, but it was about twelve or fifteen miles down in Mississippi out of Memphis. In the late '40s, early '50s, Mom and Dad bought one of those GI houses in Memphis. You know, a cracker box. I went through grade school and high school in Memphis. I went to Treadwell High School. I played fullback and defensive middle linebacker in football and catcher in baseball.

You played all the way through high school?

Yeah. In fact, I turned down some good scholarships. I met my wife, Anne, in the summer of '57 after I graduated. We married on May 31, 1958. She was fifteen and I was seventeen.

Whew, she was young.

Yeah. They said it wouldn't last, but it'll be 40 years this coming May.

That's unusual in the wrestling business.

Yeah. I think me and Bobby Fields is one of the only two that's got the original wives that I can even think of. As a matter of fact, I think they'll be married 41 years. Ann was a lucky girl. They only made one of me and she got me. (laughs)

What did you do after you graduated?

I banged around working in bakeries for a while. I had a friend who worked in a bakery and they got me on. I was working in what we called "backdoor bakeries" back then. They were little-bitty bakeries that made stuff for the bigger bakeries. I did that for just a short period of time. I met a guy that was in the appliance business ... service and refrigeration business. He and I worked together for a year or so. Then, the first of 1960, I went to work for General Electric there in Memphis and was a mechanic making taillight bulbs for cars. Tim Tyler [Marvin Hickman], who was my first partner ... his wife was working at that factory, so that's kind of the way I met him.

Had you done any wrestling at all in school?

No, not up to that point. I boxed some and fought about ten fights in the Golden Gloves. I'd do alright until I got mad, then boxing was out the window and I was wanting to kick somebody's butt. This was like in 1961. I met a guy named Billy Wicks. I had a new Triumph motorcycle. I was driving down the street and I had megaphone mufflers on it. They had taken the inside of those mufflers out to tune the bike up ... and it was loud. Billy Wick was on the sheriff's department, so he pulled me over and stopped me. He says, *"Is this one of those new Triumphs?"*

I said, *"Yeah."*

He said, *"Will it run?"*

I said, *"Yep."*

He said, *"Do you care if I ride it?"*

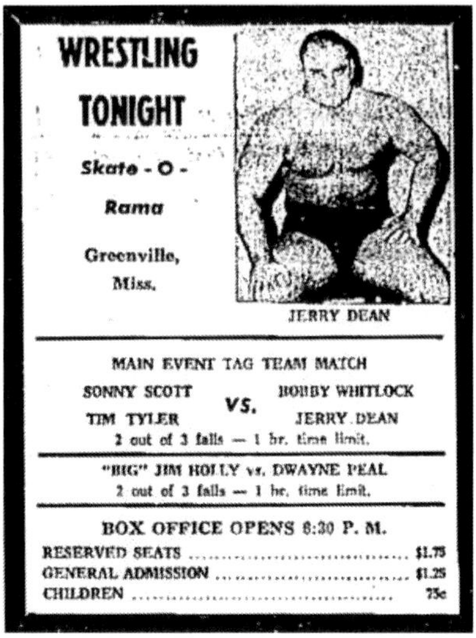

Greenville MS • Dec. 19, 1966

I said, *"No."* He jumped on my motorcycle and went about a hundred miles an hour up Jackson Avenue. (laughs) Here I am, sitting on the side of the street, with a squad car with the door open and the lights on. He come back about five minutes later and said, *"Yeah, this thing will run."* I got talking to him and he said, *"We work out with a guy named Jimbo Stewart on Friday and Saturday nights. We wrestle a little bit."* Then he told me he used to wrestle professionally. He invited me up there and, of course, I went.

Did Jimbo have a school?

No. He had a big building out back of the junkyard there where they used to rebuild motors. They put a ring up in there. Sam Steamboat, Wicks, and a lot of the guys worked out in there.

Rocket Monroe worked out there, too, didn't he?

Right. The first night I met Maury High [Rocket Monroe] was the first night I went up there to work out. Of course, they skipped my butt all over. I came out with no meat on my head, elbow, or anywhere else. I probably weighed 230 then, so I wasn't used to little guys. Wicks was quite a bit smaller than I was, so I wasn't used to that happening to me. Anyhow, they slapped me around for a few weeks. Rocket introduced me to another guy that was working out during the week. A guy named Jim Holly … "Big Jim Holly." We started going over there and working out a couple three nights a week. In fact, we worked out in his garage on an old mattress. I kept working out with Monroe and Wicks and them and got to where I could hold my own.

They hadn't smartened you up at that point, though.

No, no, no.

Before you started training, did you watch professional wrestling at all?

I had never been to a match in my life. I had no interest in it whatsoever. Rocket Monroe called me one night and said they were short a man going to Batesville, Arkansas. This was for Nick Gulas and them. So I went over there and they still didn't smarten me up. I wrestled Chico Cortez. Of course, he jumped in the ring and scared the hell out of me. All I knew to do was hook his ass and not let him go ... and that's what I did. I hooked him and, I mean, I hooked him good. (laughs) When he got close enough to me, I hooked his neck, reached down and hooked his leg, and took him over. Once I cradled him, I didn't let go. I held on for dear life.

Did the referee count him down?

The referee didn't know what to do because the match wasn't two minutes old. The referee kept going around and going around until Chico finally said, *"Shit, I give up!"* He stood up right in the middle of the ring and yells, *"Somebody smarten this guy up!"* He was mad because I hooked him and didn't let go.

What exactly *did* they tell you before the match ... just to get in there and do your best?

Yeah. They didn't tell me anything. Just that I was wrestling a guy named Chico Cortez. It was more of a rib on him than it was on me. Anyhow, that went on for two or three weeks. I went to Batesville and Hayti [Missouri]. I worked with an old Mexican named Carlos Mendoza, one of the nicest guys in the world. I also worked with Pepe Lopez. They didn't put me in there with nobody except for Mexican boys. Carlos just kind of free-handed me until I got ahold of him 'cause he knew they hadn't smartened me up. When I got ahold of him, he just took a bump and took the count.

Did they finally sit you down and lay it out?

Yeah, they did. Jim Holly and them finally smartened me up because I had got to the point where I was hurtin' people. Like I say, even at the workouts, I began to hurt people. Holly and them called me in and said, *"Look, this is the way it is."* That made it more difficult for me because now I had to learn how to do my stuff without hurtin' anybody.

What was your reaction to the information?

It was kind of embarrassing to me because I had snatched people around pretty bad. Of course, you've gotta understand. Wicks' personality was (pause) ... you know, they can talk about the history of wrestling ... where it started and all. But the truth was, back in the '50s and '60s, the Welchs, the Fullers, and the Fields were a bunch of tough suckers. Wicks was one of those tough suckers. I mean, Wicks' pain threshold was just unreal. When they broke you in, you broke in kickin' butt. See, the thing they wanted to do back in those days was make sure you had enough guts to do it if it come down to it. If you didn't have enough guts to do it, they never would smarten you up. You had to kind of earn it before they'd teach you anything. I didn't even learn to take bumps and stuff until after they smartened me up.

How many shows would you say you had been to before the night you worked with Chico?

None. The night I worked against Chico was the first live wrestling match I'd ever been to in my life.

You're kidding! You never saw even one match?

No. I had no concept of what ... you see, the thing was, Scott. I got into the business accidentally. It wasn't one of my dreams.

You couldn't have known what to expect, so were you nervous?

I was scared. Yeah. As far as I knew, everything was a shoot ... and all those people were there. Then Chico got in the ring, jumped up and down, shouted and carried on. I thought, *"This goofy son-of-a-bitch is gonna kill me."* I just found my spot and hung on.

Who started teaching you at that point?

Rocket Monroe, mostly. Jim Holly and a guy named Jim Strebel. There was two brothers named Strebel and one of 'em worked under the name Bobby Hart. Not the famous one. Strebel was just a big, clabber-butted fat boy who never went anywhere and never worked anywhere except right around Memphis. He promoted some around Memphis in the late '50s and early '60s. Jim Holly was a big, old sucker that was tough as wet-rock. There was another guy named Eaton ... not Bobby Eaton, but I can't think of his first name. After they smartened me up, Rocket and I wrestled each other all over the country up there. I wrestled around there locally for a couple of years.

I'll tell you a funny story. Buddy Wayne — Dwayne Peal — was running Jonesboro, Arkansas [and] Marianna, Arkansas ... five or six little towns around there. Tim [Tyler] worked exclusively for Buddy for several years and they got to booking me with Buddy. The first time I met Gene Dundee [Gino Sannizzaro/Flash Monroe], Buddy picked me up to go to Jonesboro one day. Gene Dundee was in the car. He was in the back seat. Buddy introduced him to me and said, *"This guy's deaf and dumb. He can't talk or hear."*

I thought, *"Well, okay."*

Buddy and I had a conversation all the way to Jonesboro and Gene didn't say nothin'. I finally asked Buddy, *"How does this boy do interviews and stuff? You know, he can't talk or nothin'. How the hell do you get finishes across to him?"*

He says, *"Oh, we do it with sign language."*

We got to the arena. Buddy Wayne popped the trunk. I went around and got my bag out, then reached and got Gino's. When I handed it to him, he said, *"Thank you,"* then turned around and walked into the building. I thought, *"Well, you good-for-nothin'. I've had it now."* They ribbed me the whole way that he was deaf and dumb.

You went to Atlanta in '63, didn't you?

I went down for some shots ... just in and out. Another story I'll tell you. I went to St. Louis for Bobby Bruns. Rufus R. Jones was on top at that particular time. On this particular show, there was me, Terry Funk, Jack Brisco, and Skandor Akbar. All of us had only had about ten matches. They got me working with Rufus R. Jones. Of course, Rufus Jones' thing was, if you throwed him into the turnbuckle, he'd come out and wiggle his butt, shake and shimmer, jump up and down. I got hot. I said, *"Listen. You get the people laughing during one of my matches and I'll kick your black ass all over this arena."*

He's saying, *"Hey, man. That's my thing."*

I said, *"Well, your thing ain't makin' no fool out of me."*

I got stiffer with him. The referee finally come to me and said, *"Hey, let him do his thing."*

I told him what I told Rufus Jones. We got back to the dressing room and he comes in there and he says, *"Look, man. That's the only thing I can do. That's my gimmick."* I kind of understood, but I got hot as hell. That's all he could do. He couldn't work a lick.

I also promoted around Memphis for a couple of years. I had a little town ... Malden, Missouri. It was just a little old building and two stores, and we sold that thing out every Saturday night. I had Red Donovan, who worked as Eric von Brauner — he was on the fire department — Bobby Whitlock, Al Galento, and a kid named Jimmy Hyde. Carl Reed, who later was the original Randy Tyler, worked under the name Rick Neal. He was my number-one heel. That was before he worked as Randy Tyler. He was almost ten years older than I was and died in 1990 of breast cancer. The trips weren't long and I was paying good.

How long did you promote there?

Probably a couple of years. We were doing good. Herman Sheffield helped me open up Tupelo [MS]. I also ran Batesville and spot shows down there.

Who was Herman Sheffield? That's a name I'm not familiar with.

He used to be a referee for Nick in years past.

He must have worked the far southwest end of the territory because I've never heard of him.

Right. He had a lot of ties in Tupelo. I went down there and met with him and he helped me open up in the National Guard Armory. Nick and them never drew a dime down there. We was drawing three or $4,000. This had to be between '64 and '66. We ran Batesville on Thursday night and Tupelo on Friday night.

Were you still running Malden?

Yeah, we ran Malden on Saturday night. Then I met a guy named Bill (pause) ... up at Fisk, Missouri. I can't think of his last name. He used my name and took a bear around for a long time.

Was he the guy who came in for Nick in the '80s as "Rip Tyler" and had the bear?

Yeah. That was him. He went to Charlotte as Rip Tyler and done a job every time he got in the ring. Later on, we were fixing to go into Charlotte. I called Jim Crockett Senior and asked him what the hell was going on ... why he let this guy screw things up. Crockett said that it wasn't any problem. They'd just change my name.

I said, *"No, you're not gonna change my name. You're gonna change his."* I don't know what they changed it to, but I finally got him for using my name. I booked him in Dothan, but he didn't know it was me. He showed up early with the bear and I kicked his ass all over the arena before anybody got there.

When did Tim Tyler come into the picture?

I started working some spots for Nick [Gulas] and Tim called me. He said Nick had called him and wanted a team. Tim bleached my hair and we went to work for Nick as Rip and Tim Tyler. Up to that point, I had always worked under the name Jerry Dean. Let me tell you something. Tim was a hell of a ring general. He knew psychology. I mean, he really had a knack for psychology. He could get your ass killed. I learned the psychology of the business from him. And believe it or not, the guy was a hell of a worker. I don't think he ever got the credit he deserved for being the worker that he was. He had a bad car accident and got cut nearly half in two. It messed his lungs up. Even after the accident, he went back and was still one hell of a performer.

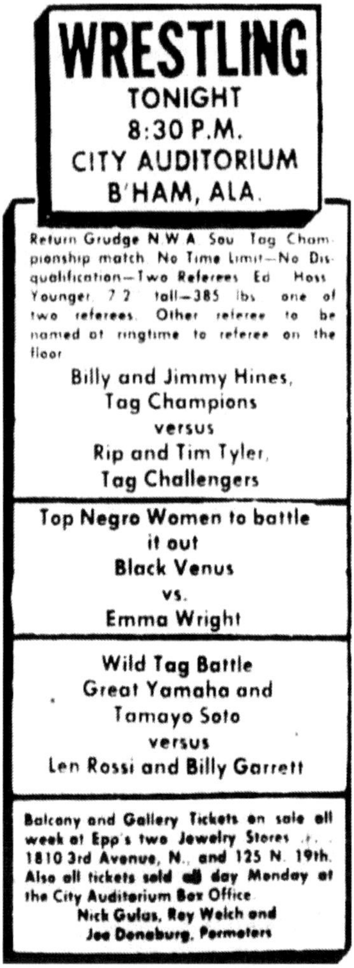
WRESTLING
TONIGHT
8:30 P.M.
CITY AUDITORIUM
B'HAM, ALA.

Return Grudge N.W.A. Sou. Tag Championship match. No Time Limit—No Disqualification—Two Referees. Ed Hoss Younger, 7'2" tall—385 lbs. one of two referees. Other referee to be named at ringtime to referee on the floor.

Billy and Jimmy Hines,
Tag Champions
versus
Rip and Tim Tyler,
Tag Challengers

Top Negro Women to battle it out
Black Venus
vs.
Emma Wright

Wild Tag Battle
Great Yamaha and
Tamayo Soto
versus
Len Rossi and Billy Garrett

Balcony and Gallery Tickets on sale all week at Epp's two Jewelry Stores 1810 3rd Avenue, N., and 125 N. 19th. Also all tickets sold all day Monday at the City Auditorium Box Office.
Nick Gulas, Roy Welch and
Joe Doneburg, Permoters

Birmingham AL • June 19, 1967

Were you excited about branching out to another territory?

Yes, I was. I had a good job at GE [General Electric] and had been with them almost five years. We had just bought a new home. It was a big move as far as financially. What really made me quit was, they knew I was wrestling at night and I had enough seniority to work the day shift, so the supervisor decided to put me on eleven [at night] to seven, which meant I couldn't work the shows. I worked there eight months after they changed my shift, then I went to 'em and told 'em, *"If you don't put me back on day shift, I'm leaving."* Of course, they didn't, and I left.

I'll tell you something, Scott. I met a lot of good people in the business. There's a lot of good people, and a lot of bad people, too. But there was a lot of good people. There was a lot of intelligent people in the business. People like Len Rossi, a very intelligent person. And Tim Tyler ... like I said, he never went anywhere much, but Tim Tyler was a hell of a ring general. He'd go someplace and get over, then he'd have to go home. I really don't know why, but that's just the way it was.

I'll say this. So many guys are bitter about aspects of the business. I've never seen anybody forced to put a pair of tights on. I've never seen anybody forced to drive to an arena. You always had the option. The guys that sang all the sad stories are the guys who had an option at any time to say, *"Hey, that's it."* Fortunately, I had learned the appliance business. I had an occupation.

I don't know how long Tim and I were in Nashville, but we weren't there too long. It was a matter of months. We were selling Nashville out and drew the biggest house [John] Cazana had ever had in Knoxville. Chattanooga was doin' good business and Birmingham was poppin." They put both sets of belts on us, but Nick cut our pay by about half. We worked against the [Billy and Jimmy] Hines brothers in Birmingham and sold it out. They got 250 and we got $125. If we had been getting what we should have made, we'd should've made five or 600 a week. If I remember right, we made three or 350. For instance, like in Birmingham, he'd give us $125. The rest of the shows, maybe 75.

The feud between the Tylers and the Hines brothers kicked off in late May 1967. For their first meeting — May 29 — promoters moved the card from the Municipal Auditorium to Rickwood Field to accommodate the anticipated surge in attendance. The following week, 5,106 packed the auditorium to see Rip and Tim win the Southern tag team title from the Hines duo. The crowd increased to 5,386 the following week as the Hines boys took back the belts.

Back in those days, we made Memphis TV on Saturday morning. We'd get on an air freight and fly to Nashville, make Nashville TV at twelve, get in the car and drive to Chattanooga, make Chattanooga TV at four, get in the car and drive to Birmingham, make Birmingham TV at eight. Then we'd turn around and drive back to Memphis. For the whole thing, you made a whoppin' 50 bucks. It would have been okay if we'd have been makin' money during the week ... but it wasn't worth it. We went to the office that Monday and told Nick that he was gonna get off the pocketbook or we were leavin'. He told us to get out of his office, so we took both sets of tag belts, throwed them down on the floor, and walked out. A short time after that, we called Lee [Fields] and came to Mobile.

Were those the first titles you held?

Right.

Was that exciting to you?

Yeah, it was. A big deal. I felt like I was the cock-of-the-walk. You have to realize that I never idolized anybody in the business because I had never watched the business. Most guys who were in the business never had their mind geared to business ... to making money. I always did. My main, ultimate goal was, what am I going to come home with? So I handled my career a hell of a lot different than a lot of people did. I walked off and left situations that I probably could have made money out of, simply because going into it I didn't have the gut feeling that they were going to do the thing right, or they were going to hustle us around. Back in those days, buddy, they'd hustle you out of your pants. Mine was strictly, what can I get to my family.

A lot of guys put the booze and the girls before the business, too.

That's one thing. When Eddie [Sullivan] and I got together, I did all the talkin' for him. And I did all the hell raisin' [with the promoters]. He knew that I was either gonna get it done or we were on our way out.

Who was it that worked as Ed "Hoss" Younger in Nashville around that time?

They just brought him in for a few shots, but it was Stanley Frazier.

I should have figured that. Before we go on, did you work with Tarzan Tyler earlier in your career?

No, no. Tarzan and I never worked together. Tim just gave me the name when we first went to Nashville for Nick. I only met Tarzan Tyler one time.

Did it bother Tarzan that you were using the Tyler name?

No. It didn't bother him because when I met him, I was on top. After he watched me in the ring, he never said anything, yay or nay.

Here's a memory test. Do you remember the next time you returned to Nashville?

We came back to Nashville when Lee ran opposition. That was all a big work. Roy Welch is Lee Fields' uncle. Nick and Roy were having problems at that time. They were trying to split up and divide the towns, and Nick wound up with Nashville. Roy conned Lee into coming in there and running opposition against Nick, to take Nashville away from him. Lee and them deny it, but it was definitely a work. We went in there and drew money. The first night we were in there, we packed that sucker.

Did it drop after the first week?

No, no. We drew every time we went there. I've always been a businessman, so that's what blew my mind. We were packing the Hippodrome. They only ran two or three times and that was it. We had the town made and had a TV station begging us to put our tape on the air. Once the word was out that Lee was running opposition against Nick ... hell, every guy in the country wanted to come in there and work. Later on, I think there was a time when Nick was thinking about changing his promotion to fall in with Lee or something. Rocky McGuire and I went to Birmingham a couple of times. It may have been Montgomery, to talk to Nick about the deal for Lee, indirectly. I don't remember all the details of it. I worked with Tojo [Yamamoto] in the opening match one night.

After they quit running, you came back a month later ... to work for Nick. What brought that about?

Tim and I went to Pensacola, but after three weeks or so, Tim all of a sudden decided he had to go home. I mean, just overnight. He had to go home. Carl Reed, who had worked for me in Mississippi, was a pretty good heel. They brought him into Pensacola as my partner. (pause) [Carl wrestled as Randy Tyler.] We went up there for two or three weeks. It was just a short period of time ... probably a holiday deal, but I don't remember whether Lee sent us up there. It must have been because it wasn't too long after that we came back and Randy got his leg broke.

How did that happen?

He took goofy bumps. He took a bump into the turnbuckle and went back over the ropes, hung his leg in it and broke it. That was against Bobby Fields and somebody else. We went to the Pensacola TV station the next week and Lee and Bob Kelley came into the dressing room. They said, *"Look, we want to get you another partner."* They gave me three names to choose from ... and I chose Eddie Sullivan. They said, *"Well, he's been beat."*

I said, *"I don't care. The guy can work."*

That's when the team of Eddie Sullivan and Rip Tyler was born.

Basically, what happened was, I had to put Eddie over ... twice. I was leavin', so I'd do the job for him. Eddie's a good Joe anyhow. Being partners in the wrestling business is kind of like being married. In those days, you spent more time with your partner than you did your wife. He was so easy to get along with and he busted his ass in the ring. Once we had the TV match in Pensacola as a team, and the contrast between me with the blond hair and him with the black hair ... from that point on, we knew we had something good.

What year would that have been?

I think that was in 1970.

You worked as one of the Golden Terrors, didn't you?

Eddie Sullivan & Rip Tyler

Yeah. When Randy and I first came back to Mobile, that was Lee's idea. The Tylers had been there and split up, so they brought us back as the Golden Terrors. We worked two or three months that way before they finally took the hoods off us. I hated the mask. Oh, I couldn't work under it. Blow up? Oh, man! I always had good peripheral vision and the mask screwed it up. I was seeing cockeyed and everything else, so I finally told them, *"Take these things off or I'm gonna take 'em off."* Smitty [Curtis Smith] worked under a hood his whole career. So did Tarzan Baxter. To a lot of guys, it was just like putting their tights on. I just could not tolerate it. Eddie done well under it. For years after Eddie and I got together, they'd introduce him as Eddie "The Masked Man" Sullivan. He'd wear a mask to the ring, then take it off. I don't know what for, but it was one of those things he did.

There was also a run in Atlanta ...

Rocket Monroe and I. (pause) Let me see if I can tell you exactly what transpired. [long pause] Uh, you got us in Atlanta when?

The summer of '70.

Yeah, that's right. Rocket and I were over there about six weeks. Let me think this through. Okay, in Mobile, Alabama, Eddie and I were wrestling Cowboy Bob Kelley and the Medic, Tony Gonzales. Burrhead Jones was refereeing. Tony double-crossed Kelley and left the ring. We're kickin' the crap out of Kelley and a black guy jumped in the ring. Of course, Burrhead was refereeing. I'm standing there looking at this guy, face to face. I realized it wasn't Burrhead. We had an all-out riot. I got hit with a root beer bottle and it busted my head wide open. Tony got cut several times. I drove from Mobile back to Pensacola to the Baptist Hospital, with a Holiday Inn towel wrapped around my head. The floor of the Volkswagen was full of blood when I got there. It took 120 stitches to close it up. I already had the starting date in Atlanta, so I went in. Bobby Shane and I were working a single in Savannah and the stitches come out of the thing, so I took two or three months off to heal. Eddie and I wound up back together and we were together from then on.

In 1972 or so, we got into it with Lee over something, and we went to Montgomery for Bill Golden for a few months. We got there and Bill had his kid, Jimmy Golden, on top, and they wasn't drawin' any money. We was talkin' about it in the dressing room. We told Bill, *"Look, man. As long as these people know Jimmy's your son, and you're putting him over all the time, you're not gonna draw any money."*

He says, *"What do you think we ought to do?"*

Eddie says, *"Well, we need to let the people know that Rip and I aren't gonna put up with any of your bull. When you go out and do an interview, we're gonna come out and break it up. I'll slap you and tell you to get your punk kid out there and we'll mash the pimples off his butt."*

So, when we got to the interview, Eddie slapped Bill completely across a desk he was standing in front of. I mean, knocked the hell out of him. And the people bought it! They had never run the big Coliseum in Montgomery because they never could draw enough to get in there. We run that sucker and popped it wide open. We worked against Jimmy Golden and the little guy from New York that used to be Roberto Soto's partner ... [Pepe] Perez something or another … a little Puerto Rican. Then we got Bill Golden in a six-man and beat the shit out of him. The next week, we sold it out. I'm talkin' about the big Coliseum. He came and gave us 250. We left and went back to Mobile for a short period of time, then went to Oklahoma.

We got to Oklahoma and Grizzly Smith was booking the territory. Grizzly was a pure-bred Texan and didn't like Mexicans, so he tried to split Eddie and I up. They pushed us for awhile, and we were gonna do business, but all of a sudden they decided Eddie was a Mexican. He started sending Eddie to spot shows and put me with Bob Sweetan. That lasted for a few weeks and I finally went to him and told him, *"I come in here with Eddie. He's my partner. If you're not gonna use us together, then we'll leave together."* We left and went back to Mobile again.

To me, though, Eddie just never came across as the stereotypical Mexican.

Let me tell you something. He did at one time. I used to jump his butt royally. I told him, *"The only person that knows you're Mexican is you. If you're gonna let that hold you back, then there's something wrong with you."*

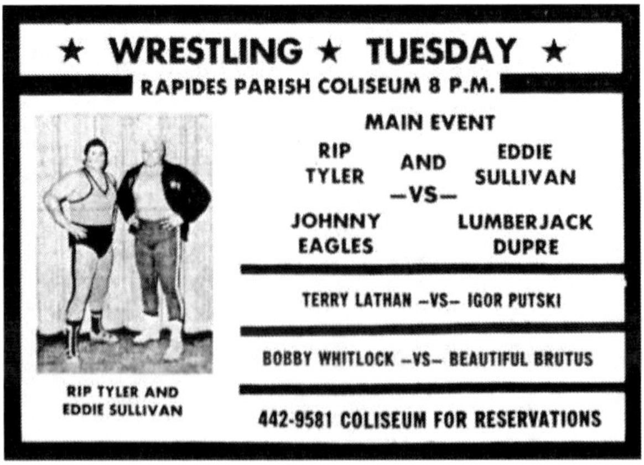

Alexandria LA • May 1, 1973

I'd get mad at him if he brought it up. I said, *"Do you have Mexican written on you somewhere?"*

"Well, no."

"Then how do these people know what you are?"

Rocky McGuire paid me 60 bucks in Dothan one night and paid Eddie 40. He said, *"Just keep your mouth shut to the damn Mexican."*

I got McGuire in a bar and told Eddie right in front of him what Rocky said. He said, *"Are you two guys married?"*

I said, *"The man's my partner. You're gonna pay him the same thing you pay me or we won't be here."*

I got Eddie to put the first dime he ever saved in the bank. He never saved a dime in his life, so we started taking ten dollars out of a payday and putting in the bank. When he left to go to Seattle in '74, he had $4,000 in the bank.

Not too long after we got back to Mobile, Dean Silverstone showed up in Panama City. He came to the motel after the matches and talked to Eddie and I about going to Seattle. Of course, that's a long way, especially in a new territory. He gave me a percentage of the territory to come up and book. We started looking for some young guys to take with us that worked southern-style. Randy Rice was one of those that we picked.

Was he already working as Randy Tyler?

No, he was working as Junior Rice. Tiny Frazier — Stanley Frazier — broke him into the business. We got up there and had Lumberjack Luke, Eddie Junior, and a guy named Paul Goforth to referee. I can't remember who the original eight was, and Silverstone and I have argued about this for the last two years. Anyhow, we went in and got the TVs all set up and cut some tapes. That southern-style of wrestling popped that sucker wide open. We scared Silverstone to death. He wasn't used to seeing that kind of heat in arenas. I was up there maybe six weeks and called my wife. She just said she wasn't movin' to Seattle. I did Silverstone kind of dirty, in a sense. I told him I was gonna go home and get my wife and kids. What I was gonna do is come home and try to talk her into going up there because I could see the thing was fixin' to go.

Meanwhile, Treach Phillips called me and said LeRoy McGuirk wanted to talk to me, so on the way through from Seattle to Pensacola, I stopped by Tulsa and saw LeRoy in the office. LeRoy was wanting me to come in and book. I told him I was on my way to Pensacola, so let me talk to my wife. I still hadn't really let Seattle go at that time. I got to Pensacola and my wife was still upset about the Seattle deal, so I knew if I was gonna see her and my kids, I was gonna have to stay around close. I took the job in Oklahoma and I never went back to Silverstone. I did him real dirty in a way, but I helped him organize the territory, helped him get the TVs on the air, and got the flow of people. I continued to send him talent even after I took the book in Oklahoma.

Did Lee Fields have a problem when Dean came into his territory and started recruiting talent?

I don't think Lee knew it. I think if he had, there might have been a problem. Dean made us a good guarantee and was gonna pay our moving expenses. Silverstone's good people. He's a first-class act.

How did things go in Oklahoma?

Good. Ken Mantell was there. I brought Buck Robley in. We worked a hell of a deal (pause) ... I took the strap off of [Danny] Hodge [and put it on Mantell]. LeRoy and everybody else was raisin' hell about it.

Who gave you permission to do that?

LeRoy finally said, *"Just do with it what you want to. It's not drawing any money, anyhow."* Hodge had held the title for such a long time. I worked a deal in Jackson, Mississippi, on the 19th of December and switched the strap. To a sellout house, I might add. Hodge began to mean something on the card, but I kind of double-crossed him in a sense. I wanted him to stay down on the card a while, so I worked my program with Robley and Mantell. We did some serious business with them.

Monroe LA • Aug. 13, 1974

Did Hodge have any problem with the scenario?

No, no. You know, a lot of guys had a lot of problems with Danny. I never had a minute's problem with Danny. Never. Not in the ring or out of the ring. Realistically, if a guy's really got his head in the right place, it's what's in your pocket at the end of the night. I'd rather work underneath you and make a hundred fifty dollars than I would be on top and make 75. I don't care where I'm at on the card. Just pay me. We had a good run in Oklahoma. LeRoy McGuirk was damned good to my wife and kids and he was good to me. I made more money there than anywhere else. But, hey! We were selling out Jackson, Monroe, Alexandria. Baton Rouge was doing tremendous business.

I brought Randy Rice in [as Randy Tyler] and kept us underneath as heels, to step up in case somebody dipped out on me. I had taken the North American heavyweight strap off of Tank Morgan and put it on Arman Hussien. They told me putting it on a black was gonna kill the belt, but Hussien drew business with it. I took it off Arman Hussien and put it on Bull Ramos. [Bob] Sweetan was in there, Terry Lathan, Chief Thundercloud, Johnny Eagles, Black Bart, Mr. Ito, Oki Shikina. Chuck O'Connor [John Studd] was in there at that time. Kansas City sent Bobby Backlund in for us to break him in.

What was Backlund like in those days?

A hell of a nice kid. You know, he was a hell of a shooter. At the time, though, he had a hard time making the transition with the working concept. But he was a hell of a nice boy ... *"Yes, sir. No, sir."* Ted DiBiase was in there at that time. I haven't talked to Ted in several years, but he was a class act. If you talk to him, tell him I said hello.

I will. Had Bill Watts eased his way in at that point?

Watts had been in, but left and went to Atlanta. I left when he started to take over. LeRoy told me in the office that he was gonna sell part of the territory to Watts, and to Fritz. I said, *"I can't work with Watts."*

He said, *"I don't think you can, either."*

What Watts did was, he tried to con me. I had the North American heavyweight belt and I was supposed to work in Vicksburg against Hussein. Watts had come in the office on Monday, so I didn't go to Tulsa that day. LeRoy called and told me it was a swerve. He said, *"I'll pay you five hundred. Just don't go to the show."* So I didn't go to the show. Watts didn't get a chance to beat me.

Panama City FL • Feb. 19, 1976

Watts was going to shoot on you?

Watts couldn't shoot my butt.

They had a fix with the referee?

Yeah. Watts couldn't carry my jockstrap. I just didn't want to put him over. LeRoy didn't want me to put him over. Anyhow, I gave my notice and left. I talked to Lee and came back here to help Bob Kelley with the book from '76 to '78, and then they sold out to Ron Fuller.

That's when I slapped Randy Poffo [Savage] across the dressing room. I had Ted Heath and John Foley in here and was getting 'em over. Heath was Foley's son-in-law. I had the Poffos [Randy and Lanny] with Angelo [Poffo] on the main event. Foley could go and Heath wasn't bad himself. The Poffos couldn't put their finger in their butt. The Poffos went to the ring with blackjacks in their tights. About the middle of the match, they started beating Heath and Foley on the head with blackjacks. Screwed my whole main event up and my whole program. So when they got back to the dressing room, I went back and told 'em, *"You guys get the hell out of here."*

They said, *"Well, they was trying to stretch us."*

I slapped that Randy all the way across the dressing room. *"I'm gonna do more than stretch you, boy. Get your stuff and get out of here. You won't never work here as long as I'm here."*

Angelo had an old gun, but Eddie [Sullivan] did, too. Eddie reached over and put his hand in his bag and said, *"You'd better do what he says. You'd better get the hell out of here."* We paid 'em and they got the hell out.

Years later, Eddie was in Phoenix and the WWF was down there. Randy come up, and the first thing he asked Eddie was, *"Where's Rip?"*

"Oh, he's still down in Pensacola."

"You remember the night he slapped me all the way across the dressing room?"

Eddie said, *"Yeah, I remember."*

Randy says, *"I remember, too. That's the only man alive that ever slapped me like that. He wouldn't do it again."*

Eddie said, *"Yeah, he would."*

So he still hadn't forgot it after all those years. He had it coming. We were doing business and he screwed my whole program up. Plus, they busted Heath and Foley's heads up. Of course, if Foley had of known it, Foley could have beat both of 'em.

Records show you put Eddie Mansfield over for the Gulf Coast belt.

No. I never dropped the strap to Eddie Mansfield. I never put Eddie Mansfield over. I refused to. If the records show that, they must have given it to him. We had a battle royal down there after Ron Fuller and them had bought Lee out. They had a battle royal booked in Mobile and I was supposed to go over. It wound up with me and Mansfield in the ring. He got smart-mouthed with me. Jimmy McGuire was refereeing. I showed him parts of his body he never could see before. Ron Fuller was on the outside of the ring and kept telling him, *"Mansfield, keep your damn mouth shut."* I made him look sick because I didn't like him anyhow. He was one of those guys that was in the business that had no place in the business. I wasn't gonna put him over. I had worked too hard in this area to develop my reputation and I could see no money coming out of it.

I couldn't keep working for Fuller and them. They turned me babyface. Dennis Stamp and I went to Dothan as partners against the Blue Yankees. Bob Armstrong come back in the dressing room and said, *"About the middle of the first fall, so-and-so is going to slam you. You grab your hip, start hollering, walk off and leave the ring."*

I said, *"My first night as a babyface and I'm gonna walk off and leave my partner. Bob, do you like that finish?"*

"Well, yeah."

I said, *"Well, then you do it."*

He said, *"We can change it."*

I said, *"No. If you like it, you do it. I'm not going to."*

Then Stamp got smart with me, so I slapped him. Fuller sent word over to the dressing room. *"Give us a finish."*

I said, *"No, if that's what you guys have in mind, you don't need me."* I packed my bags and left. I went the long way through the crowd, making sure everybody saw me leave. That was the last time I worked for the Fullers.

You and Eddie Sullivan were together for quite a few years.

Yeah. Altogether, I think Eddie and I were together for eighteen years. We made so many trips to Japan and back.

Tell us a little about winning the International tag team title while you were there.

Well, we had been going over there and had just got into their [Japanese] way of working, which is to beat the hell out of each other. They had a big tournament for the title and brought a lot of guys in for it. They were gonna put the straps on a couple of Japs. The night before the final match, they came to us and told us they wanted to put the straps on us. It's funny, but the night that we won the titles [Fukuyama, June 7, 1976], they told us they were gonna play the anthems. They were gonna play the Japanese anthem first,

Eddie Sullivan and Rip Tyler in Japan

then the United States national anthem. If you've ever heard the Japanese national anthem, it's "clunk, clink, clunk, clunk ..." You know. We were in the ring and all these dignitaries were around. AP, UPI, the whole nine yards. So they start this "clink, clunk, clunk." You hear that all over the country, but at that time, we didn't realize it was the anthem. Eddie and I are carrying on and cuttin' up. They took pictures of us laughing and it made both AP and UPI. They slandered us for no respect to the anthem and all that stuff.

Ohhhh. Major heat.

Yeah, but we just didn't know. When we got back to the dressing room, there was someone like a senator back there. He spoke good English, so we explained that we didn't know. They should have cued us, or told us what the anthem sounded like. We had no idea. Of course, we knew we had screwed up once we heard them start playing the United States national anthem.

After you left Fuller, where did you work?

Eddie stayed there for a few more months after I quit. I still had my heating and appliance business, Vaughn Appliance Services, in Pensacola, so I'd go in and out of Oklahoma. In 1976, Ann and I bought a restaurant and that thing liked to have killed us all. I still had a hand in the [wrestling] business and couldn't stay around. While I was on the road, they [employees] stole us blind.

In '85, you and Eddie went to Phoenix, didn't you?

Yeah. Eddie promoted some shows there. I went out there and made the tour of San Diego and around through Vegas. I think we worked two shows there. I stayed in the appliance business until ... I think it was '87. Ito [Hiroshi Ueda] approached me about the WOW [World Organization Wrestling] deal. I took that on and owned forty percent of it.

Did Ito have a lot of money backing him?

Ito had a big conglomerate out of Japan. See, the idea of the whole thing was that we were gonna make tapes here in this country and send them to Japan. It was so expensive to buy TV time and make tapes in Japan. We were gonna bicycle Japanese boys in and out of here, work the angles, and send the tapes back to Japan. We'd follow up by sending the Japanese and American boys back to Japan. To keep people around, I had to run some local shows, so it got to be an expensive operation. I think they dropped over half a million dollars on the thing in a period of a year and three months. It just got down to where the money just ran out. I was on 33 stations at the time and we were fixing to syndicate the thing on more than 100 stations. I flew to Atlanta on Thursday to talk with RCA in Atlanta. Coca Cola and Borden's Milk was going to pick up the spots. I flew back home, and when I got up the next morning, they called and told me to shut it down.

Gino Sannizzaro — Flash Monroe — owned ten percent of it. We figured we needed $33,000 to make our TV productions, pay the bills, and get the thing syndicated. Once we got it syndicated, then the $1,800 dollars a week, but we just couldn't swing it.

Where did you tape your shows?

I had an old commercial building in Pensacola on Border Street. I converted it into a TV station, with the lighting, the backdrops, and the flags. The whole bit. I had Channel 15 out of Mobile come in. A guy named Marshall Hart directed the thing for me. I had to smarten him up, of course, to get what I wanted out of it. I had Pat Barrett at one time as the color commentator. I finished up with Rick Stewart, who was one hell of a TV man. He was one of the best on the air.

Did you still own the appliance business during that time?

Yeah.

Why did you sell it?

It just got to be a hassle, Scott. We made good money. I had some good years in the appliance business. I stayed off almost a year. Eddie come to town one time. Dick Dunn, Eddie and I went out to the beach. Dick said, *"Look, I'm selling insurance. I have a friend who managed the office here in Pensacola. Why don't you go by and talk to him?"* I had sold insurance back when I was a very young man. I went down there and went to work for them. Eleven months later, I was managing an office in Gadsden, Alabama. I stayed with them until they sold out. I moved up here to my place and took nearly another year off. Then another company come along and made me one of them offers you can't turn down. I went to work for them and that's when I got my back broke.

How did that happen?

I fell off a porch. It was five foot high. I broke my back in two places. From Jan. 25, 1995, I had a hell of a time. Of course, I just recently got my Social Security and Medicare started. It just kicked in. I was 57 last September.

And you were diagnosed with cancer just a few days ago.

Yeah. I asked the doctor, *"How is it?"*

He said, *"Not good."*

I said, *"Well, if it ain't good, it's bad."*

He said, *"Yeah, it's bad."* He started crying.

I said, *"Look, don't pussyfoot around with me. Tell me what's going on."*

He says, *"It's your liver."*

I said, *"Is it all over?"*

He said, *"It's all over."*

I said, *"Well."*

He said, *"I want to call your family."*

I said, *"No, you don't call nobody."*

I spent the night and resolved it. It was a long night. It was a long night, but I resolved it. By the time my wife and girls got there the next morning, I told them. They all, of course, are taking it hard.

I went to a cancer doctor this past Monday and he basically told me the same thing. They wanted to see if it was in my stomach or my esophagus, so they did the light deal down there. My stomach and esophagus was clean. My pancreas, gall bladder, kidneys ... everything's fine. So it's in my colon. It's gone from my colon to my liver. My back's been so bad so long that I was hurting, but I attributed it to the back. My back's been so bad that I've been down and stayed down for two or three days. By the time it got so bad that I virtually couldn't tolerate it any more (pause) ... I got to where I couldn't eat. I'd take two or three bites and feel like I had a five-course meal. So, by the time I realized it was more than my back, it was done too late. Hell, by the time I knew I was had, I'd been had.

You know, I'm just gonna take it a day at a time and see where it leads. I'll tell you like I told everybody else. I've had a good life. I'm kind of like Elvis Presley. *"I did it my way."* I'm gonna miss it all.

Well, let's pray for a miracle.

They happen, but I'm pretty much a realist. We'll go with it day to day. I hate it for my wife's sake. This son-of-a-gun. Right now, as bad as I'm hurtin', I wouldn't want you or nobody else to come down. I stay in total misery 24 hours a day.

Let's pray you make it to the reunion in March.

Well, that's gonna be a tossup ... a real close call. We didn't tell nobody for a few days ... to give the family time to absorb it all. Ann called Eddie. I didn't want him to hear it second-hand, you know. Then I called Bill [Bowman] and them and told them to give us a couple days. We're fine now. We'll take it a day at a time and go forward. It's (pause) ... uh, just one of them deals where I'm gonna have to do the job. There's just no other way to put it. (laughs) It's not like I haven't done a million of them. (laughs) I don't have any options. Tim [Tyler] called me last night. He started crying.

I said, *"Hey, have you got a bad heart?"*

He said, *"Yeah."*

I said, *"You could be dead tomorrow, so don't worry about it."*

But realistically, Scott, you have to understand this. It's okay. I told Tim, *"You've gotta remember one thing, man. If it's okay with me, then it's okay with everybody else."* It's really okay. I can deal with whatever. If I'd have had a vote, though, I'd have voted the other way.

Why don't you rest and I'll give you a call later in the week.

Okay, son. Whenever you want to. We're just gonna hang in there. Take care, Scott.

Rip and I made plans to continue our talk a few days later. He had other memories and views of the wrestling business that he wanted to talk about, but two days later, he began three consecutive days of chemotherapy treatment. The therapy took its toll and Rip never felt well enough to talk after that. He remained in bed for most of the two weeks that followed the treatment before he passed away.

Rip Tyler passed away at his home in Flomaton, Alabama, of liver cancer on Dec. 3, 1997, at the age of 57. His funeral was held at the Harper-Morris Memorial Chapel in Pensacola and he was buried at Pensacola Memorial Gardens.

Rip was a former coach of the Brent Baseball Park Senior League and a member of the Flomaton United Methodist Church. He was also one of the founding members of the Gulf Coast Wrestling Reunion. He had two daughters, Julie and Cindy.

TITLES

Southern tag [TN '67 w/Tim Tyler]
U.S. tag (AL)
'67 w/Tim Tyler;
'67 w/Randy Tyler;
'72 & '76 w/Eddie Sullivan)
Gulf Coast [AL '71]
U.S. tag [LA/OK '73 w/Eddie Sullivan]
Western States tag
[WA '73 w/Eddie Sullivan]
North American [OK '74]
Mid-South Brass Knucks [LA/OK '74]
IWE IWA tag
[Japan '76 w/Eddie Sullivan]
International tag
[AZ '85 w/Eddie Sullivan]

We Remember Rip Tyler

I met Rip for the first time at the Gulf Coast Wrestler's Reunion in 1993. From our first handshake, Rip made me feel as if we were old friends. In the ensuing years, we stayed in touch, and though we were friends for only four years, I felt as if we had known each other for many years. He was very supportive of my efforts and always made it a point to tell me how much he appreciated what I was doing in regards to recording the history of the wrestling business.

During the previous two years before his death, Rip invited me to spend the day prior to the reunion with him and Ann, but I was unable to make it either time. We made firm plans to do that in 1998, but it wasn't to be. That's just another example of how important it is to cherish and nurture friendships while you have the time. If you wait for tomorrow, it might be too late. We have many friends that come in and out of our lives during our lifetime, but some mean more to you than others. Rip was one of those to me.

Thanks for being a good friend, Rip. I'll always have warm memories of you. wRESTle in peace, brother.

— **SCOTT TEAL**

He went to bed after he talked to you, Scott. That was about all he did that day. He'd been hurting for the last few years ... probably more than we knew. The last month was a nightmare. It happened so fast. But even when he was in pain, he'd have everybody laughing over the silliest stuff. He had a unique sense of humor. He saw everybody at Thanksgiving and was joking with the grandkids. After that, his mind kind of went because his liver wasn't functioning. He was only that way two or three days. He died real easy. He had a peaceful look.

There was quite a few of the wrestlers there [at the funeral]. It's like having an extended family, which makes it easier. He loved that wrestling reunion. Rip, Bob Kelley, Terry Lathan and Lee Fields got together and started it where Lee sells his cars, in the other barn. Lee said, *"Nobody's going to come to this. You're just wasting your time."* It fooled him. They're going to do a tribute to him this year at the reunion. My daughter and I said, *"Do something funny. Don't make it sad."* That's what he'd want.

— **ANN L. VAUGHN** [wife of Rip Tyler]

I was working on the Shelby County Sheriff's Department when I first met Dean. I saw this kid riding a Triumph, so I pulled him over. He wasn't doing anything wrong. I was getting ready to buy a motorcycle, so I checked out every motorcycle I saw on Jackson Avenue in Memphis. I asked if he'd let me try it out and drove off for a little while. We got talking, so I invited him to work out with us over at Jimbo Stewart's garage. We worked out every Sunday morning at ten o'clock.

I'll never forget the first time I worked with Dean in a live match. It was on TV. He was a little scared, which you always are the first time you're on TV. He said, *"Take it easy on me, will you?"*

I told him, *"Ah, just pretend like we're in the gym."*

He says, *"Oh, God. Not that!"*

We got in the ring and I locked up as stiff as I could. We had a good match, though. He turned out to be a pretty good worker.

In all the years gone by since the '60s, our paths never really crossed again. He went off and made some big money in wrestling. Of course, the last year I wrestled full-time was in '59, which was my best year. I didn't see him until the reunion in '93. I went down early and stayed at his house every year after that. Dean and I would have our own little mini-reunion.

— **BILLY WICKS**

On the night he died, he went to bed after they brought him back to the house. He woke up about two in the morning and his wife and two daughters talked to him. He got up to go to the bathroom, went back to bed, laid down and died. That's a good way to go, I guess.

There was at least 250 people at his funeral. He had his church people there. And there was a full enclave of wrestlers ... the Fields brothers and their wives, Jack Welch, Roy Lee Welch, Lester Welch, [Fabulous] Moolah, Mae Young, Diamond Lil, Donnie Fargo, Ken Lucas, Curtis Smith, Eddie Sullivan, Jack Donovan, Terry Lathan, Norman Frederick Charles, Ricky Fields, Bob Kelley, Anne and myself. It was a good service and he looked great.

— **BILL BOWMAN**

There are only a handful of people who, when you meet them, create such an overwhelming impression on you that they actually change your life forever. Rip Tyler was one of those people who came into my life. After meeting him in the early '70s, he changed my life so it would never be the same.

Rip drove from Pensacola to Seattle to "assist" in starting the Seattle territory, which had been dark for two years. His "assistance" included the book, the talent, the program, and the dressing room headaches. We were on about twelve TV stations at the time and, between them and dealing with arena owners, my time was really limited, so having him handle the talent was greatly appreciated.

To get Rip and his crew to come from the South to the Northwest, I guaranteed them $350 a week. The first week, of course, their guarantees came from my pocket. The second week, there was just about enough from the box office receipts to pay all the guarantees. By the fourth week, the boys on top were earning $600 a week. After two months, some of the talent was earning close to $900 a week. After three months or so, something happened that brought us even closer to Rip. He gave me his notice. He came up to me one night in Walla Walla [WA] and said *"Dean, this territory is going to pop. I'm glad I helped you get it started, but I have to go back home."* Maybe most people wouldn't have understood his reason, but I did, and it made me respect him even more. *"Anne,"* he said, *"doesn't want to move here, so I have to get back to her, my home, and family."*

Here was a quality that is something foreign in the wrestling business ... the importance of home and family. I never forgot his reluctance to leave, but I completely understood. Maybe that was part of the reason I loved the man. He was one of a kind.

— DEAN SILVERSTONE

I went to Oklahoma and was going to wrestle there with Jack Donovan as my tag partner. Jack didn't show up, so I called Rip and told him to grow a beard. He was going to be my brother. My wife had told me that this guy she worked with at the GE plant was trying to wrestle. When I called, I told him to quit his job and we'd go to Nashville. They weren't drawing very good, but things popped after we were there for about six weeks. Unfortunately, we weren't making any more money. I went to Nick [Gulas] and Roy [Welch] and said, *"If you don't give us more money, we're leaving."* They didn't, so we left. We went to Florida, but they didn't use us to the best of our ability. They had us working in single matches.

Rip was a good worker. We had different styles. I was into the acrobatics, which you didn't see a lot of back in those days. We had a real smooth team and there was never any jealousy. We split it up on the wins and the losses. He had a lot of good ideas in the ring. He'd get a little overboard once in awhile, but he was easy to talk to and would listen to advice. Plus, neither one of us did any partying or drinking. We might have a beer, but we didn't get drunk. We had some good days together. I had the opportunity to make bigger money working for Buck Robley in Arkansas, though. We figured on getting back together later, but Rip started booking in Oklahoma, so it never panned out. He had a couple of other partners after that, anyway. We lost touch for a while. I saw him again when I went to the reunion in '94, just before I had my heart surgery.

— TIM TYLER

Rip helped Hulk Hogan out when Hogan first broke into the business down in Panama City, Florida. Most people don't realize this, but Hulk Hogan got the idea of his leg drop from Rip Tyler. I don't know where Rip got the idea, but that leg drop was his trademark. Of course, when Rip did it, he went ten feet straight up in the air with it. There's nobody that could do it like he could.

Bob Kelley actually started the Gulf Coast Wrestler's Reunion. I was in the repo business and Kelley was in the wrecker business. We'd get together and talk. He said, *"You know. We ought to call a few of the boys and get together for a barbeque."* Rip was the first one we called. He was all for it. He jumped right in the middle of it. He gave a lot of input on ideas, schedules, how the money was to be handled. Rip always had a forward motion.

— **TERRY LATHAN**

I was in Pensacola when I first met Rip. When I first met him, he was leaving the territory, so he had to work with me and, of course, they had him put me over. A year or so later, I went to Tennessee. He was there, and again, was getting ready to leave. Jerry Dean was the name he was using there. They put me over him there. When I left Tennessee, I went back to Pensacola and he was there. When they asked him to find a partner, he said, *"Well, if I've gotta get a partner, I want that damned Mexican for a partner because I ain't puttin' him over no more!"*

In my opinion, Rip was a fantastic worker and a good partner. One thing about the Ripper. He didn't like to be second-best in the wrestling business. He did not like that. He either wanted to be part of the promotion, or be on top. That was good for me because I never did say a whole hell of a lot ... unless I got ticked off at somebody. Then I'd voice my opinion, but it usually wasn't very nice.

After we got out of the business, we stayed in touch. We called each other two or three times a month. We always had something to talk about. If we'd run out of things to talk about, we'd relive the past in the wrestling business. Frank Morrell and I do the same thing. We weren't partners near as long, but I had a great time with Frank, too. I drank a lot of beer with those two guys. Rip and I raised hell, but it was always just the two of us. It wasn't a whole gang of guys. We just liked to play pool, drink a few beers, play music. Or we'd go to the room, watch TV, and eat bologna sandwiches.

We borrowed a little money from each other from time to time, but I think when it was all over with, there probably wasn't fifty cents difference. We always paid each other back and never borrowed large amounts. He knew my likes and dislikes, just like I knew his. He was a sweetheart of a guy. I'd never seen him back down from anybody, and I've seen him get in some pretty rough scrapes with marks and wrestlers both. By the same token, he had a heart of gold and was easy going. He was a big teddy bear. That's the way I'll always remember Rip. I'm going to miss him.

Me and old Ripper ... we were together so long that he was kind of like a brother to me. The last time I talked to him, we were talking and his voice was real weak. He said, *"I'm gonna tell you something, Sully."* He always called me Sully. He said, *"I'm gonna tell you something, Sully. I never had a brother, but the good Lord introduced me to you. As far as I'm concerned, you're my brother."*

— **EDDIE SULLIVAN**

And, finally. Rip wrote the following for an issue of Dean Silverstone's reunion newsletter:

TEAMWORK

by Rip Tyler (also by Eddie Sullivan)

It's amazing how many people demand that everything always be fair! But life just isn't always that way. For instance, as a tag team, Eddie Sullivan and I were perfect for one another. As a rule, if we wrestled for 30 minutes, you could pretty well figure out what we'd do. Most of the time, I'd be in the ring for 25 of the 30 minutes. Eddie would tag in, do five minutes of highspots, and then tag back out and I'd work the remainder of the match. Now, you might look at that as being unfair to me. After all, I always did most of the work. But let's look at that.

Fairness had nothing to do with it. I had the stamina needed to work a 60-minute match, if I had to. Eddie, on the other hand, would work for five minutes and blow-up. It wasn't that he didn't want to pull his share of the match. It was just that he wasn't conditioned to last long in a lengthy match. But during that five minutes, before he ran out of gas, Eddie had the crowd on their feet. He was great at what he did during those five minutes. I was more than willing to do most of the work because he contributed his share to the success of the team in those five short minutes.

And that's how life is. It may not always seem to be fair, and some of us may feel that we pull more than our fair share of the load, but we all have our individual strengths and weaknesses that contribute to the overall picture.

(clockwise from top r.) 1) Rip Tyler & Eddie Sullivan in Japan; 2) Eddie & Rip show off the IWE/IWA tag team belts; 3) Rip & Tim Tyler; 4) Dick Murdoch, Rip Tyler & Bruno Sammartino in Japan, 1971; 5) Rip & Randy Tyler w/mgr. Homer O'Dell

SCOTTY WILLIAMS

Edgar L. Williams
The Flying Scotsman

This interview, conducted by Scott Teal in Aug. 1999, was originally published in issue #42 of *Whatever Happened to ...?*

When and where were you born?

I was born in Hollywood, California, on Oct. 26, 1913. I'm 85 years old ... older than water. (laughs)

What were your parents' names?

Curtis and Gertrude Williams. My mother's maiden name was Gideon. My grandfather was the first mayor of Springfield [MO]. They called him Sleepy Jim Gideon because, when he was in the Cavalry, he'd fall asleep on his horse and let it follow the one in front of him. I think he was an attorney, too.

So you grew up in Springfield?

Well, I was born in California ... me and my oldest sister. There was eleven of us kids. The rest of them were born here in Springfield.

Why did your parents move to Hollywood?

They went there for a honeymoon and just decided to stay. My mother's folks lived on East Elm Street. That's where the Gideon home was ... a great-big, two-story home. It was beautiful. I used to get up on the stair steps and slide down the banisters.

Where did you go to high school?

Here in Springfield on Central Street. They called it Central High. I went through college, but the way I went through was in the front door and out the back. (laughs) No, I just went to high school.

(laughs) What did your dad do for a living?

He was a farmer. He bought and sold mules with a guy there in town, too. That farm was out on South Fremont, but the Cadillac place is moving out there now. It's gonna be built up and all the old memories will be gone. Nine of the kids were born there.

How many of your siblings are still alive?

Eight. My dad ... he lacked a few months of being a hundred years old when he died, and my mother was 92 when she died. I'm 85 and I'm in good shape yet. In fact, I had two wet dreams last night, and if I hadn't gone to sleep, I'd have had another one. (laughs) I told my doctor that and he got a kick out of it.

(laughs) Did you play any sports as a kid?

I went out for wrestling. I had a guy who tried to teach me, but he couldn't teach me much because I could beat him. I was a country boy. I was young, but I was strong from plowing all the time ... working the handle bars on those cultivators. I was in shape. I could whip those little ol' city boys. When I got older, I went to Little Rock, Arkansas, and the guy down there who promoted wrestling got me started.

How old were you when you first took notice of wrestling?

I must have been sixteen years old … something like that. That was when I went to Little Rock.

What took you down there at such a young age?

I just got a wild hair and left home. I got to making a little money and started sending some home to my folks. That got over good with 'em because they weren't makin' much on the farm. I hated to farm with a passion. I didn't want to follow them mules all day and walk behind a walkin' plow.

Did you ever see a live wrestling show before you left Springfield?

I don't believe I did.

There was an Oliver Gideon who used to promote in Springfield, Missouri. Was he a relative?

That was my cousin. Him and Miles Walker promoted here for a long time. Oliver was the one who kind of got me started in wrestling. When I was about eighteen, he sent me down to Little Rock. I went to work doing odd jobs for Tony Bernardi, who was promoting down there. He ran Little Rock, Hot Springs, and little towns nearby.

Oliver was an attorney and worked for 42 years in local government, including Springfield's city director of revenue. An interesting side note is that Oliver's wife, Dorothy Jo Gideon, was married to Bob Barker of *The Price is Right* fame.

Miles Walker was an inspector on the Missouri Athletic Commission. He was a deputy clerk of the Greene County Magistrate Court in Springfield and promoted wrestling at the Shrine Mosque from 1942 until the time of his death on Feb. 16, 1957.

I started working out in the ring. A lot of professionals would come in and would work out with me, teach me things. I worked out, worked preliminaries, put the ring up. I was always in good shape. I weighed around 190 when I started, but my best wrestling weight was around 210.

Red Roberts was working out there at the time, too. Tony sent the two of us to Tennessee for Roy Welch. Gus Wisbar broke into the business at the same time that I did ... down in Dyersburg, Tennessee. Then I went to Portland, Oregon, and Don Owen took a liking to me. I averaged about 100,000 miles a year. I've had 52 different cars. I've been in every state except for Maine. I wrestled in Cuba ... in fact, the promoter still owes me a hundred dollars.

Did you work anywhere while you were training?

I never had a regular job in my life.

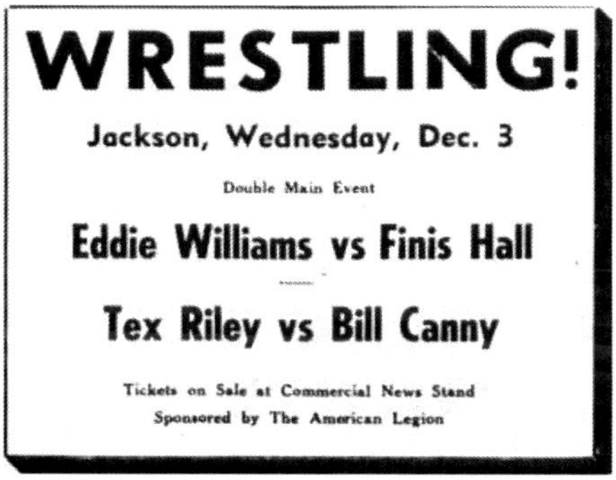
WRESTLING!

Jackson, Wednesday, Dec. 3

Double Main Event

Eddie Williams vs Finis Hall

Tex Riley vs Bill Canny

Tickets on Sale at Commercial News Stand
Sponsored by The American Legion

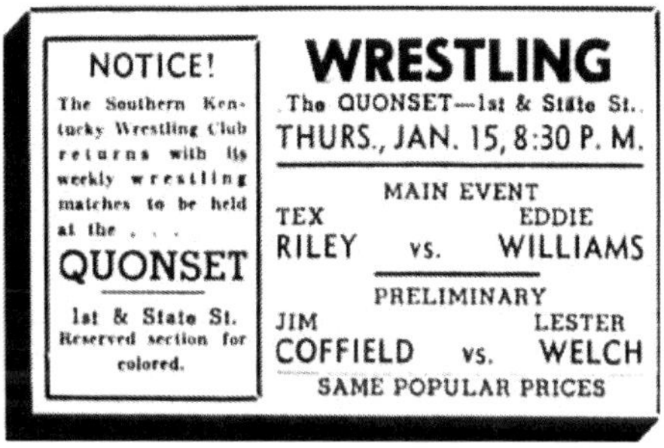
NOTICE!
The Southern Kentucky Wrestling Club returns with its weekly wrestling matches to be held at the . . .
QUONSET
1st & State St.
Reserved section for colored.

WRESTLING
The QUONSET—1st & State St.
THURS., JAN. 15, 8:30 P. M.

MAIN EVENT
TEX RILEY vs. EDDIE WILLIAMS

PRELIMINARY
JIM COFFIELD vs. LESTER WELCH

SAME POPULAR PRICES

(l.) Jackson TN • Dec. 3, 1947
(above) Bowling Green KY • Jan. 15, 1948

No kidding!

I never had a job I could be fired off of. I had a camper business on the side after I quit wrestling. This old boy got on my nerves. I asked him if he knew Argo. He said, *"No, I don't believe I do. Argo who?"*

I said, *"Argo blank yourself." (laughs)* I cleaned that one up a little for you. (laughs)

(laughs) I noticed that.

He said, *"We'll see about that. You won't be here long."* He went down the hallway to see Wayne Tripp. He was gonna try to get me fired. (laughs) Wayne says, *"I can't do anything about it. It's his company. He owns the place and I work for him."* (laughs) That was funny. It backfired on him.

Do you remember some of the guys you worked with early in your career?

Tony Galento, Red Roberts, Martino Angelo.

What did you parents think about you wrestling?

They didn't like it until I started sending home some money. Once they saw that I wasn't getting hurt and was taking care of myself, they thought it was alright.

Did you begin your career as Eddie Gideon?

No, Eddie Williams. The only reason I used Eddie Gideon was when there was another Williams or two in a territory. The people would get us mixed up. I'd just do that until I left the territory and went somewhere where the other Williams' weren't, then I'd go back to my regular name.

You switched back and forth from Eddie to Scotty.

I have Scots, Irish, English and Welsh blood.

I've also seen references to you working as Freddy Williams.

That was a mix-up. The newspaper guy got it wrong. I have a brother named Freddy, though.

And what about Tom Tracy?

I went to Dallas [Feb. 1938] and they had two other wrestlers named Williams, so they changed my name to avoid any confusion. The funny thing was, they just took it upon themselves to do it. I didn't even know what my name was until I got there.

Did I read somewhere that you worked in the AT shows?

Carnivals?

Yes.

Yeah, I was with Curly Spears. That's where I got a lot of experience, taking on all comers. You know, getting up and ballyhooing. The barker would get those country boys up on the bally and they'd look at me, lookin' like a little, ol' city boy. They figured they could beat me, especially when they had the chance to win a dollar a minute to stay with me. The maximum time limit was five minutes. I'd beat 'em as quick as I could so we didn't have to pay out any money. I was in awful good shape then. I had good wind ... you could hear it all over the building. (laughs)

(laughs) How long did you stay with the AT show?

I was with 'em for six months. I went out a couple of summers.

Did you use a stick [plant] in the crowd?

No. I just took on all comers. They charged ten, fifteen cents to get in. We did take Red Roberts once in a while. We'd wrestle when we couldn't get anybody else [to challenge].

Did you box, too?

I never did box. I thought too much of my chin. I had a black eye once. A guy said, "*How did you get that?*"

I said, "*I ran into a man with awful large hands.*"

What were the living conditions like?

I slept in the ring, in the tent ... then Curly had a big motor home. He'd let me sleep there sometimes. He had his own trucks, too.

Where did you eat?

They had a cookhouse, so I'd eat there sometimes, but I'd also go to restaurants. Curly had his own tent, so I ate with them a lot. He had good cookin'. Of course, most of the food was good.

On the average, how many times a day did you wrestle?

Oh, four or five times a day ... as long as we had guys who would take us on. I guess there were times when we'd use an outside man. If we didn't have any challenges, he'd come in and wrestle. A dollar a minute was good money. That's back when people would work all day in the fields for a dollar. There were times when, if it was the last night and a guy got over good, I'd let him beat me. I wasn't gaining anything by beating him. They didn't know me and I was leaving town, so it built up his name in his hometown. "*Why, he beat that carnival guy!*"

Did you work anywhere else in the carnivals?

Once in a while, I'd go over to the "pitch 'til you win" with a handful of pennies. I'd pitch 'em and got to where I could pitch pretty good. The owner would pay me, or give me a prize, which, of course, would help encourage other people to pitch pennies. I'd give him the prize back later. You've got to have marks, so I'd play the mark.

What was your favorite finishing hold?

Oh, I'd use a flying head scissors quite a bit ... and body slams.

You worked as the Silver Star for a long time.

Yeah.

And in 1951, you worked for one night as the Masked Red Marvel in Chattanooga.

(laughs) It was a short career. They unmasked me the first night. I didn't want to wear it, anyway. I was too good lookin'. I didn't want to cover my face. (laughs)

Scotty came into Chattanooga to wrestle another masked wrestler, the Purple Flash, in a tournament match to determine a Southern light-heavyweight champion. 1,800 fans were on hand to see the 205-lb. Scotty unmasked. Purple Flash, who was unmasked by Roy Welch a few months later that year and revealed to be Eddie (Pat) Malone, had a long run for the Nick Gulas-Roy Welch company.

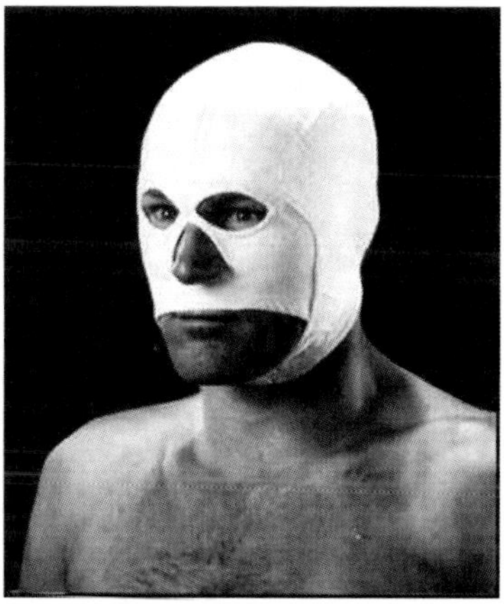

The Silver Star

Did you find it hard to work with a mask on?

It didn't bother me. I had one with the chin cut out, so I could breathe alright. It fit good and tight. Before I'd go in the ring, I'd wet it. Of course, it would get wet from sweating pretty quick, anyway.

You wrestled clean for most of your career, but did you ever have any problem with fans?

No, but it got to where there were a lot of girls hanging around. They'd give us a police escort to the ring. The girls would follow me up there, reach up and kiss me, hug me around the neck, grab me down low ... Oohh! They'd scream and go on. (laughs) That wasn't too tough to take, though.

Where did the promoters bill you as being from?

Springfield. I represented my town all over. Everywhere I went ... Springfield, Missouri.

Do you remember anyone dying in the ring?

Oh, yeah. Eddie Baker died in Mississippi. A guy [Roy Welch] body-slammed him on the mat ... and he just laid there. The guy thought Eddie was playin' possum, so he picked him up. When he did, he noticed he was awful limp, but still thought he was faking it, so he slammed him again. Eddie still laid there. He was dead.

Did you do any booking or promoting?

A little bit, but not much. I helped a few guys out with the booking. I didn't care to get into that. It's a lot of work to promote. Back then, you had to set your own ring up, then take it down. You had to set all the chairs out. When you leave, you had to clean the arena up and leave it like you found it.

You hauled the ring around for someone, didn't you?

Yeah, Tony Bernardi.

I read a statement you made in an old newspaper article that you held a version of the world title. Where was that?

That title started in Portland. It was really a junior heavyweight title. I think Don Owen has the belt.

You wrestled in the Army, too, didn't you?

Yeah, but the only reason was it got me out of a lot of duty. (laughs) I was stationed at Camp Crowder.

Why did you leave wrestling?

My age. I got into the camper manufacturing business. I made 354 campers in all.

What did you do after that?

Well, I retired and got a little woodworking shop in Springfield. I just take it easy. I bought me a nice house. I'm still single.

You've never been married?

No.

Do you have any regrets about your wrestling career?

No. I enjoyed my days in wrestling and always tried to make the best of it whenever I went in the ring. I never had a problem getting booked and made a good living at it. I got on top and was making good money. I didn't blow it. I put a lot of it away in the bank.

What was your best payoff?

The biggest I ever got was $2,150. The least I ever got was 65 cents. (laughs)

What do you do now that you're retired?

I do woodworking. I also like sports cars. I have a 1970 MGB and play around with it a little bit. It's a collector's item and in perfect shape. If I wanted, I could start for California in it tomorrow. I may not get there, but I could start. (laughs) They used to rib Jack Dillon about his car. He didn't know anything about automobiles, so they told him he had to change the air in the tires every once in a while because it got stale. He took it to a service station and told the attendant to put fresh air in the tires. The guy gave him some lip, but Dillon told him to just shut up and do it. The guy charged him a dollar for changing the air in his tires. (laughs)

Do you stay in touch with any old friends from wrestling?

No, I never really ran around with anyone in particular. We have a guy here in town who used to wrestle professionally. He has a big cauliflower ear and owns a jewelry store. I don't know his first name, but he goes by Manoli. They inducted me into the Missouri Hall of Fame. I got a big trophy and write-up.

The "Manoli" Eddie refers to is former wrestler Mike Pappas, real name Manoli Savvenas. Mike and his wife, Valerie, have owned Manoli's Jewelers since 1979.

Thanks for taking the time to do this interview, Eddie.

I sure enjoyed talkin' with you. Don't let this be the last time. I don't go to bed until late, so call whenever you want. If you're ever in Springfield, I've got an extra bedroom. I live by myself ... me, my dog, and my cat.

Scotty was a World War II U.S. Army veteran in the medical corps during the European campaign, including service during the Battle of the Bulge. After the war ended, he was an athletic coach and sports trainer in Euroope and helped manage the first football game held in Nuremberg Stadium in Germany.

His wrestling career spanned from 1933 to 1968. He was inducted into the Missouri Sports Hall of Fame on Jan. 24, 1999.

He passed away on March 23, 2008, and was buried at Rivermonte Memorial Gardens in Springfield, Missouri.

TITLES

World junior heavyweight [OR]

ALIAS

Eddie Williams
Eddie Gideon
Scotty Williams
Tom Tracy
Freddy Williams
Silver Star
The Red Marvel [TN '51]

A special thanks goes out to Terry Evans for putting us in touch with Scotty in 1999. Terry and Scotty were good friends from the first day they met.

TIM TYLER

Marvin Hickman

This interview, conducted by Scott Teal in July 1998, was originally published in issue #38 of *Whatever Happened to ...?*

Tell me a little about your childhood, Marvin.

I was born in Bradford, Arkansas, on March 10, 1932. That was 66 years ago. My parents' names were John and Artis Hickman. They farmed for a living, so I was raised on a farm, pickin' cotton and strawberries. I went to Bradford High School, but quit in the ninth grade to go in the Army. I wanted to get off the farm, so when I was fourteen, I signed up. I signed my mother's name, then wrote her a letter after I left. I told her not to say anything because it would get me in trouble. They read the articles of war to me and that's kind of a rough deal if they want to push it. I was scared they was gonna catch me for making a fraudulent enlistment. They could put you in the federal penitentiary. They didn't try to discourage it that much, though, because they needed bodies.

What was your mom's response?

Oh, she said she wouldn't get me out if she could. (laughs) She thought I was better off. I was always a kid with a lot of ideas ... wanting to experiment, wanting to do this, to do that.

Before going into the service, did you participate in any sports?

I tried basketball and didn't like that a bit. I did a lot of street fighting. We was in the country, but I got to where I was whipping everybody for a quarter. I told them to give me a quarter and I'd jump on anyone they wanted me to. (laughs) I didn't like organized sports too much, but I liked to fish. I didn't get into wrestling until I was eighteen years old.

Tell me about your time in the service.

I did my basic training in San Antonio, Texas. After six weeks, I shipped out and went straight to Japan. That was in '46. I went to Yokohama and lived in tents for three or four weeks. There was snow on the tents. I was transferred to Tachikawa and spent the rest of my time there. I tried to get in the Airborne. I had to sign up for Ground Forces unassigned and they put me in the damned Engineers. I actually didn't have a lot to do. I took care of equipment and stuff like that. They had about 30 or 40 Japanese mechanics working, so I'd just watch them. They were real good. They had an interpreter. Of course, I learned to speak the language pretty good. I had one hitch over there where they put me in the shock troopers. That's when the Berlin airlift was going on, so I had to train for that. Our job would have been to go in and knock out all communications and transportation facilities until the main troops got there. In other words, it was a suicide job. (laughs) I wanted to get into the Airborne, so I wanted to take some jump training. They said, "*You don't need any training. You're not gonna jump but one time.*" (laughs)

How long did you stay in the service?

Three years. Twenty-eight months of it was in Japan. I was in Fort Hood, Texas, for six months and was in Field Artillery. Of course, they tried to encourage me to re-enlist, but Vietnam was coming up about that time. I could see the writing on the wall. They was wanting me to stay, so they offered me a captain's commission to come back in. I was married by that time and my wife didn't want me to go, so I got out. (laughs) I wouldn't have made a very good captain if I let my wife make my mind up. (laughs) I went to barber school and worked at that for four years.

Did you own your own shop?

I worked at the Navy base in Norfolk, Virginia. I came back and worked at my brother's barber shop, then decided to get out. I was working out at the gymnasium and taking judo. The guy running the gym was Sam Platania. Sam was a pretty good wrestler. He came out of New York and had a couple of college degrees. He taught school and done a lot of things. He got shot when somebody tried to rob him. He whipped their ass after he got shot. Sam said, "*There's a couple of guys here that want to work out with you.*" I didn't know who they were because I didn't go to the matches, but it was two professional wrestlers. I worked out with them and beat 'em. That was shoots.

Who was it?

One guy's name was Alan. The other (pause, laughs) ... I really don't want to (pause, laughs) ... well, his name was Dwayne Peal [who later wrestled as Buddy Wayne]. I don't want him to get pissed off at me saying that, but Dwayne knows I could beat him. I could beat him then and I could beat him now. (laughs) Anyway, Sam said, "*You ought to go up to Ellis Auditorium.*" That's where the wrestling was in Memphis. They had just started up and was drawing about three or 400 people. Les Wolfe was still there, but Buddy Fuller had taken it over. They said, "*Go challenge a professional wrestler.*"

What they was doing at the time was have a spectator come out and challenge a pro. They had it real organized. If you're dumb enough to walk in there and challenge somebody, they're gonna put the toughest son-of-a-bitch they've got in there. So they put me with Charlie Carr. [March 16, 1959] Hell, he beat my ass in four minutes ... made me give up. (laughs) He put enough pressure on that it was hurting. I'd been beating all the other guys in the gym, so, afterwards, I went to the dressing room just as quick as I could. I was figuring on getting dressed and getting the hell out of there because I was embarrassed. It was certainly a lot different than I thought it was gonna be.

Charlie came on up there and gave me a lot of praise, and he smartened me up that night. I couldn't believe it wasn't a shoot because all I ever knew was shooting. He asked me to come and work out with him, so I worked out with him for three years. There was ten to fifteen people coming up to the gym to work out with me and Charlie. (laughs) I'd line 'em up. I'd stand 'em in a line, beat one of 'em, and say, "*Next!*" (laughs) I was a real smart ass. I'd beat 'em and stretch 'em. Once in a while, I'd kind of hurt one. Charlie was standing there once and I didn't know he was behind me. I started to rip that guy and Charlie says, "*Nah-ah!*" He made me turn him loose. (laughs)

Joe McCarthy was another tough guy around at the time.

He was a real funny thinker and was well liked, not to mention that he was tougher than hell. I had to wrestle him in the dressing room every week. Actually, his wife's name was Jo. I forget what his was. He didn't like that, so he made his wife take his name and he took Joe. (laughs) You know Roland?

Roland Criswell?

Uh, huh. That's his brother. Anyway, I was in Florida and held the world tag belts with Tarzan [Tyler]. I strutted around, thinking I was doing great things. I run into Joe down there. He was just refereeing. I went down to Texas and there was a little town on the ocean.

You must mean Corpus Christi.

Corpus Christi. That's right. Joe come in as the world light heavyweight champion. I was on the number-one spot [opening match] on the card. He says to me, "*You're a peacock today and a feather duster tomorrow.*" He was a peacock there and I was a feather duster. It was turned around from Florida. Joe was quite a fellow. Sputnik called me the other day. He talked to me for 45 minutes and never took a breath. You don't ever get your point in because he gets 'em off your mind. I told him that I was building him up a little in this story, then I said, "*Which you never did do for me, you bastard.*"

What did he say?

Oh, he says, "*God bless you. I wanted to say this and I wanted to say that.*"

When did you break into the pros?

I turned pro in '58, which was right about that time. I worked out with Charlie Carr at the gym about three hours a day for three years. I met Sputnik Monroe during that time. Monroe didn't actually break me in, but we run together and had a lot of fun together. We done a lot of crazy stuff. I had a new car (pause) ... he mentioned dropping a guy on the hood ornament of a car. [*Whatever Happened to ...? #35*] I think he was talking about my '59 Pontiac. I was doing a lot of refereeing, wrestling, filling in here and there at that time. The houses in Memphis jumped from 300 and $400 to ... well, Billy Wicks and Monroe drew $18,000.

Did Charlie also teach you to work?

No, he taught me to wrestle. There wasn't a hell of a lot of difference in working and shooting in those days, as far as the moves were concerned. You could take a guy down, put a top wristlock on him, and if he would sell it proper ... you could get a riot going with a top wristlock. Just a simple move or hold. Just keep hammering on that deal, and after a while, the fans get to believing it. I guess Monroe taught me the bullshit of the business. Monroe got to taking me on the trips and helping me. A lot of the stuff I did was Monroe's stuff. Put that comment in there in big, dark letters. I want that son-of-a-bitch to be able to read it. (laughs)

They used the "challenge a wrestler" gimmick in Memphis for several months during that time.

Carlton Hazelwood was another big guy who challenged the wrestlers. He was a tough son-of-a-gun. I never wrestled him, but I know he wrestled the boys and there was some of them who couldn't beat him. He went ahead and become a professional wrestler. They smartened him up. I think it was kind of hard to smarten him up. He later became a doctor.

Did you work a full-time job while you were training?

I worked part of the time, but quit and started refereeing. That's the way I made my living. After Charlie and I worked out together for several years, I got to traveling with Buddy Fuller and Les Wolfe, doing a little promoting and stuff. I went down to El Paso, Texas, and opened it up. Buddy Fuller and I was partners. Charlie came down there and stayed with me. He was a hell of a guy. [Sputnik] Monroe mentions him slightly in his interview, but Charlie played a big part in my life, and Monroe's, too. He had a lot to do with it. They liked me, so I should have stuck to it [promoting in El Paso], but I wanted the glory. (laughs) By that time, Les [Welch] had gone back to doing what he was doing ... roping cattle and training horses. Buddy would leave town for five or six weeks and let me run the show. I worked out the finishes and everything.

I don't find any records of you wrestling in Memphis at the time.

When that happened, I was going under the name of Randy Roper. I think Monroe gave me that name. You might mention that. I hope it makes the son-of-a-bitch feel bad because he didn't talk about me much in his interview. (laughs) He gave me a lot of good pointers and kind of pushed me along. As far as I knew at the time, it was good advice. (laughs) But you know how the wrestling business is. You don't know whether they're helping you or knocking you. I worked in and around Atlanta as Randy Roper [April 1964], but didn't do much. Of course, you never can work for the promoters that got you started. They won't give you a break. I grew up in Memphis in the business. They knew me before I was a wrestler. Once they know you before you start, they don't ever give you a good break. You have to get out away from 'em. I was talking to Buddy [Fuller] down there and I said, "*Hey, why not hook me up with Buddy Colt? He and I would make a good team.*" Fuller wouldn't do it because he remembered me as Randy Roper, the good ol' hometown boy.

He booked me in Atlanta with Eddie Graham. Before we went out to wrestle, I heard Fuller tell Eddie, "*Go out and beat him in about five minutes.*" I went out there and ... well, you know how stiff Eddie was. He knocked the piss out of me. (laughs) Well, I just made a little comeback on him. He loved it! He stayed in there with me fifteen minutes, and we were supposed to go five.

Atlanta GA • Aug. 7, 1964

I heard Eddie ask Fuller. "*Who is that kid? I like the way he works.*" (laughs) I was stiff with him. That's what he liked. (laughs)

Buddy said, "*Oh, he's just a hometown boy from Memphis.*"

About two or three weeks after that, I went into the office and I said, "*Buddy, I need to give you my notice. I'm gonna leave. I can't do no good here. You're not giving me no break at all.*" The business was mostly about politics. If I hadn't known Buddy Fuller, I wouldn't have never got in the business, but he would jack you around more than anybody in the world.

I had talked to Texas and Oklahoma and both of them wanted me to come in. While I was in Buddy's office, Eddie called and Buddy said, "*He's standing right here.*"

I got on the phone and Eddie asked, "*Can you be here Thursday?*" You know, in just a few days. "*Have you a black beard and white hair. You're gonna be a Tyler, Tarzan Tyler's brother. Just pick out your first name.*" I never met Tarzan. I said I'd be there and asked what the deal was. He said, "*We're gonna make you world* [tag team] *champion.*" I went on in there and everything worked out pretty good. I had a son named Tim, so I told them, "*I'll just be Tim Tyler.*" We run a year and they never did beat me.

Dickie Steinborn's daddy, Milo Steinborn, was promoting Orlando. He says, "*Get down on the floor and do some pushups.*" I did some pushups, just to please him. He said, "*Put some paper down. Don't breathe that dust. You look like you just crawled out from under a rock. You don't have any sun or nothing.*" (laughs) He wanted me to get a little juice there one night. I bled all over the place. He came back and says, "*I thought you were gonna bleed to death. That's the best job I've ever seen anyone do.*"

Who showed you?

It was probably Monroe (pause) ... geez, I hate to keep puttin' that son-of-a-bitch over. I suppose he's the one that taught me to do that. How to carry it in my mouth, how to tape it to my finger, all that stuff. That brings up another funny story. Pancho Villa [Bobby Lane] ... he never had done it, so he was gonna let me. He said to me, "*Now don't cut me very much.*" (laughs)

I had him in a headlock and dropped the blade. I said, "*Oops. I have another blade here, but I don't have any tape on it. I can cut you pretty good with that one.*"

His eyes got wide and he said, "*Oohh, shit! Let's just forget about it.*"

Tampa FL • Nov. 3, 1964

He liked to have fainted. He didn't want to do it. You know, a lot of those guys used to blade in their nose. I did it all over. I was wrestling old [Dwayne] Peal one time. He was promoting Jonesboro and I was working with him. He said, "*Turn me loose so I can do something.*" (laughs)

I said, "*If you get loose, you'll* be *doing something.*"

He was always worried about me not getting enough blood. One night, he wanted me to get blood and he kept on and on. "*I want you to get blood and I want it to look good.*" He said it several times. When he'd sell a hold, he used to stick his tongue out when you choked him. So I got blood and got on top of him, making a little comeback. I got him down and got the blood, then let it drip onto his tongue and down his throat as I choked him. "*Is that enough?*" (laughs)

Tarzan and I were coming out of Jacksonville one night with John Smith and Boris Volkoff. You'd hit Highway 1 around Ocala and cut back across to Tampa. Volkoff was driving. He says, "*John! Where the hell is the highway?*"

And John says, "*It's Highway One.*"

Volkoff said, "*Damn! We passed Highway One twenty miles back.*"

John says, "*Well, maybe it's the next Highway One up here.*" (laughs)

He says, "*You'd get lost in a telephone booth.*" (laughs) They'd cuss each other all the time.

Then Freddie Blassie come into Florida and they started pushing him. Blassie was a good self-promoter, you know. He was one of the best. Maybe *the* best. Of course, Monroe was good at it, too. They put Blassie in there with Tarzan and started booking me out, so I left and went to Texas.

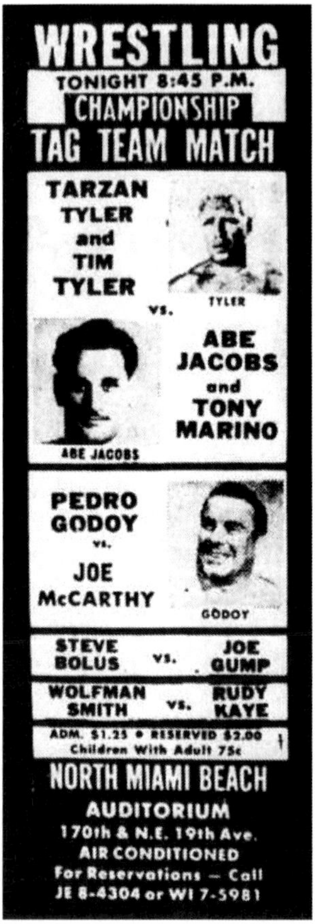

Miami Beach FL
Nov. 13, 1964

From there, I went on to Oklahoma. Jack Donovan was gonna come down to Oklahoma and tag with me. He was a blond, I was a blond. We both worked close enough, but there was enough difference that it would have been an interesting team. He never showed. I went in there and worked a few matches, waiting for him to get there, but he never got there. LeRoy McGuirk's the one that wanted us to go as a team. In fact, he's the one that called Jack. Jack got a start date, but didn't show up. [Lou] Thesz came into Oklahoma. LeRoy called him Louis. LeRoy asked me, "*Do you mind working with Louis?*" I didn't care. He said, "*We're gonna try to do something. We don't want to beat you even before we get started.*"

It turned out that somebody else showed up and wrestled Lou that night, but I got paid for the trip and didn't work at all. LeRoy was a real good guy.

I made my best money working under Eddie Graham, but as far as a person who was on the level, it was LeRoy McGuirk. LeRoy was a steady guy who didn't flip-flop on nothing. If he started you out to build you up, he went through with it. He ran his programs and there wasn't no miscues. Eddie Graham was a great finish caller. He could work out a deal. You had to be real good to work for him. If you couldn't remember all the steps, criss-crosses and punches, you didn't stay long. Anyway, since Jack Donovan didn't show, I picked up the phone and called Rip [Tyler], who was still Dean Vaughn then. I knew he was trying to get a break and was decent. I figured we'd make a team, so we went to Nashville and sold it out for several weeks in a row. Then I told Nick in Birmingham, "*Pay us more money.*" I think the payoff was about a hundred dollars apiece. He wouldn't, so we left that night. Nick said, "*I made you guys the champions,*" and this and that. I just threw the belt back over my head and said, "*That don't mean nothin'. Money's what we're after.*" The next morning, we went to Nick's office and threw the belts on the floor of his office."

I never did a lot of arguing with promoters. I'd just leave. I went back to Florida when Lester Welch was the booker. They wanted me to referee, so I said, "*Nah. I'll just go home.*" Rip and I went back to Florida for the Field brothers ... the Mobile end. They wasn't booking us real good. I don't think they liked me at all. Rip was a good learner and a good tag team partner. We traveled together and (pause) ... I think you mentioned in your last issue that we did Birmingham TV at eight o'clock at night. [*Whatever Happened to …? #34*] Hell, it was twelve o'clock midnight. We'd make about three TVs, then go to Birmingham and make it at twelve o'clock. We was going there once on Highway 75. I went blind as a bat. We had just had a match with Jackie Fargo and Len Rossi. We didn't even take our tights off before we left. I told Rip, "*Get behind the wheel. I'm blind.*"

He says, "*Aw, bullshit.*"

I said, "*You'd better take the wheel. I'm blind as hell. I can't see nothing.*"

He took the wheel and after a while, my sight came back. We went on, worked on TV, and I never had any more trouble. Can you imagine? That was the strangest thing. I'll tell you something else that's funny. Billy Wicks told the story about driving down the road and seeing a couple of broads in the front seat of a car. [*Whatever Happened to …? #34*] He said it was Mario Galento and his first wife. Well, that wasn't Yvon Roberre with Billy. It was me. (laughs) We had been in Jackson, Mississippi, and he locked the keys in his Cadillac that night. That's the car he won in the tournament.

Buck Robley came up with some money [to start a promotion] and wanted to become a wrestler, so I gave him the name Phil Tyler.

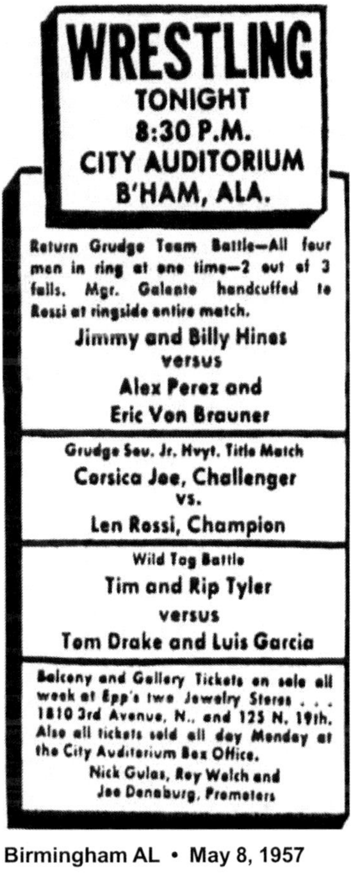

Birmingham AL • May 8, 1957

We brought him here to Arkansas and got him about eight towns going. We had a little promotion running and made pretty good money. I was calling the shots and let Robley take the credit for it. (laughs) We did everything from racing cars to getting drunk.

What was your primary town in the territory?

I guess our main town in this little territory was Jonesboro. We were selling it out every week. We'd run Blytheville, Arkansas, and towns in southern Missouri, plus spots shows. Robley was paying me a salary and I was doing real good. I was making a grand a week, so I thought that was real good. Phil was a quick learner. (laughs) Well, he was a goofy son-of-a-bitch. (laughs) He'd try anything in the world. He got to where he could take those bumps real good, which is what I did ... a lot of bumps. He got to where he outshined me. We never had any trouble with that, though. (laughs) He was welcome to go out there and take all the bumps. I'd go in and do the win. (laughs) After a while, I got tired of it and went back to working other territories.

What happened to the promotion?

Robley would get gung-ho on something, then he gets to drinking or other things. I eased on into something else and left it all with him. I don't think it lasted too long after that.

What do you feel were your strong points in the ring?

Well, I'd like to say that I was a good improviser. If we had a finish set up, like a criss-cross and a couple of hiplocks, if that screwed up, I could go into something else and make it look like we never missed anything. I helped a lot of guys to overcome things they missed or didn't remember. A lot of guys couldn't remember a finish, so I could improvise and come up with something to do. It would look as good, or better, than what they had planned. I also did a lot of acrobatics, which you didn't see a lot of back in those days. On the other hand, my weak points were that I never figured out the politics of the business. I never could hang out at the office and do business with the promoters. That includes Buddy Fuller, even though I liked the guy. He didn't want to pay the local boys. You know, just because a guy's from the same town that you're from, that don't make him a dummy. They did it everywhere.

Was there anyone in particular that you really enjoyed working with?

Billy Wicks was a real good babyface. If he liked you, and you worked with him, he was a hell of a babyface. If he didn't like you, he wouldn't put you over too good. In my opinion, he was one of the best. Not because he was there when I started, but down through the years, I can still visualize the moves that he made and the things he did and the way he sold it. He was just a good worker (pause) ... and he was stiff. (laughs)

In your opinion, who do you rate as the best worker ever?

You won't even believe what I'm fixing to tell you. I mean, the finest worker, and the loosest worker, one that would not hurt you ... I mean, you could just give him everything he wanted, and it wouldn't hurt him ... Al Galento. You could work with him all night long. He didn't make you work hard and didn't do anything that hurt you. I'd have him in a hold and I thought I was working loose. He'd say, "*Loosen up, Gabe! I'm not trying to get away!*" (laughs) You wonder how damn loose you're supposed to be. He had good heat everywhere he went. I've seen him fill up houses with Monroe.

You've mentioned your picks for best promoter and best worker. What about referees?

Sam Bass and Charlie Smith (pause) ... and Speedy Hatfield. He *was* a hell of a referee. He could make a match. And he had a lot of backing. If anything went wrong, his boys were gonna stand with him. He could make decisions in that ring that was the best for the business, and he knew what was good for the business. I'd say, all around, he was the best. He kept things going and watched everything. I've seen it when a heel would get in trouble and the people was fixing to get him. Hatfield would jump in and chew the heel's ass, then tells the babyface to fight [the heel] to the dressing room. With that babyface whipping the heel back to the dressing room, the people aren't going to get involved. As long as the babyface is winning, they ain't gonna mess with him [the heel]. Back in those days, they didn't have anything outside around the ring. No bars, no ropes. If you got thrown out, you were right with 'em.

Did you ever work under any other names?

Yeah. I wrestled under the hood in the Mobile area as [Wrestling] Pro #2. Pro One and Pro Two. What was that old boys' name that was Wrestling Pro #1?

Tarzan Baxter.

Yeah, Tarzan Baxter. I worked with him a long time. Fred Bass [Sam Bass] was the manager of that team for a while. I didn't like the mask. I didn't like it because I couldn't breathe under it and you couldn't get any expressions to the people. The only thing you had to get heat with was the mask. You can't sell expressions, either. If a guy had a good hold on you, you couldn't show any expressions of pain. Baxter loved wrestling under the hood. He worked for years as the Wrestling Pro. I don't think he ever changed his name.

Where did you get your first ring outfit?

I got my first ring outfit from K&H [Karl and Hildegard]. I had jackets made. The Fields brothers' mama used to make them for a lot of people.

What was your average weight?

I was always a small guy. I weighed 215 to 220. Tarzan weighed 284. He went to Jacksonville one night and I didn't go with him. He said some skinny guy that weighed about 140 pounds jumped up and was gonna whip his ass. The guy said, *"I'll whip your ass tonight. Your brother's not here to protect you."* Tarzan thought that was funny as hell because I was always the one that fought the jerks. He never had to raise a hand. I way always out there fighting them and getting Tarzan out of the ring. I did wrestle once at 287. I mean, I got fat. That's when Watts called me and wanted me to go to Mississippi to fill in for someone.

Did you prefer working as a heel?

Oh, that's the only way I could work. I tried working as a babyface when I worked as Randy Roper. (laughs) I'd come out on the babyface side wearing one of those nice jackets with the tassels hanging down. Those people started spitting on me and booing me. (laughs) I figured I must be a natural heel. I liked it because I knew how to get the heat and the babyfaces had to follow me in the ring. If you were smart, you'd let the heel run the show. When that didn't happen, I'd take over and make it work.

Let me explain something to you, and you'll probably remember this. The heel is the key. If the babyface gets to do too much, the houses fall. If you bring the world champion in there to beat that heel, the people will come to see it. You and the top babyface can run a five to six-week program leading up to that big match. If things dropped off, it was usually because the babyface did too much and the heel let him. Wicks was just right for Monroe because he would listen to Monroe, and Sputnik knew how to get the heat. Don't get me wrong. There were several babyfaces that were good workers. Some of the guys I worked with … like Abe Jacobs and Tony Marino ... they were two good babyfaces. Me and Rip went against Jody Hamilton and [Tom] Renesto. We made babyfaces out of them. That'll give you some idea of the team Rip and I were. Jody and Renesto were two masked guys and considered to be mean as hell. Renesto was a good navigator. He could steer Jody right into where the money was.

I was told that you were warned to hold back one night because the main event wouldn't be able to follow you.

I worked with Mario Galento in the match before the main event. The promoter was working in the main event and got pissed because he thought we were trying to steal the show. In actuality, that's what we did.

Did you ever have anyone try to get smart with you during a match?

No. Charlie Carr said I was the toughest man in the world, and he was a pretty good judge, but I don't think I'm quite that tough. I didn't have no problems with anybody. I won't mention any names, but one guy I beat about three times. He'd jump on me and try to beat me. He brought an audience to the motel one time about four o'clock in the morning.

An audience?

Yeah. He brought a bunch of people with him. He was gonna whip my ass. (laughs) I tore him up. He'll know when he reads this who he is. My wife's sitting here and she knows it, too.

Any riots that stand out in your mind?

One night in Jonesboro, Arkansas. Al Lovelock was my partner. He run off and left me amongst all those mad people. I got hit in the back of the head with a bottle and took nineteen stitches. When I got to the dressing room, I asked him why he ran off and left me. He was just scared of the riots. I went to the office and told them I'd never wrestle with Lovelock again.

Did the babyfaces try to protect you?

No, they were already in the back. Anyway, they sewed some glass up in my head. I went on back to Nashville and my head was burning. I had to get it cut back open to get the glass out. Another time, Danny Hodge and I were in Texarkana. I was supposed to run in and hit Danny. I'd screw him up, then get on out of the ring. He was supposed to get up and run me out of the ring. When I hit him, he goes down and pretends to be out like a light. He wouldn't get up. I had to grab a microphone and everything else to fight my way out. I get back to the dressing room ... and Danny makes them bring him back on a stretcher! Once everybody was out, he sits up and laughs. "*Got some heat on you, didn't I?*" (laughs) Danny and I drew a little money together.

You should have shot on Danny and taught him a lesson.

(laughs) Yeah, right. There were a few times that I tried him. I tried Lou Thesz more than I did Danny, though. He was pretty good ... real good. I still think Danny was the best, though. Lou weighed 248, roughly. Danny would weigh 215, 220. Lou would put a short-arm scissors on Danny. Danny would pick him up from a laying-down position, put him on his shoulder, and deposit him in the corner. That's strong.

Any highlights from your career that stand out in your mind?

I have some pictures of Rocky Marciano and I together. They were taken in '58. He had finished his boxing career and started refereeing. He had fears like a lot of people. He said, "*Watch my back. He's liable to try to sucker punch me and knock me out.*"

At what period in your career were you the most content?

I was working the Louisiana territory when the Fields boys were running it and was home every night. I had a match against someone one night. We'd been drinking together and was pretty drunk. When we came into the arena, we walked in together ... then we wrestled each other. (laughs) We had a great match, but if the promoters had seen us come in together, they didn't say nothing.

Did you suffer any serious injuries?

I got my shoulder broke in Dothan, Alabama. The boy I was wrestling done one of those LeRoy McGuirk roll-ups and stood me on my shoulder. He broke it, too. Things went from bad to worse. I wrestled 22 matches with a broken shoulder, and it was painful. I didn't want to hurt the business, so I was working my way out. I wanted to give them time to replace me. I left and went through Shreveport, Louisiana. Sputnik was wrestling there, so I wrestled Sputnik that night. I wanted to make one more payday because I wasn't going to have any for a while. We had a hell of a match. He was the babyface. I'm telling you the truth. There was this big old fat gal who was chewin' my ass for being so mean to Sputnik. I kept telling him that was his wife. Sputnik got tickled and had a hard time keeping from laughing. When I went to the hospital, they were gonna take some bone out of my other shoulder and put it in that one. I would have been where I couldn't move either side. I said, "*The hell with that! I'm not gonna do it.*" I just let it go ahead and heal. My right shoulder's out of whack now. It didn't grow back right. They told me I'd have to have surgery later on, but I didn't have any real problems with it.

I had a bad car wreck in the early sixties. I was going from Memphis, where I lived at that time, to Jonesboro TV, which was on Thursday. I had a friend that lived next door to me that ran a dairy-milk truck. He was gonna pass this truck. As he pulled out to pass, these people turned off this side road. He whipped the wheel and started sliding. That car hit us in the side and it broke every one of my ribs. They had to cut out half my lung and my diaphragm and my intestines were pushed up in my chest. I went back to wrestling exactly one year later.

Are your ears cauliflowered?

No. They tried to give me some cauliflower ears. All it did was make my damn head sore.

Who tried that?

Oh, Monroe was one of ‘em. They all wanted you to look like a wrestler. They’re a little gristly, but not cauliflowered like you’re talking about. Is Herb Welch still around?

He’s in a nursing home in Dyersburg.

Is he? We had worked together in Memphis and had some pretty good matches. He [Herb] went to Roy [Welch] and told him, “*You book me in there with Tyler and we’ll fill the house up.*” Roy wouldn’t listen to him because Roy had his own agenda. We’d get in the ring and I’d mess with him. I’d knock the shit out of him real hard, then I’d wait a minute and hit him again. He had that top wristlock on the mat. I reached up and hit him in the jaw. About the third time, he explodes. “*You son-of-a-bitch!*” He was hot! He let the hold go and got up and stomped me. (laughs) He was one hell of a guy. The last time I talked to him, I called him and said, “*Herb, what’s going on?*”

He says, “*Not much. Who is this?*”

I said, “*This is Tim Tyler.*”

“*Who in the fuck is Tim Tyler.*” (laughs)

He didn’t remember me.

Did you ever lose your enthusiasm for wrestling?

No. Every day and every match was exciting. I loved it. I don’t sit around and cry about it. I told Sputnik, “*Why don’t you forget that shit!*” Tears run out his eyes and he says, “*That’s my life. That’s my life, Tim.*” He couldn’t give it up. He still hasn’t given it up.

They recognized him on a show one night during the reunion. He was pretty excited about that.

I think he wanted to get slammed. He wanted somebody to slam him. I forget who it was, but they wouldn’t do it. They was afraid it would hurt him because of his age. I don’t imagine it would have bothered him a bit.

When did you have your last match?

It was in Mississippi. Cowboy Watts called me to wrestle in ... someplace just across the river from here.

Was it tough to hang up the boots?

Not really. I just walked away and that was it. I had other interests and put that to work. I got in the car business and kept that going for several years. I don’t have it anymore. In ‘94, I had a four-way bypass. I had a congestive heart, which can kill you, too. I got to where I couldn’t breathe, so they put me in the hospital and done some tests. Four arteries were stopped up. I still have a congestive heart. I have 37 percent on one side and seventeen percent on the other. It don’t seem to be getting any worse, but I’m not getting no better, either. I have good days and bad days. I’m on oxygen 24 hours a day. I can’t walk to where my truck is without giving out of wind. I don’t get enough oxygen in my blood.

Are you able to get out much?

Oh, yeah. I get out every day, just about. I have a portable [oxygen] unit that I carry with me. I hope to be at the [Gulf Coast] reunion next year. I told Sputnik I wouldn't be able to get around. He said, "*Get you a damn wheelchair. I'll push you.*" It's kind of embarrassing. You can't hardly breathe, then everyone's asking, "*Are you all right? Are you all right?*" And you don't have enough wind to tell 'em to get the hell away. They're bothering you more than helping.

Do you still sell cars?

I do a little bit. Not much, though, Scott. There's just not much going on right now. I was selling them with my son, Tim.

What is your wife's name?

Dorothy. We've been married forty-seven years. September 3, 1940. Put that in there for Bobby Fields. While I'm thinking about it, I want to order a copy of all your magazines. My son likes to read them, too. I was highly impressed with them. I let other people read them and now I don't have any left. (laughs) They never returned them.

What do you do now that you're retired?

Oh, I have a few cows and take care of them. I love to watch them eat, make babies, and make me money. I had quite a few, but sold all but four.

If you could do it over, what would you do different?

I'd live a little cleaner life. I wouldn't jack around like I did. I'd work more on the politics of the business, too. I'd like to have another shot at that. (laughs) They don't give you reruns, though. It's like Rip said when he was close to dying. He said, "*This is one bump I've gotta take by myself.*" In other words, I couldn't go out and tag team with him. That's how I took it. I couldn't help him by tagging in. He was a standup guy all through it. It surprised me a little that he did as good as he did.

Tim was living in Bauxite, Arkansas, at the time of the interview. We lost track of him after that, but heard he had passed away. However, no information can be found.

TITLES
World tag [FL '64 w/Tarzan Tyler]
Southern tag [TN '67 w/Rip Tyler]

ALIAS
Randy Roper
Wrestling Pro #2

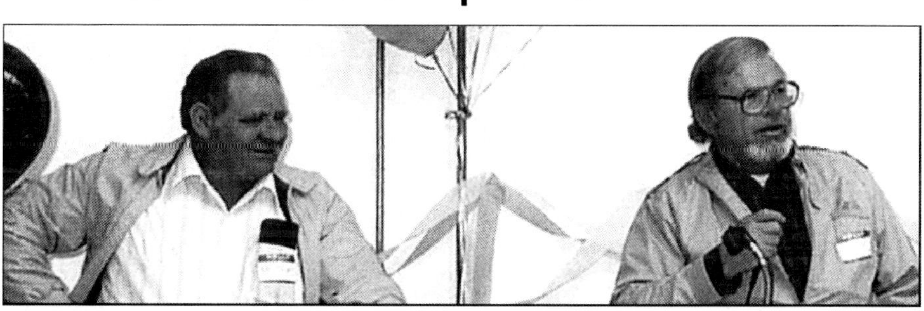

Rip & Tim Tyler at the 1993 Gulf Coast Wrestlers Reunion in Mobile, Alabama.

Two Hours in a Motel Room

The following conversation was taped in Mobile, Alabama on March 6, 1997. Present in the room were Dick Beyer, Dick Steinborn, Don Fargo, Billy Wicks, Debbie Wicks, Ted Allen, and Scott Teal.

IMPORTANT! For those of you who don't know Don Fargo personally ... regardless of how outlandish they may sound, rest assured that the stories told by and about him are probably true.

Steinborn: We were talking about the switching of names. Remember Bobby Hart? He told me this story years ago. His father, Bobby Hart Sr. (Frankie Hart), was wrestling up in Goose Bay (pause, laughs) ... what is the name of that town? (all laugh) North Bay. (laughs) Goose Bay. He says it was the first night of TV. It was live TV. He was sitting in the dressing room and he was a ribber. So the (announcer) comes in and says, *"What's your name?"* He says, *"Bobby Fart."* He says, *"What?"* He says, *"Bobby Fart."* He says, *"I can't announce that on TV."* He says, *"Well, that's what it is."* He says, *"Well, is it a dialect or something? Figh-art?" "No, Fart! Bobby Fart!"* Live TV. The guy's in the middle of the ring. *"Ladies and gentlemen! In this corner on my left, BOBBY FART!"* And Bobby ran up to him and says, *"Correction. That's Bobby Hart."*

Fargo: (laughing) He screwed the announcer.

Steinborn: Hey, I went to Indianapolis for (Jim) Barnett. He had big stars like (Dick) the Bruiser. He used to go to Detroit on Saturday night. There used to be a 12:45 plane that went back to Indianapolis. We're all on the plane and the girl is looking for her last passenger. There's like eight of us there. Here he comes. He walks up the steps like this. She says, *"Are you going to Indianapolis?"* (gruff voice) *"No, I'm going to Chicago." "Well, this plane doesn't go into Chicago."* He says, *"It goes to Chicago tonight,"* and walks into the plane. She walks to the front and I'm witnessing this from the back. It's like a theatre. (laughs) She says, *"We got this guy that blah-blah-blah."* The pilot says, *"Oh, that's Dick the Bruiser."* (all laugh) He made the trip every two weeks to Detroit. Here's what I remember.

The plane only seats about 45 or so and several of them are businessmen returning home. I'm standing in the back and, when I look up, everything's dark, except for one little light way up on the left side. It's Jim Barnett. He's got this little light on and Dick sits next to him. Dick's looking down at what Barnett's reading. Evidently, Barnett was showing Bruiser his little record book. (imitates Barnett) *"Well, you drew this here and you drew that there."* Evidently, in those days, Bruiser was so powerful that he'd say, (imitates Bruiser) *"Look, you want me at the matches? I'll be there, but I want to know what the house is and I want my money when I walk out of the building."* I think that's what they were doing. Barnett must have said, *"I'll catch you on the plane coming back from Detroit."* He got on the plane and showed him what he did in Louisville, what he did in Detroit. This is about two o'clock in the morning. All of a sudden, the quiet of the plane is shattered when Bruiser screams, *"WHAT!!!??"* (laughs) If you can imagine Woody Allen ... that's what Barnett looked like. What a cartoon Bruiser was!

Beyer: He did that all the time, though. It wasn't only in Detroit. He did that with every airplane he ever got on.

Steinborn: He always had an attache case. He had a jockstrap, which he never washed. He had a pair of trunks, which he never washed. He had a towel, which he never washed. He used to bring it in the dressing room, put it next to you, and open it up. Jeez!

Fargo: You know, he had me and Kenny Mack come up to Chicago because we were hot. We were in all kind of trouble, but we was hot. Wilbur Snyder didn't want nothin' to do with us, you know. Nobody wanted nothin' to do with us, because we was BAD, man! We were dirty and nasty, but Dick the Bruiser wanted us. We made him money, because we drew him crowds, man. I mean, we drew big crowds. We sold everything out. So he (Bruiser) tried to get us in, but (pause) ... and the guy hates me to this day.

Beyer: Verne Gagne.

Wicks: (laughs) Verne Gagne?

Fargo: He's gonna get us up there with Verne Gagne. He says, *"I want you guys to cool it. Don't eat no more garlic, don't eat onions, don't put limburger cheese on your body."* You know, he said, *"Be cool with Wilbur. I've got you guys in Chicago in the main event."* We go to the place and it's jam packed. On the way, I see a dead rat in the road.

Steinborn: (laughs)

Fargo: The head was perfect, but the rest of the body was *"Yuck."* I took it and stuck it to my chest, letting the head hang out. (laughs) Of course, we're on good drugs then. (laughs) We go upstairs and Gagne and all the commissioners are up there. Bruiser, he don't give a sh—. Wilbur Snyder is facing the floor because we're late and everything. First thing Wilbur says, *"What do you got?" "My pet rat."* (all laugh) *"It's my pet rat, man."* (laughs) That's the way I used to talk. So we sat down there and I'm pettin' the rat. Bruiser said, *"Fargo, what've you got?" "It's my pet rat, man."* Verne Gagne. *"What's he got?"* I said, *"It's my pet rat, man."* I squashed the body. Gagne puked, man. All you could hear, *"Baaaarph. Baaaarpppp."* I got fired so many times, man, (laughs) but Bruiser wouldn't let 'em do it, because we were drawin' money. We would go out when it come time and they'd play that music. We'd come out and everybody would pick us up and carry us to the ring.

Steinborn: Donnie, let me tell you something.

Fargo: Yeah.

Steinborn: With todays' crimes and skinheads and everything, you missed your calling. If it had been back then, you'd have been the leader of 'em all.

Fargo: Oh, boy. One time, we didn't feel like we were dirty enough. We see this big, old barrel of oil. This left over oil (they got from cars). We climbed in, man. We come out soaked with oil. Then one time, Wilbur said, *"I'll tell you. I'll tell you."* You know, they always had a meeting. Me and my partner, Bruiser and Snyder. He said, *"We've got to do this. I'm telling you right now, you guys, don't drink no more. You come to the ring and you stink!"* Bruiser, he don't care. *"What do you think about it?"* (calmly) *"Yeah, don't drink no more, guys."* So we stopped and got some whiskey on the way. This time we're driving a car. We're drinking the whiskey, so we thought, *"We're gonna stink, so we'd better do something about this."* We stop and get a big onion, raw garlic, and limburger cheese ... and we eat it. We don't smell each other, right? Man, we walked in that dressing room and ... WOW! We stunk everything up. Wilbur Snyder said, *"They've been drinkin'."* (all laugh) Bruiser says, *"I don't smell no booze."* He says, *"I guess not. Smell them, man!"*

You know, I'll tell you what happened one time. This is the truth, man. (laughs) In Chicago, the commissioners come in and said, *"They've gotta take a shower." "We ain't takin' no shower. I ain't taken a shower in six months and I ain't taken no shower now."* They said, *"They've got to take a shower."* Snyder says, *"They gotta take a shower."* I said, *"Okay, we're gonna take a shower, but we're not takin' our clothes off."* We went in and took a shower with our clothes on. We're in our outfits and come out soaking wet. (all laugh) We showered.

Steinborn: Let me interrupt you and let me tell a story I remember about you in California. Roy Shire was sitting on a ledge in the dressing room in Fresno. His booker was sitting next to him. Lothario is sitting next to him. Pepper Gomez is standing here. You had just got through wrestling and came out of the shower nude. You were just so (pause, laughing) ... I was sitting in the back. The next think I know, you have this cigar that's soaking wet. He goes, *"Aaaaaaaaaah."* (Reaches around to his rear end and comes back around with cigar in his hand) Shire looks up and he throws the cigar at him. Shire dives on the floor.

Fargo: I used to walk around naked and I'd take my toothbrush and put it up in the (butt) crack there. Then I'd walk around, bending over looking into thing. *"I laid my toothbrush down. Has anybody seen it? Where's my toothbrush?"* (all laugh) I've gotta tell you something really, really funny, man. If you women will forgive me. There's no foul language, but this is really funny. An old time wrestler ...

Wicks: What in the hell are you?

Fargo: No, this was one of the Welchs ... the old one, Herb. He's was old then. I used to run around the dressing room naked all the time. I always did.

Wicks: You and Red Bastien.

Fargo: He's sittin' there and he says, *"Fargo."* I said, *"What?"* He says, *"You know what you're doin'?"* I said, *"No, what?"* He says, *"You're showin' everybody in this room how big your old lady is."* (big laugh all around) Boy, that cured my ass. (laughs) He said it so calm.

Steinborn: I remember when Klondike Bill told me this story. He said he and (Don) Manoukian were gonna play a rib on Curtis Iaukea when he flew from Hawaii to San Francisco to work at the Cow Palace, and go right back that night. He used to have a little attache case with just a pair of tights and thongs. There's no snakes in Hawaii. Big Klondike Bill says, *"Manoukian and I, we went to San Francisco and went bowling early. Then we went to this snake place where you could buy these snakes and we got this snake and put him in a bag. Then we went to a movie. When we came out of the movie to go over to the Cow Palace, we looked in the bag and the snake was gone. He had eaten through the bag."* I said, *"What did you do?"* He said, *"Well, we couldn't play the rib on him." "What were you gonna do?"* He says, *"Well, we were gonna get him in the dressing room, get him aside, and just before he leaves, put the snake (in the attache case)."* Can you imagine him going back through customs? Well, that was their rib. So Klondike says, *"Well, you know my wife. I've gotta get rid of that snake out of the car. It cost me forty dollars. I took it down to the place and they went up and down and told me there's no snake in there."* He says, *"Three weeks later, he's going to San Mateo from San Francisco. You know that Chinese place on the right hand side? We stopped there for awhile. The sun was coming down, so when we get back, the snake was laying up on the dashboard."* Three weeks later. I sat back in the car with him and about five minutes later, I says, *"Bill, I got to thinking about that snake. Think about it, if you were a snake ... you get beer dropping every night, you hear stories, you crawl out every night during the matches, then crawl back in."* Bill says, *"Yeah, you're right. That snake probably liked it."* That rib would've been something.

Beyer: One of the better ribs in the business. This had to do with Vic Christy.

Fargo: Oh, Vic Christy. He was the greatest.

Beyer: When Curtis (Iaukea) just got in the business, he comes down to LA and he goes to the booking office. Jules Strongbow says, *"Tomorrow morning, Vic Christy will pick you up early. He's gonna take you to the town that you're gonna wrestle in."* They're wrestling in Santa Monica. Vic Christy picks him up in a convertible. It's a hot day. They drive all the way to San Diego, all the way to Yuma, Arizona, up to ...

Steinborn: With the top down?

Beyer: Yeah, with the top down. All the way to Yuma, which is 150, up to the desert town (pause) ... Palm Springs, another 150. So it's 450, and another hundred back. That's 550 miles. They get to the Santa Monica arena at 730 and he is roasted. He is roasted. Vic says, *"When you get done, shower quick so we can get out of here. It's a long trip back home."* During the night, Vic comes up and says, *"Hey, I've got this girl. I'm gonna go home with her. The midget will take you home."* (laughs) He (Iaukea) goes in the ring and he's working with some Oriental, and the guy chops the sh— out of him. (big laughs all around)

Fargo: Oh, God!

Beyer: Anyway, he leaves the arena and gets home in fifteen minutes ... from Santa Monica.

Fargo: You know what he did one time? Vic Christy. I can't remember the guys' name. He could throw a hell of a punch, man. A red-headed guy.

Steinborn: Wild Red Berry?

Fargo: No, not Wild Red Berry. It was another guy. Anyhow, we was working in this building that had a motel we was dressing in and it had a swimming pool. This guy was standing out there with his tights and wrestling shoes on by the pool, looking around. Christy went out there and pushed him in. Damn, he was mad! Everybody laughed. It was funny, you know. He took his shoes off and had some more he put on, then he went and wrestled. In the meantime, Christy took this guys' (pause) ... we all wore suits back then. He took this guys' suit and put it on ... pants, suit, everything. He stood by the pool. The guy comes out from wrestling and one of the guys says, *"Hey, you want to get him back? He's out there now. He's in his clothes."* (all laugh) The guy says, *"You're damned right I do!"* He went out there and pushed him in. He (Vic) had his clothes on. I can't think of this guys' name, but he got arrested for having a frog farm. The guy could throw the best punch in the world.

Steinborn: Let me tell you something that happened when I was in Europe. I was 17 years old and with my dad. We heard from an American pilot, who said that he landed in London, and the press came up to us and Primo Carnera and says, *"You understand the Zebra Kid died?"* George Bollas. Listen now. I'm in England in 1951 and I'm listening to this, as a young kid. I'm the guy that comes back to the United States and I happen to call Shire. I said, *"I heard that George Bollas died."* It happened to be somebody in the England organization who was called the Zebra Kid. I brought the infection back to the United States. I called Shire, and Shire called everybody else. I read it in the magazine about eight months later, *"He's not dead."* It was a hell of a story.

Beyer: I remember that. I don't remember where it came from, but I heard.

Steinborn: I took credit for it.

Fargo: Remember the time we were stealing hubcaps off of (Jackie) Fargo's car?

Steinborn: Oh, yeah.

Fargo: We got caught by the law, man!

Steinborn: When Florida started up, as far as wrestling, just before TV, they put he and I on first ... every night.

Fargo: Thirty, sixty, thirty, sixty, forty minutes.

Steinborn: That was my dad's idea, to give them wrestling. He said, *"In thirty minutes, you can teach them wrestling."* Then the rest of the match ... that was the old school. We were chasing Jackie Fargo in Tampa one night. Jackie has some girl. He was young at the time.

Fargo: He was Dickie Bishop then.

Steinborn: Yeah. He was doing nightclubs. I said, *"Let's put pebbles in his hubcaps, or let the air out of his tires."* So we went back in this alleyway. He says, *"I have to go to the bathroom."* He goes way back in this alleyway and, all of a sudden, here come three squad cars. *"Up against the wall!"* This cop says, *"What the hell's going on here?"* I said, *"We're not bad. We're wrestlers."* This lieutenant comes over and steps up, just like you see on TV. He says, *"Yeah, they're wrestlers. I work the matches."* (laughs) *"What are you guys doing back here?"* I say, *"Well, Jackie Fargo is over there and he has one of the girl wrestlers, so we were gonna let the air out of his tires."* He says, *"Get out of here."*

Fargo: He let us go.

Steinborn: Oh, and he says, *"I'm gonna call the promoter."* I said, *"Don't. I just got through wrestling tonight and he'll fire us."* Eighteen years old.

Fargo: They transferred us to North Carolina. All the way down, we was throwin' firecrackers. We'd put 'em in mailboxes and watch 'em blow out. He had a new convertible. We pull in to take a pee and he pulls into this grassy spot. He just had a new horn put into his car, a bullhorn. It went "Mmmmmooo." All these cows are looking.

Steinborn: (to Beyer) You know how I used to work with him? He was so strong. I loved to wrestle, like you do. I had so many broadway matches with him. You know how you get a good match? You just say, *"Don't let me slam you."* (all laugh) Before you know it, ten minutes has gone.

Beyer: Try to wrestle Moto. He wouldn't let you slam him anyway.

Wicks: (to Fargo) We came from Helena, Arkansas. You and I were in my '59 Cadillac. Bud Clardy was driving his '59 Ford Fairlane. He moons us and whips on by. You and I and Rocky Columbo. I say, *"Hey, Fargo. Get ready. Here they come."* He jumps up to the window and gets ready to drop his pants down and moon them. All of a sudden, a red light comes on. *"Sit down, Fargo. It's a cop!"* We had our beer and barbeque, on our way back to Memphis. Fargo says, *"Hey, maybe the cop wants a beer and barbeque!"* I said, *"No, Fargo. Shut up!"* I get out and walk back. *"Yes sir, officer."* He said, *"You were speeding a little bit. Let me see your driver's license. Follow me back."* We get back to a little town in Arkansas. I walk in there all by myself and he finds out I'm a wrestler. Just before I get out, here comes Fargo with a little bag. *"Hey, officer,"* he says, *"would you like a little barbeque and a beer?"* I say, *"Fargo, get out of here!"* You forgot about that, I'll bet.

Fargo: (long laugh) One time, me and my partner, Jim (Bagus), are driving down the highway eating barbeque chicken and all that stuff. I just took it and threw it out the window. A cop car come up over the hill and pulled us off to this little country town. We're on our way to Dallas, about twenty miles outside. He pulled us over and said, *"Who threw this out?"* I said, *"He did."* He says, *"He threw it across you?"* Jim says, *"Hey, man!"* I said, *"Shutup!"* And I said, *"Yes, sir."* The cop says, *"Get out of the car."* We had them guns on. The cop jumps back and says, *"Hey, wait a minute."* I say, *"Hey, man. We're the Dalton Gang, man."* He says, *"The what?"* I said, *"We're wrestlers."* He says, *"Just stay put."* He got back and called the backup. The backup came and they took us down to this little jail. I said, *"Listen, we have to go to the wrestling."* They knew who were were, finally. They said, *"Well, we've gotta to keep one of you. Which one of you threw the garbage out?"* I said, *"He did."* They said, *"Okay, we're gonna lock him up."* I said, *"Well, how much is the fine?"* The fine was like $45 and we didn't have no money on us. I said, *"I'll get the money and I'll come back. Don't worry, Jim."* Jim was young. He was only like ...

Steinborn: Jim Dalton?

Fargo: Yeah. A young kid.

Steinborn: Life is such an experience to you, isn't it?

Fargo: Huh? (laughs) It was better him than me.

Steinborn: And what happened?

Fargo: So I drove all the way up and got the $45, turned all the way back and got him out of jail. But what was funny is he was scared to death, because they put him in the only cell they had, with a black guy. And the black guy was in there for beatin' people up, man. I got him out of there, man, and we made the matches. He served my time.

Beyer: Well, he won't throw any garbage across the front of your face again.

Steinborn: That reminds me of one about the mooning. One time, I went to Athens, Georgia, and Argentina Apollo was driving. I'm sitting in the back seat. As we turn off the expressway to go up to Athens, there sits Ox Baker. He's driving like this with a big, yellow canary stationwagon and he had this big, 6-foot-3 blonde girl. He was this big, I swear, but she was this big. She had big boobs and this dolly face. We know about three miles up there's gonna be a double lane, so I told Apollo what to do. I jumped up in the back seat and put my ass right against that window. He's a big main event, he's got his arm over the seat. This is Ox's face. It looked like he just sniffed some pepper. I'm looking through (underneath). It was worth it.

I wanted to tell this story about you (Fargo). He and Jackie Fargo. When I went to Atlanta, I never knew these things existed. I used to go from Atlanta, Sunday night on Channel 17 ... this is when TV was new in Atlanta. When you went to Hogansville from Atlanta, (there is) about a half a mile you can cut off if you know the little shortcut. He tells me and a couple of other guys, *"You have to go all the way to the point, and come all the way back."* So he and Jackie cut through, pull the car over, and take all their clothes off. They put part of their anatomy between their legs (so they look like women) and they stand like this, nude, with their hair (brushed over their face), hitchhiking. (all laugh) I'm in the car with two guys from Canada. (all laugh) I swear. (laughing)

I've got to tell you one on Terry Funk. I get through in Japan. We leave on a Sunday at one o'clock. Saturday night, we're sitting in a hotel lobby. Everybody got paid and everything. Terry and I have been playing ribs on each other for years. Terry comes in and ... Terry had a funny way of walking. He drops his shoulders back and walked slew-footed. He comes into the lobby and says to Junior, *"I met these two girls. One of them looks like Sophia Loren. She's got beautiful eyes. They want us to go to this place. It's free! Come on, Junior." "I ain't goin' nowhere."* He asked Mike Paidousis. He ain't goin'. *"Dickie, come on and go."* I said, *"How much is it?" "It's free!"* (One block away), there's two geisha girls.

We open the door and it's Las Vegas. They have a big stage, big tables. I counted about 25 or 30 tables. There's men and a big mama-san. So the girls escorted us down to the best seats in the house. I'm sitting behind Terry. It's the last night. I have cash in my pocket. Who cares? The girls sit with us and the mama-san comes over. When mama-san comes over, the girls leave. I watch one girl and she goes from one table, over to that table. *"What will you have?" "I'll have a half a grapefruit."* So he gets a half a grapefruit and I get a glass of orange juice. We didn't know what was going on, right? The girls are not coming back, so (I say), *"We need to go, Terry."* The mama-san goes, *"Eighty-five dollars."*

Fargo: For the drinks!?

Steinborn: Oh, yes. Wait a minute. One drink, an orange juice, and half a grapefruit. Instead of me (making a scene), I whipped out the $50. Terry didn't even want to look at me. He still wants to be the big-shot. He walks out and the two girls are waiting for us. We walk down the stairs and, as we leave the building, there's a little alleyway with some garbage cans. He's walking ahead of me and walks past the alleyway. I say, *"Terry, Terry!"* I jumped into the alley and he comes running. When he comes around, I went WHAM! I drove him over the garbage cans and ran like hell. I went back into the lobby and Junior was sitting there waiting for us. He says, *"How is everything?"* I said, *"Everything's fine."* Here comes Terry. "Blah, blah, blah, blah."

Beyer: I have a similar story, but it's not as funny. You know Buddy Austin.

Steinborn: Oh, real well.

Fargo: Buddy Austin? The killer. He's dead now.

Beyer: We're in Japan and, on this particular trip, I've got my first wife's father. On the trip, I told him, *"Anywhere we go, you pay your way."* Anywhere we go! Most of the time, it's gonna be free, because I have a lot of freebies. As the trip goes along, everytime we got onto our train, or got onto something, somebody was coming up to Austin and saying, *"Hey, that girl Keiko* (pronounced Kay-Ko) *you're looking for, she's so-and-so-and-so-and-so."* He had put an advertisement in a magazine. He's looking for a Keiko that he met and can't find again. Keiko in Japan is like finding a Sally (in the U.S.). There's thousands of Keiko's. We're on a train going away from Tokyo on the way to Osaka. A guy comes up. *"Your Keiko is working at a club. You can get her there." "Are you sure?" "Yes, I'm positive."* We get to Osaka and, one night we're off, he says, *"You want to go with me?"* I says, *"I'll go."* My father-in-law goes, too.

We go to the club. (They say), *"I'm sorry. No Americans allowed."* They didn't allow Americans in a lot of their clubs because they don't understand the situation with girls comin', girls leavin', girls comin', girls leavin'. Mama-san coming down, writing up the check, give you a bill for $85 ... for what? That's the reason they didn't allow Americans in a lot of those clubs, but I convinced her that I knew enough Japanese that ... anyway, we get in. He wants to see Keiko. Keiko comes and sits down. Everytime you request a girl to come to the table, it's a price. Three Keiko's came. We had one beer. The bill came to $600. Two hundred for Buddy, two hundred for me, and my father-in-law's livid. Guess what? I didn't have to take him out for the rest (of the trip)! That was the greatest thing that happened to me! I didn't have to take him. Everytime I said I was going out, he says, *"I'll stay home."*

Fargo: You know, Buddy Austin was in Australia, was fooling around ...

Beyer: Oh, yeah. Is that when Pedro Morales?

Fargo: Yeah, he (hung around) with this little guy.

Steinborn: Yeah, I was there after that. They had a party and set him up.

Fargo: Yeah, it was the Mafia. They came in and shot the hell out of him, beat Morales in the face with a bottle. He lived.

Beyer: They both lived.

Fargo: Yeah. They warned him and called the wrestling office.

Steinborn: You remember Ike Eakins? He told me one time, he was in the car going to North Carolina, and he was going home. The cop pulled him over and he says, *"Let me see your license."* Ike took his license out and handed it to him. The cop says, *"This tells me that you can fish in North Carolina."* (all laugh)

Fargo: I just found out. I can fish in the ocean and it doesn't cost me nothin', because of my age.

Steinborn: Really? You waited this long.

Fargo: I'll be 69.

Beyer: Ike Eakins. We're in Lexington, Kentucky one night. He's got a pet coon. Irish Mike Clancy, myself, and Eakins drove from Columbus to Lexington. That was the night that Don Eagle was wrestling somebody and they were supposed to do something. There was a big riot, but we got out. We got the guy out of the ring, as we were supposed to do, and rushed for the car. We had the coon in the car. Clancy's got a brand-new Cadillac. This coon sh— all over that Cadillac. (all laugh) Sh— all over that Cadillac. Anyway, we're in a hurry to get away from the arena, so we take our towels out of our bags and clean the sh— up, throw the coon in the trunk with our bags, and we get away. And Clancy is livid. He is livid. Finally, we get back to Columbus. I lived at Al Haft's motel with Fred Atkins and Ike Eakins. I tie this coon outside of the door. Whitey Whittler ... do you remember these names? I'm really scrapin' some names.

Fargo: (laughs) You're goin' back, man.

Steinborn: We're with you, we're with you.

Beyer: Whitey Whittler, myself and the promoter in (pause) ...

Steinborn: Al Haft? Frankie Talaber?

Beyer: No, in Florida. Graham. Not Graham, but his name was Eddie Gossett. Eddie Gossett is in the territory. This is three or four days after this incident, so we're gonna pull a rib on Clancy. We're gonna go up, disconnect the live coon (from the chain), and put a dead coon on the end. It's gonna blame it on Mike Clancy. Anyway, we go coon hunting with Nick Roberts. Four of us ... myself, Nick Roberts, Eddie Gossett, and Whitey Whittler.

Fargo: You're goin' back to about '54.

Beyer: '54-55. We went coon huntin' and got eight or ten coons. We get back about four o'clock in the morning. We go out at midnight. This is after wrestling. We go back to the motel and Whitey Whittler comes up and he goes and gets the live coon, puts a dead coon on top of that thing. Ike Eakins got up and ... him and Fred Atkins. *"Why, the bloody bahstuds killed your coon!"* This is Fred Atkins telling Ike Eakins. So now, Ike Eakins says, *"That fu—in' Mike Clancy. That son-of-a-bit— shot my coon!"* Clancy lived in the trailer park about two miles up Route 40.

Steinborn: After he sh— in his car, right?

Beyer: Oh, yeah. This is after he sh— in his car. I can hear Ike Eakins and Atkins outside. I heard all the commotion and called Whittler. I says, *"They're* *on their way. You'd better call Clancy and tell him to get the hell out."* Because Ike Eakins ... he was a vicious guy.

Steinborn: Oh, tell me.

Beyer: He popped Whitey Whittler's eye out.

Steinborn: That's right.

He killed two men in his life.

Beyer: Anyway, the tail end of the story is that Clancy's not home. He got away from the thing. Whittler drove back to the motel and puts the live coon on the chain, takes the dead coon. When he (Eakins) gets back, there's the live coon. (big laughs)

Fargo: That would freak you out! Wouldn't that freak you out? You see a dead coon, you get back, there's a live coon! What name did you wrestle under then?

Beyer: Dick Beyer.

Fargo: Yeah, Dick Beyer. Do you remember me there then?

Beyer: Sure.

Fargo: Yeah, because I remember Whitey Whittler. Whitey Whittler opened up a little restaurant.

Beyer: Right.

Teal: Do you remember his son?

Beyer: I trained his son when he was sixteen years old to wrestle in the amateurs.

Steinborn: Donnie.

Beyer: Yep, Donnie.

Teal: He became Smasher Sloan.

Beyer: That's right. He was sixteen years old, 1954.

Steinborn: He wrestled in Fort Myers. He used to wrestle in the Armory. In all those National Guard Armories in Florida, when you come out, you got to go out in front of the people, and there's the entrance, then you go over to the men's room where the showers were. He gets through wrestling as the Red Raider. He's got the towel wrapped around him and walks out and takes a shower. He comes back out holding the mask and the towel's wrapped around him. (laughs) I was standing there watching it. A woman's standing there with her little girl waiting on an autograph. The little girl says, (in girls' voice) *"Look, mommy! It's the Red Raider without his mask on."* He takes the towel (pulls it over his head and runs for the dressing room). (all laugh)

Beyer: You talk about somebody that could throw good punches. Whitey Whittler was the best. He was the best. He could take somebody's face, go down like that, and have people out of their seat.

Fargo: He died of a heart attack.

Steinborn: Do you remember Gypsy Joe? The later one.

Teal: The one that looked like Tito Kopa.

Steinborn: That's him. The tall one. A burly chest, wrestled in Atlanta for awhile. He could throw a punch. He popped himself (when he threw a punch) and made this tremendous sound. He came into Atlanta and I thought, *"Geez, he's got a gold mine right there."* So they put me with him at first. I watched him in Augusta and he's beatin' this guy, beatin' this guy. I worked with him in Atlanta and he hit me with that thing. I fell and rolled out of the ring. He put that punch over! Charlie Smith was refereeing and he turned him around. He says, *"What did you do?"* He says, *"I'll tell you what I did."* He did the same damn thing. (big laughs all around) I sat in the audience and thought, *"You just killed the gimmick."* He was supposed to go like this (show the flat of the hand) and he went (like this). It went "Bang!" Wasted.

Beyer: Before Vic Christy died, I called him. I says, *"Vic, phone me and tape some of your stories, which he did."* That story about Curtis is on there. I've got one more about Lord Blears, then I won't tell anymore. This is in the '40s, just after the war. Lord Blears is coming into San Francisco. He comes in and they're talking in the dressing room and he said he'd love to go to the beach. Christy says, *"Hey, we'll go to the beach tomorrow. I'll tell you where to go. I'll meet you there."* He goes out to the beach and tells him where to park. Sure enough, he parks up there, looks down, and sees him (Vic). He walks down to the beach. There's a blanket, food, and everything. Tally comes down ... I call him Tally ... Blears comes down. He (Vic) says, *"Are you hungry?"* It's about eleven o'clock in the morning. He says, *"Go ahead. Have something to eat. I'm gonna walk down to the water."* He sits down and opens up a basket. These people walk up from out of the water and they say, *"What the hell are you doing?"* (big laughs all around) He says, *"Uh, this blanket ..."* and he's pointing to Vic, who was walking by. Vic says, *"I don't even know that guy,"* and starts walking up the beach.

Steinborn: You know what he did one time in Hawaii? I was sitting in a restaurant with him. I wrestled for Shire and we went to Hawaii. This woman comes in and she was wearing one of these evening (gowns). She's looking for somebody. He goes, *"Miss! Miss!"* She goes (gives a funny look). He says, *"Miss!"* Like he knows her. She comes over, he grabs his cup, and says, *"Another cup of coffee."* She says, *"I'm NOT the waitress."* (all laugh)

THE END

Also available from www.crowbarpress.com

— MASTER OF THE RING —
The Biography of "Nature Boy" Buddy Rogers

by Tim Hornbaker

In 1948, years before the "sports entertainers" like Hulk Hogan, Steve Austin, or "The Rock" were even born, a young man named Buddy Rogers went to the ring in Hollywood Legion Stadium and transformed pro wrestling forever. Billed as the "Nature Boy", Rogers, with his flambouyant personality and underhanded tactics, became an immediate box-office sensation. He was center stage everywhere he appeared, not only in fast-paced matches, but in backstage power plays.

By the late 1950s, he was an unparalleled superstar, but he had one honor yet to achieve ... the National Wrestling Alliance world heavyweight championship. To that point, the contentious environment of wrestling politics stalled his push to the ultimate throne, and only through experience did Rogers overcome the obstacles in his path until, finally, with friends in high places, he was given a title match against champion Pat O'Connor at Chicago's Comiskey Park before a record crowd of 38,000 spectators. By the end of the night, Rogers was the new heavyweight champion of the world! After the match, he strapped on the title belt, stood in the center of the ring, and in his arrogant fashion, announced: *"To a nicer guy, it couldn't happen!"*

Backstage assaults, injuries, and other events almost derailed his title reign, and in the midst of his historic run, Rogers suffered serious health problems, which as a cloud over his future on the mat. Since then, wrestling fans have asked countless questions about what really happened on that fabled evening. Author Hornbaker dissects the incident, as well as Buddy's entire life, to answer those questions and clear up some of the misconceptions and lies told about Buddy.

— Professional Wrestling and the Tennessee Wrestling Commission Volume 1, 1935-1971

by Tim Dills, with Scott Teal

Taken from two spools of microfilm that had been undiscovered for decades, these are the details of the Tennessee Athletic Commission meetings which took place from 1955 until 1980. Author Tim Dills dug deep into the files and uncovered a unique side of pro wrestling in a state that boasts a long history of fascinating mat lore. These minutes, along with other commission documents, provide details about the formation and work of the commission, and how they worked alongside the movers and shakers of the wrestling business – and boxing to a lesser degree – in Tennessee.

This book provides insight into the power wielded by influential state politicians, and how they butted heads with the men who ran the wrestling business. Their stories add a new chapter and valuable insight into the wheelings and dealings of pro wrestling.

TONIGHT! TONIGHT! TONIGHT!

by Bert Prentice & Scott Teal

Bert Prentice had a view of this business from a perspective that very few have ever had an opportunity to see. There is simply nothing he hasn't done in the business ... sold programs, set up rings, chairs and bleachers, sold tickets, ring announced, cooked hot dogs, cleaned the buildings, refereed, put out posters, produced countless hours of studio wrestling, managed, and on many occasions, wrestled midgets, women, and myself.

Bert lived his life with absolutely no filter. Not many people get to do that. One of his favorite sayings was, "What other people think about me is none of my business," and he truly lived that mantra. In fact, his haters energized him to another level. It was an amazing thing to watch.

Bert was a master of promoting pro wrestling the old-school way. In fact, he could have taught the old-school promoters a thing or two about the nuts and bolts of getting butts into the seats.

If you're a fan of pro wrestling, you won't want to put this book down until you read it in its entirety.

— Jerry "The King" Lawler

Also available from www.crowbarpress.com

This series, created by Scott Teal, features the most detailed books ever published on the history of specific wrestling cities and territories. Each volume contains a definite listing of every wrestling match we could find for each venue, illustrated with hundreds of images of program covers, advertisements, newspaper ads and headlines, and memorabilia. Also included, when available, are gate and attendance figures, match stipulations, and much more. These volumes represent an incredible amount of research that will be referred to over and over by both everyone.

v1 – Wrestling in the Garden, The Battle for New York
by Scott Teal & J Michael Kenyon

v2 – Nashville, Tennessee, volume 1: 1907-1960
by Scott Teal & Don Luce

v3 – Alabama: 1931-1935
by Jason Presley

v4 – Japan: The Rikidozan Years
by Haruo Yamaguchi, with Koji Miyamoto & Scott Teal

v5 – Knoxville, Tennessee, v1: 1905-1960
by Tim Dills & Scott Teal

6 – Amarillo, Texas, v1: 1911-1960
by Kriss Knights & Scott Teal

— Fall Guys: The Barnums of Bounce —

by Marcus Griffin, Annotated by Steve Yohe & Scott Teal

If you're like most people, who think professional wrestling was strictly "kayfabe" in the days before it morphed into "sports entertainment," then think again. In 1937, a book titled Falls Guys: The Barnums of Bounce was published. In the 215 pages written by sportwriter Marcus Griffin, the sport was exposed to the general public and the behind-the-scenes wheeling and dealing by promoters and wrestlers alike were brought to light. It was the first credible book ever published on the subject.

Fall Guys was, and still is, fascinating reading ... with one caveat. A great deal of the book was written by Griffin with an extreme bias for Toots Mondt ... his boss ... and against those whom Toots didn't like. It is filled with inconsistencies, contradiction, and ... yes, downright lies. Nevertheless, the book is the best resource of events that took place during that era, and wrestling scholars have used much of Griffin's writing as a launchpad for their own research.

That being the case, why would anyone want to read this book?

This is the annotated version, in which Yohe & Teal challenge Griffin's statements about events and correct errors that have been repeated through the years in other books and writings. They also add additional detail to the stories and the lives of the book's personalities.

Also available from www.crowbarpress.com

— Wrestling Archive Project —

by Scott Teal

This series is chock full of interviews with the true legends of pro wrestling. Scott Teal, the force behind Crowbar Press, conducted most of these interviews in the days of “kayfabe,” a time before anyone else was getting the inside scoop on the pro wrestling business, and most of the people he talked with have never been interviewed by or opened up to anyone else. Scott Teal has returned to doing what he does best — sitting down with the wrestling legends and asking them tough, probing questions that give us insight into what pro wrestling was all about in the days before “sports entertainment" became vogue. Go behind the scenes with the pro wrestling’s legends.

Volume 1: The main event is an interview with Buddy Colt, who opens the pages of his life and tells his story as he never has before. Also are Adrian Street, Benny McGuire, Dandy Jack Donovan, Dick Cardinal, Frank Martinez, Gene Dundee, Gene Lewis, Gorgeous George Grant, Ernie “Hangman” Moore, Joe Powell, Lord Littlebrook, Lou Thesz, Mac McMurray and Pepper Gomez. A massive 406 pages.

Volume 2: Killer Karl Kox, who steadfastly refused to grant an indepth interview to anyone other than Scott, headlines volume two. You’ll feel like you’re sitting across the kitchen table from Karl as he relates his life story. Also featured are Baron Von Raschke, Bob Orton Sr., Count Billy Varga, Bulldog Bob Brown, Gentleman Ed Sharpe, J Michael Kenyon, Jackie Fargo, Kody Kox, Larry Cheatham, Lou Thesz, Maniac Mike Davis.

Volume 3: A feature on one of the top heels of all-time ... The Great Malenko. A second big interview focuses on the only indepth interview ever conducted with Archie Gouldie, the Mongolian Stomper, who terrorized ring opponents (and fans) for years. Rounding out the book is an interview with Leo Garibaldi, one of the top bookers of the ‘60s and ‘70s, as well as interviews with Bill McDaniel, Buddy Wayne, Dave Levin, The Fabulous Kangaroos, Gus Raap, Leo Garibaldi, Ox Baker, Pat Barrett, Rip Tyler, Scotty Williams, and Tim Tyler.

A Complete History of Sam Muchnick’s Missouri State Championship

by Roger Deem

Roger Deem brings life to the story of the Missouri championship belt, the "crème de la crème" of pro wrestling's title belts, second only to the world heavyweight title. Deem covers everything about the title, from the creation of the belt in 1972 to its demise with the death of the St. Louis Wrestling Club in 1987. Also researched is the history of the St. Louis promotion during the time the title was in use; the genius of promoter Sam Muchnick; the behind-the-scenes manipulations that determined who would be given the opportunity to hold the title, or have it taken away; and the problems that beset the promotion both from within and without. Relive the memories of the days when St. Louis was the wrestling capital of the world and the Missouri heavyweight title was the goal of every wrestler.

Wrestling in the Canadian West

by Vance Nevada

Wrestling in the Canadian West accurately describes what it was like for those who traveled the roads on a daily basis in the unique and spectacular area of professional wrestling history. The author clearly illustrates how the business over the years has now come around full circle, as he is living it himself, and dealing with the same trials and tribulations wrestling’s pioneers faced in the area more than a hundred years ago.

— Profiles on more than 100 promotions over the past century
— Championship histories and statistical rankings
— Road stories from the wrestlers themselves, including J.J. Dillon & Moose Morowski.
— A directory of the top drawing wrestling events of all time
— Statistics for more than 200 active Canadian wrestlers
— Much, much more!!

Also available from www.crowbarpress.com

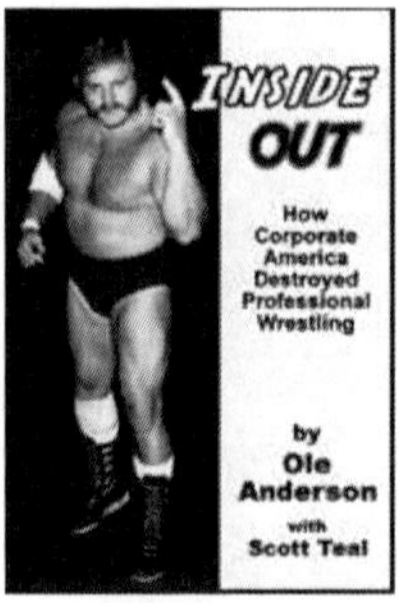

— Inside Out —

by Ole Anderson, with Scott Teal

The people who know Ole Anderson know that he is never hesitant to speak his mind — and this book is no exception. Ole tells of his feuds behind the scenes in the halls and offices of corporate giant, Superstation WTBS. In Ole's own words, *"The wrestling matches may have been staged and scripted, but there was nothing 'fake' about the corporate and legal battles."* This is a powerful story about a man who stood up to the establishment.

— "Wrestlers Are Like Seagulls" —

by James J. Dillon, with Scott Teal

For more than 40 years, James J. Dillon was involved in the world of professional wrestling. He speaks candidly on all aspects of both his career and his personal life, including his time in the WWF as Vince McMahon's right-hand man. Never before has someone from McMahon's inner circle written a book with an insider's perspective of the company. From the highs of making big money, winning championship titles, and rubbing elbows with top celebrities, to the lows of filing for bankruptcy, extramarital affairs, divorces, and drug use, no stone is left unturned.

— ASSASSIN: The Man Behind the Mask —

by Joe Hamilton, with Scott Teal

This autobiography of Joe "Jody" Hamilton takes the reader behind the scenes for a personal glimpse behind the mask of one of pro wrestling's hottest attraction — The Assassin! Joe takes readers on a journey as he tells about life both in and out of the wrestling ring—being attacked, stabbed, and shot at by angry wrestling fans; wrestling under a mask and trying to keep his identity a secret; legitimate fights and confrontations behind the scenes in the dressing rooms; and a war between two wrestling promotions in Atlanta.

— "Is That Wrestling Fake?" — The Bear Facts —

by Ivan Koloff, with Scott Teal

For decades, professional wrestling fans have asked the question – "Is that wrestling fake?" However, they wouldn't have dared ask that question directly to Ivan Koloff, whose work in the ring made believers out of the most cynical fans. In Madison Square Garden, he pinned Bruno Sammartino's shoulders to the mat and won the WWWF heavyweight title. Ivan tells the story of his life: the highs and the lows; admission of alcohol and drug abuse; reflections of a life spent on the road, and the toll it took on his body and soul; and the event that changed his life forever.

— BRUISER BRODY —

by Emerson Murray

Today, more than 18 years after his death, pro wrestling fans still talk about Bruiser Brody with reverence and awe in their voice. Hardcore fans consider him to be the greatest brawler in the history of the sport. He also was one of the most unpredictable men ever to step into the ring, marching to his own drummer and refusing to bow to anyone. Most promoters hated him, but they also loved him because fans turned out in droves to see him. This is the story of Bruiser Brody. No punches are pulled and the rulebook has been thrown out.

Also available from www.crowbarpress.com

— Wrestling with the Truth —

by Bruno Lauer, edited by Scott Teal

The story of Bruno Lauer, known professionally as Downtown Bruno and Harvey Wippleman, tells the fascinating, and often hilarious, story of his life. Direct and opinionated, he doesn't hold back anything. Even his close friends aren't safe from his scrutiny. Retracing every step of his career, this autobio is a fresh glimpse at life behind the curtain of professional sports entertainment — as much action, entertainment, heartbreak, and drama as anything inside a pro wrestling ring.

— The Solie Chronicles —

by Robert Allyn, with Pamela S. Allyn and Scott Teal

One of the most well-known pro-wrestling personalities wasn't a wrestler, but a commentator named Gordon Solie. Famous dead-pan style interviews and colorful play-by-play broadcasts of wrestling led to Gordon's induction into the WCW, NWA & WWE Halls of Fame. Background material was found in Gordon's personal files and taken from interviews with the people who knew him the best.

— Long Days and Short Pays —

by H.E. "Duke" West, edited by Scott Teal

By his own admission, H.E. West was never a well-known name in pro wrestling, but his story is a fascinating look at life on the road of a man whose only desire was to be a part of the world of pro wrestling, not matter how insignificant that part might be. Join him on his journey as he describes his time wrestling before small crowds in high-school gyms and armories, and his travels with his fellow wrestlers. West's narrative is peppered with honesty and humor, and told with humility by a man who never makes himself out to be more than he was — a wrestler whose sole purpose in the ring was to make other wrestlers look good.

— Drawing Heat —

by Jim Freedman

Freedman presents an insider's view of promoting a small, independent wrestling show ... putting the show together, setting up the ring, balancing the books, ring announcing, dealing with sports commissioners who are in the pocket of the big wrestling companies, and exactly what lures fans into arenas. Filled with wonderful characters, the focus is on Dave "The Wildman" McKigney and his wrestling bears, and his struggles and tragedies become the focus of the narrative. This is more than just a book about wrestling. It is a glimpse into a secret world unknown to most people.

— ATLAS: Too Much ... Too Soon —

by Tony Atlas, with Scott Teal

Tony Atlas was the first wrestler to be paid to learn his trade. By the late '70s, Tony was one of the biggest names in the sport and was wrestling in front of sellout crowds in the largest arenas in the country. Readers will live Tony's life through his eyes as he tells about his free-spirited and self-destructive journey through life. His out-of-the-ring stories are as compelling as those that took place inside the ring. This is the story of a man who had success handed to him—only to throw it all away—and the long, painful struggle he had to endure as he clawed his way back to the top.

Also available from www.crowbarpress.com

— The Last Laugh —

by Bill De Mott, with Scott Teal

The stories of Bill's life on the road are both hilarious and entertaining, and at other times, they are sad and insightful. His life has been filled with more backstage drama than is found in all the afternoon soap operas combined, and he doesn't pull any punches in the telling of his story. Considered by many to be a taskmaster with high expectations for his students, a softer side of Bill also reveals itself as his story unfolds. He speaks passionately about life on the road and how he missed seeing his children grow up. A fascinating memoir of one of wrestling's unique characters.

— When It Was Real —

by Nikita Breznikov

If you want to take a trip back to your childhood, your younger, less-stressful days, then journey with us back into the magical world of professional wrestling during the years 1970 to 1979 ... a time "when it was real" ... a time before Hulkamania took the world by storm. Author Nikita Breznikov tells the story from two perspectives — that of a starry-eyed fan, and as the manager and tag team partner of the legendary Nikolai Volkoff. Nikita details the matches and feuds that took place in the WWWF during the '70s and gives his insightful, often-hilarious perspective of the events that took place. Escape with Nikita as he transports you back to an era when wrestling was presented in an entertaining manner, but framed as legitimate competition.

— The Last Outlaw —

by Stan Hansen, with Scott Teal

Stan's writing is a guidebook of pro wrestling in Japan. He educates and entertains with stories about promoters and their promotions, how they operate business behind the scenes, touring the country, nightlife in the big cities, and how the sport in Japan differs from the U.S. And what would a "Stan Hansen book" be without personal stories about Bruiser Brody: how they first met, the story behind their becoming a team, spending time in the evenings on the streets and in the clubs of Japan, and his own, personal insight into the "real" Bruiser Brody.

— NIKITA: A Tale of the Ring and Redemption —

by Nikita Koloff, as told to William Murdock

Nikita Koloff, better known as the "Russian Nightmare," stormed the wrestling world as few others have. Imposing, immovable, and unbeatable, Nikita left a trail of fallen opponents as he brought the Cold War that loomed over the globe into the ring. Nikita's name filled arenas and he captured five world titles in the process. And when he was at the top of his game, he walked away from the sport. This is not just the story of a wrestler. It is the story of a man ... a man who has touched hundreds of thousands of lives.

— BRISCO —

by Jack Brisco, as told to William Murdock

A former NCAA amateur wrestling champion, Jack had his first match in 1965 and soon became one of the top names in the wrestling business. He won both the Florida and Southern heavyweight titles and, just a few years later, took the NWA world heavyweight belt from Harley Race. Jack and his brother, Jerry, were responsible for convincing other Geor

Also available from www.crowbarpress.com

— *"I Ain't No Pig Farmer!"* —

by Dean Silverstone, edited by Scott Teal

In an era when few people were allowed into pro wrestling's inner circle, Dean pitched the idea of publishing an arena program to Seattle promoter Harry Elliott, and Dean's career as a wrestling publicist began ... when he was only 14 years old. Dean later formed Super Star Championship Wrestling, and in the process, faced anti-Semitism, unpredictable actions from his talent, crowd riots, warnings from the Hell's Angels, collapsing rings, the tragic death of one of his top wrestlers, and even a Molotov cocktail.

— The Hard Way —

by Don Fargo, with Scott Teal

As famous as he was for his ability to draw crowds to the arenas, Fargo probably was more famous for his hijinks behind the scenes. The stories about his pranks and wild lifestyle are talked about to this day by those who were witness to the events. This is the most detailed book ever written that ties together important events in wrestling history with hilarious shenanigans that went on behind the scenes. You've never read a more entertaining life story than this one.

— Whatever Happened to Gorgeous George? —

by Joe Jares

This is the story of the most outlandish personalities in sport—comic book figures with fanatical followings. Here you'll meet Gorgeous George, Bruno Sammartino, Haystack Calhoun, and a host of arch-villains, prissy lords, masked marauders, and muscle-bound mamas. Loving and hating them along the way are maniacal fans who follow them and turn the arenas into screaming, roving Theaters of the Absurd—Piccolo Pete, Hatpin Mary, and the septuagenarian sisters from Baltimore, to name a few. Then come backstage with the boys and see what the brutal world of wrestling's all about—cauliflower ears, fan-inflicted knife and gun wounds, matches fought in mud and ice cream, bloody grudge brawls, whacky practical jokes.

— BRUISER —

by Richard Vicek, edited by Scott Teal.03

There have been several "Bruisers" in wrestling history, but the name synonymous with pro wrestling for almost three decades was "Dick the Bruiser." A former Green Bay Packer lineman, Bruiser is a name people mention when talking about the golden age of the sport. Within a few months of his debut, Bruiser was cracking heads and pounding flesh from coast to coast across the United States. Words that desribe Bruiser's in-ring style are believability, belligerence, domination, unpredictability, explosiveness, intensity, and rampage. This book is his legacy.

— Pain Torture Agony —

by Ron Hutchison, with Scott Teal

Ron Hutchison, trainer of some of World Wrestling Entertainment's biggest superstars, is hailed as one of pro wrestling's unsung heroes. It is an account filled with history and insight into the fascinating world of pro wrestling, as well as tales of dreamers, muscleheads, a bomb threat, machine guns, Yakuza, midgets, and even a visit to the Playboy mansion in California. Fasten your seatbelt as Ron Hutchison, trainer of some of World Wrestling Entertainment's biggest superstars, takes you on an exciting four-decade journey into the wild, no-holds-barred, wacky & amazing world of professional wrestling.

Also available from www.crowbarpress.com

— Battleground Valhalla —

by Michael Majalahti, edited by Scott Teal

From humble beginnings in Canada, Michael, the son of an immigrant preacher, aspired to become somebody from an early age. As an outsider to his peers during his youth, Michael took the path less traveled; the road of the lone wolf. As "The Rebel" StarBuck, he became one of the most accomplished European pro wrestlers of the Y2K era and stands, arguably, as the most celebrated wrestler ever from the Nordics. His story will both enthrall and inspire you!

— THE MIGHTY MILO —

by Phillips Rogers

Fred Anspach, an amateur wrestler who worked in a supermarket, had a funny customer. The customer was a Greek waiter, five-foot-three and about as broad, egg-headed, a guy who bought apples, bananas and lettuce and lived on this diet. But when Fred made a date with his customer for a little friendly wrestling at the "Y" gym, he learned that, although Milo Popolagos looked fat, he was immensely strong and could wrestle like old Milo of ancient Greece. Maybe he's the greatest wrestler in the world, Fred thought ...

It's all here — the weekly club engagements in Baltimore, the "rassle royals" in mud or molasses, and finally, the TV wrestling shows that today are so popular with the ladies. Here too are lady wrestlers, and a strip-tease actress who catches Milo's eye, and Betty Jane Blane who objects to Fred Anspach's wrestling but, like a woman, changes her mind. The Mighty Milo you characters for whom you will develop an affection even while you smile at their mastodonic antics.

— Through the Lens ... Through the Ropes —

by Scott Teal

This on-going series features photo collections taken in the various territories during specific time periods. Most photos are being published in these books for the first time, and while some have been seen in arena programs or magazines, they have never been presented in this quality. All photos were scanned from the original negatives and put through a laborious cleaning, brightening and sharpening process so they appear in this book in the highest quality possible. These are some of the best photos available from those promotions and include publicity stills, candid shots, and action pictures from both TV and house shows.

v1 – Southeastern Championship Wrestling, 321 photos

v2 – Championship Wrestling from Florida, 253 photos

v3 – All South Wrestling Alliance (Ann Gunkel), xx photos

— Classic Arena Programs —

by Scott Teal

Now, for the first time ever, entire runs of classic arena programs are being offered in book format with each program being re-printed in its entirety. Each program has been scanned, cropped, cleaned, brightened, and sharpened so they look better than the originals. Many of these programs are being sold online for a premium, but *Classic Arena Programs* gives you the opportunity to own them all at a fraction of the cost that collectors are paying for these vintage programs.

v1 & 2 – SLAM-O-GRAM (Gulas-Welch)

v3 & 4 – Championship Wrestling ACTION (Florida)

v5 – Southeastern Championship Wrestling (Knoxville): 1975-1977

v6, 7 & 9 – Sports Pointers / In the Ring (St. Louis)

v22-24 – Jacksonville, Florida: July 1976-July 1980